Dreaming in Books

Dreaming in Books

The Making of the Bibliographic
Imagination in the Romantic Age

ANDREW PIPER

The University of Chicago Press
Chicago and London

The University of Chicago Press, Chicago 60637
The University of Chicago Press, Ltd., London
© 2009 by The University of Chicago
All rights reserved. Published 2009.
Paperback edition 2013
Printed and bound by CPI Group (UK) Ltd, Croydon, CR0 4YY

22 21 20 19 18 17 16 15 14 13   2 3 4 5 6

ISBN-13: 978-0-226-66972-4 (cloth)
ISBN-13: 978-0-226-10351-8 (paperback)
ISBN-13: 978-0-226-66974-8 (e-book)
DOI: 10.7208/chicago/9780226669748.001.0001

Library of Congress Cataloging-in-Publication Data
Piper, Andrew, 1973–
    Dreaming in books : the making of the bibliographic imagination in the
Romantic age / Andrew Piper.
        pages cm—Synthesis
    Includes bibliographical references and index.
    ISBN-13: 978-0-226-66972-4 (cloth : alk. paper)
    ISBN-10: 0-226-66972-6 (cloth : alk. paper) 1. Literature publishing—Europe—
History—19th century. 2. Literature publishing—Germany—History—19th century.
3. Books—Europe—History—19th century. 4. Books—Germany—History—19th
century. 5. Romanticism—History and criticism. 6. Communication—History—
19th century. I. Title
    Z286.L58P57 2009
    070.5094′09034—dc22

                                                                    2009006780

For Tinka

CONTENTS

ILLUSTRATIONS

ACKNOWLEDGMENTS

This book is in one sense about the communities that contribute to the making of books, a fact no less true for my own book. Its completion would not have been possible without the generous and patient assistance of numerous librarians, too numerous in fact to name here, who have taught me that without human knowledge, technological knowledge is, quite literally, a mess. I have been amply aided by individuals at the following institutions: the Rare Books and Special Collections Division of the McGill University Library, the Rare Book and Manuscript Library of Columbia University, the Carl H. Pforzheimer Collection of the New York Public Library, the Pierpont Morgan Library, the Beinecke Rare Book and Manuscript Library of Yale University, the American Antiquarian Society, the Herzogin Anna Amalia Bibliothek and the Goethe- und Schiller-Archiv in Weimar, the Staatsbibliothek zu Berlin, the Niedersächsische Staats- und Universitätsbibliothek Göttingen, and the Bibliothèque Municipale de Grenoble. It was Terry Belanger and my teachers of descriptive bibliography at the Rare Book School at the University of Virginia who taught me how to understand what a book is.

Karin Bauer has provided me with tremendous support since arriving at McGill, offering careful guidance in that process that, for lack of a better word, we might call "becoming institutionalized." I have also benefited from a number of extremely smart, savvy, and humane young colleagues at McGill, including Michael Cowan, Nick Dew, Carrie Rentschler, Brian Cowan, and the recently relocated James Delbourgo and Cornelius Borck. Jonathan Sterne has been a caring companion from the start and fundamental to my connection with the Department of Art History and Communication Studies. I want to thank all of the members of the Ottawa/Montreal working group on Romanticism, and in particular, Ina Ferris and Paul Keen, who have been enthusiastic supporters of my work from the beginning. Jon Sachs has been an anchor for me ever since crossing the forty-ninth parallel and has shown me the significance—and the fun—of talking back to institutions. I also greatly appreciate the support and acknowledgment that I have received from the Goethe Society of North America, in particular its current president, Simon Richter. John Lyon has become a valued intellectual interlocutor on all matters related to the *Goethezeit*. The members of my print culture research group, Tom Mole, Nikola von Merveldt, and Susan Dalton, have pushed my thinking into new terrain at every turn. I have benefited in particular in countless ways from the intellectual and personal generosity of Tom. He is a stellar exemplar of what collaboration means. I would also like to thank my editor, Alan Thomas, for his unwavering commitment to my work and his ability to mingle matters professional with a delightful sense of ease and enjoyment. Richard Allen, my copyeditor, provided invaluable assistance in producing a readable finished product.

Portions of chapter 5 are reprinted from *Women in German Yearbook*, volume 22, by permission of the University of Nebraska Press, copyright 2006 by the University of Nebraska Press. A shorter version of chapter 1 initially appeared as "Rethinking the Print Object: Goethe and the Book of Everything," *PMLA* 121, no. 1 (Jan. 2006): 124–38. My thanks go to Leah Price and Seth Lerer for including me in their special issue dedicated to "The History of the Book and the Idea of Literature," but more importantly for putting book history at the center of the literary map and, perhaps even more significantly, vice versa.

My former teachers at Columbia shaped this work in crucial ways, and I am indebted to the thoughts of my advisor, Dorothea von Mücke, as well as Andreas Huyssen, Kelly Barry, Stefan Andriopoulos, and Mark Anderson who made important contributions to earlier stages of this book. Wolfgang Ernst gave me much needed support in Berlin. I am also deeply appreciative of Cliff Siskin's early and continued belief in my work, his always candid advice, and of course his impeccable timing. He is a model of scholarly mentoring.

I suspect that everyone can remember at least one teacher who changed the course of his or her life and who, for this, will never be forgotten. For me, that teacher is Stanley Corngold, adopted intellectual father figure, lunch mate, and epistolary raconteur. I can think of no higher compliment to offer a professor of literature than to say: he taught me how to read.

If there is a ghost in this machine, it is Martin Eisner. Given the amount of words we have exchanged over the years on anything related to books, literature, and, well, anything, it is at times hard to know where my voice starts and his stops. Of the array of literary archetypes that are available to describe this kind of interchange—Virgil, Sancho Panza, Mephisto—none quite captures what it truly means to have a friend in letters.

Academic books, by their very nature, belong to a profession. But as my *Doktormutter* once wrote, the dividing line between professing and confessing, between public speech and private sentiment, is hard to trace. This book owes as much to the family and friends who have helped me cultivate that private sphere as it does to those colleagues who have challenged me professionally. Sam Markham has been my constant guide through book- and blogworld. Andrea Quintero my prism to the world of things. Ben Huneke, who saw this ship set sail in its initial, rather rickety state, has always been willing to lend me his critical gaze. I have been trading ideas with my brother, Tommy, longer than with anyone else in the world. There is a secret history of siblings and ideas that is still waiting to be written. My parents, Ann and Tom, have shown me, through an astonishingly deep well of patience, generosity, and humor, how to be a parent. And my two children, Eliot and Echo, have taught me that human nature is infinitely more beautiful and varied than anything that could ever be in a book. Finally, to Tinka, my friend and flight mate for life who once compared us to a sentence, I can only offer the humblest yet most honest grammatical form to convey how much I love and owe you for what you have given me, namely, that of tautology: There is no there there without you.

Bibliographic Subjects

Hypothesis: All is Leaf.

—J. W. Goethe

Surveying the changes that had been wrought on the German book market over the previous forty years, the writer Wolfgang Menzel observed in 1828: "If a citizen of the next century were to look back at the current moment in German history, he would say that we had slept and dreamt in books."[1] On one level, Menzel was offering a familiar critique about how Germans had failed to participate in the political upheavals that had emerged in France at the close of the eighteenth century. While the French were modernizing their political system, the Germans had been busy reading.[2] On another level, however, Menzel was making an acute argument about the new power of books that had arisen alongside other historic changes such as the French Revolution. For Menzel the idea of a reading revolution was a very palpable one. Books were not only endowed with the capacity to put individuals to sleep—to draw their attention away from reality—they also had the power to shape their dreams, to structure their thoughts and their imaginations. Menzel had significantly titled his essay "The Mass of Literature," and what seemed to lend the book both its soporific and supplementary force was precisely its looming ubiquity. It was the *massness* of the book in Menzel's view that had transformed it into both a problem and an enormously powerful medium that had the capacity to shape one's dreams.

Menzel's alignment of dreaming and books would of course go on to become one of the most commonly promoted identities of romantic literature.[3] Never before had so many writers written about people dreaming while reading books. To dream *in* books, however, was not only to dream *while* reading, to engage in a kind of hallucinatory reading experience in which the book itself was forgotten. To dream in books also meant to dream *in the shape of* the book as well. It was precisely the materiality of the book that provided the contours to such imagining, indeed to the imagination itself. Menzel's observation suggested the extraordinary degree to which individuals and the culture at large by the turn of the nineteenth century were becoming bookish.

In both his conviction and anxiety about the growing bookishness of Germans, Menzel was not alone. One can find numerous statements from this period in which commentators from a variety of regions worried over, but also celebrated, the importance of the book as a medium of cultural communication. As Thomas Carlyle intoned in *Sartor Resartus*, the book had become a "City of the mind, a Temple and Seminary, and Prophetic Mount, whereto all kindreds of the earth will pilgrim,"[4] a statement matched only by Victor Hugo's famous pronouncement in *Notre-Dame de Paris* that "this [the book] will kill that [the church]."[5] In Novalis's unfinished novel and updated medieval romance, *Heinrich von Ofterdingen*, it was the book that would be the first key destination for the title character's underworld journey, inverting Dante's use of the book as an image not of the underworldly inferno but of the heavenly paradiso. Stephan Schütze would write an ode to "The Origin of the Book," commemorating the book's emergence from the tree of nature, while Leigh Hunt lovingly turned over the word "book" in essays like "Old Books and Bookshops," using it nine times in the first paragraph alone.[6] Friedrich Schlegel simply called it "the age of books."[7]

If the book for these writers simultaneously marked the end and the rebirth of the sacred, for others, such as Honoré de Balzac, the book was as profane as ever because of its overwhelming proliferation. Writing in 1830 in an essay entitled "De l'état actuel de la librairie," Balzac observed, "Reading has become a necessity. The European imagination feeds on the sensations that it demands from literature like the Turk demands dreams of opium."[8] Reading books was the new European addiction. As the murderous narrator of Edgar Allen Poe's "Berenice" would say about his family library, "In that chamber was I born."[9] Or as Karl Immermann recounted in his memoirs of growing-up in Magdeburg in the early 1800s, "The sheer sight of a book would set the afflicted child in a kind of quivering curiosity. . . . The young creature lived and breathed only in print; . . . evenings were incapable of bringing sleep to those letter-hungry eyes."[10]

As Immermann's vocabulary of agitated attention suggested,[11] the process of adapting to a world saturated by printed books was neither simple nor smooth. Whether asleep, inebriated, or nervously attentive, a common element that belonged to romantic bibliographic experiences was most often one of "possession"—not simply an overwhelming desire to possess books, as in Leigh Hunt's formulation about being "wedded to books,"[12] or Isaac D'Israeli's or Charles Nodier's diagnoses of the new bibliomania.[13] There was a sense of being possessed by them as well.[14] As Goethe wrote in 1811 at the opening of his autobiography about his initiation as a young boy into this new bookish space, the media aftershocks that followed the geological aftershocks of the Lisbon earthquake were understood as an initiatory personal *Erschütterung* or shock. "In vain," Goethe would write, "the young boy tried to maintain himself against these impressions," where his choice of the word "impressions" (*Eindrücke*) crucially drew attention to the media conditions—the press and its proliferating products—that contributed to the fracturing of the young boy's sense of self.[15] The pilgrimages, addictions, marriages, and aftershocks that books provoked in the early nineteenth century not only captured the deeply intense and personal ways that books were increasingly imagined to mark us as individuals. They also highlighted how difficult and contested this process of becoming bookish truly was.[16] Adapting to books—becoming bibliographic subjects—was not something that just happened. It necessitated significant reorganizations of both social and individual identities.

This book is about the process of how we became bookish at the turn of the nineteenth century. It asks what we did with books and what books did to us when there were suddenly too many books. As historians of the book have shown, the late eighteenth and early nineteenth centuries witnessed a dramatic expansion in the number and circulation of printed books across Europe and North America.[17] It was a period that saw the rise of a variety of social practices and spaces centered around the organization of books, whether it was the emergence of the public lending library, the private family library, the reading club, or the expansion of gift-giving rituals involving books.[18] At the same time, one could also observe the rising social prominence of a number of bibliographically oriented individuals: not just authors, but also editors, translators, booksellers, printers, librarians, critics, and bibliographers all assumed an elevated professional status. Booksellers in particular would become some of the most powerful financial actors in European and American societies by 1800, with extraordinary capital investments and elaborate international networks of trading partners. To take but one example, by 1824 the Vieweg Verlag in Braunschweig had 236 trading partners in 112 European cities and a 6,500 square meter printing complex.[19] It was a period, in short, that witnessed a remarkable social investment in books, both materially and imaginatively.

In exploring the different ways that the new rules and the new realities of bibliographic communication were being worked out in Europe and North America between the years 1750 and 1850, *Dreaming in Books* approaches this problem as much from the inside of books as from their outside. It argues that one of the fundamental ways through which western cultures became bibliographic cultures was through reading literature. As books streamed in ever greater numbers from publishing houses in London, Philadelphia, Paris, Stuttgart, and Berlin, romantic writing and romantic writers played a crucial role in facilitating readers' adaptation to this increasingly international and overflowing bookish environment. Learning how to read books and how to want books did not simply occur through the technological, commercial, or legal conditions that made the growing proliferation of books possible. The making of such bibliographic fantasies was also importantly a product of the very narratives and symbolic operations contained *within* books as well. It was through romantic literature where individuals came to understand their books, and it was through their books where they came to understand themselves. This book is about this complex process of how literature shaped and lent meaning to such a new media reality.

Books: Past, Present, and Future

In revisiting the book's rise through the prism of romantic literature, *Dreaming in Books* attempts to revise our assumptions about romantic literature, the medium of the printed book, and ultimately, the future of the book. Despite the annual barrage of narratives prophesying the "end of the book" today, we continue to invest enormous social resources, whether financial or educational, in ensuring the circulation, consumption, preservation, and mastery of the book. Americans spent twenty-five billion dollars on books last year, twice as much as on any other form of media, including movies, music, or video games.[20] Europeans spent over thirty-two billion euros on books, or *forty-eight* billion dollars, which is a little under twice what they spent on music, the next largest cultural expenditure.[21] There are an estimated 117,341 libraries nationwide in the U.S., and between the major public and academic libraries (roughly 13,000), another fourteen billion dollars a year is spent housing and making books available to the public.[22] In the face of such numbers, to say that the book is dead seems absurd. At the same time that books continue to enjoy an enormously broad public appeal, they have also retained an important ritualistic private function. Whether for birthdays, schooldays, holidays, or tenure, we still count time with books. We are, in this sense, still very much a bibliographic "culture." In writing a history of the bibliographic imagination in the romantic age, I am interested in understanding the communicative foundations upon which our contemporary culture is based and to which my own book is integrally related. In self-reflexive terms, it is the attempt to ask why we continue to feel such urgency, whether personally or institutionally, to write books.

But this book is not just concerned with the emergence during the romantic period of a set of values that continue to surround how we use and think about books today. It also attempts to recover very different imaginaries of how books worked and what books did in the past. It not only engages narratives of the book's end but also those of the book's "rise" or "coming" as well. Despite much of the triumphalism and universalism that surrounds rise-of-the-book narratives—that all bibliographic cultures and ages are the same—one of the aims of this book is to follow the work of recent book historians such as Robert Darnton, Adrian Johns, Stephan Füssel, Reinhart Wittmann, and Roger Chartier to help us see how the printed book was a far more richly imagined and far more diversely used media object than we have traditionally assumed. Our understanding of the book has undergone a tremendous narrowing over time that this book hopes to correct. As media historian Jonathan Sterne has written, "To study technologies in any meaningful sense requires a rich sense of their connection with human practice, habitat, and habit. It requires attention to the fields of combined cultural, social, and physical activity—what other authors have called networks or assemblages—from which technologies emerge and of which they are part."[23]

While books had by the turn of the nineteenth century been a constant of Western cultural life for over 1,500 years,[24] what was new around 1800 was the imminent sense of too-muchness that surrounded the printed book. It was precisely this notion of the surplus of books that lent the book its cosmological identity in the romantic age—that it was both everywhere and could contain everything—and simultaneously made a unified response to such a problem increasingly difficult.[25] The book, like the society it helped reflect back to itself, was increasingly marked by a key element of heterogeneity, as different book formats and literary genres were mobilized to regulate the growing problem of bibliographic surplus. If we can indeed speak of something approximating a "Gutenberg Galaxy," to use McLuhan's well-turned phrase to signify a world dominated by the printed book, I want to argue that it happened much later than the age of Gutenberg and was far more diverse than McLuhan himself had characterized it. Indeed, as will become apparent throughout this book, much of what sustained and informed the identity of the printed book in the romantic period was a variety of *scriptural* practices that had predated Gutenberg. A history of the romantic book is by necessity a history of bibliographic heterogeneity, a history of books and not "the book."

The bibliographic diversity that was characteristic of the romantic age was nevertheless simultaneously accompanied by a growing geographic homogeneity. Where early modern book culture was marked by a prominent sense of internationalism (as James Raven has shown, for example, two-thirds of English booksellers in the sixteenth century were not English),[26] romantic book culture by contrast could be understood as initiating a complementary element of transnationalism, of similar trends taking place across different national spaces. The diffusion of illustrative practices such as lithography or wood-end engraving, the vogue for gift-books, the popularity of collected editions or novella collections, the prominent role of translations, or even the fascination with ballads, bards, and all things folkish (-tales, -lore, and -song)—however much such bibliographic phenomena contributed to different nineteenth-century endeavors of nation-making, they were never limited to a single national space. Indeed it was their translatability that was in some sense one of their most definitive features. While there were of course important regional differences as to how and when such formats and practices took shape (which each of my chapters addresses in kind), what has largely been missing from current scholarship on the history of the book are precisely such transnational accounts of the book.[27] We have a history of the book in Canada, England, Scotland, France, and Germany, but very little sense of the overlaps and interactions between these bookish communities. In drawing attention to the different types of books and the different communities who made them in Great Britain, France, the German states, and the United States, *Dreaming in Books* attempts to tell a far more wide-ranging story of the printed book's identity in the early nineteenth century. In place of understanding how the book participated in the making of the imagined communities of nineteenth-century nation states, I am interested in exploring how the printed book participated in facilitating the emergence of what Karl Guthke has called a "world-spanning consciousness" around 1800.[28] How did the international circulation of books begin to foster a transnational sensibility of local differences?

If romantic bibliographic culture has much to tell us about the past and present nature of the book, it also, I want to suggest, has much to tell us about the pressures being exerted by digital media today and thus concerns the future of the book as well. A history of the romantic book and the romantic bibliographic imagination is in this sense also a history of media adaptation. A study of how nineteenth-century individuals became wedded to or possessed by their books can broaden our perspective of the nature of "new media" cultures and historical experiences of "media transition."[29] It can offer parallels, but also differences, to our current process of adapting to communicative change. Knowledge of the book's past can be a key tool in negotiating our digital future. As Carla Hesse has argued, "The striking parallels between the late eighteenth and late twentieth centuries' cultural debates suggest to me that what we are witnessing in the remaking of the 'modern literary system' at the end of the twentieth century is not so much a technological revolution (which has already occurred) but the public reinvention of intellectual community in its wake."[30] If a basic and increasingly urgent concern of academics of my generation is how we will adapt to the pressures and opportunities that digital forms of communication present us, then a study of romantic bibliographic culture can offer an important case study for such institutional and personal transformations. How were careers and communities made—and lost—through different strategies surrounding the medium of the book?

At the same time that romantic book culture offers important parallels to contemporary digital culture, there are also important *continuities* at work between these two distinct regimes of communication.[31] While we have a tremendous amount of scholarship exploring the novelty of digital media, we have far fewer historical contextualizations that are able to put those differences into perspective.[32] This book argues that many of the most pressing communicative concerns facing us today are not unique to the digital age but emerged with a particular sense of urgency during the bookish upheavals of the romantic age. A history of the romantic book offers insights into where and when some of the most salient issues surrounding communication today emerged. What did it mean to reimagine a literary work as residing not in a single book but as part of an interrelated bibliographic network? What was the cultural status of the copy and how did it relate to a larger reformulation of notions like novelty and innovation? What did it mean to process an existing yet largely forgotten cultural heritage from one medium to another? How was one to contend with the growing availability of writing, where such availability was increasingly understood to be a problem? Finally, what did it mean to imagine creativity as an act of intermedial making, as a facility with various modes of communication simultaneously? These may sound like questions that we are asking ourselves today, but they were no less urgent in the opening decades of the nineteenth century. How they were answered then can tell us something about how to think through them today.

By attending to communicative *practices* as well as technologies,[33] then, we can begin to see not only that contemporary concerns with networking, copying, processing, sharing, overhearing, and adapting were also romantic ones, but that they came into being during the romantic age. When Menzel and others worried over the new "mass of literature," their concerns in many ways predated the widespread adoption of some of the most important technological innovations in book production that took place after 1800 (steam presses, paper machines, penny papers, stereotype, and rail distribution).[34] In this sense, we could reverse Hesse's observation above and suggest that the romantic moment offers us an interesting case of a public reinvention of intellectual community that preceded a technological revolution that was in the making.

It has arguably been the work of Jerome McGann that has done more than any other to show us how the onset of digital media has allowed us, indeed required us, to rethink the history of books.[35] The digital provides us with a critical lens to see the bibliographic with fresh eyes. But my own work is driven by an alternative desire to show us how the history of books, and romantic books in particular, can help us contextualize our understanding of digital or new media today. It insists upon a hands-on encounter with books as the central means of understanding our bibliographic heritage that is itself a part of a larger media heritage more generally. One of the sought-after byproducts of such contextualizations might just be to dislodge the hegemony of the "digital" itself that lies at the heart of models like McGann's "literature *after* the world-wide-web." In returning to the ways that the book rose to such cultural prominence in the romantic age through a variety of media interactions (as opposed to media replacements), we can hopefully move beyond the often oversimplified narratives of the "end of the book" and focus instead on the more multifaceted repositioning that currently surrounds the book today in our so-called "digital age."[36]

Is Literary History Book History?

When the contemporary Peruvian writer Mario Vargas Llosa made the claim that the future of literature depended on the future of the book,[37] he was not simply articulating what might have seemed to many writers of a younger generation a naïve and antiquarian point of view. He was also showing just how important the printed book remained in continuing to shape how we think about the category of literature. As Seth Lerer has asked, "Is the modern conception of literature inseparable from the conception of the book as the physical, commercial artifact as we know it?"[38] *Dreaming in Books* is, in a more specialized sense, about the emergence of this nexus between the book and literature. When Friedrich Schlegel argued that "a novel is a romantic book" (ein Roman ist ein romantisches Buch),[39] he was highlighting how Llosa's conviction and Lerer's concern were both fundamentally romantic ones. The very hegemony that the book achieved during the romantic period and that was articulated in the tautology at the heart of Schlegel's statement elided the complex mediations that were required to make literature's location in the book seem both natural and immediate. This book seeks to reverse that process of naturalization.

Armed with the tools and training of bibliographers and book historians, numerous literary scholars today have begun to draw our attention to the ways that bibliographic details are key determinants, but also key multipliers, of textual meaning. As N. Katherine Hayles has written, "To change the physical form of the artifact is not merely to change the act of reading . . . but profoundly to transform the metaphoric network structuring the relation of word to world."[40] Or as Jerome McGann has more flatly stated, "There is no such thing as an unmarked text."[41] Such work has inherited, whether explicitly or not, the challenges posed by poststructural theory, reformulating the fundamental semiotic openness that was ascribed to the literary work in Barthes' seminal essay "From Work to Text," to the level of the material text.[42] It replaces an "eruptive" notion of the literary work—one based on a kind of destabilizing singularity—with a notion of the work as a "circuit," "process," or "event," as some *thing* that takes shape in motion across time and space.[43] Attention to the book does not aim to reproduce a textual stability and singularity that were in fact never there, the once contested ideals of early twentieth-century Anglo-American analytic bibliography (Greg, Bowers) or nineteenth-century Germanic philology (Lachmann, Wilamowitz). Instead, it foregrounds the multiple and dynamic material identities that constitute any literary work. The book as a space of analysis underscores the very constructedness of the imaginary unity not only of the category of the "work" itself but also of that between the "work" and the "book." As F. W. Bateson challengingly asked over thirty years ago, "If the *Mona Lisa* is in the Louvre, where is *Hamlet*?"[44]

The more we come to see literature as a social process and not as a singularly generative (or autopoetic) moment,[45] the more we can begin to "recover the collectivity," in Martha Woodmansee and Peter Jaszi's words,[46] that informs the making of literature in general and nineteenth-century literature in particular. As Meredith McGill has argued, there is a "foreshortening effect of the author-concept" that an attention to the book can help us reverse.[47] The more we attend to the bookishness of literature, the more we begin to see the role that a broad array of actors, and not just authors, played in governing the production, circulation, and reception of literature.[48] What was the authorial role of such "non-authors" as publishers, editors, judges, censors, translators, and readers, to which we could add the category of "programmers" today? As these various actors pushed, pulled, reshaped, repackaged, and outright deleted literary texts in part or in whole, how did their activities participate in—and at times supersede—the making of meaning surrounding literary texts? How can the intellectual battles for the ownership and interpretation of texts that manifested themselves on the printed page tell us something about the larger social concerns of a period or place? As we gradually recover a sense of what Margaret Ezell has called "social authorship," not as an alternative to romantic print culture but as a constitutive feature,[49] we will increasingly be able to complicate narratives about the growing individualization of ideas around 1800 charted by Michel Foucault in his influential article on the history of authorship.[50] Such studies will ideally make it increasingly difficult for the term "romantic author" to serve as shorthand for the isolated, hermetic genius.

If attention to the book offers one of the more important contributions to the field of literary study today, one of the core arguments of this book is that attention to literature also has important things to offer the expanding fields of the history of the book and communication studies more generally.[51] Research on the outside of books only tells half of the story of what books could mean to their readers.[52] As Albrecht Koschorke has argued in his anthropological study of the rise of eighteenth-century *Schriftkultur*, "A media theory that seeks to explain such self-revolutionary processes as completely as possible must develop a methodology to understand the *interdependence of technological mediality and semiosis*, the narrow overlap of the 'form' and 'content' of such signifying events."[53] While we have been busy illustrating the numerous ways that literature's meaning was shaped by the printed book in the course of the eighteenth and nineteenth centuries, we have overlooked in the process the ways in which literature contributed to shaping the identities of books and the bookish identities of the individuals who used and consumed them. Where Adrian Johns has shown us the means through which scientific culture contributed to how we think about print and the printed book,[54] I am interested in exploring how imaginative works of literature have contributed to our understanding of books—and to a potentially different, or at least more heterogeneous understanding at that. If there is, as Johns tells us, a continuity between the scholarly publishing practices of the early modern Tyco Brahe and the modern Ludwig Wittgenstein, what Goethe was doing in *Wilhelm Meister's Travels* or Mallarmé in *Dice Thrown Will Never Annul Chance* fit in an altogether different story. As Garret Stewart has argued, literature becomes a social fact precisely because of the powerful ways that it is tied to learning to read books.[55] A history of literature is thus integral to a history of books.[56] Literature makes books as much as books make literature.

To address this question of how literature thinks in and about books, *Dreaming in Books* takes as one of its principal sites of attention scenes of communication in romantic literary texts. I am interested in exploring how the symbolic movements *in* texts, whether of speech, things, or people, functioned as interpretations of the bibliographic environments through which such texts circulated. My work is indebted in this regard to Bakhtin's suggestive proposal that the "utterance" and not the "sentence" should constitute the main site of literary analysis and to Michel Serres's attention to the "phatic" function of language—language use that is designed not to convey content but to establish a connection.[57] The larger aim of this study is to identify what we might call a bibliographic poetics—a coherent set of stylistic and formal concerns—that attempt to make the medium of the book intelligible and thus legible to romantic readers.[58] How did literature make sense of the book so that it in turn made sense to its readers?

If one of the central features of romantic literature was a deep attention to mobility (as in Hölderlin's notion of "the streaming word" [*das strömende Wort*]), I want to ask how such circulatory energy was deployed to interrogate new conditions of communicating in books. How did prevalent modes of speaking and listening in romantic literature—such as whispering, betraying, renouncing, reporting, retelling, projecting, overhearing, confessing, or speaking "from the heart" versus "by heart"—work in concert with the circulation of objects (purses, maps, prostheses, pendulums, dossiers) and bodies (wandering, pilgrimaging, or dissected) to grapple with the changing nature of social interactivity brought about by the book's growing ubiquity? Conversely, how did the interruptions that commonly populated romantic texts—the loud noises, the parasitical guests, the intimidating followers (Irving's "dreadful monitor")—all point, in Bernhard Siegert's words, to a more general cacography, a "reference to the channel" itself?[59] In combining an analysis of the movements and fixations *of* texts with the movements and fixations *within* texts, the chapters that follow try to illustrate the extent to which romantic literary works acted as interpretations of and interactions with the bibliographic environment in which they appeared.

Bibliographic Romanticism

In arguing for the mutual overlap of books and romantic literature, *Dreaming in Books* attempts to revise one of the most enduring images of the romantic movement, perhaps best captured in Shelley's famous dictum from his *Defense of Poetry*, "When composition begins, inspiration is already on the decline."[60] Literature, according to this view, is what happens in the mind, not on the page. As Baudelaire would later declare, "Romanticism lies precisely in neither the choice of subject nor the depiction of truth, but in the manner of feeling," drawing upon Wordsworth's earlier sentiment from the *Lyrical Ballads* that "all good poetry is the spontaneous overflow of powerful feelings."[61] In paradigmatic fashion, the hero of Goethe's *Faust* famously *fled* his book-lined study, as creativity was increasingly aligned at the turn of the nineteenth century with its fidelity to an inner vision and its antipathy to the stuff of its dissemination. As Friedrich Kittler would later programmatically argue, "Poets in the discourse network of 1800 write around their own writing; they do not write down the system itself."[62] It was precisely an attention to the book's sensual, artifactual importance, and not its intellectual significance, as Ina Ferris has elegantly recounted, that was branded a mental disorder in the early nineteenth century.[63] As Marc Redfield has shown, it was the romantic age that bequeathed us this opposition between technics and aesthetics that is in many ways still operative today.[64]

And yet in each of the historical moments that gave rise to what literary scholars have typically identified as the various national and regional romanticisms, book historians have shown us that the emergence of "romantic" literature is almost always coincident with a major upsurge in the output and circulation of books. Romanticism is what happens when there are suddenly a great deal more books to read, when indeed there are *too many* books to read. According to the opposing narratives of book history and literary history, then, what books said and what books did were related only through opposition. The very forgetting of the book that has marked literary studies on and after romanticism is thus in many ways a product of a particular way of remembering the romantic period itself. A study of romanticism anchored in the history of the book can offer us a very different view of romanticism and the notion of "literature" it has bequeathed us.

What I try to identify in the pages that follow is a group of international (and internationally minded) writers for whom the book would become a vital source of creative energy and literary innovation. Such romantic writers did not write around writing, in Kittler's formulation, but crucially wrote *about* writing itself. Their writing can be read as a philosophy of bibliographic communication.[65] As the double meaning of Goethe's hypothesis, "everything is leaf/page," suggested, romantic naturalism was merely the flipside of romantic bibliographism: not just a media fantasy but a fantasy of media as well. For the main writers that I discuss here—J. W. Goethe, E. T. A. Hoffmann, Walter Scott, Washington Irving, Sophie Mereau, Edgar Allan Poe, Honoré de Balzac, and Stendhal—the book played an essential role in the larger aesthetic aims of their work. In thinking about the nature of the book, they were thinking about the nature of literature. For such romantic authors, composition *was* inspiration.

The larger aim of this book is to see the way such romantic writers were not opposed to, or even distinct from, a larger industry that was emerging in the nineteenth century to coordinate and organize what Roger Chartier has called the "order of books,"[66] but rather to see their work as an integral component in what we might call the naturalization of the book in the nineteenth century. Their "imaginative" texts, I want to suggest, served a similar function to such bibliographic reference works like J. K. Hinrich's *Verzeichniß der Bücher und Landkarte* (founded in 1797), A. J. Q. Beuchet's *Bibliographie de la France* (founded 1811), Martin Schrettinger's *Versuch eines vollständigen Lehrbuchs der Bibliothek-Wissenschaft* (1808), or T. H. Horne's *Introduction to the Study of Bibliography* (1814) that all emerged to map and make sense of this new, and increasingly tumultuous, landscape of books. The work of romantic writers—both their books and their fictions— functioned as a key space where the changes to the material conditions of writing and communication that defined the nineteenth century could be rehearsed, interrogated, and ultimately normalized. The historical significance of such romantic writers lies precisely in the extraordinary extent to which they addressed—through books—questions posed by the immense reorganization of human subjectivity around books, what it meant in Menzel's words to "dream in books."

Romanticizing Books

Few historical narratives have been more durable than those surrounding the impact of the printed book. Gutenberg's invention, so we have been told, gave rise to a medium that made ideas more stable, repeatable, sequential, national, and above all else, individual. The printed book's physical boundedness and typographical regularity became perfect embodiments of the temporal continuity and spatial autonomy on which both the modern subject (as *Individuum*) and the political form of the nation were to be founded. The printed book was imagined to be a timeless medium, as its "rise" or "coming" did the same thing to individuals and societies in all places and in all times.

This book argues that a very different way of thinking about books emerged during the romantic period. Alongside of the book's imagined singularity and indivisibility, one can also chart an equal and opposite engagement with the fragmentary, secondary, and collective nature of books. Romantic books and romantic literature not only pointed to the cosmological identity of the printed codex, they also foregrounded the relational structure of books, that there was a bibliographic elsewhere, before, and after with which books and their texts were increasingly engaged. Whether it was Goethe's two-decade-long experiment with multiply publishing his final novel, Walter Scott's grounding of the historical novel in the transmuting of an oral archive into print, or Balzac's creation of the supernovel in the form of the *Comédie humaine*, romantic literature in books repeatedly drew attention to the problem of the "where" that surrounded the romantic bibliocosmos more generally. Unlike Walter Benjamin's claim that "the birthing room of the novel is the individual in his loneliness,"[67] novel reading and novel writing for writers like Goethe, Scott, and Balzac required attention to the elaborate bibliographic horizon in which novels proliferated and circulated.

Such romantic concerns with problems of bibliographic placement were simultaneously connected to those of geographic placement, too. Reading romantic books means reading a growing attention to the international circulation of trends and texts, to an attention to cultural "flow" in the spirit of Raymond Williams.[68] When Goethe translated for his journal, *Ueber Kunst und Alterthum*, a portion of an article from the French journal, *Le Globe*, on the new "commerce intellectuel," which was itself a translation of an article from the British *Foreign Quarterly Review* on Swedish literature and which had been published as a direct response to Goethe's own initial appeal for a new "world literature," we can begin to see the high degree of circularity that such cultural circulation had assumed.[69] Poe's subsequent appeal for the "world at large" as "the only proper stage for the literary *histrio*" would echo a larger nineteenth-century fascination with a cultural and literary globality.[70] But it is important to distinguish such romantic interest in trafficking in cultural differences from an earlier eighteenth-century emphasis on producing a cultural universality that one could see in works like Montesquieu's *Lettres persanes* or Goldsmith's "The Citizen of the World; or Letters from a Chinese Philosopher residing in London to his Friends in the East."[71] As Madame de Staël, one of the great facilitators of an international romantic literary sensibility, would write in her novel *Corinne ou L'Italie* (1807), "The world is the work of a single thought, expressed in a thousand different forms."[72] Indeed, the dislocated, translating heroine of Staël's novel would provide a model of intercultural literary making that would become crucial to the careers of numerous romantic women writers. As I discuss in chapter 5, it was through the work of such translating women where we can see not only how important cross-cultural currents were to the romantic bibliocosmos but also how communicating in books was increasingly seen not as something closed, reliable, and ultimately durable but as far more open, fluid, and as that which always seemed to slip out of control, echoing Socrates' famous critique of writing in the *Phaedrus*.[73] Geographic displacement and authorial displacement—the problem of textual ownership more generally—went hand in hand in the romantic era.

At the same time that romantic books were reformulating the complex calculus of the local and the global, romantic books and their contents were also busy negotiating competing claims to individuality and collectivity: a work's projected singularity necessarily stood alongside an increasingly elaborate collective machinery, both social and technological, that was invested in making and disseminating such works. Whether it was Goethe's notion of himself as a "collective being" (*Kollektivwesen*) or the popular suspicion that Walter Scott was a "joint-stock business,"[74] romantic books and romantic literature promoted an image of the author not only as a towering singularity but also as a member or embodiment of a corporate or communal entity. Literature in books dramatized the complex interactions between the owning and the disowning of speech that inhered in the modern bibliographic landscape, the paradox of retaining while disseminating that grew increasingly problematic the more anonymous and abstract the processes of reception and circulation became. The romantic biblio-literary field was defined in many ways by a fundamental uncertainty about the control and ownership of communication, which romantic book formats and romantic literary texts in turn aimed to address. From the miscellany's promotion of the page as a site of numerous hands, to the publisher-driven nature of the collected edition, to the translator's ventriloquism, to the perorations of nineteenth-century editors to justify the proper balance of recension and emendation as they translated a vernacular manuscript tradition into print, romantic literature and romantic books were marked by a persistent sense of a crisis of the genitive.

Finally, if this book is driven by a greater attention to a variety of border-crossings in the world of romantic books, whether of format, nation, language, or gender, I want to apply this same focus to the category of the book itself that is my ultimate subject here. The *intermediality* of the romantic book is a core component of the story of the romantic book. Whether it was nineteenth-century editors' construction of notions of "oral" or "manuscript" culture in order to make sense of the printed edition, the way gift books often depended upon promoting the scribal practices of readers (inscribing, underlining, and dedicating), or the way the use of illustrated books at the turn of the nineteenth century interwove the practices of reading and seeing (reading as a form of seeing and seeing as an act of reading images), the proliferation of the printed book during the romantic period depended upon an engagement with a variety of non-print, non-book, and non-text practices and sites. This book only begins to scratch the surface of this history of intermediality in the romantic age, but my aim is to think through the way books have been embedded in a range of social and media practices that have a history and thus can have a future. The close of my book argues that the future of the book—and by extension the future of the humanities—depend upon facilitating what we might call an intermedial literacy, the overlap of the dual categories of media and translation that were so integral to the romantic moment. In arguing for the necessary alignment of a media and linguistic comparativism, I not only want to contribute to the ongoing challenge to disciplinary boundaries today. I also want to try to help move us away from the study of individual media and draw attention instead to larger media "ecologies," how individuals express themselves and interact with one another by using a variety of different media, modes of speech, and languages.[75] How do books participate in the shaping of other media today and how does the book's relationship to other media shape how we think about books and how we "speak" in books? In thinking about what comes next, I want to emphasize the "next to" and not the "after."

At the conclusion of his extraordinary essay "The Book as Symbol," which was in many ways (and many years ago) the inspiration for this book, Ernst Robert Curtius remarked: "Here, in the Age of Goethe, we bring our journey to an end. To be sure, many examples of writing imagery could be found in the succeeding centuries. But it no longer possesses a unique, a felt, a conscious 'life-relationship,' could no longer possess it after the Enlightenment shattered the authority of the book and the Technological Age changed all the relations of life."[76] My book begins where Curtius's study ends. It was precisely during the romantic age—during the moment when it stood at the threshold of becoming the embodiment of mass communication—that the book assumed not less but even more cultural significance. It was at the very moment when the book participated in structuring human relationships in the "technological age," to use Curtius's words, that we can identify a variety of literary writers who returned with renewed energy to explore this particular communications technology—what one could do with books and what books were doing to us. *Dreaming in Books* is thus one part of a much larger story about the intimate relationship between the history of communication and literary creativity.

CHAPTER ONE

Networking

Indeed, I wanted to write that my work consists of two parts: those, which lay
here before me, and all those that I have not written. And it is precisely this
second part that is the most important.

—Ludwig Wittgenstein

Fortresses of the Spirit

On Sunday, June 28, 1896, a ceremony was held to mark the completion of
a new building for the recently established Goethe and Schiller Archive in
Weimar. It was a day of extreme optimism: reverent speeches were delivered,
Beethoven's Ninth Symphony was played, and newspapers made grand pronouncements, comparing the archive to the Library of Alexandria, calling
Weimar the Athens on the Ilm, and anointing the new structure a "fortress of
the spirit" (*Geistesburg*), "temple," "hall of honor," "palace," and "citadel."[1]
Even the *Chicago Times Herald* reported the story, remarking, "The whole
may well be named the Pantheon of German Literature—the most unique
and valuable in the whole history of literature."[2] Standing imperiously on
a hill overlooking, indeed dwarfing, the small town below it, the imposing
new structure visually articulated the cultural hierarchy it was intended to
bring about. At the core of this architectural and institutional edifice was the
emerging textual monument to be known as the Weimar Edition.

The edition had been initiated nine years earlier, only two years after the
death of Goethe's last living relative, Walter Wolfgang von Goethe, who in
1885 bequeathed Goethe's entire *Nachlaß*, or posthumous papers, to the
Großherzogin Sophie von Sachsen-Weimar. The transference of Goethe's
manuscripts from private to public hands was a sensation in philological

circles, and the duchess quickly assembled a team of six editors and over seventy assistants to begin producing a new critical edition. Thirty-two years and one-hundred and forty-three volumes later, the project would reach its conclusion.

The edition not only functioned as a "Parallelaktion," in Dieter Borchmeyer's words,[3] to the founding of the German nation—the spiritual edifice on which rested the new *Kulturnation*—it also represented the culmination of the twin nineteenth-century aesthetic ideals of personality and totality. In his preface to the first volume of the Weimar Edition, the editor Hermann Grimm wrote: "One knew the poet, but now one wanted to know more about the writer and the man. Everything about everything of the man who was so dear to every German's heart."[4] And Bernhard Suphan, head editor and director of the project, wrote in his preface: "This edition shall represent in its purity and completeness the entirety of Goethe's literary activity along with everything that has been left behind of his personal essence, a project which has for the first time become achievable now that his posthumous papers have become accessible to scholarly treatment."[5] As the proliferating vocabulary of material completeness and personal essences indicated, the exhaustive empirical recovery of the author's life along with its complete and conclusive representation in print was to provide the foundation for all future interpretation.[6] One wanted "everything about everything" about the "writer" and the "man." The book was to represent the "purity" and "completeness" of this biographical data.

The Weimar Edition thus not only captured a particular theory of literature—that its meaning depended on knowledge of its author—but also a particular theory of the printed book: that it was capable of functioning as a timeless and unchanging object, an object which was itself totemically capable of holding together the social form of the nation. In the hands of the editors of the Weimar Edition, Goethe would no longer be a fluctuating network of publications and interpretations but would become something bound and complete, like the stone walls of the new archive that housed his literary remains. As Grimm had argued in his famous Berlin Goethe lectures of the 1870s just after Germany's historic unification, lectures which would function like a précis for the new edition: "We are no longer searching [in Goethe's works] for weapons that can be used for the attainment of freedom; rather, after a successful battle for freedom, we are searching for that which can strengthen us in our achieved position and fortify us in the possession of this attained good."[7] The Goethe of the Weimar Edition was to provide the spiritual edifice that sturdied the walls of the national *Burg*.

Rethinking the Book of Everything

The Weimar editors were, on the one hand, merely continuing a theoretical and material practice that Goethe himself had initiated. No previous author had been as instrumental in framing the authorial life as the key to understanding the literary *corpus*. As Goethe would write in his autobiography, *Poetry and Truth*, "Everything that I have written to this point are just fragments of a greater confession."[8] Or as he stated even more flatly in his aphorisms, "Why does everyone envy the poet? Because his nature necessitates communication, indeed, his nature is the communication itself."[9] According to Goethe, the poet was the message. Goethe worked assiduously to preserve and order the written traces of the life that would serve as the basis of the works. He produced eleven volumes of autobiographical writings in the final two decades of his life and oversaw the creation of a personal archive that consisted of an atelier of assistants, scribes, and editors[10]—a move of self-administration that must mark a first in literary history. Goethe's relentless activity as a collector, which only increased during his late period, had turned inward.[11] As Goethe famously remarked to his friend Friedrich Soret in 1832, "My oeuvre is that of a collective being who bears the name Goethe."[12] In a very real sense, Goethe's archivization preceded the architectural foundation of the Goethe Archive several decades later.

At the same time that Goethe was contributing to his own private institutionalization—to the institutionalization of the private itself—he was also working towards the public institutionalization of his works by applying to the *Bundesversammlung*, the parliamentary body of the German states, for a *Privileg* for his edition.[13] Despite the fact that the parliament lacked the legal authority to grant such a privilege, requiring Goethe to apply individually to all thirty-nine German states, each volume's title page of the edition was adorned with the words, "Under the privileges of the most honorable German Parliament." The paratextual gesture of the privilege was an anachronistic move that pointed both back in time to the early-modern copyright system of the royal privilege—to the very origins of print literature[14]—as well as forward to a time when a national system of copyright might exist to protect against the vigorous industry of piracy that beset the German book market. Most of all, it announced the sovereignty and the nationality of this final publication, that the boundaries of the book fixed the boundaries of the author's property as well as the cultural boundaries of the German nation that did not yet exist.[15] The *Privileg*, like the archive, was intended to institutionalize and nationalize the individual writer. It is easy to understand how the Weimar Edition could imagine itself as the legitimate heir, indeed the apotheosis, of these dual authorial and national projects.

And yet this is only part of the story of publishing Goethe and Goethe publishing. If we look more closely at Goethe's late publishing practices that concluded in his final collected edition, far from affirming these author- and nation-building projects, we can see a very different set of literary and bibliographic ideals emerging. I do not wish to imply that the Weimar Edition was somehow a misguided practice or that it has not proved to be a tremendously valuable resource for Goethe scholarship. But I do want to suggest that its production rested on a particular set of assumptions about literature, about the function that the printed book had in maintaining these literary ideals, and ultimately about Goethe's privileged place in the continuation of this literary system. Its production rested, in other words, on a particular way of reading Goethe that had become institutionalized in the nineteenth century, a perspective that depended on an understanding of what literary work was and thus where it could take place.

Under what one could call an ideology of the hand—in their exclusive focus on Goethe's final collected edition, the *Ausgabe letzter Hand*,[16] or their tireless attention to the unpublished manuscripts—the Weimar editors had seen publication as a form of degradation, as a disruption to the economy of consolidation on which authorial identity and literary culture came to depend in the nineteenth century. Goethe's relationship to print, however, the *process* of his actual publishing practices, necessarily remained overlooked. Yet as recent book historians, publishers, and bibliographers such as Siegfried Unseld, Waltraud Hagen, Dorothea Kuhn, and Wolfgang Bunzel have shown,[17] few writers exhibited a greater concern for the intersections of literature and publication than did Goethe during his late period. We now have a much clearer idea of how varied, extensive, and calculated his relationship was to publication and the printed book. There was a remarkable overlap between the formal operations within his late works and the bibliographic operations that surrounded the publication of these works. The meaning of Goethe's late work was always deeply and self-consciously intertwined with the changing conditions of communication in which it was produced.

The Novel as Network: J. W. Goethe's *Wilhelm Meister's Travels*

In this chapter I want to return to precisely those bibliographic and narrative spaces that were marginalized by the manuscriptural and biographical perspectives canonized by the Weimar editors and that subsequently exerted such a profound influence on both Goethe scholarship and literary scholarship more generally. Few writers have figured so prominently in the institutionalization of biographical criticism and the subsequent veering away from the bookishness of literature that it underwrote than Goethe. In attending to the complex diffusion of Goethe's work in print, I want to focus on his final major prose work, *Wilhelm Meister's Travels* (*Wilhelm Meisters Wanderjahre*), whose publication began in 1808 with the appearance of one of the work's novellas in Johann Cotta's *Ladies' Pocket-Book* and ended with the incorporation of a second version of the "novel" into the final authorized collected edition in 1829 (at which point the subtitle "A Novel" was dropped).[18] This late work thus not only encompassed the entirety of what scholars refer to as Goethe's late period, it also arguably encompassed the entirety of the early-nineteenth-century print system, from the miscellany, to the collected edition, to translations, to periodicals, to the format of the novel itself. Few works allow us such a capacious entry into the romantic bibliographic world as this one.

At the same time, Goethe's work can also be read as one of the signal contributions to the history of theorizing the book.[19] The *Travels* attended with extraordinary elaboration at a figural and narratological level to questions of bibliographic communication. Alongside a rich network of written objects that coursed throughout the novel—maps, inscriptions, tablets, notebooks, files, letters, and a variety of fictional texts—one also encountered a number of scenes that staged complex acts of linguistic communication, such as betraying (*verrathen*), renouncing (*entsagen*), rendering (*abstatten*), or paraphrasis. Book and narrative crucially interacted in the *Travels* to address the protocols of bibliographic communication that were fast shaping the nineteenth-century media imaginary. In thinking about the nature of the novel, Goethe was thinking about the nature of the book.

For German scholars of the last twenty years, *Wilhelm Meister's Travels* has come to be seen as a landmark of the modern novel. Drawing on Hermann Broch's initial modernist reassessment,[20] scholars no longer see the vast intellectual and formal heterogeneity of the *Travels*—what Broch called its *Stilagglomeration*—as the eclectic work of an old man but instead as a key precursor to James Joyce's *Ulysses*.[21] Not only is there a wild proliferation of genres within the novel (poems, aphorisms, diary entries, letters as well as a variety of short narrative forms), there is also an extraordinary proliferation of discourses as well (myth, history, religion, the arts, commerce, medicine, geology, pedagogy, cosmology, politics, and colonialism). The travel through space in the *Travels* is always a travel through ideas.[22] Even Dostoevsky's *heteroglossia* begins to appear decidedly monological in comparison to Goethe's novelistic polyphony.

Such current scholarly interest in Goethe's novel's capacity to represent and engage with the totality of available genres and forms of knowledge would of course have been deeply resonant with a particular romantic theory of the novel out of which the *Travels* emerged and to which the *Travels'* prequel, *Wilhelm Meister's Apprenticeship*, had done much to contribute.[23] As Novalis asked in his *Allgemeine Brouillon*, "Should not the novel comprehend all genres of style in a sequence diversely bound by a common spirit?"[24] Or as Friedrich Schlegel prophesied, "In the next generation the novel will take the place of the encyclopedia."[25] It was the novel more than any other genre that captured Schlegel's theory of a *progressive Universalpoesie* with its simultaneous claims to totality and transformation.[26] As Goethe himself wrote to J. F. Rochlitz about the *Travels*, "With such a little book [!] it is like life itself: within the complex of the whole one finds the necessary and the chance, the superior and the associated, occasionally successful, occasionally blighted, through which it achieves a kind of endlessness and which judicious or reasoned words can neither completely comprehend nor encompass."[27]

In placing Goethe's *Travels* at the heart of a larger story of the romantic novel, and the novel at the heart of a larger story of the romantic book, I want to redirect the way we have attended to the novel's cultural work during the romantic period. Goethe's contribution to the history of the novel did not simply lay in his capacity to represent the novel as a discursive archive or as an agglomeration of extraordinary formal heterogeneity within a single work, which Broch had suggested was necessary to counteract modernity's antipathy to representation, its *Abbildfeindlichkeit*. Rather, the innovative contribution of Goethe's *Travels* lay in the way it decoupled the novel's claim to represent everything from the unified space of the single book, the way it transformed the work into a network. Its very stylistic heterogeneity was mirrored by, and indeed depended upon, a complimentary bibliographic heterogeneity. Novel reading for Goethe was not framed as an act of splendid isolation but required attention to the elaborate bibliographic horizon in which novels proliferated and circulated. And novel writing did not solely encompass the patient imagination of complex narrative tapestries but involved attention to the available technologies of dissemination and preservation. Writing was crucially envisioned in Goethe's late work as a "craft." Where Novalis had written down in his notebooks that his task was "to find a universe in a book,"[28] Goethe's project by contrast relocated this universe across an entire spectrum of printed books and thus redefined the literary work as something material, processual, and spatially dispersed.

In drawing attention to the novel's bibliographic foundations, Goethe was of course continuing a revered novelistic tradition that extended from Cervantes to Sterne. And in affirming the novel's cosmological claims, its capacity to represent everything, Goethe was also simultaneously drawing upon current romantic theories of the novel. But in adding a mediological dimension to these claims—that the novel encompassed not just all genres but all material forms of communication as well—Goethe was marking an important point of departure from both his early modern and early romantic predecessors. The *Travels* promoted a very different way of thinking about both the book and the novel, not as a spiritual fortress as the Weimar editors had nor as "a totality existing for itself" (ein für sich bestehendes Ganze) as Friedrich Schlegel had, nor even a series of typographical gags in the spirit of Sterne or Cervantes. Rather, book and novel were uniquely reconceived as relational, transformable, and dynamic entities. The were refigured, in a word, as networks.

Perhaps no other concept has become as ubiquitous today in trying to understand modern media and society than that of the network.[29] But we are wrong to imagine that such networked thinking is exclusively a product of the digital and that print and the book are somehow intrinsically opposed to such networked communicative logic.[30] Thinking about novels and books in terms of networks is no metaphorical anachronism. Indeed, it was precisely the creative and epistemological work of networking that novels like Goethe's were designed to produce.[31] As we will see, Goethe's making and remaking of the *Travels* through printed interactions with his reading public articulated precisely the evolutionary, collective, playable, and navigational aspects that contemporary theorists have repeatedly identified as common to the nature of networks.[32] For Goethe, the emerging concern of modern fiction was no longer simply what texts could mean, but how such mobile, evolving, collectively generated webs of writing were to be navigated.

Like all of the chapters that follow, then, this chapter sets out to demonstrate the long history of new media, the way the basic concepts we use today to understand the digital can be traced back to origins that reside in bibliographic culture. Understanding the history of networked thought will not only allow us to critically approach the ubiquity of this figure as both a cultural and epistemological model today. It will also have important implications for our own scholarly methodologies and the narratives they produce about the history of the novel. The orchestrated diffusion of the *Travels* in books alongside its rhetorical strategies that oriented readers towards such diffusions suggests that the novel's rise was as much a consequence of a coherent set of stylistic affinities as it was of the capacity of such writing to promote a particular bibliographic hegemony. The novel's success depended upon a capability not only to be everywhere at the same time but also to incubate rhetorically and narratively such imaginary everywhereness. Reconceiving the novel as a network—the very challenge Goethe's *Travels* places upon its readers—solicits us to study precisely those derivative spaces that underpinned the novel's emerging generic centrality over the course of the eighteenth and nineteenth centuries.[33] In facilitating what we might call the topological study of literature,[34] network theory draws attention not to timeless, static, and ultimately enclosed literary objects but instead to the material distributedness and connectivity of literary work.[35]

The Problem of the Where

In the summer of 1815, Goethe published a short advertisement in the German newspaper *Morning Paper for the Educated Classes* (*Morgenblatt für gebildete Stände*), entitled "Reply to an Inquiry about *Wilhelm Meister's Travels*." The advertisement apologized for the absence of the *Travels* from the German book market, whose appearance had been anticipated since the publication of the first four chapters of the novel five years earlier in Cotta's *Ladies' Pocket-Book* in 1809. The advertisement, however, did not announce the pending appearance of the *Travels* in print but instead announced another series of excerpted novellas from the novel. It did not amplify the presence of an extant work, as an advertisement typically would, but rather substituted itself for a work which would not appear for another five years.

Goethe's advertisement and the deictic problems it both addressed and performed indicated the degree to which the problem of the "where" had emerged as one of the key identities of the work called *Wilhelm Meister's Travels*. Such ambiguous locatability was not simply a matter of Goethe's incapacity to produce, a convenient way of linking the work with the aging body and mind of the writer, but rather would come to mark an intrinsic aesthetic and bibliographic feature of the *Travels* from beginning to end. The advertisement was merely one of a variety of textual strategies that Goethe used during the 1810s to complicate the identity of the *Travels*, which included the publication of six separate novellas or portions of novellas from the novel in Cotta's *Ladies' Pocket-Book* prior to the initial appearance of "part one" of the novel in 1821.

In his study of this publishing strategy, Wolfgang Bunzel has argued that "these prepublications [*Vorabdrucke*] were part of a directed strategy of publication to gain readers."[36] The dissemination of the novellas was no doubt a useful marketing tool, one that will strike us today as deeply familiar. But Bunzel's use of the term of "prepublication" makes a series of important, and debatable, interpretive choices. Not only does "prepublication" determine that these "excerpts" or *Abschnitte* were in fact excerpts—and not separate "works" themselves—but calling them prepublications also determines *what* they were excerpts of: that they were parts of the larger whole of the *Travels* that did not yet exist. At the same time, the choice of "prepublication" not only defines the whole to which these parts belonged *as a whole* (the publication known as the *Travels*), it makes such wholeness dependent upon the incorporation of these earlier parts within a unified bibliographic space. The more one emphasizes the pre-ness of the novellas, the more they only matter once they reappear in the *Travels*. To readers in the 1810s—and no doubt to the author as well—it was not at all clear where these excerpts would end up.

When we look more closely at these "prepublications," it is precisely their (a)partness—the seamless relationship between part and whole implied in the notion of the *Abschnitt*—that Goethe would address through their publication. Far from establishing the unity and the identifiability of the final publication of the *Travels* or the inconsequentiality of the individual parts themselves, the publication of the excerpts, and as I will show in the next section, even of the *Travels* itself, functioned instead as an extended investigation into the status of the "cut" or "Schnitt" upon which the notion of the "excerpt" depended. More than simple marketing—more than just amplifying a particular model of absorbed novel reading that might resonate with how we think about novel reading today—such practices aimed to reorient the activity of reading itself as far more polyfocal. As Leah Price has argued, understanding a "culture of the excerpt" is an important means of understanding a particular culture of reading.[37]

The *Ladies' Pocket-Book* and the Excerpt

When Goethe published the first four chapters of the *Travels* in Cotta's miscellany the *Ladies' Pocket-Book*, they were typographically set off from the rest of the miscellany's contributions. They were not only framed by the title page, *Wilhelm Meister's Travels: First Book*, but were also paginated in roman, not arabic, numerals, a choice we know was Goethe's and not Cotta's.[38] Like the title page, the roman numerals marked the integrity and the apartness of the *Travels* from the rest of the miscellany. At the same time, however, chapter 1, "The Flight to Egypt," did not conclude the way it would in the *Travels* when it was eventually published, but ended with the words "(Here follows in the original a letter to Natalie, through which the *Travels* are introduced and connected to the *Apprenticeship*.)"[39] Through the dual use of both parenthetical and paraphrastic speech, the excerpt concluded with the signification of an omission. The very integrity and wholeness that was typographically achieved through the roman numerals was simultaneously grammatically undermined through the parentheses that marked off a space that referred somewhere else. Such a grammar of omission was then mirrored in the contents of the chapters that emphasized their own secondarity, whether it was the novella "St. Joseph II," which was a fictional adaptation of biblical gospel, or "The Flight to Egypt," which was a textual adaptation of a cycle of images. The excerpt, which was itself composed of other excerpts, articulated its own incompleteness. There was a dizzying recursivity at work as something was excerpted from an excerpt comprised of excerpts.

At the same time that the wholeness of the part was called into question, so too was the whole to which these parts referred. Not only did the other textual space, referred to as the "original," technically not exist, the part that was excerpted from the excerpt was framed both as the introduction to the *Travels and* as the connection to its prequel the *Apprenticeship* ("through which the *Travels* is introduced and connected to the *Apprenticeship*"). This other textual space, called the original, thus marked both a beginning and a continuation of another work. It was deeply divided, in other words, between being a part and a whole itself, between marking an origin of a new work and marking this new work as a part of the larger whole of the *Wilhelm Meister* series.

Following the advertisement in the *Morning Paper* in 1815, four more publications would follow in Cotta's *Pocket-Book* before the appearance of the first version of the novel in 1821. The first publication of this second wave was the incomplete novella "The Nut-Brown Maid" (1816), which was followed by the first half of "The New Melusina" (1817) with a preface that was not included in the *Travels*. This was followed by "The Man of Fifty" (1818), another incomplete novella, and finally, the second half of "The New Melusina" (1819). With the completion of "The New Melusina" in Cotta's *Pocket-Book*, we might be tempted to think such publishing practices were not only coming to a close but were beginning to articulate a looming sense of closure. But not surprisingly at this point, things were more complicated than this. "The New Melusina" was precisely the work that Goethe invoked, but did not include, in the second part of his autobiography, *Poetry and Truth,* in 1812.[40] The appearance in Cotta's *Pocket-Book* of the second half of "The New Melusina" was thus not only a prepublication of a later work, it was also a post-publication, or completion, of the novella's first half in Cotta's miscellany and its omission from Goethe's autobiography. If the excerpt from 1810, *Wilhelm Meister's Travels: First Book,* framed the whole to which it belonged as a part through the use of omission, "The New Melusina" drew attention to the incompleteness of the autobiography, both in terms of what had not yet been published and what had *already* been published.

At the same time, this act of filling-in was also marked by an act of re-writing, as the tale published in Cotta's *Pocket-Book* was framed as a new *version* of the earlier novella that was orally recounted, but not printed, in the autobiography. "One wanted the fairy-tale," Goethe would write in the *Pocket-Book* preface to "The New Melusina," "that I spoke of at the end of the second volume of my confessions. Unfortunately I will not transmit it here in its *original innocent freedom.* It was written down much later and points in its current state to a more seasoned period than the one we were concerned with in that work. This much suffices to prepare the discerning listener. Were I to narrate that fairy-tale today, I would begin in the follow-ing way—" (*WMT,* 851, my emphasis). The filling-in of the textual omission through the publication of "The New Melusina" simultaneously produced yet another omission (the fairy-tale's first version), which was itself framed as the original ("in its *original innocent freedom*"). The origin and thus origi-nal oscillated between functioning as an omission and an excerpt.

This proliferation of excerption and the problem of where such ex-cerpts referred dated back to the very first publication in Cotta's *Pocket-Book* that would subsequently be included in the *Travels,* "The Madwoman on a Pilgrimage" (1809), a translation from an anonymously authored eighteenth-century French novella, "La folle en pélerinage." Not only did "The Madwoman on a Pilgrimage," which was published prior to the first four chapters of the *Travels* in the *Ladies' Pocket-Book,* point backwards to a prior linguistic and textual source (its French original). It also pointed backwards to a different generic and bibliographic source because the po-etic "Romance" that was at the heart of the novella had been excerpted and translated by Goethe in Schiller's *Musenalmanach* as part of a four-part poem cycle in 1798. The publication of "The Madwoman on a Pilgrimage" was thus as much an excerpt of a larger work in the future (the *Travels*) as it was the whole to an earlier excerpt from the past (the poem cycle).

Taken all together, then, the "prepublications" of the *Travels* that stretched over the course of almost fifteen years and that uniformly appeared in the format of the miscellany consisted of a translation, an incomplete "book" from the novel, half of a novella, half a novella with an original preface, an incomplete novella, and then the concluding half of a novella that had appeared three years earlier in print and that had been omitted in Goethe's autobiography published even earlier. What was the status of the "pre" in these "prepublications"? Conversely, what was the status of the "publication" itself that always pointed either forward *or* backward? In each case, the "prepublication" challenged the simultaneous autonomy of both the part and the whole to which these parts belonged. They consistently begged the question of where the *Travels* was located, as each subsequent publication only contributed to the growing sense of omission that surrounded the work itself.

That Goethe's prepublication strategy occurred solely through the bibliographic scene of the *Pocket-Book* (literally a book that could fit in one's pocket, but more specifically a small format literary miscellany) would play a key role in shaping this emerging understanding of the "work" or "publication." Not only was there a tremendous semantic investment in the *Travels* in the use of diminutive forms—through words like *Täfelchen, Büchlein, Kästchen,* and *Schlüsselchen* (little writing tablet, book, casket, and key)—but as I will discuss in chapter 4, one of the miscellany's central identities in the nineteenth century was its capacity to promote the sharedness of writing, to break down the boundaries surrounding the physical object of the book and its contents. Goethe's publications that appeared in Cotta's *Pocket-Book* were each in their own way invested in precisely this project of undoing boundaries, of reformulating the cut as continuity. And yet as I will show in the fourth chapter, where the miscellanies promoted the sharedness of writing between individuals, between one reader and another and between readers and writers, Goethe's publishing practices were ecstatically self-referential. As they promoted the increasing difficulties of isolating a work's boundaries—its excerptual qualities—Goethe's prepublications also promoted the amplification of the authorial persona that regulated and orchestrated this print performance.

The bibliographic format of the miscellany through which Goethe organized the *Travels'* prepublication would not, however, serve as a passing interest, a kind of early generic stage through which he passed on the way to a more developed or advanced genre of the novel. As I will show at the conclusion of this chapter, the media poetics of the cut enacted through the deployment of the excerpt would play a key role in the later composition of the second version of the novel. Far from simple marketing devices, the novellas and the miscellany established an important bibliographic scene against which the *Travels* would come to understand itself.

The *Ausgabe letzter Hand* and a Poetics of the Version

With almost half of the novel in print by the time it appeared in 1821, it was little wonder that readers were critical of the repackaging of already printed and remunerated works. The feuilletonist Ludwig Börne claimed that Cotta's son had told him that "Goethe pulled out all of his old stuff just to fill-up the book"[41] and Friedrich Glover charged that the whole project was driven by "base financial speculation."[42] For these early nineteenth-century readers, the first version of the *Travels* looked like nothing more than repackaged and reprinted goods. And yet as Meredith McGill has shown, such reprinting was extraordinarily common in the first part of the nineteenth century.[43] Indeed, as I will discuss in the next chapter, repetition would become a constitutive feature of the modern literary market. Like the secondariness that surrounded the *Travels* as a sequel, such republication was indicative of the larger derivative nature of literature around 1800. It would be in the works of a writers like E. T. A. Hoffmann, Washington Irving, Edgar Allan Poe, and Honoré de Balzac where such experiences of textual repetition were elaborately rehearsed, interrogated and, of course, practiced.

But Goethe's case was markedly different. Not only was there a significant amount of ambiguity surrounding the repetitiveness of the prepublications of the 1810s that were then republished in the novel, but when during the course of the 1820s Goethe decided to rewrite the novel and produce a second version (*2. Fassung*) instead of a second part (*2. Theil*) or second edition (*2. Ausgabe*), the practice of repetition surrounding the novel's publication came to incorporate increasing degrees of change. Unlike Paul Budra and Betty Schellenberg's argument that the sequel functioned as a means of producing textual stabilization and consolidation in the eighteenth century, Goethe's deployment of the sequel and sequentiality only seemed to promote the opposite effect.[44] When a second *Wilhelm Meister's Travels*, published anonymously by Johann Pustkuchen,[45] appeared almost simultaneously in 1821 alongside Goethe's, such bibliographic data marked yet another important contribution to the growing multiplication of the novel's identities. If during the 1810s there had been too few *Travels*, by the 1820s there were far too many. The persistent discomfort that surrounded contemporary readers' reception of the novel arguably was less a matter of the isolated problem of repetition that was becoming increasingly common by the 1820s than it was a product of the ambiguous relationship between repetition and change in Goethe's own publishing practices.[46] The *Travels* never appeared as either a "new" work or as a stably reprinted "classic."

In the spring of 1822, after a disastrous year of reception for the novel, Goethe would publish another advertisement in the *Morning Paper*, this time entitled "Inclined Participation in the *Travels*."[47] It was an expression of thanks to readers such as Varnhagen von Ense and Adalbert Kayßler for their publications that supported the *Travels* against the novel's numerous detractors. In acknowledging his supporters, Goethe was also acknowledging that the novel did indeed pose a problem, which he dramatically referred to as the "problem of my life." The advertisement and its appeal to the novel's readers thus suggested the important ways that "error" had become a key component of writing. As Wilhelm would say in the *Apprenticeship*, "Sadly I have nothing to narrate except errors upon errors."[48] Goethe's advertisement framed the printed book as containing the capacity for self-correction. It made writing more collective and less singular. The relational exchange that Goethe established with his readers through the 1822 advertisement was thus a means of both drawing upon, but also producing, the self-correcting tendencies—the adaptability—of print "networks."

The genre of the advertisement this time did not function as a means of self-promotion—as an amplification of an author's works as it should have—but instead as a means of self-correction, as a way of addressing some problem with the writing process itself. Like the earlier advertisement that had substituted itself for the appearance of the novel, this newest advertisement signaled yet another textual omission, this time of the novel's anticipated second part. When the novel was initially published (Goethe received his first bound copy on May 22, 1821) it bore the complete title, *Wilhelm Meister's Travels, or the Renunciants. A Novel. Part One.* An original one-volume novel would have been a bibliographic exception in the early nineteenth century, and the novel's title amplified the already existing expectation on the part of readers that a second volume would be forthcoming. But by the time of the advertisement, Goethe had abandoned the continuation of the *Travels*, which he would not resume until 1825, at which point he began to drastically rewrite and reorganize it.

In place of the second part (*2. Theil*), then, Goethe produced a second version (*2. Fassung*), which he did not publish as a stand-alone work but only as part of his final collected edition. In place of the title page to the first version that established the anticipation of its continuation, the new title page, which now spread across two pages, pointed in two different directions: the first as a frame to the larger bibliographic enterprise of the collected edition and the second as a frame to the work that followed in the next three volumes. Like the prepublications that had appeared in Cotta's miscellany, it was now the *Travels* as a whole that was framed by a larger textual apparatus. Included in volumes 21–23 of the *Ausgabe letzter Hand* in 1829, the *Travels* were not only brought into direct bibliographic contact with their prequel, the *Apprenticeship* (volumes 18–20), they also radiated out into other spaces of the collected edition, for example, in the second volume of poems (volume 2 of the entire edition) that contained a section entitled "From Wilhelm Meister." Indeed, one could read the removal of the appellation "A Novel" from the title of the second version not only as a commentary on Goethe's thinking about genre but also as a bibliographic intervention as well. By removing the generic signifier, Goethe was also removing the signification of bibliographic unity and autonomy that readers had come to imagine when they read or bought a novel. Removing the word "novel" emphasized the work's incorporation within a larger textual cosmos.

Just as the 1821 version of the novel had raised important questions about its relationship to its textual precursors, which were themselves framed as fragments, so too did the 1829 version stand in an ambiguous relationship to its own fragmentary precursors, whether it was the novel's first version or Pustkuchen's imitation. In an advertisement for the *Ausgabe letzter Hand* that appeared yet again in the *Morning Paper*, Goethe would write next to the title of the *Travels*: "The marvelous fate that this small book experienced upon its first appearance afforded the author both the desire and generous spirit to give this production renewed attention. He found it entertaining to undo the work from the bottom up and rebuild it anew, so that in something totally different the same thing will appear."[49] The advertisement was meant to address the question of whether readers were receiving a reprinted, and thus canonized, work, or whether they were receiving something new, and thus an original work. On the one hand, Goethe was arguing that the *Travels* in the collected edition was indeed something new ("to undo the work from the bottom up and rebuild it anew"). At the same time, he continued to challenge any claim to originality and autonomy for this "new" work ("so that in something totally *different* the *same* thing will appear"). The answer to whether the second (or third) *Travels* was new or the same was: both. And it is crucial that it was precisely the appearance of Pustkuchen's version that Goethe identified as the impetus behind this process of revision and rewriting (the "miraculous fate" invoked by Goethe most likely referring to its doubling by Pustkuchen).

In the same advertisement where Goethe described the paradox of innovation that surrounded the *Travels*, he also articulated his understanding of the collected edition into which the *Travels* was to be subsumed: "Of what remains to be said, it shall only be touched upon how one had occasion to give the present forthcoming edition the predicates *sämmtlich* [collected/complete], *vollständig* [complete], and *letzter Hand* [final authorized]."[50] It is here where we might expect to find a justification for the model of monumentality that would later inform the Weimar Edition. Yet something very different seems to be happening in this short advertisement. In Goethe's words, *sämmtlich* is defined as "everything that above all also appeared valuable to be shared from the papers of the author." That which has been collected is based on a criterion of value (*werth*) that defines the act of *collection* first and foremost as an act of *selection*. Instead of stressing the totality of the collection's parts, this definition of "everything" emphasizes what has been left out. Goethe continues by arguing that *vollständig* represents, on the one hand, "the author's nature, formation, and progress" (des Verfassers Naturell, Bildung, Fortschreiten) and, on the other hand, "multifaceted striving in all directions" (vielfaches Versuchen nach allen Seiten hin). Completeness encompasses both the temporal evolution of the writer ("Fortschreiten") as well as the formal diversity of his work ("Versuchen nach allen Seiten"). The edition's completeness is framed as a function of both axes of time and space, but Goethe's use of gerunds (*Fortschreiten* not *Fortschritt*, *Versuchen* not *Versuche*) emphasizes process over completion. Finally, on the term *letzter Hand*, Goethe writes: "It is principally important, however, to protect the expression *letzter Hand* against misunderstanding. Wherever it has been used, it only signifies that the author has done his last and best, without therefore allowing his work to be seen as concluded" (ohne deshalb seine Arbeit als vollendet ansehen zu dürfen). The works are complete (*vollständig*) without being concluded (*vollendet*). They are understood to extend beyond the work of the author's own hand.

The advertisement thus defined the collected edition in much the same terms as Goethe had defined the *Travels* itself that was to be included in the edition. Instead of emphasizing the unity of the works that appeared within the collected edition, the advertisement underscored their diffusion. It was precisely this reconfigured notion of completion as diffusion that proved to be such an irritant to Goethe's contemporaries. In his essay "Critique of the latest Cotta Edition of Goethe's Works" (1828), Friedrich Schütz, author of a seven-volume work on Goethe's philosophy, argued: "Is it enough to lament that of the 'hitherto dispersed publications' that Goethe invokes, only 'some things' and not, as one would very much desire, 'everything' is included in this *Ausgabe letzter Hand*!"[51] Just as it had been in the case of the novel, it was the status and the location of "everything" that was at stake in the format of the collected edition. Whether it was the novel or the collected edition, Goethe's publishing practices were crucially redefining "everything" not as a unified codicological identity but instead as a temporally and spatially dispersed process.

It was precisely the category of the version (*Fassung*), I want to suggest, that crystallized for Goethe the poetics of expansion that had surrounded the *Travels* from its inception. It enabled the work's extraordinarily high degree of intertextuality to assume a bibliographic dimension as well. The final version of the *Travels* was neither the same nor new, but belonged to a larger chain of Goethe's works that each played with this question of novelty or repetition dating back to the translation of "The Madwoman on a Pilgrimage" in Cotta's miscellany, a point that should stand as an important challenge to arguments that the *Travels* represented the shift from a novelistic poetics of the *Nacheinander* to the *Nebeneinander*.[52] In the same way that the *Travels* seemed to extend horizontally through a range of print formats, it also extended itself vertically back in time to incorporate previous versions of itself, including bibliographic parodies like Pustkuchen's or paratextual commentaries like Varnhagen von Ense's. The "version," as opposed to the "edition," articulated a particular understanding of bibliographic culture as both diffuse and increasingly interconnected. Whether it was in the form of prepublishing the fragmentary novellas or republishing the novel only as part of the collected works, we can see how the *Travels* participated in a publishing program that continually transgressed and expanded the work's boundaries so that the demarcation of the literary work became increasingly problematic.

In order to convey just how problematic, I have included a network topology of the publication of the *Travels* (fig. 1.1). Such a topology can help us visualize the dispersed nature of this work and chart the relationality surrounding the work's various "parts." It allows us to reconceive the static image of autonomous publications that the more traditional work of descriptive bibliography would produce with a more dynamic understanding of how these elements might relate to one another. Such maps—like all maps—are not without interpretation, as we must judge which publications are part of the work (the "nodes") and how these publications connect to one another (the "edges" or "links"). In both cases, these determinations are dependent not just on reading the material cues of publication history but also on how the language of the texts perform the connectivity of the bibliographic data. As I will show in the next section, attention to the growing complexity of the *Travels'* identity was not limited to its bibliographic

Wilhelm Meister's Travels (1808–1829)
A Network Topology

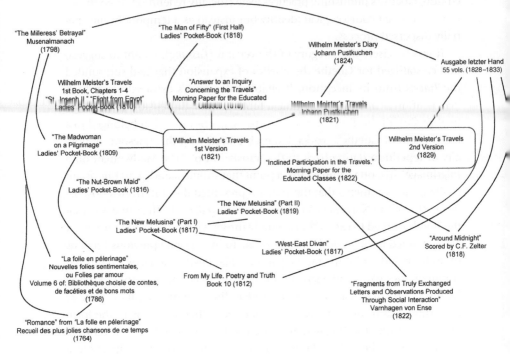

"The Milleress' Betrayal"
Musenalmanach
(1798)

"The Man of Fifty" (First Half)
Ladies' Pocket-Book (1818)

Wilhelm Meister's Diary
Johann Pustkuchen
(1824)

Ausgabe letzter Hand
55 vols. (1828–1833)

Wilhelm Meister's Travels
1st Book, Chapters 1-4
"St. Joseph II," "Flight from Egypt"
Ladies' Pocket-Book (1810)

"Answer to an Inquiry
Concerning the Travels"
Morning Paper for the Educated
Classes (1816)

Wilhelm Meister's Travels
Johann Pustkuchen
(1821)

"The Madwoman
on a Pilgrimage"
Ladies' Pocket-Book (1809)

Wilhelm Meister's Travels
1st Version
(1821)

Wilhelm Meister's Travels
2nd Version
(1829)

"Inclined Participation in the Travels."
Morning Paper for the
Educated Classes (1822)

"The Nut-Brown Maid"
Ladies' Pocket-Book (1816)

"The New Melusina" (Part II)
Ladies' Pocket-Book (1819)

"The New Melusina" (Part I)
Ladies' Pocket-Book (1817)

"West-East Divan"
Ladies' Pocket-Book (1817)

"Around Midnight"
Scored by C.F. Zelter
(1818)

"La folle en pélerinage"
Nouvelles folies sentimentales,
ou Folies par amour
Volume 6 of: Bibliothèque choisie de contes,
de facéties et de bons mots
(1786)

From My Life. Poetry and Truth
Book 10 (1812)

"Fragments from Truly Exchanged
Letters and Observations Produced
Through Social Interaction"
Varnhagen von Ense
(1822)

"Romance" from "La folle en pélerinage"
Recueil des plus jolies chansons de ce temps
(1764)

Figure 1.1   Network topology of Goethe's *Wilhelm Meisters Wanderjahre.*

operations but was motivated through narrative and rhetorical changes that accompanied the work's evolution over time. The novel's contents were designed to facilitate readers' orientation towards reading the novel according to such "expansionist" poetics, providing as we will see a kind of cartographical training. There was a navigational logic built into the novel itself.

Cartography and the Novel

In chapter 7 of the second book of the second version of the *Travels*, we find Wilhelm at the Lago Maggiore in Italy. "After our friend had discharged the preceding letter, he went still further, wandering through neighboring mountain ranges until a majestic valley opened up before him where, on the verge of a new stage of life, he hoped to conclude a few of his affairs" (*WMT*, 496). This scene marks the central turning point of the novel, mirroring in many ways Goethe's own framing of his Italian journey as a key autobiographical turning point. The enclosed space of the lake would para-doxically function as the scene of a crucial turn in Wilhelm's curriculum vitae, as the novel played on the competing notions of "revolution"—as linear change and circular repetition—that were so important to Goethe's late poetics. Indeed, in the original plan for the novel—before Cotta's pub-lishing conditions forced Goethe to transform the work from two to three volumes—the Lago Maggiore scene was to mark the end of the first volume. The biographical transition was to be amplified by the material caesura of the physical book.

One of the most defining features of the entire chapter is the way it is structured by an overwhelming accumulation of inter- and intratextual ref-erences that are most often self-referential. At the opening of the chapter we learn that Wilhelm's traveling companion, the painter, has read the prequel to the novel we are reading and is on a pilgrimage to paint the scenes of the homeland of one of its most memorable characters, Mignon. His paintings will become explicit visual citations of Mignon's songs from the *Apprentice-ship*. When this project is complete, the traveling companions then search out the characters from "The Man of Fifty," the novella within the novel. After several days crisscrossing the lake together, we learn that the widow from "The Man of Fifty" tells Wilhelm her and Hilarie's story, which is of course the novella we have just read. And finally, the chapter concludes in a moment of crisis with the painter singing, instead of painting, Mignon's song, "Kennst du das Land, wo die Zitronen blüh'n."

Far from enacting a moment of leaving behind, then, the scene of the Lago Maggiore is much more about the problem of the new beginning, enacting once again the continued tension between repetition and renewal that was at the heart of both this scene and the novel itself and that would be dramatized in what would become the new middle-point of the novel, book 2, chapter 11, where Wilhelm narratively grapples with the problem of recounting a traumatic episode from his childhood. Indeed, the impor-tance of the lake as the scene for such biographical turns (repeated with a difference in the figure of the river in chapter 11) was precisely its capacity for reflection, its ability to mediate the characters' relationship to the na-ture around them.[53] Such self-referential recursivity was of course already a component of *Wilhelm Meister's Apprenticeship* (when the *Turmgesellschaft* of the novel produces the novel we are reading, for example) and would come to be a key feature of the German romantic novel in general, which owed much of its inspiration to the revived popularity of Cervantes' *Don Quixote* (translated by Ludwig Tieck in 1799–1801).[54]

Hannelore Schlaffer has seen this scene of characters tracking down char-

acters from their books as an engagement with the problem of the trivializa-
tion of art in a bourgeois age.[55] Such a reading overlooks, however, the variety
of ways that this chapter seems to engage with the problems of reproducibility and secondarity as sources of renewal as well. The crisis of the chapter
occurs when the painter attempts to recite, rather than paint, Mignon's song.
Like the Major in "The Man of Fifty" who must move from a commonplace
culture of memorization and citation (he experiences repeated personal crises surrounding his attempt to cite a text), the characters at the Lago Maggiore must also learn to occupy a hybrid culture of versional, not citational,
secondarity. The structure of intertextuality of this scene, then, is far more
akin to what Gérard Genette would term "hypertextuality," the necessity of
the dual characteristics of absence and transformation through the act of
reference.[56] The reference in the Lago Maggiore chapter always points to a
textual elsewhere *that cannot be repeated* as signs are structured according to
increasing degrees of omission. The circle is always a spiral in Goethe.

Such readily apparent "hypertextual" moments in this chapter largely
concern the relationship between the sequel and the prequel or the frame
narrative and the novellas within the novel. And yet there is another moment that has largely been passed over by critics and that addresses the
connection between the first and second *versions* of the *Travels*—that more
nearly addresses, in other words, Goethe's relationship to publishing and
the printed book. When Wilhelm and his traveling companion at the Lago
Maggiore decide to find the characters from the novella "The Man of Fifty,"
the narrator describes their quest in the following way:

> They began crisscrossing the lake, observing the points where their friends
> tended to appear in this paradise. They had informed their skipper that they
> had hopes of seeing friends here and it did not take long until they saw a
> beautifully ornamented ship gliding towards them. They hurried after it and
> did not restrain themselves from passionately preparing to board it. The two
> women, who were somewhat taken aback, quickly composed themselves as
> Wilhelm showed them the small piece of paper and they both recognized,
> without a second thought, the arrow that they had drawn. The men were
> speedily and warmly welcomed aboard the women's ship, which occurred
> with great haste. (*WMT*, 501)

At first glance, there is little that is remarkable about this passage, a fact
that has much to do with the generic technique of description that the passage employs and that was one of the hallmarks of Goethe's late style more
generally. Remarkable is that there is nothing remarkable here. Phrases like

"and it did not take long," "a beautifully ornamented ship," and "somewhat taken aback" tell us very little, just as we are given no clarity about where such "crisscrossing" takes them in search of the women. The passage is characterized by the simultaneous communication and withholding of information, which reaches a highpoint with those concluding signs of the "small piece of paper" and "the arrow" that are not explained at all but that allow the men to enter the women's "ship."

I would like to pause for a moment and look more closely at those two signs of the "paper" and the "arrow" and the role that they play in this scene. As the narrator in *Werther* said, "Nothing remains for us to do other than to not overlook even the smallest piece of paper that has been found."[57] On one level, there is a certain logic to the idea that a piece of paper and an arrow could function as signs that facilitate Wilhelm and the painter's entry into the women's nautical salon. There is nothing contradictory, in other words, about the function of paper and arrow as communicative devices. But on another level, these signs make little sense in the context of this scene. Why would an arrow and a piece of paper suddenly transform the women's emotional state from "somewhat taken aback" to "warmly" once they have seen these objects, a process that occurs "without a second thought"?

One possible explanation of this discrepancy is supplied by the text itself, in the piece of information, "which they themselves had drawn." The establishment of contact is achieved through the recognition of one's own handwriting, as the self-reflexivity of the entire chapter is repeated in this particular scene of communication. The scene contains enough information, in other words, to allow the reader to accept its premise—women allowing men entry to their ship. But on another level, the piece of paper and arrow are deeply opaque signs. We have never before encountered the small piece of paper and its arrow in the second version of the *Travels*, and in this sense, there is an element that remains unexplained, indeed inexplicable, about them. We could say that they operate as opaque signifiers, as objects that invite and yet stubbornly resist interpretation, much like the little casket that circulates throughout the novel and that no one can open.[58]

When we turn to the equivalent scene in the first version of the *Travels*, however, we find that these two signs are in fact amply described. They function in this passage as a way of facilitating communication between characters at a distance. At the conclusion of "The Man of Fifty" in the first version of the *Travels*, Hersilie tells Wilhelm in a postscript how he will be able to find the characters of the novella (the same characters he meets in the second version on the Lago Maggiore):

> In order to show you how you can meet this lovely pair on your travels, I will
> turn to rather strange means. You are receiving in this letter a small excerpt
> of a map; when you place this piece on the larger map, the point of the
> magnetic needle that is drawn on it will direct you to the region where those
> sought-after ones have gone. (*WMT*, 126)

Thus in the first version we learn how Hersilie has constructed an elaborate
cartographical game. Wilhelm's task is to find where on the larger map this
excerpted piece fits, and when he has done this the arrow that was drawn on
the excerpt would point him where to go on the larger map. Only through
the combination of the excerpt with its original would the sign (the arrow)
make sense.

Like the opening excerpt of the novel that was initially published in
Cotta's *Pocket-Book*, it is now the second version of the whole novel that is
characterized by an omission. Instead of arguing for these signs' opacity in
the second version, then, we might be inclined to argue that this omission
in the second version is a "mistake," as the editors of the Frankfurt critical
edition have done, continuing a point of view that Erich Trunz first argued
for in his Hamburg Edition. "Goethe overlooked," write the Frankfurt editors, "the necessity in the second version to include an explanation of this
mention of the arrow and the little piece of paper both here and at a later
point" (*WMT*, 1129). However plausible it is for Goethe to have overlooked
something, the problem with such an explanation is that it depends on
a problematic hermeneutic distinction between *intentional* and *accidental*
changes to understand the process of rewriting. How are we reliably to differentiate between omissions that are "meaningful" and ones that are "mistakes," especially in a scene, a chapter, and a novel characterized by a poetics
of omission? At the same time, the argument that Goethe overlooked something reinforces, however unintentionally, the cliché that this is the work of
an "old" author who had neither the time nor the intellectual faculties left
to remember to explain something.[59] It conflates the author's identity with
that of the narrator who is in fact very often in a hurry, as in "The Man of
Fifty," whose narrator repeatedly uses the word "genug" ("enough") to stop
having to explain something.

In drawing on the explanation of "overlooking," I want to suggest that
the Frankfurt editors, whose commentary is otherwise marked by an extraordinary sensitivity to detail, have overlooked something. Like the recourse to saying that these signs are somehow opaque, the argument of
overlooking elides interpretation. The significance and thus signification of
these signs only emerges through a particular way of reading that incorpo-

rates knowledge of the material history of the novel, that reads the entire history of its publication, a reading practice that these signs are in fact aimed at bringing about.

The arrow in the second version can thus be read in its literal dimension *as an arrow*. Like the other moments set against the backdrop of the Lago Maggiore, it points the reader somewhere else, a somewhere else that I would identify in this case not as the novel's prequel or a framed narrative within the novel, but as the first *version* of the novel in which the arrow's meaning is explained. By not including the explanation of the arrow in the second version, Goethe is placing the novel's reader in the same situation as the novel's protagonist in both versions. Just as Wilhelm has to place a piece of one map on top of a much larger map in order for the piece to make sense, we as readers are invited to perform the same cartographical operations on the second version—to conceive the second version as an "excerpt" and to lay it onto a much larger map (or textual space) that would include the first version. Only then do the sign (the arrow) and the text (the map) make sense. This crucial moment of pointing—and not citing—within the frame narrative of the second version frames the second version itself not as something either "new" or "the same," but merely as part of a larger textual unit. Both sign and text are critically reconceived as "excerpts." They do not resist meaning, but radically expand the *location* of meaning across both time and space. According to the arrow and the map, the meaningful unit is always the composite and the compound.[60]

The significance of the arrow—as arrow—is not limited to this single moment in the text, however, but points to a larger concern with the symbolic more generally. As we later learn in the novel, the key that everyone is searching for to open the circulating casket is said to look like an arrow. "Here, my friend," writes Hersilie to Wilhelm upon finding the key in Fritz's pocket, "now finally what do you have to say to this picture of our riddle? Does it not remind you of barbed arrows? God bless us!" (*WMT*, 599) Goethe would include an image of this key/arrow as the only illustration to the *Travels* (fig. 1.2), suggesting just how important its visualization was to the novel. And by the close of the novel we learn that this key, which looks like an arrow, does not work as a key after all. The casket, it turns out, is only openable through the manipulation of magnets that hold down the lid. That is to say, as the key loses its keyness—and the associated hermeneutic notions of depth and penetration that go along with it—the key becomes an arrow. What is more, the element that replaces the key is the magnet, which is precisely the substance of the arrow that was described in the cartographical game of the first version (where it was called a "magnetic

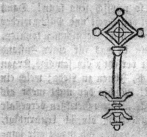

20

und mich auch wohl wieder entbinden kann; und so
wird allein die Eröffnung des Kästchens mich beru-
higen. Die Neugierde wird doppelt mächtig. Kom-
men Sie eiligst und bringen das Kästchen mit.
Für welchen Richterstuhl eigentlich das Geheimniß
gehöre, das wollen wir unter uns ausmachen; bis
dahin bleibt es unter uns; niemand wisse darum,
es sey auch wer es sey.

Hier aber, mein Freund, nun schließlich zu dieser
Abbildung des Räthsels was sagen Sie? Erinnert
es nicht an Pfeile mit Widerhaken? Gott sey uns
gnädig! Aber das Kästchen muß zwischen mir und
Ihnen erst uneröffnet stehen, und dann eröffnet das
Weitere selbst befehlen. Ich wollte, es fände sich
gar nichts drinnen und was ich sonst noch wollte
und was ich sonst noch alles erzählen könnte — doch
sey Ihnen das vorenthalten, damit sie desto eiliger
sich auf den Weg machen.

Figure 1.2   The image of the arrow/key from J. W. Goethe, *Wilhelm
Meisters Wanderjahre* (Tübingen: Cotta, 1829), 3:20. Private Collection.

needle"). In his aphorisms and observations on natural science from 1823,
Goethe would write, "The magnet is an Ur-phenomenon, which one only
needs to say aloud to have it explained; through this it becomes a symbol
for everything else, for which one need not search for words or names."[61]
The magnetic arrow is thus not one symbol among many for Goethe, but
the symbol of the symbol itself. And the crucial aspect of this symbol is the
way it is reconfigured as synecdoche.

Theories of the symbolic have constituted one of the principal sites of
critical attention in Goethe's work—and, one could argue, in understand-

ings of romanticism more generally—and the *Travels* has played a crucial role in such debates. According to Wilhelm Emrich, whose article "Das Problem der Symbolinterpretation" represents one of the most lasting and influential accounts of the problem, it is the figure of the small casket and its fundamental identification with the secret or riddle that most characterizes Goethe's theory of the symbolic. "In the literary symbol," writes Emrich, "there remains embedded a secret, an unspoken, indeed unspeakable element."[62] According to this theory of the literary symbol, carried forward by such seminal works of literary criticism as Frank Kermode's *Genesis of Secrecy*, it was precisely the fundamental opacity of literary representation that lent literature its literariness. The secret, the parable, the riddle, these all emerge as the essential communicative modes of literature.[63]

But in reading the casket and not the arrow as the central symbol of Goethe's novel, we miss the fundamental richness and novelty of Goethe's thinking about literary work. On one level, Goethe's theory of the symbol that emerged in the *Travels* had much in common with Benjamin's subsequent and enormously influential theory of allegory as the defining rhetorical device of modernity. For Goethe, as for Benjamin, the sign's referent was no longer self-evident or present within the sign itself. When the goldsmith uttered the famous words at the close of the novel, "some secrets are better left untouched" (an solche Geheimnisse sei nicht gut rühren) (*WMT,* 743), he was not simply telling us the age-old wisdom that secrets should remain secrets, thereby affirming "mystery" as a key component of the literary work. Rather, he was offering a critique of a particular mode of reading captured in the notion of *rühren* or "touch." Some secrets are better left untouched suggested that "touch" was not the best way to understand the "secret." One needed to look *elsewhere,* to sense the diffuse interconnectedness that they represented, which also explains why the goldsmith stands *back* in the moment that the container's lid opens or why his speech is reported in indirect, not direct, speech. The symbol as arrow suggests that its meaning is always somewhere *else.* Rather than undermining the riddle-like nature of Goethe's art, it drew attention to the combinatory logic of riddles. As Benjamin himself suggested, "The riddle is a fragment [*ein Bruchstück*] which makes a whole when combined with another fragment with which it fits."[64] But unlike Benjamin, for whom allegory implied the absolute arbitrariness of the relationship between sign and referent ("any person, any object, any relationship can mean absolutely anything else"),[65] Goethe's symbol of the symbol suggested that there was a particular destination, that the symbol as arrow crucially pointed *somewhere.* More than just establishing the contingency of referentiality, the "polarity" of the symbol contributed to the construction of a larger network of meaning. As both arrow and magnet, as that which points and pulls, the symbolic whole is transformed into a part or, to bring us all the way back to those initial prepublications in the miscellany, into an excerpt.

Goethe's transformation of the key into a magnetic arrow can be read as an epochal reconfiguration of the novel's intimate relationship with the figure of the key, whether it was the courtly *roman à clef* or the domestic novel's reliance on the visual space of the keyhole.[66] Goethe conceived of the novel no longer as a key to real historical persons or a spatial and psychic interiority but rather as a pointer to a codicological elsewhere. In place of the hermeneutic principles of linking a text to the world or penetrating the mystery of its meaning, the key as magnetized arrow framed reading as an art of bibliographic connectivity. The book did not point to a world or a self but to more books.

Wilhelm's cartographical training showed readers how knowledge of such larger textual universes was to be increasingly crucial to reading experiences in the early nineteenth century. Balzac's own transition to thinking of the "work" as a massive, unified "oeuvre" a year after Goethe's death in 1833 would arguably mark the highpoint of this move towards larger and larger literary systems, a tradition that one could see concluding, and unraveling, in Robert Musil's endless *The Man Without Qualities*.[67] The function of the arrow and the map in the second version of the *Travels* was to apply this principle of hypertextuality—the displacement of meaning to a textual space beyond a single work's boundaries—not from one work to another, but from one version to another of the *same work*. It crucially redefined the boundaries, and thus the classification, of the literary "work" itself. While Goethe's project anticipated in many ways other nineteenth-century projects of rewriting, most notably exemplified by Walt Whitman's *Leaves of Grass*, it also importantly grew out of an eighteenth-century culture of serial bibliographic expansion, from Klopstock's five-decade-long making of his *Messiah* to Wieland's persistent swelling of his Bildungsroman, *The History of Agathon*, to Sterne's own open-ended continuations of *Tristram Shandy*. But Goethe's project of turning the leaf or "Blatt" into a "Blättchen" (the little piece of paper upon which the magnetic arrow was sketched) asked that one observe the entirety of this process, that each subsequent bibliographic version only made sense in relation to the entirety of its previous manifestations.

Nineteenth-century readers were critical of Goethe for not including the first version of the *Travels* in his *Ausgabe letzter Hand* because they felt that the two versions constituted two *separate* works and a truly complete collected edition should contain all of Goethe's "works." As Friedrich Schütz wrote in his review of the edition, "The old text must also be reprinted in a complete edition of Goethe's collected works."[68] But this was just the inverse of the critique that readers had made *against* the inclusion of the previously published novellas in the first version of the novel. In that case, there was no difference seen between the novellas in the miscellanies and the novellas that appeared in the 1821 *Travels* and thus they should *not* have been reprinted. In either case, the works were either absolutely the same or they were absolutely different. They were conceived as finite objects and finite reading experiences. What the arrow and the map performed was the problematization of precisely this logic of sameness and difference, and they did so by arguing for the importance of the *material processes* that surrounded the literary work. They located literary work, and thus the "work" itself, not in some ideal and crucially immaterial space, but instead in the material event of publication—the circulation, distribution, and reproduction that shaped its reception. They reoriented the reader's gaze to the mobile artifacts of literary life.

The Anatomy of the Book:
The Work of Art as Technological *Präparat*

If the protagonist's biographical caesura in book 2, chapter 7 of the *Travels* oriented the reader's experience to the past permutations of the literary work in order to conceive of a more expansive and mobile literary system, then it would be another key biographical transition in Wilhelm's life figured in book 3, chapter 3, where we see Goethe's second version orienting the reader's gaze to the *future* operations that the work might theoretically undergo. Indeed, an explicit connection between these two chapters is provided by the text itself, where the image of the key that looks like an arrow is printed at the close of chapter 2 of the third book, literally pointing ahead (or more properly down the page) to the following chapter that is my subject here. The *Travels* thus expanded its identity not only back in time to encompass all prior permutations and manifestations of itself, but also forward in time to encompass its production beyond the boundaries of the author's life. It inscribed the literary work into an impersonal, deindividualized, and importantly technologized (and not organic) future.

In the third chapter of the third book of the *Travels*, we meet Wilhelm in the anatomical theater. He is recounting an important episode in his education or *Bildung*, one that will ultimately conclude in him saving his son's life at the end of the novel (and thus transforming himself into a medical doctor). Commentators have repeatedly seen in this chapter's intense interest in the human corpse—and the novel's larger fascination with the wounded body more generally—a prime example of the growing medicalization of culture at the turn of the nineteenth century so famously identified by Michel Foucault in his *The Birth of the Clinic*.[69] As Simon Richter has illustrated, it was Lessing's work on the Laocoön statue that placed the body in pain at the center of late-eighteenth-century aesthetic thought.[70] As Clifford Siskin has suggested, the medical and the literary begin to write each other during and after romanticism.[71] The anatomical sciences were thus one, albeit very important, component of this larger medical turn, and one can indeed observe the growing popularization of anatomical study in the closing decades of the eighteenth century.[72] As Barbara Stafford has argued, the cutting and classifying at the heart of anatomical practice had become a kind of epistemological leitmotif of the European Enlightenment.[73] Like the symbol of the key and its associated hermeneutical practices of unlocking and penetrating, the anatomical sciences became a potent symbol for a larger reorganization of modern knowledge around principles of objectification, penetration, and specialization that would then elicit a variety of romantic responses.

In our attention to the ways such literary representations of the body (whether in pain or dead) have been used to address the medicalization of modern culture, we have in the process overlooked the ways the figure of the body offered an important site to work through the changing realities of communication that structured both the interactions between bodies and the boundaries of those bodies. As the work of Albrecht Koschorke has done so much to show, just as changes in media technologies lead to transformations of cultural understandings of the human body—of the physical skins and interfaces that both enclose and connect us—so also is thinking about the body a key means of thinking about the impact of new media.[74] A poetics of the body is at once a poetics of media, and perhaps nowhere has this been more historically true than in the case of the book. Whether we talk of spines, headers, or footnotes, we can chart a tremendous cultural investment in the corporeal identity of the book, just as by the nineteenth century we can chart a remarkable investment in articulating the bookish identity of the human body. Goethe's attention to the corpse and the anatomical sciences thus functioned as an opportunity to reflect not just on the nature of scientific knowledge at the turn of the nineteenth century but also on the nature of the printed book that functioned like the skeletal structure to the literary work that it carried about. As we will see, in a direct reversal of the famous turning away from the book and towards the body that was dramatized on the frontispiece to Vesalius's *De humani corporis fabrica* (1543), one of the most influential anatomical handbooks in the western tradition,[75] in Goethe's drama of the anatomical theater we see Wilhelm turning *away* from the body and back towards the prosthetic object. At the heart of Goethe's project can be read a fundamental redefinition of prosthetic, and by extension, bibliographic, knowledge.

This is how Wilhelm's training begins:

> Wilhelm, who was likewise called as the next candidate [*Aspirant*], found an unsettling task [*Aufgabe*] that was placed on a clean table and neatly covered in front of the seat that was offered him; as he retracted the sheet, there lay before his eyes the most beautiful female arm that had likely ever thrown itself around the neck of a young man. He held his instrument [*Besteck*] in his hand and did not trust himself to open the arm; he remained standing and did not trust himself to sit down. (*WMT*, 602)

As the *Aspirant*, Wilhelm's character is described as the quintessential subject of *Bildung*: the modern, upwardly mobile individual whose vertically oriented desires are themselves a function of a temporally deep self. The object of such a vertical subjectivity is of course the completion of the *Aufgabe*, in the literal sense of "giving-*up*." Such personal and professional verticality, however, was equally dependent on his capacity to make spatial distinctions, here rendered as the cutting *open* of the arm that has already been cut off from the female body. The stadial development of the professional self depends on the acceptance and subsequent performance of spatial differentiations.

The translation between horizontal and vertical planes that is staged in this opening moment of Wilhelm's anatomical training and that is used to reflect on Wilhelm's own professionalization would go on to become a basic organizing principle of this chapter as a whole. Indeed, what I want to suggest is that when we attend to the elaborate spatial poetics that this chapter sets out in its dramatization of the human body—details which are usually passed over in the rush to locate the passage's historical affinities[76]—we can begin to see the way it can be read as a sophisticated rethinking of the increasingly interrelated fields of work, literary work, and the notion of *the* work itself. Wilhelm's professionalization here is integrally tied to his relationship to the status of the "literary corpus."

In a further elaboration of this translation of the horizontally into the vertically adjacent, the primary object of the scene—the female arm that is the origin of Wilhelm's personal crisis—is described, not in its capacity to point to the female body to which it was once spatially attached, but instead to a narrative history of that body: "there lay before his eyes the most beautiful female arm that had likely ever thrown itself around the neck of a young man." Unlike the *Aufgabe* that pointed upwards, the pulling back of the cover *(Hülle)* to reveal a body part articulates instead a *substrate* of human experience. Like the self-referentiality of the Lago Maggiore, the story that this arm discloses, which we learn in the narrative just prior to this scene ("A very beautiful young woman, led astray through unrequited love, searched out and found death in the water" [*WMT*, 602]), points back in time either to a female version of Werther or a former character of the *Wilhelm Meister* series, what Erich Blackall insightfully called this novel's "reckoning with Mignon."[77] As in book 2, where the figure of Mignon played such a central role in haunting the narrative, the figure of the corpse functions in book 3 like a literary mausoleum of Goethe's own works.

It is at this exact moment of not being able to make the spatio-temporal incision—severing the already severed arm and present from past—that Wilhelm is rescued by a rather mysterious figure who emerges from the crowd during Wilhelm's training. Where the narrative companion (the painter) at the Lago Maggiore had a Cervantean flavor in keeping with the chapter's overall homage to the textual games of *Don Quixote*, the anatomy scene, with its fixation on the underworld of the body, is structured according to a kind of Dantean logic as the companion functions here as a guide (and not sidekick) to lead our unwitting hero.

Wilhelm will be led to his guide's studio, where he encounters a room whose walls are adorned with prostheses. But in yet another of the horizontal to vertical reorientations that this scene performs, these objects are not artificial—and thus horizontal—substitutions for *lost* body parts but instead artificial representations of various *layers* of existing body parts to be used in anatomical training. The prosthetic, the "next to," is reformulated here as the "below." Such directional reformulations achieve a particularly intense pitch at the moment when Wilhelm encounters the sculptor's refashioning of an antique statue: "The master had cast the beautiful torso [*Sturz*] of an ancient youth as a kneadable mass and now judiciously attempted to divest this ideal form of its epidermis and transform the beautiful living creature into a real anatomical sample of the body's muscles [*ein reales Muskelpräparat*]" (607). Here we see the sculptor creating a "wet" or workable sculpture that has not yet been completely set, where the "removal" of the skin is actually a transformation of the cast's surface into the shape of the body's muscles.

In endowing the anatomical sculpture with classical origins, Goethe was on the one hand continuing a tradition that had begun with Vesalius, whose anatomized bodies were in the shape of various well-known classical poses. In making the torso the central set-piece of the anatomical scene here, he was also drawing on the eighteenth-century torso-vogue set in motion by the work of Winckelmann. But in staging the *refashioning* of a torso, Goethe was drawing on, and in the process reimagining, a familiar early-modern practice of amending, or supplementing, discovered antique fragments.[78] Such a practice would have been familiar to Goethe through his translation of Benvenuto Cellini's autobiography, which contained an episode where Cellini describes his transformation of a found antique torso into the figure of Ganymede by adding and removing various elements, which was itself then copied and passed-off as an original in the collection of Eugène de Sartiges.[79] The torso was thus not just an embodiment of potentiality, of a turn, it also captured a crucial site of cultural reproducibility and renovation. Goethe's classicism that was on display in this scene was not an imitation of antiquity but a renewal of early-modern techniques of cultural renewal.

If the torso was the quintessential site of bodily turning, Goethe, in using the word *Sturz*, which referred in nineteenth-century art-historical parlance to the torso of a statue,[80] was also endowing this figure of the turn (of troping itself) with a vertical dimension. But in a play on the idea of the fall encoded in the word (*stürzen* = to fall), the continuous downward motion of the intact, falling human body is replaced here by discrete underlayers of the body's various parts (again perhaps recalling Vesalius's handbook, where the bodies of those classical anatomical poses are gradually disrobed and dismembered as one turns the pages). The human body is endowed with the same stadial identity as the human subject.

What is arguably most remarkable about these directional reversals is that final one produced at the close of the passage, where the pouring of the "Sturz" or sculptural torso is translated into the preparation of the anatomical "Präparat." When Wilhelm refers to the prosthesis as a *Präparat*, he is using a word that technically refers to an object that has been chemically treated in preparation for an anatomical observation. But in a play on the prefix "pro" in the German *Prothese*, the *below* that the anatomical prosthesis as *Präparat* represented also captures a notion of the *before*. The *Ersatz* or replacement object is refigured here as one of *Vorsatz* or design, as the archetype crucially becomes a prototype.[81] The *Präparat* not only represents a chemical compound, it also marks a preliminary stage, a shift that is picked up in one final word play in the chapter when the sculptor instructs

Wilhelm to move from being a *Prosektor* (technically an anatomical assistant, but literally a "pre-cutter") to a *Proplastiker*, to one who constructed in advance (612).

In substituting the *Surrogat* with the *Präparat*, Goethe was vividly refashioning for his readers the identity of the technological prosthetic spaces of both the book and the novel.[82] Like the arrow and the map in book 2, the *Präparat* was a compound figure, but unlike the arrow and the map, the relational operation it performed pointed forward instead of backward. Instead of incorporating all prior manifestations into a larger textual system as the arrow and the map had done, the novel conceived as a prototype anticipated, and in some sense participated in, the production of itself in the future. Like Wittgenstein's assertion that the most important works were those he had not written, the technological *Präparat* incorporated into itself all of the forms that the work had *not yet* assumed. It not only refigured the identity of the novel as a collection, it also transformed the producer of the novel into a collective. It inscribed itself within a larger cultural process and acknowledged the numerous cultural actors who would participate in its afterlife, an afterlife that was crucially imagined to be increasingly international, much like the sculptor who was packing up his wares to take "overseas" to the American colony.

And yet unlike the criminality that surrounded the "resurrections" performed by the grave robbers who provided bodies for the anatomy business (suggestively referred to in the novel as "resurrection men"), the *Präparat* offered a more legitimate model of futurity, continuity, and "aspiration." It established a mimetic, as opposed to dissective, relationship between observer and observed, between reader and read, between one generation and the next. As in the small casket whose secrets we are told were best left untouched, one learned from the technological *Präparat* not by touching or dissecting it but by *looking* at it. There was a crucially visual dimension to one's relationship to the corpus that was being established here. At the same time that the collected compound was refigured as a part of a larger future whole that it helped to generate, its own wholeness was simultaneously affirmed and maintained. According to the didactic site of the anatomical *Präparat*, the novel and the book were neither figured as inert corpses (or corpuses) nor as timeless fundaments to secure the walls of the individual or national fortress. Instead, novel and book were refigured as prophetic, radiant, technological compounds. They were imagined as objects that transcended a single author's control and that transgressed the spatio-temporal boundaries of modern cultural spaces, reorganizing them into dramatically different, and crucially fluid, configurations.

Coda: *Faust* and the Future

Wilhelm Meister's Travels thus constituted Goethe's most extensive and exhaustive engagement with his bookish world. In the novel's deployment across a variety of bibliographic formats over more than two decades and in its elaborate refiguring of the relational identity of the symbolic object, the *Travels* had powerfully reconceived both the book and the novel as mobile, evolutionary, self-correcting networks. And yet such intense book-theoretical engagement with the art of publication was followed by Goethe's decision at the end of his life *not* to publish the second part of *Faust*. Even more than the *Travels*, *Faust* had represented the summation of everything Goethe had written in his long career, and yet its outcome was marked by a very different relationship to print and publishing. As Goethe wrote to Wilhelm von Humboldt in what turned out to be the final letter of his life:

> Without question it would give me endless joy to dedicate and communicate this earnest satire to my dear and thankfully widely recognized and widely distributed friends and to hear their replies during my lifetime. Our age is nonetheless truly so absurd and confused that I have convinced myself that my hard-fought, long persecuted efforts for this curious creation [*Gebäu*] would be poorly rewarded, ultimately driven aground, and, like a shipwreck, lie there covered over by the sands of time. Confused teachings on confused practices preside over the world today and I have nothing more pressing to do than to amplify what I have left and continue to distill my essential qualities [*meine Eigentümlichkeiten zu kohobieren*], as you now do, my friend, in your own fortress [*Burg*].[83]

After the two-decade-long adventure of publishing the *Travels*, withholding *Faust* seemed like a dramatic reversal of practice. The letter to Humboldt articulated an inversion of all of the values that had been energetically invested in the production of the *Travels*, signaling a move away from the publicity and the printedness of the literary work and a return to the isolation, autonomy, and interiority of authorship (accentuated in that word *Eigentümlichkeiten*). In the final image of the writerly *Burg*, we arrive not only at the values promoted by the Weimar Edition but also at the opening scene of *Faust* itself, with the scholar alone in his narrow, gothic study.

Goethe's withholding of *Faust* from publication has been one of the most influential pieces of evidence that has contributed to the image of Goethe as an outsider to the literary marketplace. It has contributed to our capacity, indeed our desire, to see the author as somehow immune to the exigencies of publishing and publication. And yet there is another way to understand this gesture of withholding, one that in fact underscores the importance of Goethe's conception of the work of art as a technological prototype. By the time Goethe was writing to Humboldt, he had already made arrangements with Riemer and Eckermann to have *Faust II* published as part of the *Nachlaß* edition of the *Ausgabe letzter Hand*. The private archive that Goethe had been busy putting together towards the end of his life would regulate the posthumous dissemination of his works in print. In other words, retaining *Faust* was not an act of *not* publishing *Faust* but an act of *delaying* the publication of *Faust*. It was an act of inscribing *Faust* within precisely the publishing paradigm articulated in the figure of the *Präparat* from the *Travels*: a post-author, future-oriented, technologized notion of literary work.

CHAPTER TWO

Copying

The physical sensation closest to this feeling of repetition, which sometimes
lasts for several minutes and can be quite disconcerting, is that of the peculiar
numbness brought on by a heavy loss of blood, often resulting in a temporary
inability to think, to speak or to move one's limbs, as though, without being
aware of it, one had suffered a stroke. Perhaps there is in this as yet unexplained
phenomenon of apparent duplication some kind of anticipation of the end,
a venture into the void, a sort of disengagement, which, like a gramophone
repeatedly playing the same sequence of notes, has less to do with damage to
the machine itself than with an irreparable defect of its program.

—W. G. Sebald, *The Rings of Saturn*

Making Classics

In the late summer of 1794, the German publisher Georg Joachim Göschen
invited Christoph Martin Wieland, widely regarded by contemporaries as
the German language's most renowned living writer, to a book-presentation
ceremony in Leipzig. Early one evening as the sun was setting, Wieland
was paddled out to an island that lay in the middle of a lake within one of
Leipzig's most elegant gardens. Göschen had erected a temporary classical
Greek temple in the center of the island, and inside the temple was a bust
of Wieland. Two young boys wearing Greek costume greeted Wieland, and
behind them they pulled a chariot in which lay the first volume of Wieland's
collected works. As the gilded edition was presented to Wieland, Göschen's
sister-in-law navigated the illuminated channel to the island in a gondola,
stepped out of her boat, and set a laurel wreath on Wieland's head. According to eyewitnesses, Wieland, who was known for being quite shy, was

deeply touched by the ceremony and began to weep, crown on head and book in hand.[1]

Göschen's performance must surely count as one of the most elaborate book-presentation ceremonies that we have on record, one that would make any contemporary author as much embarrassed as deeply envious. While the kind of rigorous dramatization behind Göschen's gesture might strike us as slightly comic today, the ceremony disclosed the vibrant cultural energy that surrounded the book as an object in the late eighteenth and early nineteenth centuries. More specifically, it revealed how the format of the collected edition was fast becoming the sovereign of all book formats. If the collected edition was, on one level, one part of a larger early-nineteenth-century vogue for literary collecting, from the ballad and folktale collections that I will discuss in chapter 3 to the literary miscellanies that I discuss in chapter 4, it would also emerge as one of the most—if not the most—durable and effective vehicles for regulating, institutionalizing, and stabilizing the category of literature in an age of too much literature. Like other collecting practices, the collected edition had the capacity to organize a voluminous amount of material within a defined bibliographic space. Yet unlike collected formats such as the miscellany, the critical edition, or the publisher's series, which always depended upon and negotiated the mixedness of their collectivity, the collected edition argued for a fundamental homogeneity of its contents through the overwhelming promotion of the author as the single organizing figure behind the collection. As in the Sanskrit root "samá" from which the German "Sammlung" and the English "same" derive, there was a fundamental sameness at the heart of the collected edition.[2] Such sameness was not solely limited to the spatial unity of the edition's contents—the gathering together of a diverse set of writings within one single edition—but also encompassed the edition's capacity to produce a temporal continuity through the reproduction of already extant texts. Unlike a critical edition whose very name suggested an interpretive engagement with its textual predecessors, the collected edition was based on an act of reprinting and textual continuity. A "classic" was not just an agreed-upon interpretive consensus, but as Göschen's overlap of the classical and the contemporary in Wieland's ceremony highlighted, a classic was a work whose identity depended upon a fundamental aspect of reproducibility.

In its capacity to stabilize and pass on a literary canon over time, the collected edition thus embodied arguments by pioneering book historians like Elizabeth Eisenstein, Alvin Kernan, and Lucien Febvre and Henri-Jean Martin that print contributed to the standardization and the stability of cultural knowledge.[3] It proved to be an extraordinarily effective vehicle to promote what Philip Connell has identified as the rising "heritage consciousness" of the early nineteenth century, the way such practices of collection intersected nineteenth-century historical thinking in general.[4] And in its capacity to fashion a unified literary *corpus* out of a diverse and often heterogeneous array of texts, the collected edition offered a vivid example of Benedict Anderson's theory of print nationalism, as such bibliographic operations became a potent symbol for the collective political aspirations of fashioning a national body as well.[5] The collected edition not only responded to, and in part repaired, the *spatial* disorganization of the literary and political systems of the nineteenth century, it also addressed the crisis of *traditio*, the problem of cultural durability in an age of mass-reproduced objects.

The collected edition was of course by no means an "invention" of the nineteenth century. It had played a key role in the establishment of Ben Jonson's literary fame, to name but one well-known early-modern example.[6] Göschen's enormous investment in the collected edition of Wieland's works, however, did mark a difference of degree if not one of kind. It signified an important beginning point in terms of what we might call a form of cultural capital as the collected edition came to play an increasingly prominent role in the organization of literature as a category in the nineteenth century.[7] The collected edition was no longer the relatively unique aftereffect to the drama of authorial publication or theatrical performance. It was now part and parcel of literary making. From Goethe's *Ausgabe letzter Hand* and Walter Scott's *Magnum Opus* edition of the 1820s, to Balzac's plan for the *Comédie humaine* in the 1840s, to Washington Irving's Revised Edition of 1848, to Henry James's New York Edition at the turn of the century, the collected edition not only served an essential function in the monumentalization of literature in the nineteenth century, it also became a key site of authorial creativity.[8] Alongside the quantitative expansion of each individual edition— whether in terms of the sheer number of volumes or the consumption of a publishers' resources—one could also find a corresponding quantitative expansion of the number of collected editions themselves.[9] The question in the nineteenth century was no longer who did but who *didn't* have a collected edition?

The Combinatory Spirit and the Collected Edition

Collected editions have powerfully shaped our understanding of who counts in the history of literature. The collected edition is the format from which we derive the material for reading and writing about reading on which our profession depends, and it is also the format—imperiously perched on our most prominent book shelves—from which we derive so much symbolic capital on which our personal identities depend.[10] Through attention to both the rhetorical and visual interfaces of collected editions from the opening decades of the nineteenth century—an attention to both their stuff and their style—I am interested in exploring the various meanings that were gradually attached to this particular bibliographic container. As we saw with Goethe's *Wilhelm Meister's Travels,* the collected edition was fast becoming an influential literary format that could shape a writer's work in significant ways. But far from simply promoting the author as the central fact of literary history, the collected edition also played a key role in legitimizing the experience of literary reproducibility. The very authorial singularity that the collected edition promoted was simultaneously a product of the technological reproducibility upon which it depended. Despite counterarguments by G. Thomas Tanselle and William St. Clair about the incapacity of the hand press during this period to produce the same thing twice,[11] I want to argue that what mattered to the collected edition's rise in cultural prominence during the early nineteenth century was precisely the *imaginative* possibility that something stayed the same and that this sameness was not seen as either illicit or creatively impoverished but juridically and aesthetically legitimate.

In order for the collected edition to assume legitimacy within the classificatory logic of the nineteenth-century literary system, a larger cultural reorientation had to occur around the categories of repetition, novelty, and authorial identity. The rise to prominence of the collected edition—and literary collections in general—necessitated on the one hand the acceptance of increasing degrees of sameness and reproduction within literary life on an unprecedented scale. Never before had so much of the same thing been produced, whether it was in the quantity of a single edition or in the reprinting of numerous subsequent editions of the same work. The prominence of collected editions thus depended on a taste for repetition and collection—practices that were themselves crucial features of the larger bibliographic landscape and that we can see being motivated in theoretical paradigms like Edgar Allen Poe's formulation, "To originate is carefully, patiently, and understandingly to combine," or Friedrich Schlegel's promotion of the "kombinatorischer Geist" (combinatory spirit) at the heart of Lessing's aphoristic style.[12]

At the same time, the legitimacy of sameness was dependent on an acceptance of the simultaneous presence and absence of a third party mediating these repetitive encounters between readers and authors. Like Göschen's important directorial role in Wieland's book ceremony, the collected edition also highlighted the increasingly important role that publishers were playing as makers of culture. Like Johann Cotta, Georg Reimer, or Friedrich Brockhaus in Germany, James Ballantyne, James Cadell or John Murray in Britain, Charles Ladvocat or Eugène Renduel in France, or Mathew Carey, George Putnam, or the Harper brothers in the United States, Göschen was one of numerous publishers who would play a decisive role in shaping the romantic literary establishment, whether it was through the courting of particular authors or the deployment of particular bibliographic arrangements of their works. But the collected edition's success often depended in large measure on both the acknowledgment *and* the overlooking of the fact that there was always someone else there on the page, that what counted as an author was always in some sense a collective persona. Notions like the *Ausgabe letzter Hand* were intended to efface the publisher's presence in such undertakings, to hide the presence of the publisher's own invisible hand, if you will, that extended the reach of the author's. It was not for nothing that one romantic French commentator referred to the emerging "libraire-éditeur" as the author's "evil genius" (*mauvais génie*).[13] The bibliographic repetitions that collected editions performed were also surrounded by an ambiguously available collectivity that stood behind such singular performances. The *collected* edition necessitated the reevaluation not only of what counted as new but also of the singular identity of the bibliographic subject.

Copying haunts modern culture. Whether in the form of the reproducible artwork or replicable human code, the question of the copy has been at the heart of some of the most influential cultural critiques of the past two centuries.[14] To return to the romantic fascination with repetition and reproducibility—to the figure of the return itself—is to return to the very beginnings of this fascination with technological reproducibility.[15] Doing so should not only tell us new things about the immediate concerns of romantic writers within their changing bibliographic environment. It should also help us see the copy itself with fresh eyes: not just as a vertiginous process of hollowing out some more authentic essence—what Sebald called the irreparable defect of its program—but also as the initiation of a new form of creativity, one that depended on a fundamental collectivity, on the cultivation of a new "combinatory spirit." For romantic writers, the emerging culture of the copy that informed bibliographic formats like the collected edition not only posed a significant threat to a variety of established norms and categories surrounding literary creativity. It also posed an important new opportunity for thinking about the changing nexus of communication and creativity.

Producing Corporeal Integrity (Wieland, Byron, Rousseau)

The presentation of Wieland's collected edition marked the conclusion of one of the most significant publishing ventures in the German book market at the turn of the nineteenth century. But it also marked a key beginning of a significant new trend in literary publishing, signaling a number of important changes to book publishing and the romantic understanding of the book that would endure for long after. On a physical level, Göschen's investment in the project led to numerous innovations in German bookmaking, from the flatness of the paper, to the straightness of the type, to the blackness of the ink.[16] As Göschen wrote to Wieland in reference to his edition, "You must admit that this is a masterpiece."[17] The importance of the book's physical appearance was to reflect the cultural importance of its author. Not only did such technical innovations require significant capital investments, but the sheer extensiveness of the editions themselves required an enormous commitment on the part of publishers. To produce thirty-eight volumes of an author's works as a single undertaking, as Göschen had done in the case of Wieland, was to invest an enormous percentage of resources in a single project. Göschen wrote rather dramatically to Wieland during production: "This undertaking is larger than you think. With the nature of my business activities my end stands daily before me."[18] Indeed, such editions not only taxed the financial resources of a publisher, they also often exceeded their infrastructure capacity. Cotta was forced to delay part of the publication of Goethe's *Ausgabe letzter Hand* because he was also publishing collected editions of Schiller and Herder at the same time.[19] Making classics, then and now, was a key driver of the expansions of the publishing sector.

Such editions were not exclusively about exclusivity, however. In printing these editions in numerous formats, early-nineteenth-century publishers sought to offer collected editions that were accessible to a broad reading audience. As Göschen wrote to Wieland, "Every merchant's assistant, every poor student, every rural priest, every moderately salaried officer shall be able to buy your works . . . In this way they will be read by all of Germany and will impact all of Germany."[20] In forming a literary elite, the collected edition was also contributing to the establishment of a political commons. The more collected editions unified and stabilized an author's works, the more such works could paradoxically circulate among the populace. The surge of collected editions that one can identify in the 1820s was directly related to the political and economic recuperations that were taking place after the close of the Napoleonic wars. In constructing and making available a textual body, the collected edition was also contributing in the process to the reconstruction of the national body politic as well. As the publisher Georg Reimer wrote in 1826 to one of his authors, greatly understating the case, "The public [is now] especially inclined towards collected editions."[21]

If the collected edition highlighted nascent political aspirations, it also participated in the early-nineteenth-century ideal of fashioning an image of heroic individuality on which such nation states were to be based. As much as any genre or discourse in the early nineteenth century, the format of the collected edition contributed to and grew out of the idea of literature as an index of personality. In contrast to an author's individual works, in which frontispieces often represented particular scenes or settings from the work, the frontispieces of collected editions were very often portraits of the author. In reading the collected edition, one experienced a persistent encounter with a person.

But as Tom Mole has argued, it was precisely the growing citability of such images—their capacity to circulate outside of an economy of likeness—that contributed to the promotion of authorial celebrity.[22] The vogue for authorial portraits as frontispieces disclosed an important tension between person and personality as the frame of writing, between the individual and the simulacrum of individuality that the book promoted. The romantic book became a key sign of what Deleuze and Guattari have called the emerging "faciality" of modern culture, at whose core was the commodification and thus deterritorialization of self.[23] The face for Deleuze and Guattari was not a part of the body, like a head or a hand, but something altogether separate, indeed a sign of the very disintegration of the embodied self under capitalism. "There is something absolutely inhuman about the face," they write.[24] The face emerged as a crucial icon in orienting readers' relationships to the increasingly dispersed and mediated self of bibliographic culture. The face, according to Deleuze and Guattari, "carrie[d] out the prior gridding that makes it possible for the signifying elements to become discernible."[25] In this context one can begin to understand the critical force, and enduring appeal, of romantic novellas like Balzac's "Unknown Masterpiece," at the center of which is an illegible portrait, or Hawthorne's "The Minister's Black Veil," whose protagonist covers over his face and thereby becomes monstrous to his congregation: "He has changed himself into something awful, only by hiding his face!"[26]

Where the face marked a threshold to the simultaneous autobiographization of literature and its dehumanization through the commodification of the book, genre too played a key role as an index and antidote to this new media reality. One of the most popular additions to the collected edition was the biographical sketch of the author, which almost always was placed in the opening volumes of the edition (as in Walter Scott's edition of John Dryden or Ludwig Tieck's edition of the works of Heinrich von Kleist). The 1819 edition of Rousseau's works, produced by Jean-Jacques Lefèvre, offered a slight variation of this approach when it placed the *Confessions* at the head of the edition,[27] a practice that numerous subsequent editions would follow and that replaced the traditional primary location of the *Discours* at the head of Rousseau's oeuvre (initiated by the Société typographique de Genève's 1782 edition).[28] The author's narrative self-portrait became the discursive frame to complement the visual frame of the face that shaped the reception of the author's works. The final volume of Lefèvre's edition, which marked a key turn in reprinting Rousseau, also contained a collection of remarkable expressions by the author, "Vocabulaire des expressions et locutions remarquables," not only motivating the linguistic uniqueness of this particular author but also basing the category of authorship itself on such expressive remarkability. Finally, in its competition with other posthumous editions, a competition which always rested on claims of totality and completeness, Lefèvre's 1819 edition emphasized that it was *more* complete because of the inclusion of so much *unprinted* material from Rousseau's life. In the "Avertissement de L'Editeur" in the opening volume we read: "Every editor of the collected works not only aspires to publish a pure text [*un texte pur*]; his collection must include all of his author's productions; and in order to have the advantage over his competitors, he does his utmost to procure those that have *not yet* been published" (il met tous ses soins à s'en procurer d'*inédites*).[29] The collected edition's increasing reliance on publishing the author's diaries, notes, and correspondence, which we saw vividly enacted in the production of the Weimar Edition of Goethe's works in chapter 1, was not only a way of marketing the edition's novelty and thus marketability. It also increasingly aligned the book with the category of the author's private life and away from the history of the author's publications. Such a fact was morbidly on display in the final text of the 1819 edition, "Procès-Verbal de l'ouverture du corps de J. J. Rousseau," where the closure of the collected edition was the anatomical confirmation of the death of the author.

The orientation of the collected edition around the author's life was by no means unique to Rousseau. As the publishers of Byron's posthumous 1832 collected edition argued in their introduction to the volume of juvenalia, "But every page of it is in fact, when rightly understood, a chapter of the author's confessions."[30] These were of course almost the very same words Goethe had used to describe his own works, when he wrote in *Poetry and Truth*: "Everything that I have written to this point are just fragments of a greater confession."[31] To affirm the notion of literature as confessional discourse, this same volume of Byron's works contained a fold-out facsimile of Byron's manuscript of the early poem "To D—," which opened with the line, "In thee, I fondly hop'd to clasp." The author's handwriting brought the reader through the screen of the printed page and into the heart and mind of the author himself, enacting the very desire of "clasping" encoded in the reproduced handwritten poem. In the fold-out facsimile of handwriting, the traces of the individual life literally enveloped, like a clasp, the collected edition. The synecdoche of the figure of the hand that was repeatedly mobilized in collected editions, whether through such titles as the *Ausgabe letzter Hand*, the promotion of unpublished material, or the printing of handwriting, was there to repair the corporeal ruptures (of the authorial corpus in a double sense) that the book's proliferation increasingly enacted. As Christof Windgätter has written, "The changing appearance of the book (through its mobilization, format, and geometry) collaborated with the emergence of a linguistic structure that would persistently be used, accompanied, and constituted by the antecedent presence of the human."[32]

However much such individual editions promoted literature as an index of the individual person, when one begins to look broadly at such editions, what is most striking about them is the remarkable visual uniformity that they achieved. Unlike the uniqueness of their portrayed authors, the editions themselves all began to look the same. Whether it was from one edition to the next of one author with the same publisher, as in the case of Byron's collected editions with Murray, multiple authors with the same publisher, as in Cotta's publication of the German *Klassiker*, or one author with multiple publishers, as in the case of the numerous posthumous Rousseau editions (fig. 2.1), one encounters a striking typographical regularity in collected editions. However much such editions promoted an aspect of novelty to differentiate themselves from their predecessors, they were simultaneously marked by an enormous degree of typographic sameness.

Such sameness was not only important on a synchronic level between different editions, it also mattered diachronically as well between previous editions of the stand-alone works and the collected edition that reproduced these works, a process referred to by the editors of the 1819 Rousseau edition as "l'intégrité du texte."[33] In this notion of textual "integrity," the collected edition argued for a fundamental continuity between what appeared in the collection and that which had appeared before. This sameness that underlay such textual integrity was nevertheless simultaneously positioned within an economy of novelty as each new collected edition had to motivate the novelty of what it collected. The collected edition affirmed both the sameness of the collection's parts and the novelty of the collection's whole.

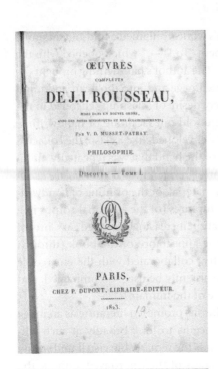

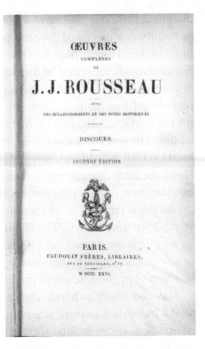

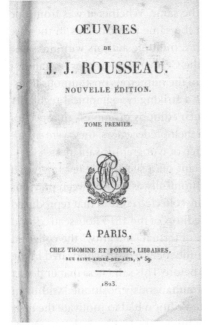

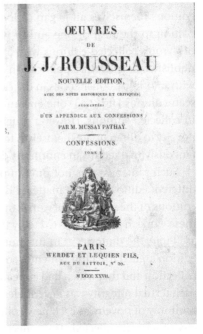

Figure 2.1 Title pages from four separate editions of *Oeuvres complètes de J. J. Rousseau* (1823–26). Courtesy of the Rare Books and Special Collections Division, McGill University Library.

And here the case of Göschen and Wieland is again instructive. Göschen's Wieland edition was not only a landmark in the history of publishing, it also marked a key moment in the evolution of German copyright law.[34] Wieland had published seventeen individual works with the Weidmann publishing house, and when he sold the copyright of his entire collected works to Göschen in 1788, Weidmann's director, Ernst Martin Graff, filed suit to challenge the legality of this move. The basic question behind the case was whether a work published within the context of a "collected edition" constituted a *new* work or simply an illegal reprint or *Nachdruck*. For years, debates about the positive and negative effects of reprinting had raged in the German publishing world,[35] a problem that was made especially acute by the absence of a unified legal system. Works published in Leipzig could legally be reprinted in Stuttgart because those cities were under separate legal and political systems. Wieland's collected works thus appeared during a particularly tense period when the boundaries of an author's and a publisher's property rights were being vigorously contested.

Both the Leipziger Bücherkommission and the Sächsische Oberappellationsgericht sided with Göschen, citing the fact that a collected edition would never come to fruition if an author's previous publishers all had to be compensated to produce the new edition. The common good of collecting an author's works together in one single edition overrode the more immediate concerns of publishers' financial remuneration. Göschen's successful defense had rested largely on his claim that a work published as part of the collected edition was essentially a *new work*. Wieland's novel *Agathon*, when published as part of the works, was not, according to Göschen, the same *Agathon*, but was to be seen as "a new object, a part of the whole."[36]

The case of Wieland's edition thus not only marked a beginning point in the emerging legitimacy of a certain kind of reprinting and textual repetition. It also signaled the way a literary work was crucially understood as a material event as well as an intellectual one. As one of the leading voices of the nascent copyright movement in the German states, Fichte had argued that the literary work was defined solely by its unique and proprietary use of language.[37] The category of the work was disaggregated from its material location. And yet Göschen's defense rested on the argument that the work's location *did* change the status and meaning and, indeed, novelty of that work. The *Agathon* of the collected works was new because it was "a new object, a part of the whole." In order to justify the reprinting of a previous work not as an act of piracy but as one of innovation, Göschen oriented both reading *and* writing as much around the physical location of the work as the operations of the author's mind. It invited readers and writers alike to see a work's meaning and thus its value as lying within a larger system of works. Cotta would later remark to Göschen many years later: "Through your publication of Wieland's works, it appears that you have taken the German book trade in a totally new direction."[38] The new direction to which Cotta referred was precisely the capitalization of repetition as a cultural and literary value.

Reprinting, Reproducibility, and the Novella Collection

In 1819, the first volume of E. T. A. Hoffmann's *The Serapion Brothers: Collected Stories and Tales*, appeared on the German book market, at the suggestion of Georg Reimer, Hoffmann's publisher. Reimer, who would emerge as one of the most important promoters of German romantic literature,[39] had previously published Ludwig Tieck's collection of already published stories, *Phantasus* (1812–16), with relative success, and he recommended the same practice to Hoffmann. Like other collected editions, the preface to Hoffmann's first volume identified the project's importance as its capacity to unite and bring together the diffuse stories published in a variety of other bibliographic formats. As Hoffmann confessed to his readers, "The publisher's request that the author collect and add to his stories and tales dispersed in journals and miscellanies . . . gave rise to this book and the form in which it appears."[40] At the same time, Hoffmann's opening also attempted to defend the novelty of this collected edition of previously published work. In agreeing that readers might find his collection extraordinarily similar to the one published just a few years before by Ludwig Tieck, Hoffmann proceeded to explain how the two collections were in fact quite different. He enunciated, in other words, the ways that *The Serapion Brothers* was different from another author's work. What he did not address was how the works *in The Serapion Brothers* related to themselves. That problem was left to the tales.

In capitalizing on the growing market for republication in the nineteenth century, Hoffmann was of course not alone. Numerous romantic writers were busy enjoying the fruits of being paid twice (or more) for the same piece of writing, and readers were willing to pay for it.[41] At the same time that Hoffmann's collection inscribed itself within a bibliographic practice of reprinting, it also inscribed itself within the literary genre of the novella collection by creating an elaborate frame narrative for the collected tales in the spirit of Boccaccio's *Decameron*. Beginning with Goethe's *Conversations of German Refugees* (1795) on through Tieck's *Phantasus* (1812–16), Hoffmann's *The Serapion Brothers* (1819–21), Washington Irving's *Bracebridge*

Hall (1822), Balzac's *Cent contes drolatiques* (1832), and Dickens's *Pickwick Papers* (1837), the genre of the novella collection experienced a tremendous rise in popularity in the first half of the nineteenth century across Europe and the Atlantic, a fact that offers an important counterweight to the importance that scholars have accorded the novel in thinking about literary form around 1800. Where the novel functioned as a key genre at the turn of the nineteenth century to explore the possibility of networking—of bibliographic everywhereness—it was the novella collection that emerged to address the problem of literary repetition and the bibliographic copy.

The novella collection might seem at first glance an odd genre through which to frame such repetitive practices. For Hoffmann's German contemporaries, it was precisely the genre of the novella at the heart of these collections that was theorized as the form through which writers could work through the problem of literary novelty, the way "modern" literature increasingly came to define itself in opposition, not in conversation, with a literary tradition.[42] Whether it was Goethe's comment that the novella was "an unheard-of event" (eine sich ereignete unerhörte Begebenheit),[43] Schlegel's description of the novella as "a story that does not belong to history" (eine Geschichte, die . . . nicht zur Geschichte gehört),[44] Tieck's argument that the novella narrates an event (*Vorfall*) "which is marvelous, perhaps singular,"[45] or Kleist's emphasis on the improbability at the heart of the novella's plot, the novella was repeatedly invested with the ideals of writing something down that had not yet come before. Novellistic writing was unheard of, lacked a history, was singular or improbable. It was the literary version of the news, the genre of geniuses.

And yet in practice, the novella *collection* was always intensely concerned with the question of narrative recycling, a problem which of course dated back to the genre's medieval founder Boccaccio, whom the romantics were explicitly invoking. Whether it was Goethe's *Conversations of German Refugees* with his retelling of Bassompierre's memoirs (which would later be retold by Hugo von Hofmannsthal), Stendhal's dramatization of his engagement with his early-modern source material and the presence of "une autre main" in his collection *L'abbesse de Castro* (1839), Balzac's imitation of Rabelaisian diction in *Cent contes drolatiques* (1832), or the fashion for refashioning folk and fairy tales in Tieck, Irving, or Hawthorne (think of the latter's *Twice-Told Tales* [1837]), the nineteenth-century novella collection seemed far more invested in investigating the problem of secondarity than novelty. It had much more in common with Alfred de Vigny's categorization of the romantic age as an age of "renaissance" *and* "rehabilitation"[46] or Friedrich Schlegel's anecdote about the Italian restorer of a painting by

Caracci who cleaned half of the image and left the other half alone.[47] Ernst Behler has called this romantic fascination with rehab and rebirth "evolutionary modernism,"[48] and one sees the important overlaps at work here between literary practices and emerging scientific paradigms in the nineteenth century.

When we turn more closely to E. T. A. Hoffmann's final novella collection, however, we encounter an altogether different set of concerns, one that we might call, following Behler, "reproducible modernism." Instead of exhibiting an interest in either pure or evolutionary novelty, Hoffmann's work seems far more interested in the question of the novelty of sameness. Rather than standing as a founding document of either a modernist mythos of avant-gardism with its continued urgency of innovation or a postmodernist mythos of adaptation and recycling, I want to argue Hoffmann's collection stands at the head of an altogether different artistic tradition concerned with the impact of technological reproducibility on modern cultural spaces. Hoffmann's collection is especially significant here precisely because it has served, through the figure of the patron saint in its title, as one of the paradigmatic works of a "visionary romanticism," where the category of literature was increasingly equated with a deeply interior, and thus highly individual, experience, just as the categories of interiority and individuality themselves were increasingly equated with those of depth and illegibility.[49]

Hoffmann would go on to figure as one of the most significant influences in the development of literature in the nineteenth century. Such impact would eventually culminate in the significance that Hoffmann played in the work of Sigmund Freud, and in particular in Freud's development of the concept of the uncanny which would form the basis of Freud's thinking about the structure of the human psyche more generally. Freud's essay on "The Uncanny," which he defined as "that class of the frightening which leads back to what is known of old and long familiar," would arguably function as one of the most influential readings of Hoffmann and this larger romantic concern with repetition.[50] And yet in transforming a historically specific bibliographic concern of Hoffmann's into a universal psychological condition, Freud was in essence effacing the important role that the book had played in shaping such imaginary experiences. Freud's essay represented a key landmark, in other words, in the nineteenth-century process of the naturalization of the book.

In taking Hoffmann as the case study for my chapter—in performing my own act of repetition—I am interested in understanding how the poetics of repetition that Freud so acutely identified in Hoffmann's work was not the function of a basic and timeless psychic structure but instead was a technique of addressing the media-technological conditions in which such psychological profiles could be generated. I want to dwell on the way Hoffmann's intense interest not with forms of *Innerlichkeit* but with forms of *Äußerung*—that is, forms of expression, exteriors, sociability, and communication—was a means of aligning his writing with the logic of reproducibility and collectivity that was coming to define his immediate bibliographic environment.[51] How did Hoffmann's poetics of the return in a collection like *The Serapion Brothers* inscribe itself within the increasingly elaborate system of reproducibility and the attendant proliferation of the literary "copy," which such collections were themselves generating? How did these literary reproductions legitimize reproducibility itself?

E. T. A. Hoffmann's *The Serapion Brothers* and the Crisis of Originality

The Serapion Brothers was published in four volumes over the course of three years (1819–21) and consisted almost exclusively of material that Hoffmann had already published in either periodicals or miscellanies. We know from Hoffmann's correspondence with Reimer that this collection was supposed to contain as much new material as old. While the preface to the first volume announced that "new contributions" would indeed be "added," from the very beginning the old always outnumbered the new and the project was overshadowed by Hoffmann's inability to produce the promised number of new works. This crisis of productivity reached its highpoint with the fourth and final volume, when Hoffmann wrote to Reimer:

> Sickness has once again inhibited my activities and drive; nevertheless the fourth part of the *Serapion Brothers* moves inexorably forward and will be, God willing, the most interesting of all, since it only contains two previously printed stories, of which the one (printed in the *Wiener Zeitblatt*) remains relatively unfamiliar to us, otherwise it contains only new work.[52]

Of the six stories ultimately published in the fourth volume, four were reprints and only two were new, one of which had been promised for the third volume but had not been completed in time. In the entire collection's twenty-eight stories that spanned four volumes and over one-thousand pages of text, Hoffmann managed to produce just three new tales (and two of these only in time for the final volume). The emphasis in his letter to Reimer of the obscurity of one of his story's previous printings (in the *Wiener Zeitblatt*)—and thus the possibility of considering it as a quasi-"new" work—revealed not only the extent to which Hoffmann participated in the vogue for reprinting in the early nineteenth century. It also showed how this work, in distinction to his earlier collections, was marked from beginning to end by a steady and growing orientation towards writing as reproduction.

The frame narrative that Hoffmann wrote for the collection (and that significantly contained a tale that had previously been published elsewhere) not surprisingly takes up this issue, or crisis if you will, of origination. It describes the reconvening of four (eventually six) old friends who debate whether or not to form a club in which they will tell each other stories that they have previously written down. In the closed community of storytellers, Hoffmann's frame explicitly echoed Boccaccio's *Decameron*. But in reading stories aloud that had already been written down, Hoffmann's collection not only captured a larger cultural shift from an oral to a written narrative culture that was consistently thematized in romantic writing. It also drew attention to the way such oral and performative tropes were deployed to understand books. If the plague that Boccaccio's narrators fled, however, had really been the plague, the plague in Hoffmann's collection was originality itself, the problem of starting anew that we know literally plagued Hoffmann during the entire production of this edition.

The collection opens with the statement by Lothar, one of the club's narrators: "Look at it how you will, one cannot deny, cannot avert the bitter conviction that never—never will something return that once was" (*SB*, 13). Opening the collection with Lothar's statement about the *impossibility* of the return suggests a very different focus to this collection than I have just intimated, one driven by a commitment to a larger romantic poetics of novelty and the impossibility of the return of the past. And yet Hoffman's rhetorical and grammatical strategies counteract precisely the content of the opening statement's assertion. In opening with direct speech, the frame narrative is framed by the positionality of its opening enunciation, as the remaining tales both inside the frame narrative and between it (the frame narrative is structured like a novella collection itself) will function as so many replies to Lothar's assertion. Indeed in that double "never" of Lothar's opening statement we can see how the absoluteness of Lothar's position, already undermined through the use of quotation marks, is further undercut through the rhetorical device of repetition (epizeuxis).

This commitment to a world defined by temporal discontinuity articulated in Lothar's opening position is first challenged in the frame narrative by Cyprian in his subsequent anecdote about the two philosophy students who, after not having seen one another for several years, resume their conversation at precisely the point where they left off:

Precisely in such a philosophical debate, precisely in that moment [*in dem Augenblick*] when Sebastian threw a decisive and powerful blow [*Schlag*] and Ptolomäus was collecting himself to reply, they were interrupted and chance willed it that they never again met in K—. . . . Nearly twenty years passed, when Ptolomäus sees a figure on the street in B— walking in front of him, whom he quickly recognizes to be his friend Sebastian. He hurries after him, taps him on the shoulder, and as Sebastian turns around, Ptolomäus immediately begins: You asserted that—enough!—he threw the blow that he had prepared twenty years ago. (*SB*, 21–22)

This anecdote would mark an essential focal point for the collection as a whole, with its various elements of deixis ("in that moment"), acoustic shock (the "blow"), and diegetic shifting ("you asserted that—enough!—he threw the blow") being replayed throughout the subsequent tales. The point of the anecdote was not that the students have the same conversation over again, but that the conversation remained the same even over vast amounts of time. There was a fundamental continuity and textual integrity at stake here. But just as the rhetorical device of repetition was used to articulate the impossibility of return in the opening sentence, the rhetorical devices of interruption (parenthesis) and omission (ellipsis) are used here in conjunction with the narratological shift from direct to indirect speech to articulate the possibility of continuity ("*you* asserted that—enough!—*he* threw the blow . . ."). What returns in the frame narrative is not the content but the frame itself, the condition of possibility of sameness.

Such concern with temporal continuity and corporeal integrity is enacted most prominently in the frame narrative in the tale about the title figure, Serapion, who will eventually be chosen as the club's patron saint. Cyprian is once again the narrator, and we learn that Serapion is a hermit whom he has met and whom he suspects of being a certain Count P**. Nevertheless, as a prime example of the psychological pathology of *der fixen Ideen*, the Count insists on referring to himself as Serapion, whom we are told is a third-century heretical Christian monk who was dismembered by the Emperor Decius during the "Decian persecution" and thrown off a cliff to his death.[53] Serapion's fidelity to an inner vision, however discordant with external reality, is what has made him such an attractive romantic hero for generations of subsequent readers. As Peter von Matt has suggested, transforming this romantic paradigm into a universal one: "Precisely because of his variety of insanity, Serapion becomes the Ur-image of the poet, the goal towards which every narrative artist should strive: to fashion everything in and out of his inner self."[54]

I want to suggest that Serapion is chosen here as the patron saint of both the collection and romanticism more generally not simply because of his visionary identity—that he represents an alternative to the technological foundations of art embodied in the figure of Councilor Krespel, for example, whose tale is also included in the frame narrative. Rather, what makes Serapion the patron saint of this novella collection in particular and, one could argue of a particular aspect of romanticism in general, is his promotion of a temporal and corporeal continuity. His survival and his corporeal intactness represent a resistance to the very problem of diffusion and change that surrounded bibliographic work in the early nineteenth century and that the novella collection as a genre was designed to recuperate. Serapion literally embodies the textual integrity at the heart of collected editions, an integrity that was understood as both a spatial and temporal unity. He is the ideal patron to this collection because he represents a particular ideal of collection itself. This continuity between the body of the saint and the body of the book is then amplified in Serapion's mode of speech, as he recounts a collection of novellas to Cyprian one evening to pass the night together during his visit. Whether figuratively or communicatively, in both who he is and what he says, Serapion quite literally embodies the genre of the novella collection.

When Cyprian returns to find Serapion again, however, he is gone. The figure of continuity and sameness has disappeared. By adopting Serapion as the patron saint to this collection, *The Serapion Brothers* substitutes itself for his absence. The book, the corpus of tales, becomes the space or corpus of repetition. According to the narrative frame to the collected edition, the work of the collection—and of the individual works within the collection—is to enact precisely this movement from discontinuity to continuity, from difference to sameness, from the impossibility of return to the legitimacy of repetition. As I will try to show in greater detail, the work of writing in the collection motivates the very practice of literary collection itself.

"The Uncanny Guest" and the Poetics of the Same

In the third volume of *The Serapion Brothers* there appeared the novella "The Uncanny Guest." "The Uncanny Guest" was not only a reused title of an earlier novella by Hoffmann's friend, Friedrich de la Motte Fouqué, that had appeared in the miscellany *Pocket-Book Dedicated to Love and Friendship* (1814). It was also a reprint of Hoffmann's own novella by that title that had initially appeared in the literary miscellany *The Narrator* (1819). On top of this, it was also a rewritten version of another of Hoffmann's tales,

"The Magnetist," that had been printed in one of his earlier collections, *Fantasy Pieces in the Manner of Callot* (1814). The reprint that reused available literary material was also a remake. Like the collection in which it appeared, "The Uncanny Guest" was marked by an accumulation of repetitive bibliographic practices, a point that one could see amplified at a figural and communicative level as well. Far from attempting to justify the category of the "version"—the variants and the transformations that were so central to a Goethean theory of art—Hoffmann's remaking was far more invested in legitimizing, through the very process of transformation, the experience of sameness. As we will see, it is precisely at those moments where the second version differs from its predecessor that it is most invested in promoting a poetics of repetition.

"The Uncanny Guest" has been a much passed-over story in Hoffmann scholarship, a point that is notable because it explicitly invokes the category of *das Unheimliche* upon which much of Hoffmann's subsequent fame has rested (Freud himself does not address this story). I suspect that such overlooking has been the product of the deep sense of unoriginality that has surrounded it and the crucial ways that originality and novelty have remained dominant critical positions within the field of literary study. But I want to suggest that the significance of "The Uncanny Guest"—what makes it in my view one of *the* key texts of Hoffmann's corpus—lies precisely in its intricate attention to the growing problem of sameness that structured the nineteenth-century literary field. Its importance resides in its capacity to take up at so many different levels simultaneously the intersection of reading and repetition that was at the heart of the romantic bibliographic world.[55]

"The Uncanny Guest" is based on Hoffmann's initial tale, "The Magnetist," and the earlier story concerns the failed marriage of Maria and Hypolit that concludes in her death on their wedding day. It begins with a family sitting around the fire drinking *Punsch* and discussing the status of dreams. The statement, "Träume sind Schäume" (literally, dreams are foam, but more loosely understood as dreams are nonsense), leads to a debate about the meaning of dreams in general, which is followed by the tale of the Baron's dream about an extremely odd Major he met during his time at the *Ritterakademie* (who was given to nighttime performances of imaginary sword fights in his garden that would conclude with him climbing trees and laughing uncontrollably). The Baron's unsettling dream concludes with the Major using a "glowing instrument" pressed against his head to see through the Baron's "innermost self" (*SB*, 146).

This tale is followed by a comic interlude on the part of the painter,

Franz Bickert, a guest for many years of the Baron's, who tells the story of a dream he had in which he was a watermark and was tortured one evening by a satanic writer. Bickert's tale is followed by Ottmar's story of his friend Theobald who used the popular eighteenth-century science of magnetism (also known as mesmerism) to win back his lost lover, Auguste. Ottmar tells us that he has learned his story from Alban, another guest at the Baron's house, and it is in fact Alban who teaches Theobald the magnetic skills he needs to win over his lover, who fell for an Italian officer during Theobald's absence at university. At the conclusion of the story, the Baron's daughter, Maria, faints and Alban enters from an adjacent room to assist her, at which point the Baron, in traditional Hoffmannian fashion, suspects that Alban is in fact the Major from his youth. The narrative breaks off at this point and is continued through a letter of Maria's to her friend Adelgunde where we learn that Alban is practicing his magnetism on her, which threatens her planned marriage with Hypolit, who is away at war. The story is concluded through an editor's account and through the inclusion of notes from Franz Bickert's diary in which we learn of the death of Maria on her wedding day and the subsequent death of the Baron (old age) and Ottmar (battle).

When Hoffmann "rewrote" his initial story, he not only reused all of the basic elements of the first version, he also crucially reversed the trajectory of the narrative. "The Uncanny Guest" begins in a similar fashion with a family sitting around the fire drinking *Punsch*, but instead of discussing the status of dreams, they tell each other stories of mysterious sounds that draw in significant ways on Goethe's earlier novella collection, *Conversations of German Refugees* (1795). The question of reference (do dreams refer to some stratum of the real) is transferred from a psychological plane to an acoustic or sensorial one. The magnetist who haunts the Baron's dreams and reappears as the family guest to seduce the young woman in the first version reappears in the second version as the "uncanny Count S—i." As in the first version, he will attempt to seduce the young woman (Angelika) away from the young man (Moritz) when he departs for battle. Upon the news that Moritz has died in battle, Angelika agrees to marry the Count, but unlike the first version where the young man and woman both die, the marriage to the magnetist is interrupted by Moritz's return, at which point the Count dies and Angelika and Moritz marry, living happily ever after (almost).

The Plot of the Returning Husband

At the most general level, both "The Magnetist" and "The Uncanny Guest" belong to the genre of stories about the problem of the returning husband.

Homer's *Odyssey* provides one of the key archetypes of this plot, and the elevation of Homer to the position of Ur-poet in the romantic pantheon (brought to life, in German at least, through Voß's translation, Werther's imagination, and Schlegel's theorization) offered the most obvious source for the growing popularity of such stories, which included Balzac's "Colonel Chabert," Washington Irving's "Rip van Winkle," and Hawthorne's "The Wives of the Dead." But the more immediate historical backdrop of the Napoleonic wars was also an important point of reference for these tales. One should never underestimate just how violent the romantic period was. The plot of the returning husband was intimately connected with postwar narratives more generally, as the corporeal and social ruptures of war were memorialized either in the character's name (*Rip* van Winkle or the early-modern example of Martin *Guerre*)[56] or his physical description (Odysseus' scar, Chabert's head wound, Guerre's missing limbs). The returning husband represented a moment of social crisis, figuring the "remembrance" of the wounded male body as a tripartite act of memorialization, social membership, and personal and psychological integrity.[57] As with Odysseus' conflict with his wife's suitors, at stake in the figure of the returning husband was the project of domestication, of how to expel unwanted guests and, in the process, how to transform *oneself* from a guest to a husband. Both "The Magnetist" and "The Uncanny Guest" were marked by a series of people who would not leave (Bickert, Alban, Count S—i), and the question that the stories posed was how to tell the difference between those who belonged and those who did not. The success of the husband's return, of moving from guest to husband, depended on his capacity to prove, in Serapion-like fashion, the continuity of his identity, that he was in fact the same person as when he left.

The story of the returning husband was thus, on one level, a remarkably effective symbolic means to reestablish the imagined inviolability of interior spaces, whether of self, home, or *Heimat*. It played a key role in the political recuperations that marked the post-revolutionary period in European and American history. But the story of the returning husband in Hoffmann also became an important means to understand the practices of collection upon which the integrity of these interiors depended. Their imagined inviolability rested on the production of temporal continuity, not so much through the deployment of physical evidence (the scar) as through the practice of narration (of being able to recount the past that one held in common). Indeed, it was precisely the mobilization of narrative material in Hoffmann—which, as we will see, depended on the fundamental mobility of narrative material itself—that compensated for the corporeal disfigurations of the veteran's body, that compensated for any visual unlikeness. Unlike Hypolit in the first version of Hoffmann's tale, whose return from battle was narrated by someone else and which resulted in the death of his wife on their wedding day, Moritz's successful reintegration rested on his capacity to narrate his *own* absence, a narrative performance that nevertheless importantly had to pass through the *other* narrators who were present. Moritz's social reintegration was produced through the collectivizing technique of narrative orchestration.

The Magnetic Doppelgänger

There is a remarkable similarity, in other words, between the figure of the returning husband and that most ubiquitous of romantic figures, the double.[58] In each case, the duel with the double is about reestablishing the integrity of the "I." It is not surprising, then, that the husband as double is himself doubled through the figure of the magnetist, the person capable of dividing the interiority of the individual subject.

The first key change that Hoffmann makes between the first and second versions of his story—what makes the returning husband's return a success and not a failure—is to make the subplot of the first version (Theobald's successful mesmerization of his lover Auguste) into the primary plot of the second, to transform, in other words, the returning husband from the magnetist's antagonist to the magnetist's pupil. We know that "The Magnetist" was written at the height of Hoffmann's interest in magnetism, a period in which he was avidly reading works like Kluge's *Essay on the Representation of Animal Magnetism as a Means of Healing* (1811), Bartels' *Foundations of a Physiology and Physics of Animal Magnetism* (1812), and Schubert's *Observations on the Dark Side of Natural Philosophy* (1808).[59] Like the attention to dreams at the opening of "The Magnetist," magnetism and the magnetist's power to control his subjects captured for Hoffmann what Hans Robert Jauss has called the larger romantic fascination with the "Not-I" that would then go on to play such a prominent role in Freudian psychoanalysis.[60] As Jürgen Barkhoff has written, "The case studies and even more the fictionalizations of mesmerism . . . are readable as ethnographic investigations into the foreign and threatening nature of inner-psychological abysses."[61] Or as Maria herself wrote to her friend Adelgunde, "Yes, even as I write this I feel all too well that it is only He who gives me the words to see myself in him" (*SB*, 166). The division of the "I" that the attention to both dreams and the magnetist's ethereal rapport with his subjects produces is also in some sense an *Ich-Verlust*, a loss of the subject's control over him- or herself.

In the vast literature on the topic, the *Doppelgänger* has most often been thought of in psychologized terms, as a sign, in Christof Forderer's words in a recent monograph on the topic, of the "diffusion of identity" (*Identitätsdiffusion*) or the "dedifferentiation of the I-Pronoun" (*Entgrenzung des Ich-Pronomens*).[62] The proliferation of literary doubles is supposed to be the most emphatic sign of the growing psychologization of literature in the nineteenth century, the orientation of the literary as an exploration of an interiority that undergoes both a remarkable expansion as well as division. The proliferation of the double within the larger historical fact of the proliferation of the book assumes a fundamentally narcissistic structure, one which Freud argued was a crucial component of the "uncanny" itself,[63] as readers were increasingly trained to see an image of themselves in their books. As Friedrich Kittler has argued, "The printed word was skipped and the book forgotten, until somewhere between the lines a hallucination appeared—the pure signified of the printed sign. In other words, Doubles in the era of classical Romanticism originated in the classroom where we learn to read correctly."[64]

I want to pause for a moment here and ask whether this all too familiar reading of the proliferation of the romantic double is not in need of some revision. If the encounter with the double in romantic fiction is most often a threatening one, why would such an agonistic figure function as a mechanism of *identification* between reader and medium? Why would the traumatic experience of one's double lead a reader to see *through* the medium of the book? Why is the double a figure of the double self, in other words, and not just a figure of doubleness more generally? Instead of a figure of narcissistic personification or psychological division, perhaps the story of the double—the story about the proliferation of sameness—offered an extremely attractive plot to address a communicative world defined by increasingly reproducible cultural objects. In capturing the crisis that surrounded the singular and the unique, perhaps the story of the double did not so much articulate some new psychological reality or a larger program of psychologization at all, but instead represented with striking precision the material reality of a new communications environment. Perhaps it captured the sheer discomfort of inhabiting a world constituted by so much of the same thing, or put differently, of a world of so little originality. The duel with the double was not so much an invitation to identify with the characters in books as it was a means of contending with the discomforts of so much cultural sameness.

Maria's comment to her friend in "The Uncanny Guest" that I cited above nicely underscores the way Hoffmann's work explicitly draws attention to such communicative concerns. When she writes, "Yes, even as I *write this* . . . ," she is indicating how a particular technology of communication and its accompanying narrative practice are implicated in this process of "I-Loss."[65] As Albrecht Koschorke has argued, a fundamental absence of language was necessary for the healing process of classical magnetism, which relied instead on invisible fluids and connective tissues.[66] This is the case in Hoffmann's "The Magnetist" for the Baron, on whom the magnetist Major uses his "glowing instrument" to create an immediate rapport with his innermost self. But in the subplot surrounding Theodor, which is then elevated to the primary plot of the later "Uncanny Guest," what matters most for the magnetizing process is not the immediacy of the contact but precisely its "mediacy" through the narration of preexisting narrative material which is "whispered" into the subject's ear. This particular magnetist plot is then reused by Hoffmann (and expanded) because it motivates the reuse of material. Again Koschorke: "If classical magnetism depended upon a fundamental transmission of energy, one century later psychoanalysis would base itself on the absolute unavoidability of the semiotic distance of its subjects."[67] To nuance Koschorke's claim slightly, we could say that if classical magnetism was about dramatizing the possibility of a sympathetic, direct contact with another, Hoffmannian magnetism (and its offspring Freudian psychoanalysis) was increasingly about the *Technik* (technologies and techniques) of literary reactivation and recollection that produced such connectivity. The fundamental principle of the semiotic distance between subjects necessitated a more general reflection on the narrative, linguistic, and material techniques that were used to shape and bridge that distance.

The Whisper, Noise, and the Acoustics of Relocatability

Hoffmann's work thus dramatizes the historical transformation of the magnetist's-psychoanalyst's-artist's control over the subject from one of immediacy to semiotic and technological mediacy. It transforms the magnetist plot, in other words, into a means of thinking about the bibliographic economy. And it will be through the remediated orality of the "whisper," I want to suggest, which replaces the natural media of "fluids," "ether," or "electricity" on which magnetism formerly depended, where Hoffmann promotes this new bibliographic culture of collection. In being both audible and inaudible, the whisper not only communicates some piece of information to the one who can hear it, it also communicates the *ambiguity* and thus interpretability of such information to those who cannot.[68] In the inaudibility of its content on both a diegetic and heterodiegetic level—

to both readers and certain characters within the story—the whisper communicates incommunicability. It is not just noise but the figure of noise. It is both secretive (*heimlich*) and unavailable. But in the audibility of the enunciation itself—an audibility without content and thus without a determinable meaning or source—the whisper as a mode of communication is also defined by its extraordinary *availability* to appropriation and thus *unheimlich*. The importance of the whisper is not simply in the way it activates a hermeneutic scenario, but the way in which such interpretive necessities are framed as a function of the increasing mobility and thus availability of narrative information.

The whisper is thus, on one level, an ideal mode of "magnetic communication" because it draws attention to the noise, and thus the channel, of any communicative channel. In a perfect articulation of Burke's scene/act ratio, the mode of speech (the whisper) corresponds here to its speaker (the magnetist), because he literally embodies the channel (he is the figure of the third).[69] If the whisper emerges as a fundamental sign of noise in Hoffmann, it is also one part of a much larger economy of unintelligible sound that lacks either source or sense. In another important variation between the first and the second versions, Hoffmann dramatically expands and alters the opening frame narrative of "The Uncanny Guest" so that instead of telling stories about dreams, the characters recount stories about sounds for which no one can identify the sound's source. Whether it is the ethereal music of Ceylon, the Spanish sigh, the rain drops without rain during a visit to an inn, or the haunting sigh of death that follows Moritz's friend Bogislav, what each story narrates is the experience of *not* being able to connect a sound with its source. Indeed, these sounds without sources in the *framed* narratives of the novella are part of a larger economy of sound without *sense* within the *frame* narrative of the novella, whether it is the verbs used to describe the fire or the "tea machine" (*zischen, prasseln, pfiffen, heulen, knistern*), the whispering that Angelika is repeatedly subjected to that we as readers never overhear (performed by a proliferation of "M"-characters, the Mother, Marguerite, and Moritz), or the series of loud, sudden noises that punctuate the story (when Marguerite drops her glass, the *Schlag* or "blow" at the door that marks the Count's entrance, and the gunshots that are described in the stories of Bogislav and Moritz).

What we have in the second novella, in other words, is a series of circulating noises that literally remain *unheimlich*, that are incapable of establishing the status of being "at home." They lack a stable frame of reference, failing to belong in a strong sense to a particular owner or a particular place. Nowhere is this *guestness* of sound and speech more emphatically on display than in the moment of the loud bang at the door while Moritz is recounting his story of Bogislav prior to his departure for war. At the moment that Moritz tells us that Bogislav cries out, "Show yourself, you demon!," we read:

> Show yourself, you demon! if you dare—I challenge you and all your spirits of hell that stand ready at your command—Now a violent blow [*Schlag*] occurred.—In that moment [*in dem Augenblick*] the door to the room flung open with a threatening rattle. (*SB*, 734)

Recalling both the "blow" (*Schlag*) and the words "in that moment" (*in dem Augenblick*) of the anecdote about the philosophy students in the novella collection's frame narrative, it is precisely at the moment of the "violent blow" in "The Uncanny Guest" that the reader's attention is suddenly stretched across three (or four) different diegetic levels. The digression, "Now a violent blow occurred," could variously refer to either the character's narrative (Bogislav), the fictional narrator's narrative (Moritz), or the frame narrator's narrative (Ottmar), or of course, as is always possible in Hoffmann, an intrusion by the (real or fictional) editor of the volume. Unlike in the anecdote of the philosophy students, however, the words "in that moment" fail to correspond to a single speaking position; like all of the other sounds in the novella, they are marked by an extraordinary availability.

This economy of circulating sounds and the growing effacement of a stable system of origins that characterizes Hoffmann's novella has much in common with the "poetics of secondarity" and the "dislocation of reference" that Meredith McGill has identified in the writing of Edgar Allen Poe.[70] Indeed, the whisper would be the central mode of communication used by the double in Poe's "William Wilson." But a signal difference between these two writers' works lies in the way such poetic dislocations in Hoffmann's later work are always bound together with a poetics of *relocation* as well. The dislocatability of language is indeed the very precondition of its relocatability. The opening anecdotes that all narrate an acoustics of availability do not simply frame the remaining concerns of the novella. Rather, they become the narrative material through which the magnetist, and later, the returning husband, will practice their own arts of repetition and recuperation. The material that is reused is marked by the availability and mobility of speech within it—in other words, *that it can be reused*. The point is not simply that there are a series of repetitions that one can trace throughout Hoffmann's text, but that these repetitions motivate the very practice of repetition itself. As we will see, the particular moment of diegetic uncertainty and polyreferentiality in the knock at the door not only points backwards to preexisting material in the collection but becomes material for future reuse as well.

The Collectivity of the Copy

This brings me to the final significant variation between these two novellas. As we can recall from my opening description of "The Magnetist," the earlier version concludes with a cascading series of perspectives, a technique used most famously in Hoffmann's "The Sandman" and congruent with Gerhard Neumann's identification of the perspectival instabilities of Hoffmann's prose.[71] At the close of "The Magnetist" we are presented with a letter from Maria, a letter fragment from Alban, a first-person narrative in the voice of an editor, and excerpts from Franz Bickert's diary. The later novella, on the other hand, does not so much do away with this polyphony as contain it. In the course of eight pages, the following speakers tell the tale of Moritz's return in the order in which they are listed: Moritz, Dagobert, General S—en, the Colonel's wife, Dagobert, Moritz, General S—en, Dagobert, Moritz, Dagobert, a letter of Count S—i received from Marguerite read aloud by Dagobert, the Colonel's wife, Dagobert, and the Colonel's wife.

The polyphony of "The Magnetist" reappears in "The Uncanny Guest," but now such voices are recorded as the orchestration of *a single figure.* Where in the first novella such multiple speaking positions seemed to radiate outwards away from a unified perspective, in the later version they always return to, or revolve around, a single coordinating figure responsible for this procedure of narrative montage.

Moritz begins this operation of narrative orchestration with the words "You know . . . ," as the polyphonic narrative performance is framed precisely by the practice of reuse, of what a listener already knows. But this act of speech points not only to preexisting common knowledge but also to the reuse of this act of speech itself, which had marked the beginning of one of Moritz's own narratives from the earlier portion of the novella ("You know, began Moritz . . ." [*SB*, 725]). When Ottmar, who in the second version is no longer a character in the story but its narrator, cries out "What! you already know my story?," such shock in the frame narrative is replaced in the novella by the *normalization* of using such preexisting material. The narration continues through a series of planned and unplanned interruptions, with Moritz guiding the transitions ("But now you continue, Dagobert") or interjecting himself ("Yes, said the Captain [Moritz] as he interrupted his friend" [Ja! fiel der Rittmeister dem Freunde ins Wort]). It is precisely this latter expression by the narrator, to fall into someone's words (an idiom for interrupting someone), that discloses most succinctly the larger narrative operation occurring here. In being spoken for, Moritz is literally falling into the words of others, as his biography is constituted through the speech of others. Moritz's role as a narrator is to coordinate the heterogeneity of these increasingly available voices—his but one among many—as though they were his own.

Bringing about this transformation from guest to husband—bringing about the legitimization of Moritz's reappearance, in other words—depends on two important, and importantly paradoxical, narrative procedures. It depends, first, on the coordination of numerous voices as a single voice, on the narrator's capacity to regulate heterogeneity in a double sense: as both plurality and difference. As the narrator's interlocutor asks in Hawthorne's "My Kinsman, Major Molineaux": "May not a man have several voices, Robin, as well as two complexions?"[72] The task of the narrator is thus twofold: to present the increasing variability of speaking positions as increasingly unified and to present the increasing foreignness of speech as proprietary. Far from reestablishing the congruence between sound and source that was marked as a problem through the opening narratives of the novella, the successful conclusion of the novella depends on the *normalization* of this suspension of the ownership of speech. The novella redefines "at-homeness" in language as the incorporation of increasing degrees of "guestness." Where Bakhtin has argued that "foreignness" is the fundamental element of all utterances, I want to suggest that Hoffmann's tale discloses the way such acceptance of the foreign in language, indeed language as something potentially foreign (and thus *unheimlich*), can be read as a crucially romantic contribution.[73]

But that is just the first operation at work here. The returning husband's legitimacy also depends on the collective legitimization of, and participation in, this practice of reuse. The condition of possibility of appropriating the words of others in Moritz's narrative is precisely the proliferation of narratives at the outset of the novella—most prominently figured in Moritz's *own* narrative—that dramatize the availability of speech, that dramatize the increasing instability of the relationship between a sound and its source, speech and speaker. The *practice* of repetition, in other words, is motivated by a preexisting *poetics* of repetition. In redeploying the very narrative techniques enacted in the earlier tales, and more significantly, in redeploying his own earlier narrative techniques, Moritz transforms himself not only into a magnetist but more importantly into a kind of collector. The magnetist is no longer necessary to the plot—he can die in the second version—because he lives on in the figure of Moritz, only now as a legitimate figure. According to Hoffmann's writing, the collector is precisely the figure capable of produc-

ing sameness out of heterogeneity and heterogeneity—a novel difference—
out of such sameness.

Again

In the early nineteenth century, following the precedent of the Göschen
publishing house, publishers were increasingly occupied with collecting,
packaging, and selling the collected works of their respective language's
most popular authors. The success of this format both derived from, as well
as contributed to, the emerging discourse of the heroic author, the organization of textual material around a single individual's life. At the same time,
the rise of collected editions had the undeniable effect of contributing to
the proliferation of copies and the experience of repetition that would become a hallmark of a modern environment of mass communication. The
format of the collected edition legitimized not only a particular way of classifying literature but also a particular practice of reproducing it as well. It
emphatically aligned reading with repetition, indeed, it figured reading as
repetition.[74]

Perhaps no other work was as explicitly and thoroughly concerned with
the collectedness of literature as E. T. A. Hoffmann's own landmark collection, *The Serapion Brothers*. And perhaps no other work within the collection organized more thoroughly the issues posed by collection than the rewritten novella, "The Uncanny Guest." In strategies that emphasized the
increasing availability of narrative property, the legitimacy of reuse, and the
redefinition of the singular as increasingly heterogeneous, "The Uncanny
Guest" marked, but also promoted, the increasing importance of collection
to the romantic bibliocosmos.[75] "The Uncanny Guest" thus coordinated an
entire spectrum of devices that one could find deployed individually in a
number of other novellas in *The Serapion Brothers*, whether it was the centrality of "aftersinging" (*Nachsingen*) in "The Bride Selection," the pluralization
of voice in "Madame Scuderi," or the dislocation of meaning away from the
body of the speaker in "The Automata."

What makes Hoffmann's work ultimately so incisive, however, is not
just the way it symbolically legitimizes a bibliographic practice but the way
it critiques this process as well, the way it asks what it means to accept
and naturalize such a system of reproducibility. In the final sentence of
"The Uncanny Guest," Hoffmann writes: "Then Angelika buried her face,
blushing in bright, rosy flames, in the breast of the superiorly happy Moritz.
That one slung his arm around his graceful spouse and whispered softly: is
there still a higher bliss down here than this?" (*Der* schlang aber den Arm

um die holde Gattin und lispelte leise: Gibt es denn noch hienieden eine höhere Seligkeit als diese?) (*SB*, 769). Through the pun on the verb *schlang* (slung) with the word *Schlange* (snake), the final image that the novella offers is of a snake encircling its prey, acoustically amplified in the consonance of all those "s" sounds (*lispeln, leise, es, Seligkeit, diese*). At the same time, the final act of communication of the novella is another whisper, precisely the mode of speech used in the magnetizing process that seduced Angelika away from Moritz in the first place. It is a deeply unsettling conclusion, accentuated by the ambiguity or outright irony of the rhetorical question (is there something more blissful than being married?) as well as the conspicuous italicization of "*Der*." The use of deixis here in place of the proper name is the final, and most suggestive, mark of this uncoupling of speech and speaker, sound and source. To whom is the narrator pointing when he says "that one"? Are we talking about Moritz or perhaps the specter of the Count that still haunts Angelika's memory? The final utterance thus repeats precisely the availability of speech, the unnecessary connection between speaker and spoken, word and meaning, that opened the novella and that was enacted in a similar deictic moment with the words, "in *that* moment." The transformation of Moritz from guest to husband—and thus the legitimacy and at-homeness of the practice of collection that was at stake in his narrative performance—is ultimately marked as an incomplete, indeed incompletable, process. The status of the husband's or the collection's identity is never completely divorced from the haunting liminality and mobility of the uncanny guest. Guestness is inscribed into the heart of this culture of the copy.

Far from depicting the practice of collection as one of fixation—that the collected works inaugurated a condition of textual or cultural stability—"The Uncanny Guest" thus argued for the essential instability of this project, that it was a drama that needed to be perpetually rehearsed. It was a fact that was born out by the reality of producing collected editions. Collected editions not only seemed to have something interminable about them—as in Goethe's collected works that continued to expand with the printing of ever greater amounts of posthumous material, from forty to sixty to over one-hundred volumes for the Weimar Edition—but each collected edition always seemed to produce another one, as in the numerous Walter Scott editions in the early nineteenth century or the various successive Hölderlin or Nietzsche editions in the twentieth. Instead of limiting the flow and overflow of literary material, the publication of collected editions contributed to the very surplus of production they were designed to control. "The Uncanny Guest" thus enacted both the consolidation and stability that collected editions were intended to produce at the same time that it deposited pieces of evidence that pointed to the necessary *failure* of such consolidation and control. It highlighted, in Sebald's words, "the irreparable defect of its program," the reality that this new communicative environment required the perpetual reproduction of artifacts to compensate for the insufficient substantiality of their reproducibility. According to Hoffmann, the dream of the stable copy always turned into something of a nightmare.

CHAPTER THREE

Processing

Until—What's this the Germans say is fact
That Wolf found out first? It's unpleasant work
Their chop and change, unsettling one's belief.

—Robert Browning, "Homer" (1888)

Printing the Past (Intermediality and the Book I)

"Everyone wants to edit!"[1] These were the words that the collector Karl von Meusebach wrote to Jacob Grimm in 1824, and they captured the voracious enthusiasm that surrounded the practice of editing in the early nineteenth century. In the years around 1800 an expanding philological community was vigorously debating the practices of discovering, transcribing, glossing, annotating, collating, interpolating, and commenting on texts that all belonged to the editor's trade. Like the growing importance of the publisher or bookseller to the early-nineteenth-century literary market, the editor represented another mediator or middle*man* (the gender is important here) whose increasing prominence correlated to the increasing sophistication of the bibliographic environment. The more material there was circulating about, the more important those individuals became who ensured the reliability of bibliographic transmission.

In their rising fascination with a vernacular literary past, early-nineteenth-century editors played an integral role in producing the creative heritage upon which the imagined communities of emerging European nation states were to be based. As Benedict Anderson has written, this was a "golden age of vernacularizing lexicographers, grammarians, philologists, and litterateurs."[2] Works like Joseph Ritson's *Scotish Songs* (1794), Friedrich von der

Hagen's *Der Nibelungen Lied* (1807), or François-Juste-Marie Raynouard's six volume collection of French troubadours, *Choix des poésies originales des troubadours* (1816–21), were key contributions in shaping nineteenth-century national imaginaries. As Hagen wrote in the preface to his edition, the publication of his medieval epic represented the "hope for the future return of German glory and world grandeur."[3]

At the same time that the work of early-nineteenth-century editors played an essential role in the shaping of various romantic nationalisms, their work was also marked by a decisive linguistic heterogeneity.[4] In editions like Wilhelm Grimm's *Altdänische Heldenlieder* (1811) or Friedrich Diez's *Altspanischen Romanzen* (1818), editors were responsible not only for the translation of material across time but also between languages and cultures.[5] Indeed, the extent to which editors were or were not like translators would emerge as one of the key problems within the early-nineteenth-century philological community.

Such cultural and linguistic diversity at the heart of the editorial project around 1800 was matched by an equal diversity of genre. In the broad array of material that they recovered and made available—the ballads, folk songs, fairy tales, chapbooks, romances, epics, and myths of an earlier age—romantic editors functioned as an essential source of literary innovation, contributing in important ways to the increasing generic mixing, the "Gattungsverschlungenheit" in Georg Lukacs's words, that was one of the hallmarks of early-nineteenth-century literature.[6] Their significance lay in their capacity to supply the expanding literary market not only with "natural," that is, nonclassical (or non-French), genres, but also "new," that is, nonprint, genres, where such novelty always depended on an implicit familiarity. Editors' insatiable appetites for locating and reproducing this dormant manuscript heritage only seemed to confirm the anatomical sculptor's prophecy in Goethe's *Wilhelm Meister's Travels* that "truly a conflict will one day emerge between the living and the dead. . . . No one of any age or any position, whether high or low, was safe in his grave anymore."[7] The popular romantic image of the grave robber (one thinks of James Hogg) was a metaphorical embodiment of all those would-be philologists roaming European libraries in search of buried manuscripts and old books.

Finally, in their detailed attention to the *practices* of transmission—of moving from a manuscript or even oral tradition of literary circulation to one founded upon the printed book—romantic editors played an essential role in contributing to a nineteenth-century media imaginary. Teasing out the relations of different communications media to literary production, romantic editors functioned much like early media theorists. Like translators or publishers, editors' work was always surrounded by questions of change, of how much change was acceptable in transmitting a text through time and space and from one communications technology to another. The editor's importance corresponded not only to the growing proliferation of material but also to the fundamental *intermediality* of literary culture around 1800. Like the translators that I will discuss in chapter 5, who occupied an important writerly space of the in-between, the romantic editor embodied a larger negotiation with historical, linguistic, generic, and medial alterity.

The Editor's Rise and Fall

The image of the heroic author that the romantic age has bequeathed us and that, at least in German, has led in circular fashion to the period's classification around a single author (known affectionately as the *Goethezeit*), has left little room for the figure of the editor, whom Nietzsche liked to call a "word quibbler" and a "dirty pedant."[8] Yet not only did editors exert a tremendous influence on the romantic literary market, numerous romantic authors *were* editors. For "heroic" romantic literary figures like Giacomo Leopardi, Walter Scott, and J. W. Goethe, editing was integral to their careers as writers (one thinks of Goethe's *Winckelmann and His Century* or his edition of his correspondence with Schiller, Scott's edition of Dryden, or Leopardi's edition of Porphyry's *De vita plotini*). Such romantic author-editors of course stood in a much longer, and much revered, literary tradition that included names like Petrarch, Boccaccio, Erasmus, and Pope, among many others.[9] There was nothing antithetical, in other words, to these dual writerly practices in the romantic period and for long before, something that most literary histories both on and after romanticism seem to have forgotten. Where Browning's late-nineteenth-century poem on Homer cited above as an epigraph to this chapter expressed exasperation over the "unpleasant work" of editors, Leopardi's early-nineteenth-century poem "Ad Angelo Mai," for example, was written *in honor* of his philologist friend who discovered numerous works by the Roman rhetorician Marcus Cornelius Fronto.[10] In a similar vein, Goethe had written to the philologist Friedrich August Wolf—the very object of Browning's ire—that his work on Homer had inspired him to begin his own experiments with the epic genre.[11] Indeed, Wolf's *Prolegomena ad Homerum* was one of the key texts that Goethe was reading while producing the first version of his *Travels*.[12] For writers like Leopardi and Goethe, it was precisely the mediating role of the editor, his "chop and change" in Browning's words, that initiated new creative spaces.

Between Leopardi's praise of editors and Browning's indictment of them, then, something happened in the course of the nineteenth century. The figure of the editor and the practices of the editor underwent a major shift in the literary imagination, from a source of inspiration to that of a problem. In this chapter, I want to return to the debates and books of early-nineteenth-century editors—to the textual margins and marginal figures of the period—to try to understand how a notion of writing as mediation was itself marginalized. My focus, however, will not be with the intra-philological question of whether this intensification of editorial activity at the turn of the nineteenth century produced any major methodological innovations within the field of editorial theory, a debate that has received an enormous amount of scholarly attention and that depends on a teleological view of editorial work.[13] Rather, I want to cross the disciplinary boundaries that have traditionally walled off a history of scholarship from a history of literature to see how editing and authoring, creating and correcting, were in fact integrally intertwined with one another during the romantic period. How did editors produce authors at the turn of the nineteenth century, not simply within the confines of their own editions but in the way such editions made varying notions of authorship culturally available? How did editorial theory and editorial work contribute to a broader understanding of what an author was and what an author did?

A history of romantic editing is important today because it allows us to see a parallel moment when questions about the movement from one communicative regime to another were felt with increasing urgency. The project of reformatting a print literary heritage for a digital environment necessarily entails an understanding of the protocols through which such preservation has until now been guaranteed. As Jerome McGann has argued, "We are thus entering a period when the entirety of our received cultural archive of materials, not least of all our books and manuscripts, will have to be reconceived."[14] Understanding the acerbic debates and the professional stakes of the romantic experience can help us contextualize the often contentious arguments that surround today's projects of digitization. But they can also show us that those stakes are indeed quite high because they impact not only who controls archives but also who counts in the hierarchy of institutional power. They impinge upon notions of authority and expertise and highlight how such categories are integrally related to ideals of communication.

But a history of the *relationship* between editing and authoring is also important because it can show us the myriad ways that the processing of available artistic material, Browning's chop and change, can serve as an essential source of literary creativity. Indeed, showing the historical contingency of the differentiation of editorial from authorial thinking can help us see with renewed clarity the importance of "processing" to a contemporary media landscape in which we have ever greater amounts of material at our disposal and increasingly sophisticated technologies to transmit and transmute that material. Resurrecting the editor and the edition as influential sources of literary making can highlight the importance that knowledge of the technological protocols of communication can and should have for writers.

Immaculate Reception: From *Erneuung* to Critical Edition (Tieck, Hagen, Lachmann)

In 1803, Ludwig Tieck produced an edition of medieval courtly love songs, *Minnelieder aus dem schwäbischen Zeitalter* (Love Songs from the Swabian Age), a work of 220 poems that included many of the best-known German medieval poets such as Walther von der Vogelweide and Hartmann von Aue. Jacob Grimm would later say that it was Tieck's *Minnelieder* that inspired him to dedicate himself to the study of old German poetry.[15] On the one hand, Tieck's turn towards early Germanic documents was a continuation of an emerging historical awareness of local cultures that had largely been inspired by Herder's edition of *Volkslieder* (1778), which was itself indebted to Percy's *Reliques of Ancient English Poetry* (1765), and that had subsequently fanned out across Europe. The year 1803 was also the one that saw the publication of the final volume of Walter Scott's *Minstrelsy of the Scottish Border*, and one year later Charles Nodier's *Essais d'un jeune barde* appeared, an eclectic collection of translations, imitations, and essays on both folk and contemporary poetry. A year after that Clemens Brentano's and Achim von Arnim's landmark romantic collection of ballads and folksongs appeared under the title *Des Knaben Wunderhorn* (1805–8).

As the historian of scholarship Rüdiger Krohn has argued, however, Tieck's *Minnelieder* also marked the beginning of a new tide of what came to be known neologistically as literary *Erneuungen*, modernizations that hovered between the various modes of translation, paraphrase, and imitation and that found their French equivalent in what came to be known as "le genre troubadour."[16] As Tieck explained in his introduction to the collection, he did not leave his literary sources in their original state but crucially made changes to them such as updating words, adding stanza divisions, and erasing place names to give the work a more universal feel. If his courtly love songs were in important ways different from their originals, they also were not pure transformations into modern German either. He changed some, but not all, of his Middle High German words and left those untouched that the reader could intuit.[17] His edition required, he said, "that the reader should meet him halfway, just as he too approaches the reader halfway as well."[18] One could find Tieck's editorial practices fictionalized on English terrain in Ann Radcliffe's gothic novel *Gaston de Blondeville* (1803/1826), where the editor/narrator tells us in similar fashion: "The following is a modernized copy. . . . In this copy, Willoughton endeavoured to preserve somewhat of the air of the old style, without its dryness. . . . However, he often retained the old words, where they did not seem to form too glaring a contrast with the modern style, and, now and then, somewhat of the quaintness of the original."[19]

Like Radcliffe's fictional edition, Tieck's actual edition depended on a theory of translation, on the mutual crossing over (*über-setzen*) between languages and time by both reader and writer. In transforming his original, Tieck's aim was to make these dormant literary texts more available to a contemporary reading public. As Walter Scott would similarly argue, praising George Ellis's abridgments in his *Specimens of Early English Metrical Romances* (1803), "Mr. Ellis has brought the minstrels of old into the boudoirs and drawing-rooms, which have replaced the sounding halls and tapestried bowers in which they were once so familiar."[20] Tieck's editing participated in a romantic theory of enlivening past documents, a vitality that was thought to be a central feature of such documents themselves, whether it was the "lively movement" (*lebendige Bewegung*) that Joseph Görres ascribed to the corporeal performances of old German *Meisterlieder* or the geographic circulations of metrical material that Jacob Grimm claimed were one of the most "refreshing and comforting gifts of God."[21] If in changing his original Tieck's aim was to emphasize, as he said in his introduction, that there was truly only "Eine Poesie," in simultaneously preserving the foreignness of his original he was also capturing the irredeemable pastness, the historicity, of such literary origins that was essential to the romantic imagination.[22]

In its interventionist approach to its source material, the *Erneuung* was the latest example of the long, and often revered, tradition of interpolations and conjecture that surrounded the practice of editing. As F. A. Wolf had said of Homer's editors, "It is by this sort of emendation, or rather criticism, that all critics once were rivals in Homer, or rather with Homer."[23] Or as Richard Bentley put it in his edition of Horace (1711), "For us, reason and the facts are worth more than a hundred manuscripts."[24] Like its editorial forerunners, the *Erneuung* required literary talent to replace and not just annotate the "foreign" words of earlier manifestations of the German language. As Clemens Brentano wrote to his collaborator, Achim von Arnim, upon reading the Grimms' collection of fairytales, "After reading this book, I truly sensed how correctly we proceeded with the *Wunderhorn* and the extraordinary talent that one could ascribe to us; the fidelity that one finds in the fairytales reads rather poorly."[25] Talent was prized over fidelity, judgment over artifact. The romantic modernization thus participated in—and one might say concluded—the long editorial tradition of equating editors with authors. To those who practiced the art of *Erneuung*, it was supposed to embody both old and new, that the old was a form of renewal and that correcting could induce creating. To its coming detractors, however, the *Erneuung* was an example of neither.

Four years after the appearance of Tieck's *Minnelieder*, Friedrich von der Hagen, who would later hold the first chair for German philology at the newly founded University of Berlin, produced an edition of the *Nibelungenlied*,[26] a work whose growing reputation as the German *Iliad* made it one of the most important—and contested—texts of the early nineteenth century. Hagen's edition became one of the most popular, as well as the strangest, examples of this method of literary *Erneuung*. In a review of the edition in the *Heidelbergische Jahrbücher der Literatur*, Wilhelm Grimm said of Hagen's work, "It is a modernization that is worse than the original and yet not even modern."[27] The problem with the practice of *Erneuung* to its detractors was that, like the word *Erneuung* itself, it seemed to stand outside of time. The *Erneuung* neither represented its source, what Tieck called the "essential character" of the language, nor did it represent a unique poetic voice of the present. "The language that appears here," wrote Grimm, "is such that has never lived in any particular age."[28] The *Erneuung* did not seem to belong to anyone or any time.

To its many critics, the *Erneuung* thus involved both the wrong kind and the wrong quantity of change. It brought the reader too far away from any kind of stable textual origins, from either its medieval context in which it was first produced or the early nineteenth-century world in which it was being reproduced. One could find the same critique leveled in François-Juste-Marie Raynouard's review of Legrand d'Aussy's popular edition of *Fabliaux ou contes* that had appeared initially in 1779 and was later reissued in 1829. In the *Journal des Savants*, Raynouard wrote of the reissued edition: "After analyzing these works . . . the author should have communicated such curious and interesting details in his notes not through translation but in meticulously referring to the original texts."[29] It was precisely translation's problem of linguistic change—and the infidelity to one's sources it suggested—that posed a problem for early-nineteenth-century editions.

If romantic editors were increasingly becoming critical of their predecessors' predilection for altering their source texts through the once honored practice of conjecture, romantic editors could also be charged with the equal and opposite problem of too *little* change. In the battle between Friedrich von der Hagen and the Grimm brothers to produce a new edition of the *Edda*,[30] Hagen was the first to obtain the thirteenth-century Codex Regius manuscript from the Copenhagen Library and was thus the first to market.[31] Three years later, the Grimm Brothers produced an edition of the *Edda* that was a translation into German.[32] The charge that Wilhelm Grimm leveled this time at Hagen, perhaps as a veiled justification for the significant amounts of change that surrounded his translated edition of the *Edda*, was that Hagen's edition was no "edition" at all—it was simply a manuscript in print: "What Herr Professor v.d. Hagen offers here is nothing more than a reprint of his manuscript copy" (ist nichts als ein bloßer Abdruck seiner Abschrift).[33] Hagen's crime was that he had not changed his sources enough. When Hagen produced what he called a "critical edition" (*kritische Ausgabe*) of the *Nibelungenlied* in 1816 to answer his critics of his *Erneuung* from 1807,[34] this time it was philology's rising star, Karl Lachmann, who leveled the same charge that Grimm had: "We must now thank Herr v.d.H[agen] for the careful and qualified reprint [*Abdruck*] of one of the best manuscripts, but we can by no means speak of an edition of the Nibelungenlied that would be deserving of this name."[35]

Hagen had explicitly called his edition a "critical edition" and had emphasized his review and comparison of numerous manuscript sources, the *recensio* that was increasingly understood to be at the heart of producing an "edition."[36] By the 1820 edition, Hagen would list over eleven manuscript sources on which his edition was based. But in both his title and his introduction to the edition, it was clear that even with the surplus of manuscripts—or perhaps because of this surplus—Hagen's primary concern lay with printing the single oldest manuscript as accurately as possible. "The premise stated there," he writes of his earlier 1810 edition, "to use the oldest and best manuscript as the basis [of this edition] must now be much more strictly and precisely applied. The St. Gallen manuscript is thus printed almost word for word, letter for letter" (xxv). For Hagen, as for his humanist predecessors, the authority of a new edition rested as much on the authority of his sources as with the activity of the editor himself, a point still operative today as one can still find modern editions of the *Nibelungenlied* that are reprints of the St. Gallen manuscript.[37]

For editors like Lachmann and the Grimms, however, manuscripts were seen not as perfect records of an original work but instead as corrupted variants or incomplete fragments of a lost origin. There was in essence a theory of media and mediation embedded in Lachmann's thinking: the written document constituted a fall from the garden of the author's mind. Fidelity to a single manuscript meant infidelity to the original author or work. The *Abdruck* or reprint of a single manuscript meant that the editor had not engaged his source material enough. For something to be considered a "critical edition" not only required that the editor's engagement with multiple sources result in a single, best text, but that such engagements with the material legacy of the text were to be dramatized on the printed page. The critical edition rested on the paradoxical idea that it was only through the practice of transformation that the editor could recover something that was originally there. The more the editor did, in other words, the more he disappeared from the author's text. Unlike their humanist predecessors, whose interventions often encircled and seemed to overtake their primary texts, as in Scaliger's 1604 edition of Catullus' collected works (fig. 3.1), which was itself indebted to a medieval practice of manuscriptural glossing, early-nineteenth-century editors were rapidly typographically moving to the margins of their books, and specifically the footnotes, even as they were still present in practice within the main body of their texts.

To his contemporaries, Hagen's edition was thus marred by the fact that it contained too few marks. Like Hagen, Raynouard had similarly invoked the necessity of consulting numerous manuscript witnesses for the making of his groundbreaking edition of troubadour poetry (1816–21). "It is indispensable," writes Raynouard in a note to the text, "when one wishes to publish or translate the works of the troubadours, to consult the different manuscripts, to examine and judge variants with taste and critique."[38] But like Hagen, Raynouard had omitted such critical activity from the space of the printed page, a fact that would later be criticized by Raynouard's Prussian follower, Friedrich Diez, in his subsequent edition, *Die Poesie der Troubadours* (1826).[39] There was a paginal immaculateness to these earlier editions that needed to be discarded, or better, framed, a blank space that needed to be typographically bordered by the work of the editor. Between the late 1810s and early 1830s, the critical edition emerged as the bibliographic format that motivated but also regulated the interventions of editors into their source materials at the same time that it visually and typographically contributed to their marginalization. Christof Windgätter has argued that "at the end of the eighteenth century a form of writing emerges on the printed book's page that is no longer categorized by its multi-dimensional segmentation [as in medieval or early-modern editions], but rather a unidimensional progression."[40] But in its promotion of a bifurcated rather than unidimensional page, the critical edition was not simply participating in a romantic reorganization of bibliographic knowledge as a form of "channel-

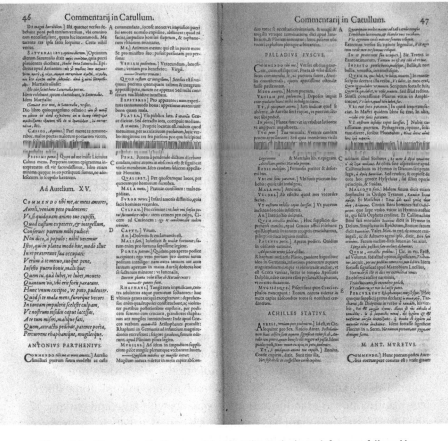

Figure 3.1   One can see the Roman original in italics in the lower left corner followed by
sections of subsequent commentary. C. Val. Catulli *Opera Omnia* (1604), 46–47.
Courtesy of the Rare Book and Manuscript Library, Columbia University.

ized" knowledge. It also dramatized a space of vertical reading of multiple
variants that overlay one another in complex ways. Fluid reading was juxta-
posed here with thick reading.

The peculiar genius of the duality behind the critical edition was that
it reorganized the competing demands of editorial and authorial activity
that surrounded editorial work. The former intermingling of mediation and
origination that had surrounded both editorial and authorial work was now
rigorously separated out into two distinct practices and paginal spaces—
that were nonetheless still related to one another only now according to a
kind of causal logic. The more you were confronted with the one (originality), the more you needed the other (editing). As Lachmann wrote in his

review of Hagen's failed critical edition, "From an ample number of good manuscripts we should represent a text that lies at the basis of all of these texts, which must either be the original itself or come very close."[41] And in the preface to his second edition of *Iwein* (1843), he would write even more passionately: "I have sought to give the words of the poet as precisely and originally as it appeared possible to me; so that a relatively educated reader must only read what has been printed in order to have the impression of immaculate reception [um den Eindruck rein zu empfangen]."[42] Through an attention to the numerous and various records of the literary text—through an attention, in other words, to the historical exigencies that underlay the text—the editor's ultimate goal was to locate the original work and thus bypass history.

In the course of the early nineteenth century, German and European print editions thus moved away from practices like the *Erneuung* or the "genre troubadour," where the editor intervened directly in the work by transforming the original work's language. At the same time, they also moved away from the *Abdruck*, where the editor printed a single (and most likely oldest) source as accurately as possible (a practice that, today, has gained increasing currency with the New Philology).[43] Instead, German editors moved towards the category of the "critical edition" to accommodate the competing demands of mediation and originality that surround the edited work. The representational practices of the critical edition were (and continue to be) designed to *differentiate* the tasks of authoring and editing, to create two separate spaces where their respective activity could be observed without interference from the other, indeed, where their distinct practices in fact produced one another. Unlike their humanist predecessors, whose titles often invoked the genealogy of editors and editions that supported their own edition and thus blurred the boundaries between authors and editors,[44] early-nineteenth-century editors were busy constructing textual and typographical borders between these two kinds of writerly work.

Unlike the *Erneuung*, evidence of the editor's practice in the critical edition was pushed beyond the boundaries of the work proper, either to footnotes, prefaces, or more commonly to the back of the book. And unlike the *Abdruck*, where the editor's activity was supposed to be as limited as possible, the editor's work in the critical edition was voluminously on display, as in G. F. Benecke's edition of Wirnt von Gravenberch's *Wigalois: Der Ritter mit dem Rade* (Berlin: Reimer, 1819), with its sixty-four-page preface, two-hundred fifty-six-page dictionary, and almost one-hundred-page commentary, or Lachmann's edition of the works of Wolfram von Eschenbach, an unprecedented *tour de force* of textual notation (fig. 3.2), a practice that

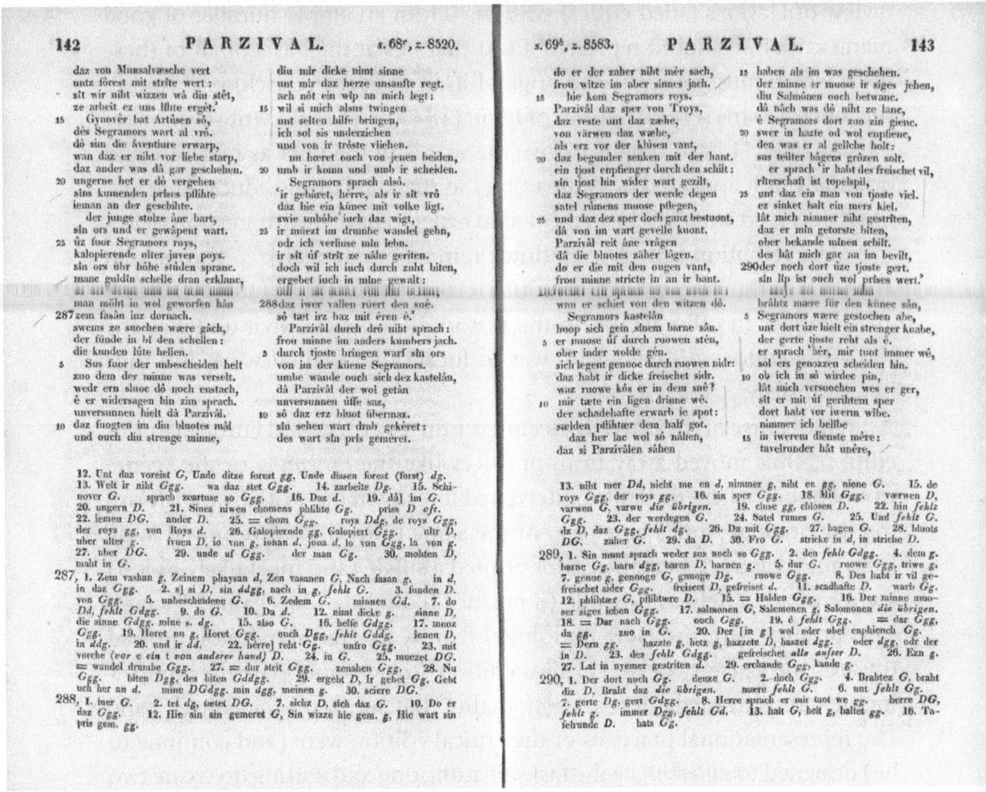

Figure 3.2   Karl Lachmann, *Wolfram von Eschenbach* (1833), 336–37.
Courtesy of the Klassik Stiftung Weimar, HAAB/Koe III 121.

arguably reached its apex with the recent publication of an edition of Büchner's *Danton's Death* in which the 160 page play is followed, rather than surrounded by, 1,480 pages of textual commentary.[45] Through its emerging textual apparatus, the critical edition was designed to produce a Herculean image of both author and editor who worked according to very different principles and very different places on the page. On the one hand, there was the editor reconstructing the routes of transmission and the acts of transformation that surrounded his text, and on the other, there was the author, overwhelmingly defined by originality in both senses of the word—as someone whose work was as near as possible to his original intent and as someone whose work was deeply original (that is, innovative) and who thus warranted the attention of scholars, publishers, and readers. Only the differentiation of authoring and editing and the *simultaneous* presentation

of their practices in distinct paginal spaces allowed the reader to experience Lachmann's paradoxical ideal of "immaculate reception." As with any
edition, the editor produced the author, but with the critical edition, the
equation worked according to the logic of revelation: the more the editor
did, the more one saw the author emerge in all of his original and singular
splendor.

Walter Scott, the Ballad, and the Book

The notion and nature of the "critical edition" that had emerged largely out
of the field of Germanic philology in the early nineteenth century—and
that, to be sure, owed much to an earlier classical philological tradition
through figures like Wolf and Heyne—would go on to exert enormous influence in the field of textual criticism down to today. As one scholar has
remarked, only slightly tongue-in-cheek, "In the case of editorial theory,
we are all Germans."[46] But the story of the rise of the critical edition and
the fall of a particular typology of the editor only tells half of the story of
how editors produced authors in the romantic age and for long after. It
may show us the methodological and typographical distinctions that were
taking place across the pages of printed books, but it does not help us see
how editing and authoring more nearly overlapped. To understand that part
of the story I want to turn the clock back to a time (the 1790s), an author
(Walter Scott), and a genre (the ballad) where we can see how these issues
were being worked out in very concrete and often deeply paradoxical ways.
To move from German to Scottish terrain is of course to follow a key cultural circuit of the romantic age. As Goethe would later write to his Scottish
translator, Thomas Carlyle, "I have to repeat that perhaps never has the case
arisen where a nation has concerned itself and taken part so intimately with
another as the Scottish does now with the German."[47]

During the late 1790s, Walter Scott began touring the border regions
of Scotland with his friend, John Leyden, to collect recitations of Scottish
ballads. Such activity mirrored with remarkable fidelity a similar project
undertaken by Goethe and Herder over twenty years earlier, when they traveled to the region of Alsace and began recording the folksongs that would
eventually contribute to Herder's *Volkslieder* (1778).[48] Two decades later one
could find the same exploratory poetic ethnography in the work of Charles
Nodier, who, as the municipal librarian in Ljubljana under Napoleon, began recording and promoting Illyrian ballads in his periodical, *Télégraphe
officiel* (1812–13).

Such renewed interest in the ballad as an articulation of an often distressed local culture—one believed to be imminently passing away—was not simply a transnational phenomenon that took place at different times and in different places. It was also crucially an inter-national one of influence and circulation, especially between German and Scottish culture.[49] During the years of his ballad collecting excursions, Scott was also at work translating German balladeers like Gottfried August Bürger, and both Scott and Bürger were inspired by Herder's edition of folksongs and ballads from across Europe that had appeared two decades earlier, an edition which itself derived from Herder's initial interest in Percy's *Reliques*. Indeed, as Hannelore Schlaffer has shown, such bardic translations could be seen operating on a visual plane as well. Bürger's collection of ballads, which contained the version of "Lenore" that Scott would eventually translate, used as its frontispiece the same image of the wandering minstrel that had initially appeared in Johann Joachim Eschenburg's translation of Percy's collection.[50] Scott's reimportation of such anglo-inspired Germanic balladeering would then be imported *back* into the German states as his *Minstrelsy of the Scottish Border* would serve as a key influence on Brentano and Arnim's *Des Knaben Wunderhorn*.[51]

As a witness to the new international attention to the local, the ballad would go on to play an essential generic role in the development of romantic poetry.[52] Whether it was Goethe and Schiller's ballad year of 1797, Coleridge and Wordsworth's literary "experiment" of the *Lyrical Ballads*, or Victor Hugo's opening salvos in the wars between the classicists and the romanticists with his *Odes et ballades*, the ballad repeatedly served as a poetic opening that attempted to mark a creative opening. With its inherent appeal to the oral and the medium of the body (ballad comes from the Provençal *ballada*, or dance tune [*Tanzlied*]), the ballad came to stand in a post-Rousseauean fashion for all things natural, original, and prelapsarian.[53] Goethe, we remember, called the ballad the "Ur-Ey," or original egg, of poetic genres.[54] As a hybrid between a sung performance and a print object, the ballad became the preferred genre to mediate between the increasingly commercial aspects of the book trade and the seemingly evanescent authenticity of folk culture. Indeed, it became the ideal poetic vehicle to translate the commercial into the natural, the topical into the timeless. As Paula McDowell has argued, it was precisely the romantic ballad revival itself, with its programmatic exclusion of the print broadside in favor of the oral recitation, that helped produce a notion of "orality" and oral culture that is still with us today.[55]

If the ballad was on the one hand one of the most emphatic signs of a greater romantic fascination with orality and the originary, it was also a key index of a romantic attention to intermediality.[56] As both a print object and a record (or basis) of a sung performance, the ballad was also tied to questions of textual illustration. Not only was the early-modern broadside ballad often an illustrated sheet well into the eighteenth century, the romantic ballad collection would be at the forefront of the rise of illustrated books in the 1820s and 30s. When book illustrators sought to make their mark, it was the genre of the ballad they most often turned to first. Walter Scott's figure of the sorcerer "page" in *The Lay of the Last Minstrel* was not simply a sign of a greater romantic equation of the act of reading with that of visual hallucination.[57] It was also a key incorporation of the ballad's very real intermedial identity at the level of poetic figure.

Despite a wealth of research today that is attuned to the mediality of the romantic ballad revival, what much of this work has overlooked is the ballad's bookishness and, by extension, the way the ballad was a key object in early-nineteenth-century editorial debates. As Steve Newman has shown, in the new critical context of the mid-twentieth century the ballad was thought to be *the* literary genre to initiate readers into reading literature in books precisely because it was imagined to be a *non*-bookish genre, a critical move imported wholesale from the romantic era.[58] But few genres were as tied to debates about making books as the ballad was by the early nineteenth century. The ballad revival was always intensely mediated through the bibliographic practices of collection and correction. The ballad was in this sense not the genre where we learn to read in books, but the one where we learn to read the logic of *books* themselves.

In her groundbreaking work on categorizing the ballad as a "distressed genre"—as that which has been made old—Susan Stewart has shown how the ballad's cultural work during the long eighteenth century was its capacity to "mean historically," to mean time.[59] But I want to add to Stewart's claim and argue that the ballad's other significance, at least to the romantic project at the end of Stewart's timeframe, was the way it dramatized the problem of textual transmission through books, the way it signified as a genre not just time itself but the dual problems of literary ownership and textual stability that were at the heart of an expanding early-nineteenth-century editorial culture. The ballad foregrounded a range of problems surrounding the commonality of literary property in an age of the printed book and the editor's role in producing, protecting, and pirating such poetic commons. How could poetry belong to an individual and still belong to a public at the same time? What was the role of the editor in navigating these questions of propriety, property, and dissemination? And finally, how did such editorial concerns intersect with authorial concerns through such notions as tradition, heritage, and innovation?

As a translator of German ballads, an editor of Scottish ones, and an author of historical novels that straddled both English and Scottish culture, Walter Scott was one of the great mediating figures of the nineteenth century. In returning to Scott's early editorial project, *Minstrelsy of the Scottish Border* (1802–3), I want to show how his editorial work was not a phase through which Scott passed on his way to becoming a full-fledged author but offered instead the conditions upon which such authorship would later be achieved. The *Minstrelsy's* importance to the later novels is most often understood as a kind of archival well, from which Scott would later draw to develop his novels' elaborate plots. The novel was in this sense understood as the prosification of poetic genres like the ballad and the *Volkslied*, participating in a larger nineteenth-century narrative of historical progress at the level of genre.[60] But I want to suggest that it was the problematic ownership of narrative property that surrounded editorial work and that Scott's *Minstrelsy* itself dramatized that became a key "source" for Scott's poetry and novels. As Maureen McLane has suggested, it was precisely the impossible presence of minstrelsy as a poetic practice that necessitated and in some sense authorized the figure of the editor.[61] Not only did the figure of minstrelsy and the genre of the ballad highlight with unusual clarity the contests of textual attribution during the romantic period, but Scott's figure of the "border" as the location of such poetic creations also drew attention to the difficulties of such literary specification.

Scholars of Scott's work have repeatedly drawn attention to the way it participated in a greater nineteenth-century obsession with borders, whether of time or space, from the making of national or imperial borders, to the borders of history, to those of language (most notably between Scots and English).[62] But while we have been vigorously debating Scott's role in shaping the nineteenth-century consciousness of nation, empire, or time, we have been ignoring Scott's place in a literary culture that was overwhelmingly concerned with *textual* borders, with the boundaries within and between books. We have overlooked not only the origins of Scott's own career, which began in the editor's laboratory, but also the larger concerns of a literary market that was increasingly beset by an editorial culture that was ransacking its textual past and debating how to do it. With so much material reappearing and so many hands involved, how was one to tell the difference between what belonged to whom, especially in an environment in which the very categories of belonging and authenticity were at the heart of such nationalist editorial projects? What were the visual and discursive protocols that were to determine the successful transmission and attribution of writing in the nineteenth century, whether to a person or a place?

It was precisely this problematic relationship of the specificity of poetic language to either person, place, or book that would be dramatized in the making of Scott's ballad edition and that would then reemerge in his novelistic productions, indeed would become the ground of his writerly fame. Rather than trace an intra-genre genealogy of the novel that passes through the complex intersections of romance, national tale, gothic and historical novel as others have already done,[63] I want to understand the way the novel, and Scott's novels in particular, emerged in the early nineteenth century within a bibliographic context that was programmatically attentive to the transcription, correction, and reproduction of historical narrative material. If for Goethe the novel took shape—both materially and rhetorically— through an engagement with the entirety of nineteenth-century bibliographic modes of communication, for Scott the novel—and the historical novel in particular—took shape in its negotiation with the bibliographic format of the edition and its investment in marginalizing the mediating practices of the editor. The novel thus represented less the prosification of poetic genres like the ballad as it did an engagement with the intense process of bookification that such genres underwent at the turn of the century.

The Borders of Books: *Minstrelsy of the Scottish Border*

Walter Scott's edition of Scottish ballads, *Minstrelsy of the Scottish Border* (1802–3), began to take shape as a book when he wrote to the printer John Ballantyne: "I have been for years collecting old Border ballads, and I think I could, with little trouble, put together such a selection from them as might make a neat little volume, to sell for four or five shillings."[64] Both Ballantyne and Scott were at the beginning of their careers, and the *Minstrelsy* was to serve as a showcase of Scott's editorial and Ballantyne's printing ability. Unlike the relative lack of splendor that surrounded the publication of Herder's *Volkslieder*, for example, Scott's ballads were printed in octavo with an elegant title page that combined a noticeably large amount of text (there are twenty-one lines of text versus seven for Lachmann's Wolfram edition or eight for Hagen's *Nibelungen Lied*) with a typographical uniformity that also utilized an array of alternating font sizes (fig. 3.3). The pages for the texts were then characterized by a vast amount of white space, a true sign of bookish luxury. As a physical object, the *Minstrelsy* was designed not only to appear as singular and unique as possible, it was also designed, through the

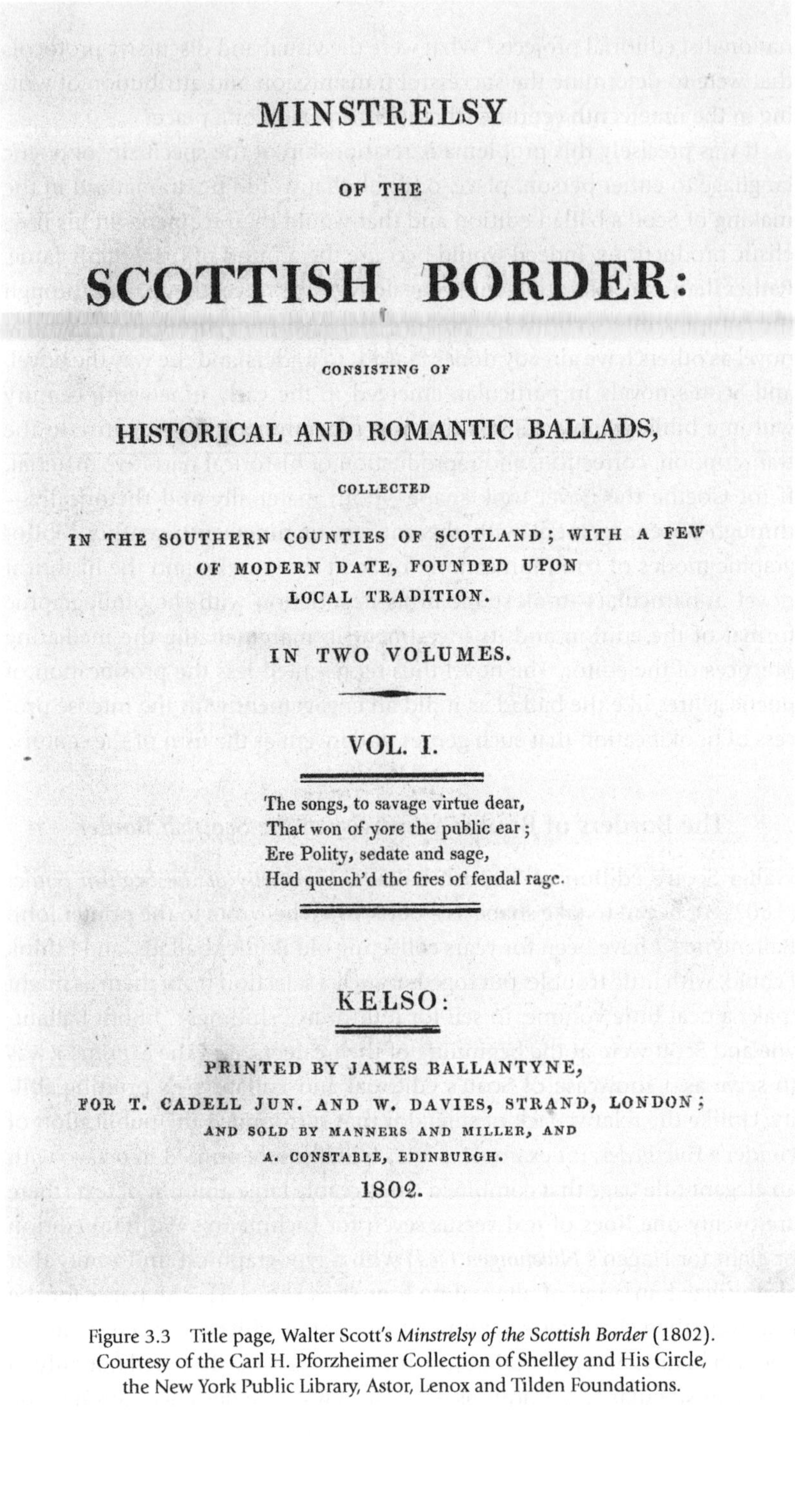

MINSTRELSY

OF THE

SCOTTISH BORDER:

CONSISTING OF

HISTORICAL AND ROMANTIC BALLADS,

COLLECTED

IN THE SOUTHERN COUNTIES OF SCOTLAND; WITH A FEW
OF MODERN DATE, FOUNDED UPON
LOCAL TRADITION.

IN TWO VOLUMES.

VOL. I.

The songs, to savage virtue dear,
That won of yore the public ear;
Ere Polity, sedate and sage,
Had quench'd the fires of feudal rage.

KELSO:

PRINTED BY JAMES BALLANTYNE,

FOR T. CADELL JUN. AND W. DAVIES, STRAND, LONDON;
AND SOLD BY MANNERS AND MILLER, AND
A. CONSTABLE, EDINBURGH.

1802.

Figure 3.3   Title page, Walter Scott's *Minstrelsy of the Scottish Border* (1802).
Courtesy of the Carl H. Pforzheimer Collection of Shelley and His Circle,
the New York Public Library, Astor, Lenox and Tilden Foundations.

effacement of editorial marks on the page, to embody Windgätter's notion of the emerging "channelization" of reading around 1800 and that we saw at work in Tieck's edition of *Minnelieder* or Hagen's edition of the *Nibelungenlied*. As Scott would later write in a review of John Todd's variorum edition of Spenser (1805), criticizing the early-modern inspired practice of cumulative commentary, "To conclude, we are well aware that the trade finds their advantage in publishing what are technically called Variorum editions of celebrated authors. It saves copy money, saves trouble, saves everything but the credit of the unfortunate poet. . . . It is impossible that the ordinary reader can form a just judgment of the text, which is absolutely borne down and overwhelmed by the dull, dubious, and contradictory commentaries of so many uncongenial spirits."[65] Unlike early-modern editions with their encircling layers of commentary, the romantic edition was supposed to free the reader's imaginative engagement with the text.

At the same time, such typographical exclusivity of Scott's edition (in both the elegance and the relative absence of type) included another level of omission: that of musical notation. In Joseph Ritson's *Scotish Songs* (1794), for example, the poetic texts were very often accompanied by musical notation, typographically representing the "oral" origins of the ballad genre. In a similar fashion, the frontispiece to numerous ballad collections deployed the figure of the wandering minstrel playing his lyre for a select audience. Such "reliques" were understood to belong to a pre-print, pre-bibliographic culture of literary circulation and thus shaped in important ways a larger romantic fascination with the media of song and voice. Scott's collection, on the other hand, excluded such calls to musicality. There was no musical notation, and the frontispiece illustration was of a castle ruin, emphasizing instead the material fragments that underlay this print artifact. The *Minstrelsy* visually foregrounded the editorial work of textual archaeology on which such collections were based instead of the primary orality from which they derived. It drew attention through its visual semantics to the collective practices of making artifacts instead of the singular practices of melodic performance.

This tension between singularity and collectivity in the physical make-up of the edition was also enacted through the title Scott chose for it. When Scott used the word "Minstrelsy" in his title he was explicitly drawing on Percy's theory of ballad production from the *Reliques*.[66] According to the Minstrel theory, ballads were not the work of some collective folk but the product of individual bards who performed for chiefs or lords. In this, Scott stood in stark contrast to German editors like Achim von Arnim who were busy formulating theories about popular collective authorship, as in Arnim's essay

"Von Volkslieder," where he invoked the poet as a "Gemeingeist, ein *spiritus familiaris*."[67] The Minstrel theory emphasized the fact of sovereignty—of both production and reception—over against any sharedness or collectivity that might surround such traditional songs.

At the same time, by referring to his collection as "of the Scottish Border," Scott was following Percy's lead in another way—in Percy's suggestion that the Border region was the cradle of Scottish balladry.[68] In grounding his ballad collection in a single local culture, Scott was participating in a larger trend of publishing folksongs and ballads whose monocultural or nationalist trajectory stood in stark contrast to the cosmo-provincialism of someone like Herder's collection.[69] Again, the emphasis was on singularity and not plurality. But while the "border" signified, on the one hand, a particular geographical and political region within Anglo-Scottish history, the border also signified, in a more general sense, no space at all.[70] The very site, the very particularity on which this edition was supposed to be based was in fact ungrounded. Its singularity was simultaneously constituted as liminality.

The genre of the ballad that formed the core of Scott's collection of minstrelsy exhibited at the level of genre the same tension found at the level of both book and title. As a deeply narrative poetic form, the ballad favored third-person narrators and the direct speech of characters over and above the lyrical "I" for which romantic poetry would become so famous. There were no heart-felt lamentations, no single guiding consciousnesses, no interiors here. As tales told in the third person according to a standard and mostly unwavering rhyme scheme, they were designed for collective ownership, to be passed around from person to person.

When we turn to the content of this form, a similar focus emerges. Taken together, the ballads dramatize a relatively homogenous body of material that concerns tales of battles, stealing, and revenge, tales of fairies and elves, tales of mothers who kill their children or knights who steal their brides or wives who cheat on their husbands. As Max Kommerell has pointed out about the ballad in general, what all of these themes have in common is the problem of legitimacy, as they enact the transgression of various ethical, corporeal, or property boundaries.[71] The border ballads were most often, and not unsurprisingly, about the problematic status of cultural, social, and personal borders. They were about the difficulties of establishing—and protecting—singularity and ownership.

Moving further into the text, we can see how this delicate balancing act between the proprietary and the commons is further enacted in the margins of Scott's edition. The *Minstrelsy* opened with a long, one-hundred and ten page introduction, and each ballad was accompanied by introductory notes as well as endnotes. Like the editor of the emerging critical edition, the editor here was overwhelmingly present at the bibliographic frames of Scott's edition. The individual introductions to the ballads described the numerous sources from which Scott had drawn, putting on display the collating as well as completing that he did as an editor. In a number of cases, Scott the editor tells his reader that he has produced a more "complete" version, participating in those twin pillars of editorial work, addition (new variant readings, new supplements, new editions, etc.) and completeness (the conjectures and montage used to fill in textual gaps and to finish fragments). Such attention to completeness would be the guiding spirit behind Scott's subsequent editorial project of producing an edition of Dryden's works. As Scott would write to George Ellis about this planned edition, "But in making an edition of a man of genius's works for libraries or collections . . . I must give my author as I find him, and will not tear out the page, even to get rid of the blot, little as a I like it."[72]

Scott's footnotes, on the other hand, departed from what would become the standard use of footnotes in the critical edition. Instead of explaining the variant readings that supported his ballads—they did not record the exclusions and corruptions that the editor of multiple sources invariably faced—Scott's footnotes were only used to translate or explicate foreign (most often Scottish) words. The paratextual elements of Scott's edition thus suggested a gradual, if incomplete, movement of the editor beyond the boundaries of his primary text and towards the margins. He was largely concerned with collating and comparing his primary sources, but he was also concerned with translating and completing his text according to aesthetic criteria. He was both at the margins and in the text at the same time, mirroring the editor of both the *Erneuung* and the critical edition at once. The *Minstrelsy* thus not only captured a certain spatial liminality of the Scottish border, it also represented a temporally liminal moment between competing notions of editorial practice. Like the middling heroes that would populate so many of his novels (Edward Waverley or Henry Morton), Scott was once again crucially in the middle.

In order to illustrate how this friction between the commons and the singular achieved an ultimately revelatory intensity within the works themselves, I want to concentrate on one ballad in particular, "The Sang of the Outlaw Murray," which Scott chose to open the first edition of his ballad collection (later replaced by "Sir Patrick Spens"). It tells the story of how John Murray became the Sheriff of Ettrick Forest in the sixteenth century, which we know was a remarkably autobiographical choice, as Scott had been appointed Deputy Sheriff just three years earlier. According to Scott's introduction, on the other hand, it was said to be at the head of the collection because "this Ballad appears to be among the most ancient offered to the Public in the present collection."[73] Instead of autobiography, then, the ballad apparatus offered another competing motivation, that of chronology, for the placement of "Murray" at the outset of the collection. By placing the oldest first, the ballad collection was lent a developmental logic, mirroring the larger social commitment to the notions of *Bildung* and betterment that the romantic age so persuasively produced. At the same time, when we look more closely at the content of this ballad, a third possible motivation emerges as to why it was chosen as the frame to the collection. As the tale of an "outlaw," "Murray" was essentially about the problem of property and legitimacy, about the difficult operations involved in moving from out-law to in-law. In this sense, it was a ballad about ballad collections and thus an ideal ballad to begin one.

It is when we turn to the poem itself, and specifically Scott's rendering of the poem, where we find a fourth, and by far the most significant, possible reason for this ballad's location at the head of the collection. Stanzas forty-nine to fifty-one do not appear in any other version of the ballad prior to Scott's version (Scott himself writes in a note that "this and the three following verses [49–51] are not in some copies" [23]), and can thus be read in some sense as proprietary material, as Scott's personal contribution to this collective text (whether Scott personally authored them is not my concern here, but is the subject of considerable debate). In these three stanzas, a character named Sir Walter Scott, Lord of Buccleuch, appears, who challenges Murray's acquisition of the Forest. The stanzas read:

> Then spak kene lair of Buckscleuth,
> A stalworthye man, and sterne was he—
> "For a King to gang an Outlaw till,
> Is beneath his state and his dignitie.

> "The man that wons yon Foreste intill,
> He lives by rief and felonie!
> Wherefore, brayd on, my Sovereign liege,
> Wi' fire and sword we'll follow thee;
> Or, gif your Courtrie Lords fa' back,
> Our Borderers sall the onset gie."

> Then out and spak the nobil King,
> And round him cast a wilie ee—

"Now haud thy tongue, Sir Walter Scott,
Nor speik of reif nor felonie:
For had everye honeste man his awin kye,
A right puir clan thy name wad be!" (16)

In the very lines that are unique to Scott's edition, we find that Scott's name appears ("Now haud thy tongue, Sir Walter Scott"). It is in fact one of several instances in Scott's edition where a character from the Scott family emerges, most often when the ownership of property is at stake.[74] On one level, we could say that Scott's construction of this ballad makes its autobiographical function even more explicit, serving as a means of suggesting his own genealogical rights to the property whose stewardship he has just been accorded. But on a more general level, the appearance of Scott's name in lines unique to Scott's edition—lines that appear at the transactional center of the opening ballad where the ownership of property is being negotiated—performs an authorial function. The name functions like a kind of signature here, marking this text, and this collection, in some sense as *Scott's* text and *Scott's* collection. The sovereignty of the fictional "sir" in "Sir Walter Scott" (it would be many years before Scott acquired his baronetcy) only underscored the supposed sovereignty of this edition. In the opening ballad to Scott's collection questions of personal and familial property are deeply intertwined with questions of literary property.

And yet when we look at the last four lines spoken by the king to Sir Walter Scott, this very possibility of sovereignty is precisely what the language of the ballad calls into question. At the moment that the editor's name appears in the text to make a claim of ownership, he is instructed to remain silent ("Now haud thy tongue"). However, the passage does not tell us that he has no right to claim ownership, but that the very category of ownership and ownness upon which such claims are based has been suspended. He cannot speak of "reif" (robbery) or "felonie" because he is operating in a state of the *absence* of legitimate ownership, of the possibility of possessing one's "awin kye" (own cattle). Scott is making an important point here about the inherent difficulties or contradictions of applying commercial notions of private ownership to a space of collective goods. In a world of cattle rustling—or ballad collecting—how was one to ground oneself in a notion of legitimate property? Better to hold one's tongue on that score. At the same time, the very line that suggests the commonality, not the singularity, of property is metrically distinct from the rest of the ballad with five feet instead of four. In the passage that stands out in Scott's edition, the line about one's own property literally stands out from the rest of the ballad. And yet the final word that participates in the stanza's rhyme, "kye," the word that denotes property, is a distinctly Scottish word, pointing to a common space whose singularity and cultural uniqueness is what the ballad collection is designed both to capture and produce.

This otherwise simple passage thus performs a series of complex, and importantly contradictory, operations. In invoking the name of Walter Scott in a passage unique to Scott's edition, the passage confers a kind of authoriality on the edition. It emphatically endorses the uniqueness of this particular edition. And yet in the sovereign's command for the editor to hold his tongue, it also anticipates the emerging early-nineteenth-century consensus of the marginalization of the editor. It enacts, in other words, Lachmann's principle of immaculate reception. The editor was precisely the figure who should not speak in a poem. At the same time, the sovereign's speech calls into question the very conditions of sovereignty, the possibilities of ownness and ownership ("For had everye honeste man his awin kye"). It highlights the internal contradictions of asserting principles of proprietariness within an *edition*. Where Lachmann had argued, following Wolf's work on Homer, that early Germanic literary works like the *Nibelungenlied* were the product of multiple hands,[75] Scott's edition was arguing this for the format of the edition itself. And nowhere was the conflict between the proprietary and the commons more pronounced in this passage than in the fifth line of the third stanza cited above, where we experience rhythmic singularity alongside semantic commonality.

It was precisely in the *addition* where we can see Scott offering his readers a crucial moment of self-reflection about the nature of the *edition*, about the contradictions and the tensions that surrounded textual ownership in the practice of editing in the early nineteenth century. It was in the transactional heart of the opening entry in a collection of ballads about the border where Scott teases out the contradictions surrounding the uncertain boundaries of literary property inherent in the "edition." Whether here or on the title page, the name of Walter Scott was enmeshed in the competing imperatives of the proprietary and the common *in a world of common property*. The passage enacted precisely the editor's dilemma between producing an *original* edition, something his own, and an *authentic* edition, something decidedly not his own. The editor was caught between making too many and too few changes to his material, thereby assuming either the position of author or of the reprinter, or worse, the plagiarist. The editor was always there, like the Walter Scott who discretely emerged in the body of the text, but he was also not there, like the Walter Scott instructed to hold his tongue. According to the logic of this passage, the editor's activity was supposed to efface its very presence. That logic mirrored the very terms of the debate that followed over German editorial theory and Scott's own later editorial practice in his editions of Dryden and Swift—"I will not castrate John Dryden," said Scott.[76] Like the figure of the bookseller that I discussed in chapter 2, the reader to be discussed in chapter 4, or the translator of chapter 5, the editor was one more ghost in the textual machine of the romantic book.

Narrating Editing: The Historical Novel and the *Tales of My Landlord*

When Scott invented the persona of Jedediah Cleishbotham as the fictive editor of the novels that would appear under the heading *Tales of My Landlord*, he was not only drawing attention to a professional continuity in his own life, he was also participating in a long and illustrious novelistic tradition. The editor lived a vibrant life throughout eighteenth-century fiction, from Swift's use of "Richard Sympson" in *Gulliver's Travels*, to Prevost's use of "M. de Renoncour" in *Cleveland* (1735), to the numerous editor-figures of the epistolary novel exemplified by Goethe's *Werther* (1774) or Laclos's *Les Liaisons dangereuses* (1782).[77] Such substitutions of the author by the editor dated back to Cervantes' claim that *Don Quixote* was merely the Spanish translation of a work written in Arabic by Cide Hamete Benengali. The editor's function was to affirm the ownership of the text by a particular individual (Gulliver, Werther, Cleveland) and to disaffirm the ownership by another individual, the author. The editor-function was an effective vehicle to combine the novel's dual claims to the suspension of referentiality (through its fictiveness) alongside its affirmation of referentiality through "realist" narrative techniques.

If Scott's drawing on this tradition through the persona of Cleishbotham highlighted an important generic continuity on the one hand, it also underscored an important personal and professional continuity as well. Cleishbotham was not only an echo of Scott's former self as an editor, he also embodied in many ways the concerns Scott continued to have as a *historical* novelist, where the intersection of fictionality and facticity common to all novels was most intensely compressed. As Scott's numerous prefaces to the *Magnum Opus* edition attested, the Waverley Novels all depended to one degree or another on the transcription, correction, and completion of found objects.

But what makes the prefaces and opening chapters (which served as prefaces) to the *Tales of My Landlord* series so important to the history of the novel is not the singular figure of Cleishbotham but the *accumulation* of narrative personae responsible for the tales that he oversees. Not only do we have Peter, or Patrick, Pattieson, who is the compiler of these tales, which Cleishbotham has merely selected and sent to a bookseller (who is himself a "counterfeiter of voices"), but we have the various narrators Pattieson cites, such as Old Mortality, Mr Dunover, Halkit, Hardie, Dick Tinto, and of course the Landlord himself, to whom these tales somehow belong, along with a host of nameless corroborating narrators such as the weavers, tailors, moorland farmers, traveling merchants, honorable families, bishops, gamekeepers, and a laird or two that Pattieson names in the opening chapter of *Old Mortality*, to which we could add the "real" sources that Scott later cites in the introductions to the *Magnum Opus* edition, such as Joseph Train, Helen Lawson, Mrs. Goldie, and the volume *Sketches from Nature* by John M'Diarmid. That is to say, Scott's novels, like the preface to his ballad collection, exhibit the very multiplicity of sources upon which the composition of the historical novel is based. They highlight the collecting and the collectivity that was at the heart of both projects, whether edition or novel. This explicit foregrounding of such a transmissional poetics drew attention to the mediating figure responsible for the interweaving of these textual parts. In highlighting the plurality and not the singularity of the novel's sources, Scott was highlighting the role and the practices of the mediator responsible for their collation.

Fiona Robertson has made the point that the Waverley Novels were intimately concerned with problems of historical and political legitimacy.[78] In highlighting the question of legitimacy in Scott, Robertson has drawn our attention to one of the central recurring themes that run throughout Scott's work. But in her analysis Robertson does not address the ways in which the Waverley Novels and the *Tales of My Landlord* series in particular were also thinking through questions of *textual* legitimacy. The prefaces to the *Tales* creatively frame the problem of textual ownership, the difficulty of attributing speech to a particular individual, which we already saw prefigured in the primal scene surrounding the name of "Sir Walter Scott" in the opening ballad of Scott's *Minstrelsy*. They highlight the way the "achievement of literary authority," as Ina Ferris titled her study of Scott,[79] was a product of one's relationship to a given textual tradition.

Indeed, this fundamental problem of attribution (which was of course a basic problem surrounding the Waverley Novels in general with their "anonymous" author) is articulated in the very framing title Scott used for the series within the series, *Tales of My Landlord*. Where the double possession expressed through the "of" and the "my" in the title asserts on the one hand an assurance of ownership, that these texts belong to someone, such titular cues of possessive assurance are also undermined in the prefaces, where it is made clear that they do not in fact belong to the landlord in any direct sense of the word. The landlord, the stated owner of property, merely functions as drinking partner and interlocutor of both Cleishbotham and Pattieson, just as it will also become impossible to determine with precise specificity to whom "my" in "my landlord" actually refers, whether Cleishbotham or Pattieson. The title, *Tales of My Landlord*, refers neither to the landlord's tales nor to a particular tenant (the referent of "my") but instead, as the title pages to the novels make clear, to a citation from *Don Quixote*. The title does not point to that which it contains (narratively or contractually) but to another book altogether.

Such contractual ambiguities of possession—of the *of* and the *my*—are then amplified not only in the first series in *Old Mortality*, which concerns the fate of a covenant, but again in the second series in *The Heart of Mid-Lothian*, where in the first chapter the singular narrator of Old Mortality, after whom the novel in the first series is named, is replaced by the triumvirate of Mr Dunover, Halkit, and Hardie. When the narrator shifts from an external to a character-bound narrator through the introduction of the narrative "I" in the opening of *Mid-Lothian*'s second chapter, the reader is faced with the dilemma of whom this "I" refers to, where possibilities range from the three overturned narrators named in chapter 1 to the two compilers, Pattieson and Cleishbotham, named in the preface. A similar trajectory away from the singularity of direct speech towards increasing degrees of indirection could be typographically observed in the first series' use of quotation marks to surround the entire first chapter—to affirm that the chapter's contents belonged to the single character Peter Pattieson—which are then absent from the opening chapter of *The Heart of Mid-Lothian* in the second series. When poststructuralists like Deleuze and Guattari write that "language in its entirety is indirect discourse,"[80] we can see how such seemingly universal sentiments about the nature of language and narration were being prepared in the historical cauldron of the romantic historical novel.

The empty "I" that stands over, or at the heart of, *The Heart of Mid-Lothian* not only captured a fundamental feature of Scott's authorial project that dated back to his injunction to Walter Scott the editor to hold his tongue in the *Minstrelsy* and continued through his enduring anonymity in the Waverley Novels. It also, I want to suggest, captured a fundamental feature of the narrative organization of this signal romantic novel in particular, where the plural significations articulated through the empty "I" are graphed onto the figure of the "heart" that is at the heart, so to speak, of both this novel and of a nineteenth-century notion of subjectivity that was increasingly being produced through the reading of novels.

In the reconceptualizations of the human body that took place around 1800, the identity of the heart was, not surprisingly, integral to such corporeal reconfigurations and the communicative poetics they subtended.[81] The question that surrounded the human heart was whether it was to be understood as the center or core of the human body or as a circulatory relay. In the opening chapter of Scott's novel in which the figure of the heart is put through a rapid series of puns, we learn that the "Heart of Mid-Lothian" refers to an architectural structure that is both a prison and a tollbooth, a container *and* a relay. We can see how the novel enacts precisely this medico-cultural tension between the heart as a signifier of a closed container and the heart as a signifier of a network node. This figural dichotomy between the heart as center and relay (amplified in the dual meaning of "mid" as *in the center* and *in between*) was then threaded through the novel through the use of two competing figures of speech (about speech) that depended on the figure of the heart: to say something "by heart" (to incorporate, store, and repeat it) and to speak "from the heart" (to reveal or confess something). In the latter case, the heart is the origin of an original mode of speaking, and in the former, the heart stands for a practice of transmitting something not one's own. In each case the heart is a guarantor of reliability and authenticity, but the reference of this reliability shifts from something outside to inside the self.

The figure of the heart was thus connected to a variety of communicative practices that would emerge as central points of tension during the early nineteenth century and that would include the categories of confession, sympathy, and sentimentality, as well as those of memory, memorialization, collection, and commonality. As Andrea Henderson has highlighted in her reading of the novel, Scott's *Heart* was intensely concerned with the tensions between legitimate and illegitimate circulation,[82] participating in what Deidre Lynch has identified as a longer novelistic tradition defined by an attention to both the commercial and social circulations that inhered in an emergent market economy.[83] Just as in Scott's historical narrative poem *Marmion*,[84] for example, one could break down the characters of the *Heart of Mid-Lothian* into two groups, those that embodied illegitimate movements (Madge, Staunton, Effie) and those that remained "steadfast" (Jeanie, Butler, Jeanie's father), where the former seemed to disappear and the latter always to return home, completing the circuit that they began like Scott's first hero Edward Waverley. As Jane Millgate has argued, "Journeys in [Scott's] fiction rarely follow the unidirectional pattern of the simple picaresque. Coming home to the father or the place of the fathers is an essential element in his characteristic design. . . . London cannot provide a conclusion."[85] This sense of circularity and closure that informed so many of Scott's novels, and *The Heart of Mid-Lothian* in particular, has no doubt been one of the reasons why much recent scholarship on *The Heart of Mid-Lothian* has focused on its participation in constructing British nationalism.[86] The closed routes of the characters' travels in the novel are meant to reenact the closing of the nation's (or empire's) borders.

What I want to focus on instead is not the way such circulatory logic reinforced emerging national or imperial mentalities or, as Henderson and Lynch have suggested, facilitated romantic subjects' adaptation to the commercial circulations of an ever-expanding market economy. Rather, I want to focus on the way these questions of circulation and circularity, transmission and reliability, were deployed by Scott to address the increasingly urgent problem of textual circulation and ownership, of how to attribute language to a person (or a nation) as so much material passed out of a literary commons and into the hands of editors and authors. And here the punning passage on the heart in the novel's first chapter is again instructive. When Hardie asks, "Why should not the Tolbooth have its 'Last Speech, Confession, and Dying Words'?"[87] the question that this question poses is, What are the rhetorical and technological conditions that are capable of generating the speech act of "confession" itself, of aligning the heart—and by association the novel that was called a heart—away from speaking *by heart* and towards speaking *from the heart*? In place of the numerous narrators that the novel deploys at its opening, how can the heart speak *itself*?

"By Heart" v. "From the Heart" in *The Heart of Mid-Lothian*

In order to try to answer these questions I would like to concentrate on two key scenes that concern the performance of a confession—that concern, in other words, the very production of singularity that would provide the conditions of both *The Heart of Mid-Lothian's* success and of course Scott's own career. The novel tells the story of Jeanie Deans whose sister, Effie, has been accused of murdering the child she had out of wedlock and who sits in the "Heart of Mid-Lothian" awaiting her fate. Jeanie can free her sister on a legal technicality if she perjures herself in court, but she ultimately does not. Instead, after her sister is sentenced, she undertakes a voyage on foot to London to gain a pardon for her sister from the queen, where the eventual overturning of the judicial decision mirrors the overturning of the coach at the novel's opening that led to its being written down in the first place. The overturned case, in both cases, leads to a new narrative reordering of existing documents. Upon being freed, Jeanie's sister will once again disappear, as the novel continues to rehearse two different forms of being "wayward."

In chapter 2, volume 2, Jeanie responds to a written communiqué that requests her to meet her sister's seducer, George Staunton, late one night at Muschat's Cairn in St. Leonard's Chase. We are told in the novel that this enclosed space is also crucially a storied space, much like Washington Irving's Sleepy Hollow (on a discussion of both hollows appears in the next chapter), and while there are numerous legends that belong to this space, the Cairn in particular is named after Nicol Muschat, who brutally murdered his wife. "With all of these legends Jeanie Deans was too well acquainted, to escape that strong impression which they usually make on the imagination" (*HM*, 135). Like Hoffmann's living room, it is the natural setting in Scott that is denoted by the presence and power of such oft-repeated tales. Landscape is marked as a narrative archive. And like Hoffmann's magnetist who both occupies and activates the storied space of the living room, the conversation between Jeanie and her interlocutor will revolve around the status and the utility of what one has been told. The performance of the conversation corresponds, in Kenneth Burke's terminology, to the scene in which it is acted out:

"But you said there was a remedy," again gasped out the terrified young woman.

"There is," answered the stranger, "and it is in your own hands. The blow which the law aims cannot be broken by directly encountering it, but it may be turned aside. You saw your sister during the period preceding the birth of her child—what is so natural as that she should have mentioned her condition to you? The doing so would, as their cant goes, take the case from under the statute, for it removes the quality of concealment. I know their jargon, and have had sad cause to know it; and the quality of concealment is essential to this statutory offence. Nothing is so natural as that Effie should have mentioned her condition to you—think—reflect—I am positive that she did."

"Woes me!" said Jeanie, "she never spoke to me on the subject, but grat sorely when I spoke to her about her altered looks, and the change on her spirits."

"You asked her questions on the subject?" said he eagerly. "You *must* remember her answer was, a confession that she had been ruined by a villain—yes, lay a strong emphasis on that—a cruel, false villain called—the name is unnecessary; and that she bore under her bosom the consequences of his guilt and her folly; and that he had assured her he would provide safely for her approaching illness.—Well he kept his word!" These last words he spoke as it were to himself, and with a violent gesture of self-accusation, and then calmly proceeded, "You will remember all this?—That is all that is necessary to be said."

"But I cannot remember," answered Jeanie, with simplicity, "that which Effie never told me."

"Are you so dull—so very dull of apprehension!" he exclaimed, suddenly grasping her arm, and holding it firm in his hand. "I tell you," (speaking between his teeth, and under his breath, but with great energy,) "you *must* remember that she told you all this, whether she ever said a syllable of it or no. You must repeat this tale, in which there is no falsehood, except in so far as it was not told to you, before these Justices—Justiciary—whatever they call their blood-thirsty court, and save your sister from being murdered, and them from becoming murderers. Do not hesitate—I pledge life and salvation, that in saying what I have said, you will only speak the simple truth." (*HM*, 140–41)

In distinction to the very tales that make a "strong impression" on Jeanie in this cavernous landscape, George Staunton's tale does not make a lasting impression on Jeanie because she has not heard it before ("But I cannot remember that which Effie never told me"). In invoking frames of reference such as "it is in your own hands" or "nothing is so natural," Staunton attempts to reverse the very unnaturalness of facts such as Effie's own act of child-murder at the heart of this dialogue, Muschat's act of murdering his wife that was memorialized where the dialogue occurs, or the prospect of a future dialogue where she will say what she has not been told. Alongside this invocation of ownness at the heart of the confession, Staunton will nevertheless reveal the indirection at the heart of his method ("the blow which the law aims cannot be broken by directly encountering it")—not just indirectly freeing Effie by a legal loophole, but also the use of indirection itself to achieve this end, that is, the control of Jeanie's speech through his own. Staunton's project is not simply to control Jeanie's confession but to control confession itself. "In saying what I have said, you will only speak the simple truth." And yet unlike the oft-repeated tales that make a "strong impression" on Jeannie—that bear some truth value—Staunton's tale is a *novel* statement and therefore must remain untrue.

Staunton's project of trying to control Jeannie's confession, staged of course in the middle of the night in a space of illicit backdrop, is threatening not because of its illegality—the perjury at its heart—but because of its communicative rationale, that it would redefine *confession* as the speech of *someone else*. The following chapter opens with an epigraph from *Hamlet* concerning the character of Ophelia: "She speaks things in doubt, / That carry but half sense: her speech is nothing, / Yet the unshaped use of it doth move / The hearers to collection; they aim at it, / And botch the words up fit to their own thoughts" (*HM*, 143). While the epigraph points towards a chapter where we will learn of the Ophelia-like madness of Madge Wildfire—the fool turned foolish because of the trauma of losing her child as a young woman (murdered by her mother to save her honor)—the citation also points backward to the previous chapter as well. It highlights the risks of Staunton's project, of reducing Jeanie's speech, and her speaking from the heart, to "nothing," to something, in other words, that does not correspond to the heart of the speaker as a source and thus allows others to "botch the words up fit to their own thoughts." Like the natural precipice at the conclusion of the novel that almost claims Effie's life (vol. 4, chap. 12), it is precisely this communicative precipice of speaking "nothing," of speech that cannot be attributed to a stable source, that must be negotiated in the novel.

If we turn to the famous confrontation between Jeanie and the queen in chapters 10 through 12 of volume 3, we see a similar moment of an attempt to control Jeanie's confession, only this time the operation is far more successful (it results in the desired pardon for her sister). In place of Staunton as the directorial figure, it is now the Duke of Argyle who will orchestrate Jeanie's confession, and in place of the Scottish court of law as the site of this confession, it is now the court of the English king to which Jeanie will petition her sister's case. We must remember that the very conditions upon which Jeanie acquires the duke's assistance as a mediating figure in the first place depended on her own capacity to properly utilize mediation. It was only when she presented the document entrusted to her by her fiancé Butler, which explained the Argyle family's indebtedness to Butler's family, that the effect of her presentation to the duke achieved its desired goal. In repayment for being entrusted with this document, Jeanie will perform another act of mediation in return by writing in Butler's Bible (*HM*, 247).

In response to this media performance, the duke agrees to arrange an audience with the queen, who refers to herself as a "medium": "Your Grace is aware, that I can only be the medium through which the matter is subjected to his Majesty's superior wisdom" (*HM*, 334). The mediality of the queen is the further continuation of *all* of the characters' mediality in this scene, as both Jeanie and the duke function, each in their own way, as media (to which one could add the queen's attendant, Lady Suffolk, who was then sleeping with the king but was also the former lover of Argyle). "Now I have done for you," says the duke to Jeanie, "what I would certainly not have done to serve any purpose of my own—I have asked an audience of a lady whose interest with the king is deservedly very high. It has been allowed me, and I am desirous that you should see her and speak for yourself. You have no occasion to be abashed; tell your story simply as you did to me" (*HM*, 328). Yet the duke will continue: "Just say what you think is likely to make the best impression—look at me from time to time—if I put my hand to my cravat so—(shewing her the motion)—you will stop; but I shall only do this when you say anything that is not likely to please." To which Jeanie replies, "But, sir, your Grace, if it wasna ower muckle trouble, wad it na be better to tell me what I should say, and I could get it by heart?" "No Jeanie," the duke concludes, "that would not have the same effect."

Who is the medium here? The duke arranges the connection ("I have asked an audience of a lady") but also orchestrates the performance ("look at me from time to time"). Jeannie is merely the vehicle for her sister's case, but she is supposed to speak *from* the heart, not *by* heart ("tell your story as simply as you did to me"). The success of the performance depends, as it will for the queen who will communicate it further to the king and as it did for Jeanie's handling of someone else's document to gain the queen's audience in the first place, on the delicate balance between mediation and originality, saying someone else's story *as though it were your own*. It depends, in other words, on the delicate balance of the "by heart" and the "from the heart." In place of George Staunton's "In saying what I have said, you will only speak the simple truth," we have the duke's assurance to Jeanie's question, "wad it na be better to tell me what I should say, and I could get it by heart?": "No Jeanie, that would not have the same effect." In moving from Staunton to the duke, from the Cairn to the Court, we are always moving in the direction of increasing direction, but such direction is always still fundamentally coupled in *The Heart of Mid-Lothian* with the art of indirection.[88] Only in this way, to return to the Shakespearean epigraph above, will one's listeners be moved to "collection": in both the sense of giving alms for such a narrative performance and in terms of becoming a collective. It is this particular type of media performance that will result in both financial reward for the author and the generation of a reading public.

In exchange for her performance of mediation as origination, Jeanie will be rewarded with "a little pocket-book" (*HM*, 343). James Chandler has identified this scene as a paramount example of the romantic investment in the "case" as the essential genre of historiographical discourse, to which Scott's historical novels become some of the most important narrative contributions (to which we could add the centrality of the "casket" in Goethe's *Travels*).[89] But rather than see the case here as a representation of a more universal notion of the case, I want to unpack this object in Scott in a more literal and material sense, to look inside, as it were, what is actually there on the page. As we saw in chapter 1 and as I will show in the next chapter, the "little pocket-book" was an extremely important bibliographic format for organizing literary material in the romantic period and one of the chief identities that gets associated with it is as a space of sharing and exchange. *When Jeanie writes in Butler's Bible*, and is highlighting the way writing in books at the turn of the nineteenth century continued to play a crucial role in establishing a network of reciprocal obligations through books, nowhere more prevalent than in "little pocket-books." When the queen gives Jeanie this book in which we later learn she has inscribed her own name, "Caroline," she is not only participating in a popular nineteenth-century bibliographic practice, she is also drawing attention to the complex mixture of sharing and owning that surrounded such medial practices of inscription.

When we turn to the inside of the book as case, we see how the contents correspond to the container in which they appear. Inside the pocket-book we find, along with the queen's inscription, the "usual assortment of silk and needles" and "a bank-bill for fifty pounds." To put it more abstractly but no less suggestively, what we find inside the book is handwriting (the inscription), printed writing (the bill), and the tools for producing texts/textiles (the silk and needles). We could organize these symbolic items even more concretely by saying that what this book does that is given in exchange for Jeanie's oral performance is replace the oral performance itself with a written one that is based on the practices of collection (the silk and needles that are used to piece together the textile), circulation (the bank-bill), and *shared* ownership (the inscription).

In the introduction that Scott writes in 1830 to *Old Mortality*, he recounts a tale told by his friend Mr. Walker about how in exchange for being delivered out of Locher Moss, in which he was lost, he recited a headstone's epitaph that concerned his guide's family that he knew "by heart" and that he then proceeded to write down for his guide. This anecdote that was added to the introduction to the opening series of the *Tales* models, in other words, the very same operation that we see occurring in *The Heart of Mid-Lothian*, as we move from a culture of memorization and recitation to one of writing and exchange. But the crucial difference between these two episodes is that the exchange of the "little pocket-book" for Jeanie's oral performance does not so much mark a transition from a state of orality to that of writing as it models a mode of text-making and text-transmitting that *combined* the principles behind these two regimes and that were associated with the figure of the heart. Jeanie's audience with the queen highlights the profound ways in which speaking *from the heart* was not opposed to, but necessarily incorporated with, speaking *by heart*. Scott's novel dramatized, in other words, the necessary overlap between the practices of preservation, transmission, and attribution that were underwriting the novel's rise to prominence in the nineteenth century.

Producing Singularity

Scott's concern with the reliability of confessional speech—with the alignment of speech with the individual heart—would continue through the conclusion of the *Tales of My Landlord* in *The Bride of Lammermoor* (1819) that appeared along with *A Legend of Montrose* in the third series of the *Tales*. Like the ballad "The Sang of the Outlaw Murray," or Scott's narrative poem *Marmion*, *The Bride of Lammermoor* concerned a case of the dispossession of inherited property, and, like *The Heart of Mid-Lothian*, it was also simultaneously concerned with the control of a young woman's speech (Lucy Ashton) and the reliability of the signed document (her engagement letter to Ravenswood versus her marriage certificate to Bucklaw). When Ravenswood intones upon returning in a fit of rage, "Is *that*, madam, your hand?,"[90] we are meant to see the proliferation of signatures as a challenge to authenticity and certainty surrounding written documents. Lucy then throws into the fire the letter of engagement along with the gold locket she had "concealed in her bosom" (252). Through the gesture of the discarded text and locket (or case), writing in *Lammermoor* is divested of both its "gold standard" and from its quality of being from the heart. It is replaced by writing as a site of competing interests and voiceovers. At the conclusion of the scene of Ravenswood's claim to Lucy's love, Lucy's mother remarks: "Master of Ravenswood, you have asked what questions you thought fit. You see the total incapacity of my daughter to answer you. But I will reply for her, and in a manner which you cannot dispute" (252). Unlike Jeanie Deans, who speaks for herself through others (the duke and the queen) and for others through herself (Butler and Effie), Lucy's voice and the possibility of her confession is completely occluded by the speech of Lady Ashton. In either case, whether as tragedy or comedy, speaking from the heart—the mode of confessional speech that was the cornerstone of an eighteenth-century poetics of sentimentality—is reconfigured in Scott's romantic *Tales* as incorporating increasing degrees of mediation. Personal speech is aligned with the increasing bookishness of subjectivity.

Many readers have argued for the importance of Scott's *Minstrelsy* for his later fictional works, a point already noted by Lockhart in his introduction to the posthumous edition of Scott's works, where he writes: "In the text and notes of [the *Minstrelsy*], we can now trace the primary incident, or broad outline of almost every romance, whether in verse or prose, which Sir Walter Scott built in after life on the history or traditions of his country."[91] Yet the *Minstrelsy*'s influence for Scott's later work was not simply a matter of its content, that it provided a rich amount of material that Scott then later rewrote in prose. Rather, it also lay in the way it enacted the problem of rewriting itself that would remain at the heart of Scott's fiction—and its configuration of the "heart" as a shared, not singular, space. The *Minstrelsy* enacted the persistent irresolutions surrounding the borders of literary property, and it highlighted the negotiations between mediation and originality in writing. The opening addition to Scott's edition ("Now haud thy tongue Sir Walter Scott") prefigured numerous scenes of the contested ownership of documents and speech that suffused Scott's poetry and fiction, and, I would argue, were the grounds on which his success depended. The signature, the heart, the confession—these were all techniques of articulating singularity in *The Heart of Mid-Lothian*, of motivating its own as well as its author's singularity in the literary market. And yet they were also simultaneously constructed around a series of mediating, and thus plural, figures such as the duke, the queen, and Jeanie herself. Creation and originality, speaking *from the heart*, were always inseparably intertwined with mediation and rewriting, speaking *by heart*. Like the critical edition and its increasingly pronounced capacity to construct the originality of its authors, Scott's fictions too increasingly motivated the principle of the proprietary as the heart of writing by pointing to the art of mediation as the necessary precondition—the heart—of origination. In preparation for the publication of his final, authorized collected edition, Scott would produce a voluminous editorial apparatus to accompany his works. Like the sovereign who undid a concept of sovereignty in the *Minstrelsy*, the inscriber of headstones who never received a headstone in *Old Mortality*, or, finally, the persistent interweaving of the *by heart* and the *from the heart* in *The Heart of Mid-Lothian*, this final act of auto-editorialism was at once the grandest of all gestures of producing one's own singularity as well as the perfect confession of where this incredibly singular, original, and influential literary project began: in the act of editing.

CHAPTER FOUR

Sharing

"What hands are here?"

—Shakespeare, *Macbeth*

Assorted Books: The Romantic Miscellany
(Almanacs, Taschenbücher, Gift-Books)

"Sharing is more difficult than you think."[1] This was the advice offered to the Major by his friend in Goethe's novella "The Man of Fifty," and it concerned the difficulties of transmitting the *Verjüngungskunst*, the art of rejuvenation, that the Major required to retain his vitality for his niece who, in a typical Goethean fantasy, had fallen in love with him. "The Man of Fifty" had initially appeared in part in 1817 in Cotta's *Ladies' Pocket-Book*,[2] and it was a story that was in fact largely concerned with the problem of the part—with the parting, imparting, and parting with things. It would later be included in Goethe's last novel, *Wilhelm Meister's Travels* (1808–29), where it would achieve its fame as one of his most important prose works. And yet its initial placement within Cotta's miscellany disclosed an important fact about the culture of nineteenth-century miscellanies: that the question of the part, imparting, and parting with—in a word, *sharing*—was integral to the miscellany's success as a literary format in the nineteenth century.

In the first half of the nineteenth century whether in France, England, the German states, or the United States, a vast amount of writing was circulated through eclectic collections of poetry, short fiction, essays, and anecdotes. Like the format of the collected edition, the nineteenth-century miscellany served a crucial ordering function in an age of too much writing. But unlike the collected edition, the miscellany was not organized around the unifying figure of the author but instead, as Barbara Benedict has suggested, around the figure of the reader.[3] Where the collected edition aimed to canonize its author and in the process create a literary canon, the miscellany was far more a document of the carnevalesque impulse to undo such rules, standards, or means. With the absence of any obvious organizing principle and the simultaneous presence of high, low, and outright weird texts, the romantic miscellany authorized the reader to create the linkages between such cultural strata. Like the stitching that bound together the loose leaves of the book, it was the reader who provided the intellectual threads that connected the book's diverse parts. As Leah Price has argued, anthologies and miscellanies "determine not simply who gets published or what gets read but who reads, and how."[4] In their capacity to slice, select, condense, combine, and reproduce, miscellanies' prominence during the romantic period reflected, as Ina Ferris has shown in the case of Isaac D'Israeli's *Curiosities of Literature*, the continued importance of the elsewhere and the afterward, transmission and excision, to romantic literary culture.[5]

In addition to the work of Benedict, Price, and Ferris, recent work by Kathryn Ledbetter, Meredith McGill, and Seth Lerer in English, York-Gotthart Mix, Hans-Jürgen Lüsebrinck, and Siegfried Wenzel in German, Armando Petrucci in Italian, and Ségolène Le Men in French have put the miscellany back onto the literary map.[6] In doing so, they have drawn our attention to the important role that the miscellany has played within the history of literature and the history of the book, either as a printed book in the early modern period or as a manuscript book from antiquity to the middle ages. Indeed, there is something almost intrinsic to the identity of the book and the disorder of the miscellany, the way the miscellany embodies the etymological origins of reading as an act of gathering—as both a collecting together and an intermittent plucking. But while the miscellany may be, on the one hand, a timeless bibliographic format, a unique type of miscellany does emerge during the romantic period, one that has traditionally been classified according to different names depending on which language one works in. We speak of *almanacs* in French, *Taschenbücher* in German, and *gift-books* or *literary annuals* in English, a diversity of nomenclature that I suspect has had much to do with why the study of these books has been so nationally focused. While there were of course important differences between these regional articulations of the miscellany, I want to suggest that there was a fundamental continuity in the cultural work that such miscellaneous books performed during the romantic period.

In drawing upon the much older book format of the "almanac" or "calendar" that appeared in yearly installments, nineteenth-century literary miscellanies were drawing upon one of the oldest available bibliographic genres and thus engaging in that familiar romantic quest for origins. As Leigh Hunt said in his introduction to the English miscellany *The Keepsake* (1828), "The history of Pocket-books and their forerunners, Almanacks, Calendars, Ephemerides, &c. is ancient beyond all precedent: even the Welshman's genealogy, the middle of which contained the creation of the world, is nothing to it."[7] But in mapping such serially appearing collections onto the seasonal rhythms of nature—most visibly in the calendrical tables that so often appeared in these books' frontmatter, as in this example of the *Almanach des dames* from 1811 (fig. 4.1)—the romantic miscellany was not only participating in the naturalization of literature and the book so familiar to romantic readers. It also played an important role in marking the transition from the cyclicality to the seriality of cultural production that would become a hallmark of both nineteenth-century literature and twentieth-century mass media more generally.[8] At the same time, in the small size captured in the notion of the *Taschenbuch*—the book that could fit in one's pocket—the miscellanies articulated the increasing reproducibility and affordability of printed books that brought with them a growing sense of a loss of control. The miscellaneous pocket-book's identity as an early form of popular culture would later be captured not only in the German and French words for modern "paperbacks" (*Taschenbuch*, *livre de poche*) but also in the choice of *Pocket Books* as the title for the first American paperback imprint in the twentieth century.[9] As one could see in a popular image of the "Scholarly Traveler" from 1820 who was surreptitiously placing a small book in his pocket (and being caught by a dutiful dog),[10] the "pocket-book" was increasingly associated at the turn of the nineteenth century with problems of regulation, authority, and control.

If the notion of the "Taschenbuch" captured the growing availability of the book and related problems of hierarchy and control, it was the appellation of "gift book" that captured the particular way that the circulation of these books was being inscribed within an affective economy of gift exchange. While books had always functioned as gift objects, the miscellaneous "gift book" was emerging at precisely the moment when books were overwhelmingly being defined by their status as commodities.[11] In replacing a system of anonymous circulation with a more intimate system of exchange between friends and family, the gift book was a means of compensating for, but also propelling, the new commercial proliferation of books. With titles like *Penelope*, *Almanach dédiés aux dames*, or *Frauentaschenbuch*, miscellanies' orientation towards female readers was not just a means of capitalizing on a rapidly expanding reading audience but was also a means of locating the

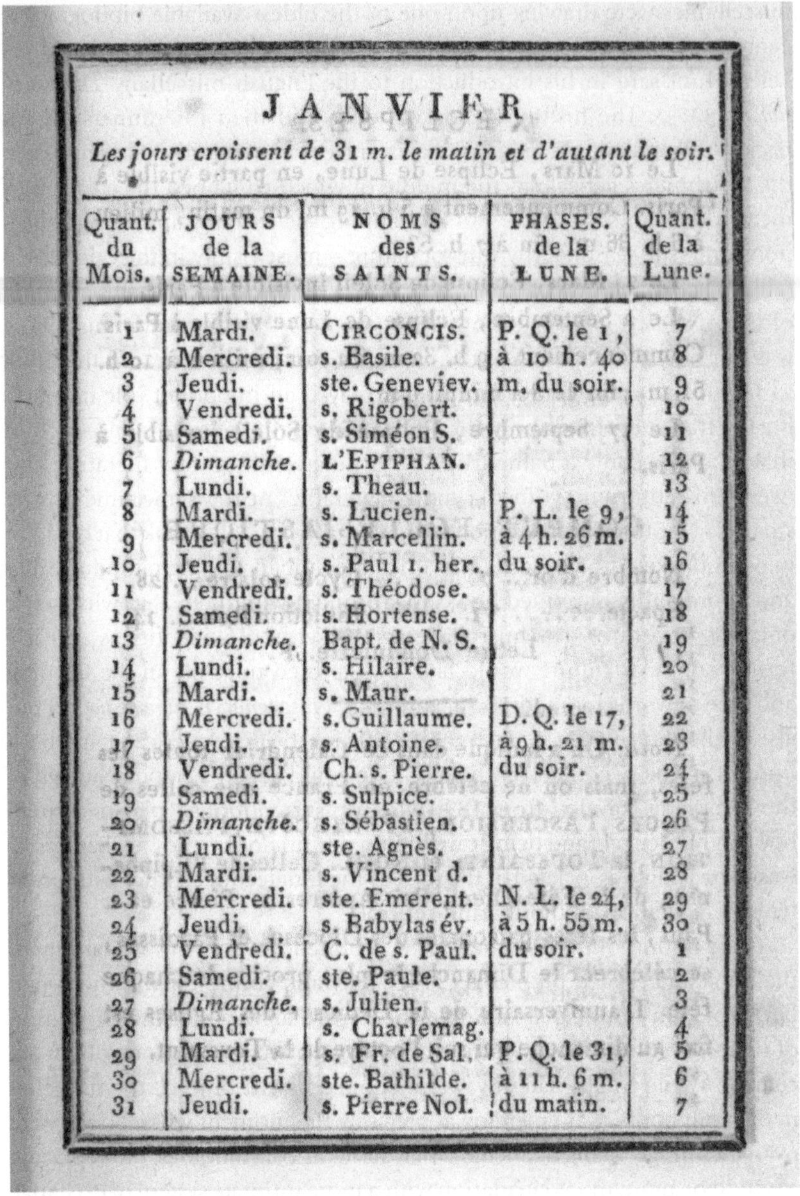

JANVIER

Les jours croissent de 31 m. le matin et d'autant le soir.

Quant. du Mois.	JOURS de la SEMAINE.	NOMS des SAINTS.	PHASES. de la LUNE.	Quant. de la Lune.
1	Mardi.	CIRCONCIS.	P. Q. le 1,	7
2	Mercredi.	s. Basile.	à 10 h. 40	8
3	Jeudi.	ste. Geneviev.	m. du soir.	9
4	Vendredi.	s. Rigobert.		10
5	Samedi.	s. Siméon S.		11
6	*Dimanche.*	L'EPIPHAN.		12
7	Lundi.	s. Theau.		13
8	Mardi.	s. Lucien.	P. L. le 9,	14
9	Mercredi.	s. Marcellin.	à 4 h. 26 m.	15
10	Jeudi.	s. Paul 1. her.	du soir.	16
11	Vendredi.	s. Théodose.		17
12	Samedi.	s. Hortense.		18
13	*Dimanche.*	Bapt. de N. S.		19
14	Lundi.	s. Hilaire.		20
15	Mardi.	s. Maur.		21
16	Mercredi.	s.Guillaume.	D. Q. le 17,	22
17	Jeudi.	s. Antoine.	à 9 h. 21 m.	23
18	Vendredi.	Ch. s. Pierre.	du soir.	24
19	Samedi.	s. Sulpice.		25
20	*Dimanche.*	s. Sébastien.		26
21	Lundi.	ste. Agnès.		27
22	Mardi.	s. Vincent d.		28
23	Mercredi.	ste. Emerent.	N. L. le 24,	29
24	Jeudi.	s. Babylas év.	à 5 h. 55 m.	30
25	Vendredi.	C. de s. Paul.	du soir.	1
26	Samedi.	ste. Paule.		2
27	*Dimanche.*	s. Julien.		3
28	Lundi.	s. Charlemag.		4
29	Mardi.	s. Fr. de Sal.	P. Q. le 31,	5
30	Mercredi.	ste. Bathilde.	à 11 h. 6 m.	6
31	Jeudi.	s. Pierre Nol.	du matin.	7

Figure 4.1   Calendar page, *Almanachs des dames* (1811). Courtesy of the
Rare Book and Manuscript Library, Columbia University.

book within household economies of sentimental affection, a key means, in other words, of domesticating the book.[12] Perhaps more than any of the other formats discussed in this book, the romantic miscellany had a decidedly interpersonal function. Despite these various functions, what all of these books had in common of course was the *mixed* nature of writing that appeared within them. They reflected, and indeed celebrated, at the level of the book the growing heterogeneity of writing within the larger literary market. In doing so, miscellanies represented a powerful challenge to assumptions about the book's capacity to promote a notion of sequential or fluid reading. As the editors argued in the miscellany *Curiositäten-Almanach* of 1825, which was dedicated to "friends of encyclopedic entertainments," such collections were expressly for people who read "fragmentarisch."

Common Right v. Copyright

It is precisely the mixedness at the core of writing in the miscellanies that I want to explore in this chapter, a mixedness understood not just as the diversity of form but as the diversity of ownership. By returning to the bibliographic scene of Goethe's reflections on sharing—by reading the linguistic and material codes of this particular genre of books—I want to suggest that the book format of the romantic miscellany functioned as a particularly acute space in which the mutual relationship of sharing and owning (a common right and copyright to writing) could be rehearsed during the first half of the nineteenth century. How *was* one to share writing with someone else, to have it in common without losing it completely? With so much written material moving about with ever greater ease, how was one to reliably negotiate the complex contours between the mine, the yours, and the ours? Sharing was integral to writing's diffusion in the nineteenth century, making it increasingly available at the same time that writing's availability made sharing that much easier. But the more writing was shared and shareable, the more difficult it became to claim something as one's own. The more one shared, the less one paradoxically had to give away. As Goethe suggested, sharing *was* more difficult than one thought.

Following on the work of Martha Woodmansee, there have been numerous compelling studies in the course of the last two decades on the origins and evolution of the notion of copyright, the long and contentious process of establishing the conditions for the proprietary ownership of ideas that emerged out of the eighteenth and early nineteenth centuries.[13] What we know less about are the numerous ways that this period emphasized the sharing, and not the owning, of information. As Natalie Zemon Davis has argued in an essay that remains a key contribution to the history of intellectual property, "We have concentrated on the book as a commodity rather than on the book as a bearer of benefits and duties, on copyright rather than common right."[14] In our emphasis on the proprietary, we have overlooked how sharing has served as a crucial practice for literary and intellectual innovation both during and after the romantic period. At the same time, we have overlooked just how complicated and contentious such a practice was and continues to be, the complexity of trying to work out the principles of parting, imparting, and parting with something. How was one to conceive of a discrete medium like the book as something "held" in common?

Few issues have become more contentious today in our emerging environment of digital communication than that of sharing. The more material is shared and made shareable, the more criminalized such practices become.[15] There seems to be a growing disconnect between the needs and habits of various creative communities and the way we are choosing to regulate those interactions. By turning to the history of a *common* right and not a copyright to writing, we can begin to see how our current predicament over file sharing is not something distinctly new, but reflects a persistent problem that has always surrounded writing as an allographic art, as an art form that can be reproduced without degrading or changing its value.[16] With each new innovation in writing technology, with each new contribution towards the *reproducibility* of writing, the question of sharing only seems to emerge with renewed force. Rather than offering another trenchant critique of the current institutional exuberance for ever stricter mechanisms of copyright,[17] by identifying the richness of a literary and intellectual tradition of sharing and sharedness, we can begin to understand contemporary digital practices not as essentially aberrant but as standing in a long and legitimate history. We can begin to see how sharing and owning should not be seen as agons, as mutually exclusive of one another—as they are increasingly understood today—but as standing in a necessary, mutual, and always tangled formation with one another.

When we take into consideration the romantic miscellany in its entirety, when we attend to a range of paratextual elements such as bindings, frontmatter, and dedicatory leaves along with the texts that such material aspects enclosed, we can observe the intricate ways that romantic miscellanies were addressing questions of sharing and the sharedness of writing during a crucial moment of historical change in the conditions of writing. Miscellaneity in the romantic era was intimately related to questions of partiality and commonality that surrounded the problem of sharing writing. Where critical and collected editions contributed to the differentiation of literary property, the format of the miscellany strongly responded to a social need to have literature in common.

As I will show, such questions were first and foremost articulated through the presence, whether real or imagined, of handwriting in the miscellany. Whether it was their nature as gift books, the ubiquity of blank dedicatory spaces within them, or in some cases the elaborate white space for diary entries or notes, romantic miscellanies were often typographically designed to invite readers to write within them. Unlike Laurence Sterne's use of handwriting, who signed copies of the first edition of *Tristram Shandy* to keep it from being pirated,[18] the miscellanies used such invitations to handwriting, not to authorize the printed book, but instead to frame the book as a shared space, either between one reader and another or between readers and authors. The singular identity of the hand in Sterne's sHANDy (whether it was the author's autograph or those famous wavy lines that I will discuss in chapter 6) starkly contrasted with the commonality of hands in the miscellany, often captured in the familiar miscellany subtitle, "by several hands."[19] As we will see, the residual technology of handwriting in the miscellanies was not principally a form of autography, a guarantor of individuality, but an indication of commonality. Where the figure of the face played a crucial role in the constitution of the collected edition and readers' identification with such books, it was the contested meaning of the hand and its dual capacity both to clasp and to give that served as a key corporeal site in the self-definition of the romantic miscellany.

In contributing to a growing body of work that has drawn attention to the manuscriptural spaces within or alongside printed books,[20] my aim is to expand our notion of romantic bibliographic culture to include observations of the *simultaneity* of various writing technologies within what we have traditionally called "print culture." As Margaret Ezell has illustrated in her study of late-seventeenth- and early-eighteenth-century manuscript literature, handwriting continued to have an important role to play in literary communities even with the ascent of print in the eighteenth century. In Ezell's words, "public" did not always mean "publication."[21] And as a number of scholars of the romantic period have shown, handwriting continued to play an important role in literary culture well after Ezell's timeframe into the nineteenth century, whether it was the centrality of manuscript to Poe's poetics ("MS. Found in a Bottle," "The Purloined Letter" or his planned periodical, *Stylus*), the renewed popularity of commonplace books known as literary "albums," or the important role that letter exchanges played in shaping audience feedback.[22] As Wilhelm wrote to Nathalie in Goethe's *Travels*,

"One has no idea how much people write today. I'm not even talking about what is printed, although that is still plenty. One can only imagine what is circulated in silence through letters and essays about the letters, news, stories, anecdotes, and descriptions of individual lives."[23] If Wilhelm's observation was true and manuscript production far exceeded print in the early nineteenth century, can we still reliably speak of a "print culture"?

Rather than conceive such manuscriptural work as an *alternative* writerly space to print in the nineteenth century,[24] however, I am interested in exploring the ways that handwriting and printed writing were brought into intimate contact with one another, the way these two very different technologies could literally overlap one another in the space of a single book. As we will see, the invitation to handwriting in the miscellanies did not serve a compensatory function—an articulation of an alternative, human space in a world of mechanized, mass-reproduced objects—but served instead as a kind of initiation into a way of thinking about writing more generally within the printed public sphere as a space of commonality. Such paratextual elements of miscellaneous gift books were then complemented by the literary contributions to these books—a poetics of miscellaneity if you will—that motivated the shareability of writing. The all-important romantic figure of the hollow and a variety of techniques of formal omission would become the formal ground where miscellaneous writing explored and promoted the divisibility and the commonality of writing. Reformulating the written work as a share was not a means of capturing some larger sense of modern fragmentation, but was the precondition, indeed the foundation, upon which a culture of intellectual ownership was being built in the romantic period and that found one of its most successful articulations through the bibliographic genre of the romantic miscellany.

Book-Keeping and the Inscription
(Intermediality and the Book II)

In the introduction to the first issue of the English miscellany *The Keepsake* (1828), Leigh Hunt would write:

> What renders a book more valuable as a keepsake than almost any other, is, that, like a friend, it can talk with and entertain us. And here we have one thing to recommend, which to all those who prize the spirit of books and or regard it above the letter, can give to a favourite volume a charm inexpressible. It is this: that where such an affectionate liberty can be taken either in right of playing the teacher, or because the giver of the book is sure of a sympathy in

point of taste with the person receiving it, the said giver should mark his or
her favourite passages throughout (as delicately as need be), and so present,
as it were, the author's and the giver's minds at once.[25]

As one of the few extended reflections on the miscellany that we have, Hunt's
essay has a kind of programmatic character about it, an attempt to frame
for nineteenth-century readers why this format mattered. In aligning the
category of the book with that of friendship Hunt was drawing on a familiar
strategy that dated back at least to Erasmus's effort to frame the commercial
printed text as common property, beginning with his choice of "Friends
hold all things in common" as the opening of his adage collection.[26] Equating the book with a friend was not simply a way of enlivening the dead
letter on the page, as Hunt suggested ("like a friend, it can talk with and
entertain us"). It was also a way of replacing the anonymous distribution of
mass-produced objects through buying and selling with a model of intimate
circulation of personalized copies among friends, however paradoxical such
a notion of the "personalized copy" might have been. *The Keepsake* was intended not to be kept for oneself but to be given away, shared among friends
and family. The discourse of friendship and the practice of gift-giving under
which miscellanies like *The Keepsake* were produced and circulated were
intended to counteract precisely the anonymity of mass circulation that the
format itself was engendering.

Perhaps no other practice facilitated this mode of intimate exchange
more than *inscription*, the placement of the giver's handwriting alongside,
or in front of, the printed text.[27] As Hunt intoned, "One precious name, or
little inscription at the beginning of the volume . . . is worth all the binding
in St. James's."[28] Numerous miscellanies contained a printed space or even
a special leaf designed to allow givers to dedicate these books to their recipients. Whether it was ornamental presentation leaves, as in this copy of the
Atlantic Souvenir from 1827 (fig. 4.2), or dedicatory poems that included a
blank space to write in the dedicatee's name, as in this copy of the *Taschenbuch der Liebe und Freundschaft gewidmet* (Pocket-Book Dedicated to Love
and Friendship) for 1811 (fig. 4.3), miscellanies consistently used white
space to encourage their users to write within them. Unlike the white space
of critical editions that functioned as a kind of immaculate border insulating the author's work from that of the editor, white space in the miscellanies
was an invitation to cross the boundaries between reader and author and
produce the presence of multiple hands on the page.

And readers responded in kind. If we turn to individual copies housed in
the rich collection of literary annuals at the American Antiquarian Society,

Figure 4.2   Dedication page, *The Atlantic Souvenir* (1827). Courtesy of the Rare Books Division, the New York Public Library, Astor, Lenox and Tilden Foundations.

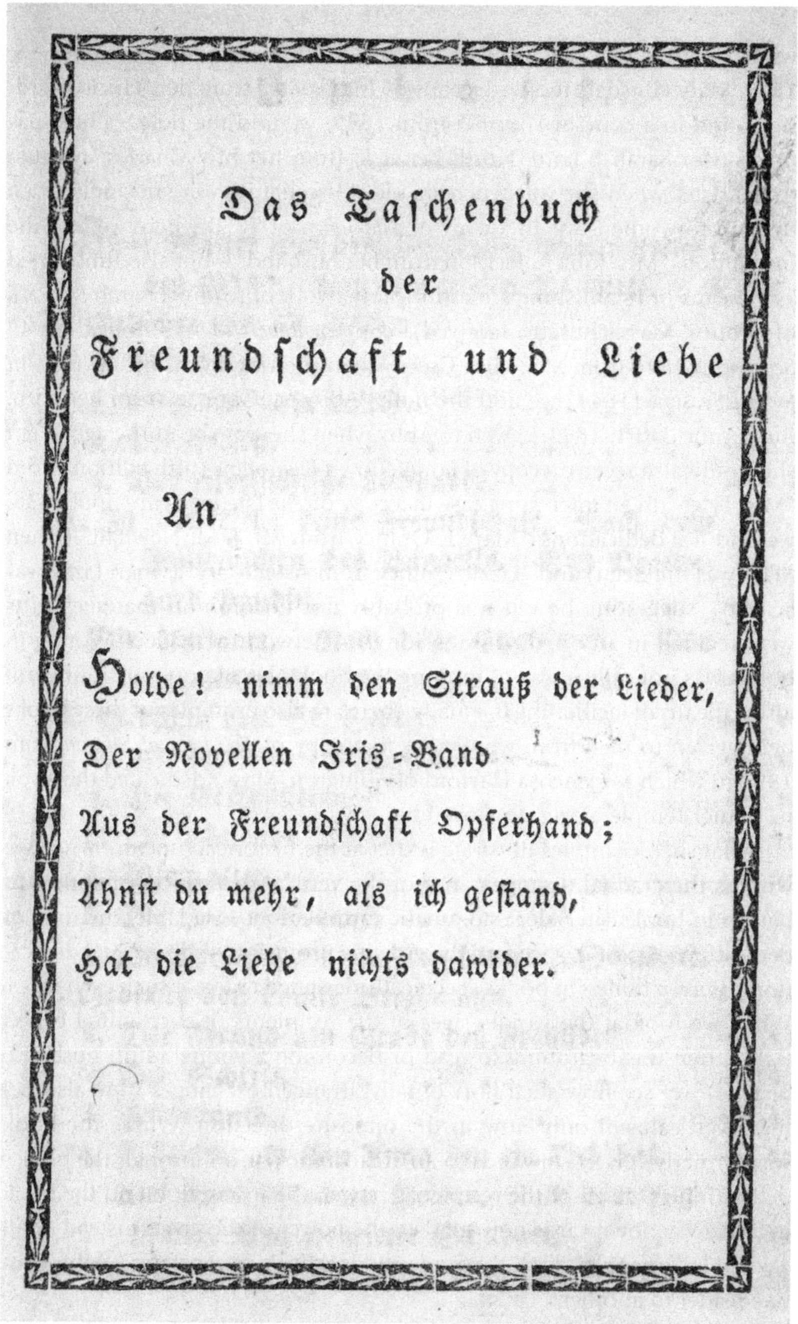

Das Taschenbuch

der

Freundschaft und Liebe

An

Holde! nimm den Strauß der Lieder,

Der Novellen Iris-Band

Aus der Freundschaft Opferhand;

Ahnst du mehr, als ich gestand,

Hat die Liebe nichts dawider.

Figure 4.3 Dedicatory poem, *Taschenbuch der Liebe und Freundschaft gewidmet* (1811). Courtesy of the Klassik Stiftung Weimar, HAAB/Ff1-90.

we find numerous instances of readers' inscriptions. On December 25, 1849, Mary Hinsdale received a copy of *The Garland* from her "Uncle Beardsley," and in a copy of *Hyacinth* from 1849, we find the note, "Christmas present for Sarah J. Lord, North Berwick; from her bro. Charles," written to his sister when she was ten years old. Miscellanies were not only given by men to women—as in a copy of *The Token* of 1830 where we find the inscription, "Mrs. Julia A. Jackson from her husband"—but also functioned as a means of establishing a matrilineal network of reading. Sarah M. Park of Groton, Massachusetts, received a copy of *Robert Merry's Annual for All Seasons* in 1840 from Mrs. Eliza Green when she was seven, and in *The Gift for All Seasons* (1844) we find the note, "Abby M. Gourgas from her afftn. Aunt Anne. Jan 1, 1843," given to Abby when she was six. At the age of ten she would also receive a copy of Longfellow's *Evangeline* (fifth edition) from "Mrs. Tyler." In an interesting case in a copy of *The Literary Souvenir* of 1838, we find *two* dedications, "Mary F. Quincy from Mr. J. M. Newhall" (when Mary was nineteen) and "Lizzie Quincy from sister Mary" (when Lizzy was sixteen), suggesting how it was probably not uncommon that such gifts were regifted in an ongoing extension of a network of readers. Writing in books was not only a way of limiting the book's circulatory possibility but also a means of facilitating it. Finally, there are also examples of these books being given to men from women, as in a copy of *The Rose of Sharon* from 1852 in which Miss Achsa Hayford of Abington, Mass., dedicated the book to Daniel Temple Noyes on November 25.

What such examples illustrate is that at the historical juncture when we witness the gradual disappearance of the vertical dedication of author to patron in books (in Balzac's dramatic formulation: "Madame, the time of dedications is past"),[29] we find the growing profusion of horizontal dedications *between readers* in books specifically designed to foster such exchanges. When we look at the various ages of the recipients of such gifted books (when one was beginning to read or becoming a young adult, husband, or wife), we see how such horizontally arranged exchanges were also being reverticalized, only now in the opposite direction. Where the book was formerly "given" upwards to an aristocratic patron through the book's dedication as a sign of the recipient's power, the inscription and the book it gave away downwards now marked the power of the giver. Instead of an acknowledgment of debt, the romantic inscription transferred debt from one reader to another.

On one level, the inscription was part of a larger cultural matrix in which the acquisition and deployment of handwriting played a pivotal role in the socialization of nineteenth-century readers and writers.[30] As we know from nineteenth-century handwriting handbooks, the production of manuscript involved an extraordinary investment of one's body to the execution of this technology (usually involving various techniques of bondage).[31] If handwriting manuals served as treatises on the incorporation of writing—of bringing the letter into the body—miscellanies and their inscriptions, on the other hand, served as sites for the opposite process of bringing the body into the book and, by association, the world of books. Unlike printed dedications of authors to patrons, which inscribed the private into an otherwise public mode of address, the handwritten dedication—writing in a book—endowed this seemingly private mode of address with a certain publicness. But the important message that it communicated, beyond any well-wishing included in the often prescribed dedicatory lyrics, was that the printed writing in the book was something that was fundamentally shareable between readers. The inscription conveyed the ease with which printed books could be transferred from one reader to another, shared in the sense of held in common.

Hunt's introduction went one step further to motivate another kind of writing in books and thus another mode of shareability: that between *author* and reader. When Hunt instructed owners of the book to further "mark" the text beyond the inscription ("the said giver should mark his or her favourite passages throughout (as delicately as need be)"), this act of handwriting was understood not as an act of giving away, but conversely, one of taking. Instead of authorizing the shareability of books, such marking with the hand authorized the shareability of ideas within them. It instructed readers on how to make the ideas in the book their own property, just as their "property" was importantly being framed as a selection of someone else's ideas.

The inscription thus functioned as a starting point—a portal—to initiate more writing in books. But where the handwritten inscription emphasized the importance, and the singularity, of the material object of the book (this copy is special because it bears the handwriting of a friend), Hunt's invocation for readers and givers to move beyond the inscription and to mark-up the text was a way of prizing the book not as an object but as a bearer of ideas ("to all those who prize the spirit of books and or regard it above the letter"). The individual book was transformed in Hunt's injunction into a space of literary work. When Hunt concluded this invitation to write in miscellanies with the words "and so present, as it were, *the author's and the giver's minds at once,*" he was granting to handwriting an extraordinary power, suggesting that the reason to write in books was to endow writing in books with an authorial status. By marking the book with one's hand, the giver—or more generally the reader—was in some sense making the ideas *her own.* Her markings would create a new work within the material space of the book; she would occupy, as Hunt suggested, the same space and thus the same status as an author.

According to the textual economy of the miscellanies, then, writing was not only a product of more writing, it was even more significantly founded on the critical act of selection and an economy of credit and debt between giver (as both author, friend, or parent) and recipient. Following Hunt's directions, when the giver shared a selection of readings (a miscellany) gleaned from a particular selection of texts (another miscellany), she was modeling an activity for the receiver to create her own miscellany within the miscellany. She was illustrating for her how to participate in this system of marking one's debts and forwarding one's credits. Whether handwritten or print, writing in the miscellanies was conceived as miscellaneous, as a practice of (medial and transactional) mixing. It was always a share and thus shareable.

Hunt's instructions to mark-up these books was not only a rhetorical extension of the typographical frame of their dedicatory leaves. It was also an extension of a more general visual logic in the miscellanies' frontmatter that encouraged readers to mark their books. There was an intimate connection between the cosmos of book formats that all fell under the heading of the "miscellany" and typographical invitations to get readers to write in books, whether it was financial ledgers, as in this copy of *Taschenbuch der Liebe und Freundschaft gewidmet* (1805–7) (fig. 4.4) or the *American Ladies' Calendar* (1818); diary spaces, as in this copy of *Le Souvenir* (1826) (fig. 4.5); or, finally, wallet bindings that were common to miscellanies and into whose pockets readers could place their own writing (fig. 4.6). Goethe had done this, for example, in his many shipments of his writings to his English translator, Thomas Carlyle, where he would place his own poems in the pockets of the books' bindings (one of which was called "A Likeness," and was an exquisite comparison of the practice of translation to a vase of cut flowers).[32] In all of these cases of writing in books, readers' writing was importantly being framed as a part—a share—of a larger universe of writing. Typographical spaces like the accounting tables or diary sheets encouraged readers to learn to narrate their own lives—to *re*count and thus *ac*count for their actions—but such tabular autobiographical spaces were taking place not in blank books but in books with other writing in them. There was a transactional logic to writing that was encoded in the "in" and the "out" of those accounting tables. Indeed, the table to calculate credit and debit was the logical visual extension of the dedication page itself that established a fundamental bibliographic debt between readers. In framing readers' writ-

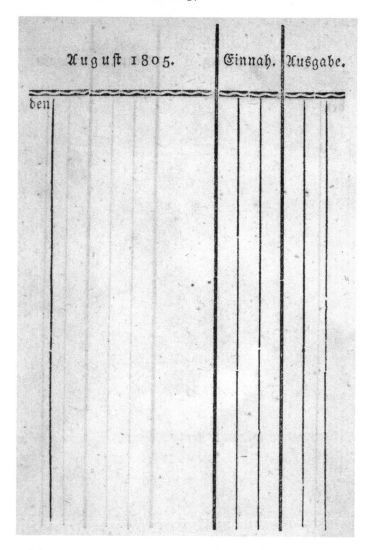

Figure 4.4   Financial ledger, *Taschenbuch der Liebe und Freundschaft gewidmet* (1805). Courtesy of the Klassik Stiftung Weimar, HAAB/Ff1-90.

ing according to the logic of book*keeping*, then, writing was not framed as an act of keeping books, of possession, but as a way of mapping lines of exchange.[33]

Yet unlike the popular early-modern commonplace book that was comprised of the collection of textual parts, the romantic miscellany did not take excerpts of what was "out there" and inscribe them "in here" in one's

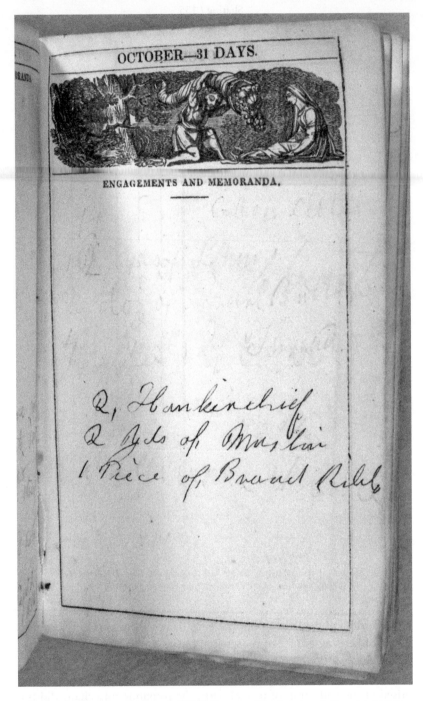

Figure 4.5   Diary page, *Le Souvenir* (1826). Courtesy of the American Antiquarian Society.

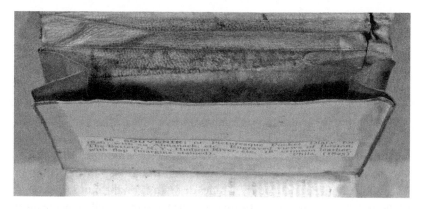

Figure 4.6   Wallet binding of Prudence Carter's copy of *Le Souvenir*
(1826). Courtesy of the American Antiquarian Society.

own personal book. Rather, it inscribed the individual into a book *already
composed* of textual parts.[34] As in Lucy Walsh's copy of *The American Ladies
Pocket Book* (1818) or Edward King's copy of *The Gentleman's Annual Pocket
Remembrancer* (1816), which bear their readers' annotations, the act of writing took place no longer on the blank page of the commonplace book but
on the printed page of the miscellany. Far from signaling the repersonaliza-
tion of the printed book, handwriting was an entry point into an interpersonal public space. Handwriting did not arrest the circulation of the book
in the romantic period but was its very precondition. In Prudence Carter's
copy of *Le Souvenir* (1826), for example, we can see how her own annotations mingle with those of another, William A. Howard of Charlestown,
who has written occasional poems on the theme of friendship on the tissue
papers that cover the book's images. When the Major in Goethe's "The Man
of Fifty" looks over his commonplace books in order to select a citation to
adorn his poem that is to be sent in a pocket-book (a *Brieftasche*) woven by
the beautiful widow, we can see how Goethe's novella was staging precisely
this bibliographic transition from the handwritten collection of one's own
writing to the "woven" collection of the writing of others.

The inscription that framed writing with one's hand in the miscellanies
thus functioned as a crucial counterpoint to the romantic fascination with
the autograph. The inscription captured the fundamental sharedness of
writing—that it could be owned and given away, that it was (im)partable—
that was then to be amplified in a reader's underlining, markings, or occasional notes, each act of script capturing the partiality and the appropriatability, not the proprietariness, of what was in a book. An inscription was

importantly *not* a signature. It depended on a fundamental legibility and thus communicability. In engaging with the figure of the hand that surrounded the book's identity more generally—the way the book depended upon being "at hand"—the inscription capitalized on a different notion of the hand as that which greets rather than grasps.[35] In chapter 1, we saw how the hand was endowed with a certain narrative depth through the figure of the anatomical sculpture in Goethe's *Travels*. And in chapter 2, through the repetitive use of the key word, *schlagen*, we saw how the hand that populated the Hoffmannian novella was depicted as the striking hand—as that which dislodged and dislocated—a move that would later be picked-up in Théophile Gautier's poetic study "Études de Mains," on the murderous hand of Pierre-François Lacenaire. The image of the hand that would emerge most popularly in romantic miscellanies, by contrast, was understood instead as the *exchanging* hand (as in the German *handeln*). In another poignant bibliographic scene in Goethe's "The Man of Fifty," which we remember had initially appeared in part in Cotta's *Ladies' Pocket-Book*, the novella's two young lovers jointly clasp a book in order to read aloud one evening as their hands gradually overlap and their joints (*Gelenke*) begin "touching quite naturally in secret."[36] In Goethe's bibliographic imaginary, grasping turns to guiding (*lenken*), owning to forwarding.

Hollow Texts, Textual Hollows

The possibility of such bibliographic mutuality, of handwriting that both personalized and pluralized the book, was crucially dependent on a typographical program that privileged empty space. As we have seen, the bibliographic format of the romantic miscellany was propelled by its own withholding of print and a simultaneous advancement of techniques that framed such omissions. The promotion of the partiality of the page was not limited to the typographic frames of the printed book, however, but was amplified by the texts that accompanied these paginal absences or textual "hollows." What I am suggesting is that the very predominant poetics of the hollow in romantic miscellanies can be read as a reply to the typographic hollows that predominated in those miscellanies. Miscellaneous prose in the early nineteenth century, and its detailed attention to hollow spaces, became a key force in this process of acculturating readers to understand writing and the book as fundamentally shared spaces.

The first exhibit I want to turn to is a relatively late one, but all the more revealing for being so because it has an entire tradition behind it that it deftly incorporates. In Edgar Allen Poe's "The Pit and the Pendulum," which was published in *The Gift* for 1843, the story's protagonist is threatened first by a fatal descent into a deep pit and then by being strapped to a table as a pendulum with a razor-sharp edge swings above him and slowly descends "designed to cross the region of the heart."[37] The hero's heart is alternately threatened by a "pocket" and "periodicity," the twin identities of the miscellany format for which Poe was writing and which he exploited throughout his career with great skill. The reader's double in Poe is under siege by the mechanization of inscription (the writing machine) as well as the claustrophobia of the book (the pit). He reels between the double threat of the technologization and the sensory isolation of reading, which Poe's narrator will call "the state of seeming nothingness" (135). Absence and inscription, the hollow and writing, are brought together here within a mutually informed economy, nowhere more suggestively on display than in the flickering black and white figures of the judges whose grotesquely thin white lips are set against their black robes and "writhe with a deadly locution" as the protagonist's "sentence" is passed (133). The outcome of writing's writhing "sentence" is either enclosure or dissection, and the only gesture that will rescue the reader at risk is the touch of a human hand on his arm at the story's close ("that of General Lasalle"). The book's handedness resurges in Poe as that which rescues the endangered sociability of the reader in an age of too many books.

Almost two decades earlier in another story about a pocket—and a hole in that pocket—we can see how the hollow is imagined not as the condition of a subjective falling apart that must be repaired but as the precondition of a new social configuration. In A. F. E. Langbein's "The Misunderstanding," which appeared in the German miscellany *The Narrator* (1824), we learn of the tale of a misdirected love letter written by a young woman, Antonia, who has been banished to a convent. When a bishop's undergarment, which is in need of repair (there is a hole in the pocket), is brought to a nun named, Agathe, instead of the tailor, Agath, we learn that Antonia hides a love letter to her forbidden lover, Anton, in the pocket. When the underwear is returned to the bishop, he finds the letter and at first assumes it is from the nun, Agathe. The scandal of a bishop receiving a love letter from a nun is soon replaced by knowledge of the scandal of the forbidden correspondence between Antonia and Anton. The bishop will not only deliver the letter to its proper addressee, however, but in a twist of plot that will result in the happy end so common to miscellany writing, the bishop will then marry the two young lovers. In this tale by an author who was also a recently appointed censor for the newly created *Oberzensorkollegium* in Berlin, the pocket with the hole in it—the double hollow that allows for the misdirection of communication—is figured as the medium through which social reparation is produced.

The social and medial recirculations generated by the text(ile) with a hole in it in Langbein would later be translated by Balzac into a shift from one mode of circulation to another. In "La Bourse" (The Wallet), which initially appeared in volume 3 of the second edition of Balzac's miscellaneous collection of tales, *Scènes de la vie privée* (Paris: Mame et Delaunay, 1832), the story's hero, who is a painter, finds that his wallet or money purse has been stolen. It is only as the story unfolds that he realizes that it has been replaced by a new wallet given to him by the young woman he is secretly in love with. The pocket or purse here is transformed from the quintessential site of monetary exchange to one of gift exchange, as the money bag itself becomes a gift. The tale of the pocket enacts precisely the cultural work that pocket-books were designed to perform during the romantic age. A key component of Balzac's narrative is the way this reformulation of the container from commodity to gift serves as the initiation of the female figure into the world of (visual) art. Here Balzac introduces an intermedial spin to the scriptural work of the miscellany that will be taken up in my final chapter.

Perhaps no other writer in the early nineteenth century, however, worked more assiduously on, and became more categorically famous for, the problem of the hollow than Washington Irving. In addition to the thematic resonance of the hollow in "The Legend of Sleepy Hollow" (with its "sequestered glen," "spacious coves," and "fearful darkness") that would be picked up again in the "deep inlet" at the opening of "The Devil and Tom Walker" or the dangerous "eddy" that collected fables at the expense of truth in "Hell Gate" ("In seeking to dig-up one fact it is incredible the number of fables which I unearthed"), one also encounters the syntactic hollows performed by Irving's deployment of the dash, for example in "Rip van Winkle": "In place of these a lean bilious looking fellow with his pockets full of hand bills, was haranguing vehemently about rights of citizens—elections—members of Congress—liberty—Bunker's hill—heroes of seventy six—and other words which were a perfect babylonish jargon to the bewildered Van Winkle."[38] Here we see how the typographical blank enacts the estrangement of a political and rhetorical consensus. Like the fluidity of those handbills stuffed into the pockets of the speaker, language too has become unanchored, swirling about in pieces. Or finally, consider the narratological hollow in a work like "The Student of Salamanca," which thematically revolved around alchemy, "the grand secret," and the quandary of partial knowledge. At the very highpoint of the story—in the duel between

Don Antonio and Don Ambrosio—Inez, the heroine of the story, faints, producing a narrative break that is followed by a retrospective.[39] The unity of narrated time gives way not only to a degree of anachrony through the use of analepsis (the narrative retrospective that predates the duel) but also to a new focalization as we shift from her perspective to that of Antonio's. At the same time, the narration assumes a far greater degree of paraphrasis, a résumé or summing-up of events that leaves out a great degree of detail. The narrative hollow—her moment of unconsciousness—is conjoined with a narrative projection and filling-in of information that she could not otherwise have known but that itself is continually marked by what it excludes.

"The Student of Salamanca" is of particular relevance here because of the way it is also a key witness to the instabilities that surrounded the international circulation of texts in the early nineteenth century. As a story that was both thematically and narratologically invested in the figure of the hollow or *Leerstelle*, it drew attention to the *textual* gaps that were also prevalent between print editions circulating across the Atlantic. As Irving's later editors tell us, "The Student of Salamanca was almost entirely rewritten between the drafting of [the first American printer's copy] and the publication of [the first English edition]. . . . There is no clear point at which an editor can say, 'Here is the finished text of Bracebridge Hall [to which it belonged].'"[40] In the vexed world of American reprinting, numerous variants, both great and small, crept into the books of Americans. Irving's rush to send off his manuscript to the States before it was "finished" was itself an attempt to protect himself against the intellectual piracy that beset the American book market. And it is telling that Irving's revisions to "Salamanca" most often took the form of precisely the kind of narrative filling-in dramatized by his own narrator in the story after Inez loses consciousness. Revision was formulated according to Irving as a kind of projection.

The career of Washington Irving is significant here because both his fame and subsequent marginalization within the European and American romantic canons have rested on the overt miscellaneity that surrounded his writing, whether generically or nationally understood. Unlike his "young American" followers whose identities were often emphatically linked to a particular place, Irving was, for much of his career, a far more itinerant cultural collector. At the same time, few writers were more associated with the genre of the miscellany and the "short story" that emerged out of this format than Irving.[41] Indeed, he would one day become a miscellany himself: *The Irving Gift* of 1853. Like the genre of the miscellany, no writer has seemed both so central and yet so marginal to literary history.[42] Irving is at once the father of the short story and of the American Renaissance as well as a deeply derivative writer whose work was far surpassed by his followers, a patriarch, like Rip van Winkle, always out of sync with his place and time. In trying to address the diminution of Irving within American literary history, Paul Giles has suggested that it is largely a function of nationalist critical perspectives. "Irving is perhaps the best example," writes Giles, "of an American author whose stature is diminished by a forced affiliation with agendas of literary nationalism, but whose subtleties can be appreciated more readily once he is situated within a transnational context."[43] Michael Warner, on the other hand, has suggested that Irving's troubled reception is a function of Irving's own "rhetoric of anachronism" and the problematic relationship to futurity staged in his writing.[44]

What I want to suggest, by contrast, is that Irving's sinking fortunes have a bibliographic rationale, that the decline in his reputation has been closely related to the decline of a bibliographic format with very distinct gender associations and with which his writing was most intimately associated. The ambiguity of his patriarchy, in other words, was tied to both the femininity and the secondarity of this bibliographic genre that had little in common with the later critical biases of a profession that rested on very different bibliographic and gender foundations. In resurrecting Irving around the genre of the "short story" and not the miscellany, we overlook in the process the tremendous diversity and the remarkable derivative quality that surrounded his writing. Irving is, in this sense, a truly "American" writer because he is so indicative of the derivative nature of antebellum literary culture. But in this, he is also an indicative romantic writer, too, a sign of the way numerous local cultures were working out a new calculus of international indebtedness and ownership (the "in" and the "out" of the gift-book's ledger) in a changing bibliographic landscape. The derivative that promoted the practice of derivation—as though such derivation was one's own—was precisely the complex romantic point of Irving's literary program.

The proliferating gestures of thematic, syntactic, and narratological hollowing-out that one encountered in Irving's miscellaneous writing were thus intimately related to the nature of the bibliographic genre to which his prose corresponded. Both depended upon a fundamental opening-up and carving-out of the bibliographic text. As we would see time and again, Irving's hollow texts were counteracted by recurrent figures of "projection," of throwing-forth and filling-in. Whether it was the prevalence of the gun's discharge at the opening of "Sleepy Hollow," the gun as the sign of Rip van Winkle's discovered untimeliness, or the fact of the headless horseman's thrown head as the cause of Ichabod Crane's disappearance (a head that was itself, we are told, removed by a canon ball), the thrownness (*projectere*) of Irving's miscellaneous poetics provided an imaginary template against which readers could learn to negotiate the sharing and the shareability of writing that inhered in miscellany culture. In order to look more closely at the way this nexus of projection, the textual hollow, sharedness, and miscellaneity worked in Irving's writing, I want to turn to a contribution Irving made to the miscellany *The Gift* for 1836. By entering into Irving's piece in great detail, we will be able to see the elaborate ways that a short work like this made sense of the bookish culture to which it belonged—the way it made writing in miscellaneous books intelligible to the readers of those books.

The Problem of the "Of": Washington Irving's "An Unwritten Drama of Lord Byron"

The reading world has, I apprehend, by this time become possessed of nearly every scrap of poetry and romance ever written by Lord Byron. It may be pleased, however, to know something of a dramatic poem which he did not write, but which he projected—and this is the story:—[45]

This is the opening of Washington Irving's "An Unwritten Drama of Lord Byron," which appeared in *The Gift* for 1836 and was based on information that Irving had recorded in his journal in 1825 under the heading "Unpublished note by Capt. Medwin."[46] The note that Irving received and then transcribed in his journal was based on Medwin's conversations with Byron in Italy about a play that Byron intended to write that was itself based, so Irving tells us, on a play by Calderon entitled *Embozado de Cordova*. No such play existed, but Calderon's *El Purgatorio de San Patricio*, which was based on a long tradition of reusing the St. Patrick myth (beginning most notably with Marie de France), was translated by Shelley and read by Byron, who eventually incorporated elements of it into his *unfinished* drama *The Deformed Transformed*.[47] To begin to recover the story of "An Unwritten Drama" is thus to create a micro-literary history, a chronicle of the borrowing, sharing, misreading, transcribing, and transforming of words that constitutes the field of literature.

But what does it mean to write about something that has *not* been written? There is something wonderfully strange about the title of this work. In its emphasis on the *unwritten* and not the *unfinished*, Irving's piece posed an initial problem of genre, a problem whose availability was a function of the format of the miscellanies themselves with their constant jostling of genres. Was this work by Irving fiction, philology, literary criticism, biography, or all of the above? He begins by invoking the "scraps of poetry" of Byron's writing, aligning his work with the manuscript-hunting editors and philologists that I described in chapter 3, only instead of resurrecting a distant textual past they are now contributing to the making of contemporary celebrity. At the same, when he writes, "and this is its story," he assumes a narrator's stance, transforming his contribution from philology to fiction. Irving's opening mirrored with remarkable precision the fictional editors of so much romantic fiction and seemed to hover in that same ambiguous space of referentiality. And yet instead of a twice-told tale, a retelling of what has already been recorded, what we are about to hear is something that has *not* been written. At first glance it looks like the exact inverse of Borges's "Pierre Menard," whose title character's crowning authorial project was to write *Don Quixote* word for word *again*. Instead of writing the same work, Irving writes a work that does not yet exist.

The opening to this work is as remarkable as its title, and its function seems precisely to *make an opening*. The passage begins with the words, "The reading world," a replacement of the more familiar, "Dear reader,"[48] as we move from the very outset from a scene of individual to mass communication, from a closed to an open system. The first verb of the opening sentence's main clause, "has . . . become possessed" (which amplifies, but also reverses the agency of the initial verb, "I apprehend") performs a clever parody of the ideals of completion and ownership—the possibilities of closure and enclosure—that suffused projects of nineteenth-century collection and that we saw parodied in Poe's "Pit and Pendulum." To want "every scrap of poetry and romance ever written" was indeed to "become possessed." *Possession* and *apprehension* embodied the bibliographic obsessions of the nineteenth century at the same time that they illustrated the impossibility of such projects in a world of overproliferation. To offer an *unwritten* drama was both to feed this possession of possessiveness as well as to confound it: how could you possess that which had not been written? To whom did the *unwritten* drama belong? It was to call the whole project of possession—the genitive case in the title ("*of* Lord Byron")—into question.

We are offered something that is both there and not there at once, Byron's but also Irving's, a poem "which he did not write, but which he projected." It is "an unwritten drama *of* Lord Byron," at the same time that another "I" emerges merely five words into the story ("The reading world has, *I* apprehend"). The key word that Irving uses to negotiate this predicament of possession—the very predicament that makes Irving's authorial project possible—is that verb "project." The author is equated no longer with a *creator* in Irving's piece but instead with a *projector* in a double sense: as someone who projects or throws forth so that others will write (here represented by the proper name Byron) and as someone who projects—who fills in and also amplifies—what others have *partially* written (here represented by the proper name Irving). Equating writing with projection was a crucial means of participating in the larger romantic alignment of writing with sketching, captured in the German *entwerfen* (to draft, but also literally to throw forth). Reformulating writing as projection, as an *Entwurf*, established writing not only as a shared practice (collaborative *and* partial, transactional *and* creative) but also as a crucially intermedial one as well. As the *un*written drama is written, the *un*published note published, writing is reconceived as a practice of media translation. In place of the striking hand of Hoffmann or the greeting hand of Goethe, here we have the throwing hand of Irving, as the author—or each author—is only one component in a larger technological "project." The thrownness of writing at the piece's opening establishes an opening for more writing.

The story that Irving goes on to tell concerns a Spanish nobleman, Alfonso, whose passions have become "ungovernable" and who is soon plagued by a mysterious figure who remains "masked and muffled up" and who follows Alfonso "at every turn" ("like the demon in Faust, he intrudes in his solitude"). The pursuer destroys Alfonso's "zest" ("the sweetest cup of pleasure becomes poison to him") and soon Alfonso suspects that this demon is seducing Alfonso's lover. A duel ensues and Alfonso kills the pursuer only to learn that he is himself: "The mask and the mantle of the unknown drop off, and Alfonso discovers his own image—the spectre of himself—he dies with horror!"

Byron's/Irving's tale belonged, of course, to the rapidly expanding corpus of works about the *Doppelgänger* in the first half of the nineteenth century and that I discussed in chapter 2. If the double captured a more general concern with reproducibility and sameness that inhered in the emerging nineteenth-century mediascape, the crisis of singularity at its heart also disclosed, on a more specific level, something essential about Irving's project of "projection." It was precisely the conditions of the "diffusion of identity" and the "dedifferentiation of the I," in Christof Forderer's words,[49] that were not only at the heart of writing the unwritten but were integral to the format of the miscellany in general that increasingly encouraged readers' participation in the space of the book. Irving's story of the double—of the reproducibility of both subjectivity and writing—was thus also explicitly about the "ungovernable," about the difficulties of order and classification that such a system of writing produced. That is one reason why the crowd plays such a crucial role here ("he follows him in the crowded street, or the brilliant saloon; thwarting his schemes, and marring all his intrigues of love or ambition"), a theme that derived from Irving's own "The Mysterious Stranger" and would be further elaborated in later stories of the double such as Poe's "The Man of the Crowd" or Grillparzer's "Der arme Spielmann." That is why the concluding event that leads to the hero's downfall is the disruption of the dance: "In the giddy mazes of the dance, in which Alfonso is addressing his fair partner with the honeyed words of seduction, he sees the stranger pass like a shadow before him; a voice, like the voice of his own soul, whispers in his ear; the words of seduction die from his lips; *he no longer hears the music of the dance*" (emphasis added). The order of the dance ("the giddy mazes") gives way to the disorder of the crowd, the hero's form-giving powers of orchestrating intrigues disappears ("marring all his intrigues") along with the orchestrating power of the music *that he can no longer hear*. The harmony of the dance is replaced by the disharmony of the whisper, the key mode of communication from Hoffmann's "The Uncanny Guest" that I discussed in chapter 2. Following this whisper, "the words of seduction die from his lips," as we no longer know the content of speech. Speech is crucially hollowed out here, as closed forms like the "intrigue," "scheme," or "dance" are replaced by forms without form that challenge notions of governance and singularity and that were essential to this previous social and narrative order. A story concerned with an omission (the unwritten) and that opens with an opening about openings (the projection) is no less about openings and omissions (the whisper, the unheard, the crowd).

Irving's story (if we can call it that) ends (if we can say that) also in proto-Borgesian fashion:

> How far the plan he had in view agreed with the Spanish original, I have not been able to ascertain. The latter was said to be by Calderon; but it is not to be found in any edition of his works that I have seen. My curiosity being awakened on the subject, I made diligent inquiry while in Spain, for the play in question, but it was not to be met with in any of the public libraries, or private collections; nor could the book-sellers give me any information about it. Some of the most learned and indefatigable collectors of Spanish literature informed me that a play of the kind, called the Embozado of Cordova, was somewhere in existence, but they had never seen it. The foregoing sketch of the plot may hereafter suggest a rich theme to a poet or dramatist of the Byron school.[50]

We are offered a textual universe that consists of a chain of writers (Irving, Byron, Calderon) at the same time that the status of each preceding node in the network is called into question. The drama that Byron did not write, which Irving is merely summarizing and thus not "writing" (in the sense of creating), is based on a drama that Calderon himself might not have written. Like Byron's unwritten drama, Calderon's drama is said to exist but has never been seen. Irving consults all of the relevant nodes of the print economy (the library, the book-seller, the collector), but the textual gap continues to exist. The conclusion of the story creates yet another opening, an opening that depends on the precondition of a textual omission. The incapacity of Calderon's work to be possessed seems to be the very condition upon which its continued circulation depends, much like Irving's own project that is intended to motivate the possibility of future writing ("The foregoing sketch of the plot may hereafter suggest a rich theme to a poet or dramatist of the Byron school"). The bibliographic economy is conceptualized, like the crowd in the story, as necessarily incomplete, unwhole, and open.

To summarize Irving's story, and to interpret it, is to perform a rather dizzying feat of repetition: like Susan Sontag's "Description (of a Description)," we are summarizing a summary (articulated most forcefully in the vague temporal markers that populate Irving's story, such as "at first," "by degrees," "at length," "soon after," "at every turn"). But Irving's summary is not intended as a *summa*, a totality, but instead as a *projection*, as something to produce more writing. In an insightful essay on nineteenth-century miscellanies, Laura Mandell has argued that miscellany contributions very often dramatize what she calls an act of "productive consumption," where "the poems, stories, and pictures in literary annuals are often about viewing, listening to, and reading works of art."[51] On one level, we could say Irving offers an exemplary instance of this. (Balzac's "The Purse" would of course be another example of the heroine being initiated into the aesthetic sphere.) But it is precisely the element of sharedness that suffuses these books and their contents that problematizes the dualism of Mandell's terms of producing and consuming. Sharing stands outside of the binary logic of both production and consumption, challenging such market rationale from within. In calling his story "An Unwritten Drama *of* Lord Byron," Irving was emphasizing the ambiguity surrounding the ownership of literary property, challenging the possibilities and even the legitimacy of possession that demarcated the twin, autonomous spaces of production and consumption. At the same time, in calling his story "An *Unwritten* Drama of Lord Byron," he was also demarcating a space for future writers to call their own. Just as the origin of Byron's work (Calderon) could not be recovered, the origin for Irving and future writers was not there either. Writing what was *unwritten* was a way of simultaneously affirming and effacing the work's own origins, its indebtedness and sharedness to another writer. Like the complicated semiotics of the inscription, Irving was both inviting the practice of textual sharing at the same time that he was producing boundaries to facilitate the paradoxical sense of originality, a space of one's own, within this shared space.

Sharing Sharing: Poe, Hawthorne, and Mrs. Chamberlain's "Jottings from an Old Journal"

In a review of Hawthorne's *Twice-Told Tales* written for *Graham's Magazine* in 1842, Poe would address the remarkable similarity between Hawthorne's "Howe's Masquerade" and his own "William Wilson." "In 'Howe's Masquerade,'" writes Poe, "we observe something which resembles plagiarism—but which *may be* a very flattering coincidence of thought."[52] Poe's accusation of plagiarism was odd on two accounts. Hawthorne's story had appeared in *The Democratic Review* in May 1838 *before* Poe's had appeared in *The Gift* in late 1839 and then shortly after that in his collection, *Tales of the Grotesque and Arabesque*, in 1840. It is possible that Poe did not know about the initial publication of Hawthorne's tale and, overlooking the nature of the collection's title, took its subsequent reprinting in the *Twice-Told Tales* as the first occasion of its appearance. Or perhaps he was accusing himself of plagiarism: Poe never in fact says *who* the plagiarist is.

But this notice is odd, or perhaps disingenuous, on another level because of the fact that both Hawthorne's *and* Poe's tales were very clearly based on Irving's "An Unwritten Drama," which had appeared four years earlier in *The Gift*. Indeed, Mary Shelley's adaptation of Byron's play, suggestively titled "The Transformation," had already appeared in the 1831 British miscellany *The Keepsake*, suggesting how Irving's invocation of an unwritten space had itself already been written. When Poe writes that Hawthorne's line "And lowered the cape of the cloak from his face . . . and let fall his sword upon the floor" mirrored his own "His mask and cloak lay where he had thrown them, upon the floor," what he did not mention was that both "paralleled" (as Poe called it) a line from Irving that read, "The mask and the mantle of the unknown drop off, and Alfonso discovers his own image."

The resurrection of Irving's (or Byron's) tale and its contribution to the making of the future canon of American literature depended in part on its capacity to dramatize such textual transmission, whether it was symbolically within the tale (as in the reference to Calderon) or bibliographically within the literary market. "An Unwritten Drama of Lord Byron" was initially preprinted in the *Knickerbocker Magazine* in August and then in *The New York Mirror* in October of 1835 before *The Gift* appeared towards the end of that year, a not uncommon strategy of a work appearing in more than one publication in a single, short span of time. Based on the available evidence, however, bibliographers suspect that the versions that appeared before the version in *The Gift* were in fact *re*printed from the later miscellany,[53] which means that this story about sharing was not only capable of sharing itself with other authors in the future but had the capacity to engender its own material predecessors as well. It orchestrated its future amplification—its *re*writing and *re*printing—not only through a very distinct poetics but also through the strategic material practice of *pre*printing.

Washington Irving's story about textual sharing and textual hollows was thus shared with remarkable success within the nineteenth-century world of books. In doing so, it paradoxically contributed to the singular fame of two of the period's best-known American authors. The inter-authorial repetitions at the heart of Irving's retelling of Byron's own literary recycling were translated in Poe into *intra*-authorial repetitions that depended upon the explicit denunciation of literary borrowing. As Poe would write in his review of Hawthorne in praise of stylistic repetition, "Without a certain contiguity of effort—without a certain duration or repetition of purpose—the soul is never deeply moved."[54] Or as he would later explain in "The Philosophy of Composition": "In carefully thinking over all the usual artistic effects . . . I did not fail to perceive immediately that no one had been so universally employed as that of the refrain . . . [where] pleasure is deduced solely from the sense of identity—of repetition."[55] Beauty for Poe was a function of writing's internal repetitiveness, a form of auto-amplification and self-projection that eschewed writing's allographic potential.

Poe and Hawthorne bear witness to the paradox of a poetic program of singularization that could grow out of a miscellaneous book culture of commonality. Indeed, as we saw in the case of Walter Scott, the ballad, and the novel, such commonality was in fact the precondition of such singularity. One could find a similar program at work in German romantic writers like Clemens Brentano, whose landmark novella "The History of Virtuous Kasper and Beautiful Anne," which appeared in the gift book *Gaben der Milde* (Gifts of Clemency) (1817–18), eschewed a feminine culture of shared textuality in favor of a masculine, monumental literary aesthetic written in stone.[56]

But I want to conclude by way of highlighting how Irving's program of sharing, and not just its content, could itself be shared. Rather than contribute to the singular fame of the heroic author, such techniques were simultaneously being employed in nineteenth-century miscellanies to *engender* new classes and new communities of writers.[57] Turning to one final example of miscellany writing, "Jottings from an Old Journal" by Mrs. S. A. H. Chamberlain that appeared in *The Rose of Sharon* (1852), we can see the way such textual sharing embodied in Irving's piece had become programmatic in the miscellanies by mid-century—as both widely prevalent but also as a way of rhetorically programming the function and meaning of these books.

"Jottings from an Old Journal" was the story of two women who had recently spent time together reading aloud from *Reveries of a Bachelor* (1852) by "IK Marvel" (Donald Mitchell)—"you had followed me from kitchen to parlor, book in hand."[58] After one departs, the other chances upon a journal after "rummaging in an out-of-the-way closet" that belongs to an anonymous woman ("the dainty penmanship, and certain other unmistakable signs, prove her to have been . . . upon *our* side of the *gens humana*"). The remainder of the story consists of excerpts from this "old journal" ("I send you a few random leaves in place of the spoiled 'Reverie'").

In its movement from sociable conversation to the sociability of transcription, "Jottings" mirrored the same intermedial moves with which Irving's piece had begun, from the unwritten drama to the written account. The writer was equated here with that of the philologist and the act of writing with that of transmission. But where Irving and the philologists were busy explaining the various libraries across Europe where their manuscripts had been found, the domestic "closet" (out-of-the-way to be sure) is framed as the archival source of women's writing. At the same time, whether as oral performance or silent reading, sharing texts is framed as a means of escaping the confines of domestic work ("I made pastry and listened to the memories of his early days"), a way of substituting one form of home-work for another.

Ultimately, however, the significance of "Jottings" is the way it charts a trajectory of making something public and thus enunciates a process of making publics. The interior, interpersonal space of domestic affection and reading aloud gives way to a mediated space of distance, silent reading, and random "leafing" as women move from readers to authors, the handwritten culture of journaling remediated in the format of the printed gift-book. The word "jotting," which the *OED* tells us made one of its earliest appearances in Scott's *Waverley*, not only captured the marking of the page solicited by the medium of the gift-book. It also captured the miscellaneity at the heart of these books, drawing attention to the textual mixing that was on display in Chamberlain's story as well as to the haphazard nature of the personal accounts that were being "jotted" down. Jotting and gender had much to do with one another. If the similarity between Irving's "An Unwritten Drama," Poe's "William Wilson," and Hawthorne's "Howe's Masquerade" highlighted the capacity of Irving's text to produce a masculine poetics of singularity (that was itself based on textual repetition), the *continuity* between Irving's "An Unwritten Drama" and Chamberlain's "Jottings from an Old Journal" reflected the opposite potential of texts like this to move across genders, to create the rhetorical and bibliographical conditions of such intergender openings that would be a key means of enabling women's entry into the professional world of writing. As the text itself suggests and as I will show in greater detail in the next chapter, the rigorously closed-off feminine space of "jottings from an old journal," a space that would later be canonized through a work like Virginia Woolf's *A Room of One's Own*, paradoxically derived from the necessary and fundamental sharedness, not ownness, of writing. It depended on the openness of "the reading world" to recreate the intimacy of a new "dear reader."

To conclude, then, however small or partial this particular miscellany entry of Irving's might have been—indeed precisely because of its synoptic and partial nature—I want to suggest that it stands as an ideal entry point for understanding the complex logic of sharing and owning that surrounded romantic miscellanies more generally. Unlike Irving's more famous "tales," pieces like "An Unwritten Drama" have not been anthologized with any regularity (if at all) and have most often been treated as textual anomalies in the critical literature. As the editors of Irving's critical edition write, "No information is available as to the impetus which led Irving during the summer of 1835 to prepare his sketch for publication in an elegant gift-book. . . . Since he was extremely busy—revising and proofreading the second and third volumes of The Crayon Miscellany, purchasing and renovating a home, and overseeing the researches of his nephew Pierre for Astoria—it seems unlikely he would have written the work at this time unless solicited to do so."[59] At work on more important miscellanies of his own, we have little idea why he would contribute a ten-year-old journal entry to another miscellany. Like the blank spaces that populated the miscellanies, Irving's contribution to *The Gift* is read as a kind of unmotivated blank space within Irving's own corpus of miscellaneous writing, itself a persistent blank space in the narrative of American literary history.

And yet "An Unwritten Drama" has much to tell us about the bibliographic importance of Irving's writing in general, whether it was the doubling of "Rip van Winkle," the borrowings of "The Art of Book-Making," the incompletions found in "The Student of Salamanca," or the textual hollows of "A Legend of Sleepy Hollow" or "Hell Gate." They each in their own way contributed to a culture that was motivated by making writing more available. At the same time, the formal and bibliographic evidence surrounding "An Unwritten Drama" suggested the important ways that this piece was engaged with the unique culture of miscellanies in which it appeared. It illustrated that this was not a random contribution to randomly organized books—miscellaneity *in extremis*—but rather a very considered piece of writing that engaged with the principles of writing encoded in these increasingly prominent bibliographic objects. In exploring a notion of writing as projection—and all of the related, technologized ideas of amplification, division, processing, calculation, and computation that accompanied it— Irving's work was engaging with the sharedness of writing that the miscellanies themselves were in the process of promoting but also trying to control. Like the miscellanies, Irving's work made sharing a central principle in the creative process, and like the miscellanies, it attempted to negotiate textual openings as well, to carve out through such shared spaces writing spaces of one's own. As a part itself, it attempted both to impart and part with writing. To rephrase Goethe with whom I began, "An Unwritten Drama" suggested that sharing was not only more difficult but also far more important to the romantic bibliocosmos than we have traditionally imagined.

CHAPTER FIVE

Overhearing

"I still don't understand! If you listened at his door, you must have heard two voices."

"No, we heard only his voice. There were strange noises, but we thought they came from him too."

"Only his voice! But how is it that you didn't hear . . . her?"

—Stanislaw Lem, *Solaris*

The Problem of Open Source

At the age of ten, the lyric poet Elisabeth Kulmann (1808–25), who lived and died in St. Petersburg, spoke Italian, French, Russian, and German, and by age fourteen the list included Latin, Greek, English, Spanish, Portuguese, and modern Greek. She was reciting Tasso at eleven, translating Horace at twelve, and reading Homer at fourteen. She composed almost every one of her poems simultaneously in three languages: German, Italian, and Russian. Into German she translated Anacreon and portions of *Paradise Lost*. Into Italian, some of the *Iliad*. She was a woman who traveled in languages, a "remarkable meteor" as her biographer said,[1] whose career was unfortunately cut short: she died at the age of seventeen.

Of course Kulmann offers a fascinating case for any study of translation. There is no one language in her writing that emerges as her first language or "mother tongue." She never translates from a "source" language into a single "target" language. At the same time that she lacks a mother tongue, her poems also curiously lack a mother text. Kulmann named her book of poems after the ancient Greek poet Corinna (who it was said defeated Pindar five times in poetic contest), but in the early nineteenth century there were no extant poems by Corinna, nothing of Corinna's that Kulmann could have read. While the queen of poets for a young woman writer in the early nineteenth century would more often than not have been Sappho,[2] Kulmann invokes a female predecessor who lacks a literary corpus. Like the translating, bicultural heroine of Madame de Staël's *Corinne ou l'Italie* (1807), who leaves behind no textual legacy and who might have been a possible source for Kulmann, there was no work by the ancient Corinna for Kulmann to translate or to transform. Poetry begins in this case with a genealogical absence. It begins with the absence of source language altogether. Yet this absence is filled in by the song Kulmann chooses for Corinna to sing in the title poem of the collection. It is the story of Daphne and Apollo, where Daphne escapes her pursuing lover by being transformed into a laurel tree—the laurel that will adorn Apollo's lyre of poetry. Daphne survives— and poetry begins this time—through the woman's metamorphosis and her silence. Kulmann invents a text for her textless literary predecessor in three different languages, but the invented text is actually a borrowed text that tells the story of disowning one's own voice, of going silent. It now signals a crisis of target language.

In her fascination with the multiplicity of languages and translating between them, Kulmann was very much a part of her age. Few periods have been more transfixed by the practice of translation than that of the romantic.[3] As Clemens Brentano famously declared in his novel *Godwi*, "The Romantic itself is a translation."[4] Or as Goethe put it with familiar hyperbole, "Every translator is a prophet among his people."[5] Translations such as Alfred de Vigny's *Othello* (1829), which served as a pivotal literary turning point between the failure of Hugo's *Cromwell* (1827) and the epoch-making success of his *Hernani* (1830), Hölderlin's *Antigone* (1804), which was produced on the threshold to his psychic unraveling and thus became the ultimate signpost of romanticism as the sleep of reason, and Coleridge's *Wallenstein* (1800), which appeared in the same year as the expanded second edition of the *Lyrical Ballads*, were just a few signs of translation's capacity to serve as a crucial, and even necessary, accompaniment to literary innovation in the years around 1800. As Ezra Pound would later say, "Every allegedly great age is an age of translations."[6]

If translations and translating were closely aligned with the formal innovations of the romantic period, they were also intimately connected with the expansions of the book trade. With no international copyright agreements in place until the close of the nineteenth century and informal bilateral agreements only operative by mid-century, translations were cheap and thus very profitable to produce. As we will see, translations played a key role in a number of new publishing ventures in the nineteenth century, helping satiate the growing demand for new content while circumventing the costs of authorial advances. Translations and translators came to stand in the romantic age for a new industrializing world of letters.

As they enlarged the reading material available to romantic audiences, translations also helped consolidate the collective identities of those audiences. Translations were importantly intertwined with the rise of a national consciousness across Europe and North America. As Franco Moretti has argued, one of the principal reasons for translation's prominence in the early nineteenth century was its capacity to contribute to the process of cultural homogenization and centralization necessary for the constitution of emerging nation states.[7] In this regard, translations played a similar role to the nation-building work of collected editions. In place of an early-modern competition of vernaculars, as Peter Burke has argued,[8] where public business was often conducted in numerous languages simultaneously, the rise of translations in the early nineteenth century played a key role in importing and domesticating the foreign, in smoothing over such linguistic differences. In responding to the increasingly mass, and monolingual, reading public, romantic translations contributed to the standardization of European cultures.

And yet in emphasizing its capacity to assimilate, we overlook translation's ability to estrange, to draw readers' attention somewhere else. A crucial component of translation's facility to innovate in the early nineteenth century (and of course beyond) lay in its ability to foster an alternative international literary imaginary, to transcend such local and locatable boundaries. Translations drew attention to the foreign as much as they made such foreignness intelligible to domestic audiences. Where the early modern competition of vernaculars had been underpinned by a stabilizing notion of *translatio imperii*—translation as an orientation towards classical origins—romantic translation by contrast was marked by an increasing transactional complexity. A new kind of competition of vernaculars emerged that coincided, or competed, with the stability of the mother tongue, a point strongly evoked by the criss-crossing vectors of Kulmann's own linguistic interests. As the editors of *The Edinburgh Review* triumphantly stated in 1832, "Till near the middle of the eighteenth century what had been long called the 'Republic of Letters' existed only in name. It is not truly applicable but to the present period, when the transmission of knowledge is rapid and easy, and no work of unquestionable genius can excite much interest in any country without the vibration being quickly felt to the uttermost limits of the civilized world."[9] Translation was the mechanism behind such inter-

national cultural "vibrations." As Goethe would write to his Scottish translator Thomas Carlyle in 1827, "Whatever one may say about the inadequa-
cies of translation, it remains one of the most important and honorable
occupations in the whole world [*in dem allgemeinen Weltwesen*]."[10] As David
Damrosch has argued, translation was and continues to be an essential category for thinking about world, as opposed to national literature, for thinking about the world as a world-being (*Weltwesen*), in Goethe's terms.[11]

Kulmann's interest in the multiplicity of languages and the complexi-
ties of moving between them thus captured something essential about the
romantic age. But in her acute attention to questions of gender—and the
twinned problematic of source and target language—Kulmann's translations also mark an important entry point for thinking in new ways about
the role that translation played during this period. Numerous women writers were active as translators during the romantic period, contributing in
important ways to what Margaret Cohen and Carolyn Dever have identified
as women's efforts at "eroding the comforting ideal of the mother tongue."[12]
And yet despite the widespread activity of romantic women as translators,
we still have surprisingly few studies of their work from this period.[13] While
we know much about A. W. Schlegel's Shakespeare, Percy Shelley's *Faust*
(and now Coleridge's!), or Friedrich Hölderlin's Sophocles, we know little
about Fanny Tarnow's George Sand, Felicia Hemans's Goethe, or Louise
Colet's Shakespeare. In her work on gender and translation, Sherry Simon
has asked whether discussing women as translators is a way for women
writers to lose their voice, whether it does not reproduce a gender hierarchy
of men as producers and women as reproducers.[14] As Lori Chamberlain
has shown, translation has for so long been coded as a feminine writing
practice that the study of women translators might simply perpetuate such
dichotomies.[15] After all, as feminist scholarship has increasingly made us
aware, it was precisely during the romantic era when women were writing
and publishing extraordinary amounts of "original" material, altering the
literary landscape in crucial ways.

These are important concerns to bear in mind, and yet in leaving translation out of women's literary history we recreate a generic hierarchy that
does not do service to women's writing or literary history more generally.
Readers read literature—whether in translation or in their native languages.
To attend to the history of translation is to contend with a spectrum of
books that deeply mattered to readers and writers. And as Simon's work
has done so much to show, the more we uncover about women's writing in
particular and the important position that translation has played as both
a practice and an idea within it, the more translation becomes a space to

recover, not lose, women's voices. As a growing body of theoretical work on the relationship of women's writing to translation has argued,[16] translation captures the mediations, displacements, and contradictions that surrounded, and continue to surround, women's place in the literary market. Such work, which is emerging in many cases from the bilingual concerns of Canadian scholars, foregrounds aspects of women's writing that have been at the heart of some of the most major trends in feminist literary history, whether it is Catherine Gallagher's stress on the poetics of dispossession in women's writing, Susanne Kord's illustration of the problem of the proper name for emerging professional women writers, Joan DeJean and Nancy K. Miller's emphasis on the "displacements" in the making of women's literary traditions, or Margaret Ezell's proposal about shifting the site and definition of "publication" and "public" in order to recover women's contributions to the world of writing.[17] Translation is an ideal space to contend with such problems of literary displacement.

But where Ezell cautions us about using nineteenth-century models of commercial publication to understand early-modern women authors who were writing outside of commercial networks, I would like to suggest, as Carla Hesse, Elizabeth Eger, and Margaret Cohen have recently done,[18] that we have not been attentive *enough* to the commercialism of women's writing precisely in the nineteenth century. If the years around 1800 have traditionally been understood as marking the emergence of the professional woman writer (not as an exception but as a norm), I want to explore how such professionalization—the generation of a literature of one's own so to speak—very often transpired through an engagement with the extremely mercantilist practice of translation, with a literature *not* one's own. It is in the liminal space of translation where we can see these writers working through the problems of "going public,"[19] of negotiating the ambiguous and shifting specificity of the public's boundaries at the turn of the nineteenth century. With their detailed attention to questions of identity, communication, and the availability or looseness of narrative property, the translation projects of romantic women can be read as extended reflections on the categories of publicness and publication (*Öffentlichkeit* and *Veröffentlichung*) that surrounded the changing nature of their bookish world. Translation allowed women writers to explore the possibilities, as well as the risks, that the increasing openness of these categories entailed for new classes of writers. Going public was always a means of exploring the complicated process of making new publics.[20] Translation was both a vehicle for invention and appropriation as well as a means of vanishing and effacement, at once a public and deeply private mode of communication. It represented the difficulties surrounding categories like ownership and commonality that accompanied a world of increasingly available cultural material. Rather than present a history of women writers' full emancipation at the outset of the nineteenth century or their continued exclusion well into the twentieth, my aim here is to illustrate the strategies through which they negotiated between these two poles, the way translation served as a crucial site for writerly negotiation itself.

In what follows, I will traverse a variety of translation projects by women writers from the opening decades of the nineteenth century in an attempt to resituate translation within the history of books and women within the history of romantic literature. In keeping an eye on how women's translational work differed from that of men during this period, I want to draw attention to the specific ways that women's translations initiated new modes of thought concerning the overlapping fields of translation, books, and the making of print publics. Like their male counterparts, women translators were vigorously engaged with the transmission of literary works across time and space in the early nineteenth century. They, too, were actively participating in the accelerating availability of printed books after 1800 and the increasing circulatory complexity that accompanied such availability. But where translation projects by men seemed far more invested in a poetics of appropriatability—in the belief that translation was ultimately a means of making something one's own (as in Novalis's formulation, "metamorphosis of the foreign into something one's own, appropriation [*Zueignung*] is the ceaseless business of the spirit")[21]—women translators seemed far more committed to exploring precisely the difficulties of such poetic possessiveness. Like the miscellanies that I discussed in chapter 4, women's translations broke down the consolidation of the authorial persona between the covers of the book that was enacted in formats like the collected edition discussed in chapter 2 or the critical edition of chapter 3. Translations by women were part of a larger trend of women's writing in the eighteenth and nineteenth centuries that aimed to challenge existing cultural unities, resisting in sophisticated ways, as Deidre Shauna Lynch, April Alliston, and others have shown, the assumed boundaries of the fatherland or the mother tongue.[22] Translation became a vehicle to promote the increasing openness of romantic book culture as a means to gain entry into books. At the same time, it provided women an occasion to reflect on the challenges that such openness posed, whether it was in creating a work, a literature, or even a public of one's own.

Today, an increasingly urgent sense of the endangered nature of privacy has emerged as one of the most salient and pressing issues surrounding modern media.[23] Where Balzac had placed on the title page of his novel, *Le Père Goriot* (1835), the epigraph "All is true" (from Shakespeare's *Henry VIII*),[24] today we might be inclined to say that "all is public." Such concerns, I want to suggest, were already beginning to take shape in the romantic age. As Tom Mole has shown, the problem of celebrity and its attendant cult of revelation can be traced back to the opening decades of the nineteenth century.[25] Romantic writers increasingly worried over but also capitalized upon this new culture of endless personal disclosure.[26] The work of women translators becomes particularly significant in this context because of the way they repeatedly and trenchantly addressed the internal tensions behind the growing sense of openness surrounding the printed book. On the one hand, the book's openness and availability made room for new writers and new readers. Translation drew upon and also promoted the availability of writing in books. It facilitated the making of new publics. But on the other hand, the persistent openness that surrounded translation and the book—indeed the book as a translational space—also threatened a sense of personal ownness and autonomy. A public founded upon private availability in books increasingly came to be seen as something potentially dangerous, especially for women.

In turning in the second half of this chapter to an intricate body of translations by the German romantic writer Sophie Mereau, I want to explore the way her texts return time and again to the motif of overhearing to think through the intersecting fields of translation, gender, writing, and the book.[27] Mereau's translational work is significant precisely because of the way it shows us how overhearing is part of privacy's—and thus publicity's—story and the way that story is tied to how books were being understood at the turn of the nineteenth century. For privacy to be constituted and to be known, it must be overheard (and not heard). But the knowledge of overhearing also marks privacy's end: if all is overheard, nothing is private. Overhearing, one of the oldest literary tropes on record, thus came to serve as a kind of metatrope for modernity: it both marked out the dividing line between those all important modern categories of public and private *and* signaled their erasure. In circling around the question of overhearing, Mereau's translations provide an extended theoretical reflection on the changing availability of personal narrative as a key feature of modern society and on the role that the printed book played in constructing such cultural logic. The trope of overhearing united the historical looseness that surrounded translation with the growing openness that was coming to surround the printed book. The overheard story in translation became an ideal case to think through the dichotomy of the book's capacity to operate as a crucial motor of social and cultural change *and* as a threat to individual autonomy and subjectivity. The significance of Mereau's translational work was not its unmitigated breakthrough into publicness but its persistent questioning of the efficacy of publicness as a public good.

"Le commerce intellectuel"

"Today people are united by their interests; civilization fosters among itself a useful exchange of knowledge and products."[28] Such were the opening words of the Paris paper *Le Globe*, founded in 1824, and they pointed to the enthusiasm that surrounded the increasing commercial orientation of culture that facilitated the growing mobility of language and ideas. Translation was to be the motor of this new "commerce intellectuel," an essential practice in bringing near what was far.

Such enthusiastic pronouncements about the growing internationalism of intellectual life were mirrored by the realities of the book trade, where translation came to play an increasingly pronounced role in the market for printed books. From the 1790s onward in England, booksellers who supplied popular fiction for circulating libraries such as the Minerva Press increasingly relied on translations, just as one could observe a rash of Schiller and Kotzebue translations during this same decade as a means of responding to the French revolution via the German stage (referred to by Wordsworth as those "sickly and stupid German tragedies").[29] The vogue for German plays in English publishing was the vanguard of a much greater attention to the German literary world after 1800. As the *Critical Review* remarked in 1807, "So great is the rage for German tales and German novels, that a cargo is no sooner imported, than the booksellers' shops are filled with a multitude of translators who seize with avidity and without discrimination whatever they can lay their hands on."[30] In the German states in the 1820s, whole series began to emerge after the deleterious effects of the Napoleonic wars that were devoted to translation, such as the Gebrüder Schumann's "Taschenbibliothek der ausländischen Klassiker." Alongside such miscellaneous series, one could also find in the 1820s the appearance of major, and often multiple, translation projects of multi-volume collected editions of British authors, from Shakespeare to Scott to Byron. In the first third of the nineteenth century there were almost as many translations into German from any language as in the entire eighteenth century combined.[31] And as Norbert

Bachleitner has shown, the number of translated novels produced between 1820 and 1845 increased fourteen times, while the number of novels only increased by a factor of three.[32] In the French case, scholars such as José Lambert, Lieven D'Hulst, Katrin van Bragt, and André Lefevere have documented the integral role that translation played in the 1820s in facilitating the rise of romantic writing.[33] Between 1820 and 1830 there were more translations produced in France simply from one language (German) than there were from all languages in the German states during the same decade.[34] Finally, this rise of translation was not limited to the European continent but was also crucial to the development of American literature and what was ultimately called the "American Renaissance." In the voluminous landscape of American periodicals, reviews or translations of German literature increased from fifteen in 1800 to thirty-six in 1830 to one-hundred thirteen by 1841,[35] the year in which the Boston-based newspaper *The Dial* began speaking of "this German epidemic."[36] The prospectus for the international-minded periodical *Brother Jonathan*, whose circulation reached 32,000 in 1840 and whose novel "extras" included with readers' subscriptions were largely driven by foreign imprints, contained the epigraph, "He comes, the herald of a noisy world, / NEWS FROM ALL NATIONS lumbering at his back."[37] In the market for American books, the year 1840 also saw more literary works in translation than works by American authors, with offerings ranging from the *Arabian Nights* to *Don Quixote* to *Faust*.[38] The bibliographic data seem to bear out satires like Cornelius Mathews's *The Career of Puffer Hopkins* (1842), where two publishers discuss the idea of founding a new press: "We shall pirate all foreign tales regularly; and where we can purloin the proof sheets shall publish in advance of the author himself; shall in all cases employ third-rate native writers at journeyman-cobbler's wages, and swear to their genius as a matter of business; shall reprint the old annuals and almanacs, systematically, as select extracts and facetiae, and shall reproduce their cuts and illustrations, as new designs from the burin of Mr. Tinto, the celebrated Engraver."[39]

The satirical references to piracy and the exploitation of translators (the natives) in *Puffer Hopkins* revealed an important book-historical fact about romantic translation: that before the Berne Convention at the close of the nineteenth century, a reliable system of international copyright did not exist (although bilateral agreements of varying degrees of effect were often instituted by mid-century). Understanding romantic literature as tightly linked to the rise of limited-term copyright, as William St. Clair has done in his study of the romantic "reading nation,"[40] overlooks in crucial ways that a large portion of the literary environment was *not* subject to the concerns and pressures of copyright. Attending to the reading *nation* excludes considerations of the nature of authorial property *between* nations.[41] Where "original" literature during the romantic period vigorously promoted the protocols of ownership surrounding writing, translation increasingly came to stand for a writerly space defined by a loss of authorial control.

Once again the bibliographic facts bear this observation out. The translation of Walter Scott into German, for example, was a thriving industry in the early nineteenth century, with translations appearing in ever shorter time spans after the date of the original publication. But by the time of *Peveril of the Peak*, the novel appeared in translation into German *before* it appeared in English. Similarly, Willibald Alexis (a.k.a. Wilhelm Häring) produced at least one novel, *Walladmor*, that claimed to be a Walter Scott translation but was in fact an original work.[42] In similar fashion, the Gebrüder Franckh, publishers in Stuttgart, published the play *Octavia* as though it were a translation from the French, although it had originally been published by Kotzebue in German through another publisher only a few years earlier.[43] Such international textual deregulations were not limited exclusively to the field of translation, however, as one could often find an author's suppressed material appearing abroad in the original language that one could not find in one's homeland. The booksellers of Parsons and Galignani in Paris were some of the most prominent practitioners, where their "English, French, Italian, German and Spanish Library" often published works by Byron in English that one could not buy in London, explicitly advertising their wares as such. And there was of course the celebrated case of Diderot's *Rameau's Nephew* that first appeared in print in French as a translation of Goethe's translation into German, which had appeared several years earlier and which was based on a manuscript that had been smuggled out of the royal library in St. Petersburg by a friend of Schiller's, although the French edition suppressed its true source and claimed to be based on Diderot's original manuscript.[44] Just prior to its publication in German, Goethe would write to Schiller: "My greatest comfort in this matter is that I can say: *sine me ibis liber!* because I do not wish be present everywhere it goes."[45] In invoking Ovid's well-known saying from the *Tristia*, "without me, book, you will go [into the city]," Goethe was of course referring to his desire to disassociate himself from the rather scurrilous nature of Diderot's work. But he could just as well have been referring to the scandalon of translation itself, to the looseness of authorial control that surrounded the international circulation of texts in the early nineteenth century and the resulting ethical loosening of public speech that it seemed to facilitate.

Women, Translation, Transnation

If translation was beset by a problem of looseness at the turn of the nine-teenth century—an identity that dated at least as far back as the seven-teenth century with the emergence of *les belles infidèles*, a term that referred to a French school of loose translation—I am interested in drawing at-tention to the way women translators from this period both mobilized such looseness to generate authorial openings for themselves as well to identify the risks such looseness posed to them as writers and individuals. The dislocations of literary nationalisms that were at the heart of women's translations became a means of exploring the problematic of dislocation itself. The loose textuality surrounding translation provided an ideal occa-sion for the "revision" (in Adrienne Rich's terms) of existing canons and literary hierarchies that would be a necessary component of becoming publicly valued writers. At the same time, such looseness—understood as the unemphatic attribution of person to text—also constituted the very grounds of women's continued marginalization and invisibility within the literary market.

To take a closer look at this tension surrounding translation, I want to begin by looking at a translation of the *Odyssey* by Hedwig Hülle which appeared in 1826.[46] Whether it was through Johann Heinrich Voß's ground-breaking Homer translations from the early 1780s, Werther's fictional mus-ings on Homer in Goethe's European bestseller, or Friedrich Schlegel's later influential theorizing in *Gespräche über die Poesie* (1800), the Homeric epics would become some of the foundational works to motivate the formal revo-lutions in German poetics that occurred at the turn of the nineteenth cen-tury. Hülle's experiment almost half a century after the rebirth of Homer in German literary circles implied a series of reversals from the Voßian-Werther revival, first and foremost in her choice of rhyme and meter. While Voß had draped Homer in dactyllic hexameter, a form made popular through Klopstock's argument that it was precisely the dactyl and not the iamb that was the rhythm most closely related to the German language,[47] Hülle used the much shorter and swifter form of rhyming iambic tetrameter. If the form of Hülle's translation could be read in one sense as an answer to Voß, it was also in conversation with its immediate poetic environment. Faust's opening monologue in the rhyming couplets of *Knittelvers*—also iambic tetrameter—was naturally one important source for Hülle (as was Schil-ler's "Hero und Leander"), but so was the larger nineteenth-century revival of Shakespeare that exerted a constant pull on German poetry to be more English and thus more iambic. In the same year as Hülle's translation of

Homer, Dorothea Tieck's translation of a portion of Shakespeare's sonnets appeared in the journal *Penelope*.

In engaging with the image and status of Homer, Hülle had inserted herself into one of the most influential poetic projects at the turn of the nineteenth century. But in place of Werther's fantasy that Homer's works offered an ideal image of the patriarchal home or Friedrich Schlegel's universalizing notion of Homer as the "poet of poets," Hülle saw in Homer's Odysseus the playful trickster capable of reversing fortune at numerous turns. Her own playful translation (called a "treie Nachbildung" in the title) importantly contained not just one but two proper names on the title page, not only her married name (which despite appearances [*Hülle* = mantle or cover] was not a pseudonym) but also her birth name of Hoffmeier, which asserted, while not a purely matrilineal nomenclature, at least a pre-marital female identity. Her translation also significantly did not begin with an appeal to the muse, as her source text did, but with the word "Hellas," effacing in the process one of the more prevalent, and restrictive, notions of femininity as the silent inspiration of the male poet. After her translation, Hülle would go on to produce an epistolary novel, *Seraphine* (1830), a collection of poetry and poetic translations (1836), and edit a yearly literary almanac for children (1833–37). Woman as muse here turns into woman as professional author. Translation, like the fortune-reversing hero of the work Hülle chose to translate, became a means of reversing not only the text's particular *fortuna* but a woman's relationship to writing more generally.

If Homer represented one of the central points of attraction for nineteenth-century German translators, then it was of course Shakespeare who occupied another key node.[48] While we have a great deal of work on the so-called "Schlegel-Tieck" edition of Shakespeare's works, named after A. W. Schlegel and Ludwig Tieck, we have very few readings of the Shakespearean engagements of Ludwig's daughter, Dorothea Tieck, who translated six plays for the edition and became the first author to translate the entirety of Shakespeare's sonnets into German.[49] While the sonnet—and in particular the translation of sonnets—played an important role in romantic poetic production in both England and the German states,[50] Shakespeare's sonnets always occupied an uncomfortable position within such sonnet revivals. The romantics' circumvention of Shakespeare's sonnets was part of a persistent uncertainty about the sonnets' position within both the Shakespearean "corpus" and the literary canon more generally.[51] The gender reversal of Shakespeare's sonnets to a young man, the fundamentally dialogical structure of this epideictic genre (the relationship of the "I" and the "you" that was at the core of the sonnet form), the focus on begetting and offspring in Shakespeare's opening set of sonnets, even the ambiguity or plurality of the speaker in the sonnets' opening "we" ("From fairest creatures we desire increase")[52]—such aspects of the Shakespearean sonnet posed problems not only for romantic poetic theory. They also posed significant openings for a woman translator to think about and articulate her art. In place of what Goethe saw the Shakespeare of the plays offering his readers—what he called "das Eigenthümliche unsres Ichs" (the essence of our self),[53] that which we most own as ourselves—the sonnets by contrast were intently concerned with what J. W. Lever called the "antinomies of being,"[54] the problems of giving, taking, borrowing, mortgaging, copying, leasing, wasting, procreating, you *and* I. To take up the translation of Shakespeare's sonnets in their entirety was in some sense to reflect on the problem of supplementarity, of how a work, a corpus, a canon, or even a public was to be closed, constituted, and completed.

And Dorothea Tieck's translations responded in kind. Whether it was her reformulation of the "you" as a gift in the opening sonnet, the equation of being with respite in the thirteenth sonnet, or the rewriting of writerly metaphors like "engrafting" into that of "encircling" (*umgeben*) in sonnet fifteen, Tieck's sonnets continually promoted the contingency and the circularity of the translator's task. There was a vorticular structure to her sonnets' relationship to their source text that stood in stark contrast to the owning and appropriating promoted by her male counterparts' thinking about translation.[55] In place of Shakespeare as a middlepoint (Ludwig Tieck) or a sun (Dumas), Dorothea Tieck's translational universe was neither Ptolemaic nor Copernican, but rather relational and mutually constitutive.

In their Homer and Shakespeare translations, Dorothea Tieck and Hedwig Hülle were engaging the work of two of the most important writers that came to define the horizon of "classics" for romantic literature, altering the image of these precursors in important ways. While women translators were actively engaged with the transmission and thus rethinking of literary classics, whether it was Felicia Hemans's translations of Petrarch, Lope de Vega, or Camões into English or Aloïse de Carlowitz's prizewinning French translation of Klopstock's epic *Messiah*, they also participated in the circulation of contemporary literature across Europe, nowhere more visibly on display than in the translation of novels, from Fanny Tarnow's translation of fifty volumes of French and English novelists into German to Sophie de Maraise's more than twenty volumes of Walter Scott translations into French. In their work as novelistic translators, women writers adhered to both a model of literal and loose translation, freely enacting the "chop and change," in Browning's words, that was advocated, for example, by Wilhelmine von Gersdorf in the preface to her translation of Catherine Maria Sedgwick's *Redwood: A Tale* (which was falsely attributed at the time to James Fenimore Cooper), where she compares the translator to a gardener with pruning sheers.[56] Women explicitly revised the plots of their male sources, as in Therese Huber's invented ending for Jean-Baptiste Louvet's *Émilie de Varmont, ou Le divorce nécessaire* (original 1791, translation 1794), where Emilie remarries in the German translation but not in the French original.[57] But they did so to their female sources as well, as in the example of Isabelle de Montolieu who during the 1820s resentimentalized Jane Austen's desentimentalization of the novel.[58] Far from exhibiting a failure or travesty as some critics have contended, Montolieu's translational work should be read as an important witness to Margaret Cohen's argument about the conflictual social production of the novel at the turn of the nineteenth century.[59] In her over fifty volumes of translation, Montolieu's work was an attempt to reinvigorate through translation a particularly "feminine" literary aesthetic that was gradually being infringed upon by a more "masculine" historical and realist poetics. At the same time, the remarkable number of women who were involved as translators of one of the great exemplars of this new historico-realist poetics, Walter Scott—Sophie de Maraise (23 novels), Fanny Collet (19 novels), Sophie Mayer (12 novels), Elise von Hohenhausen (3 novels and the ballads)—should give us pause to ask whether such involvement was a sign of the actual accessibility of the historical novel for women readers and writers (contrary to what scholars have often asserted) or whether such involvement articulated a large-scale effort of literary co-opting. Why so many women were drawn to Scott's novels as translators and as readers remains a key question in the history of gender and genre and awaits a study unto itself.

If translation functioned on one level as an important site for literary revisioning—for the pruning of literature's "protuberances" in Gersdorf's words—it also provided the occasion for women to explore questions of place and voice, what Barbara Becker-Cantarino has called women's pivotal engagement with the problem of "Mündigkeit," the dual conditions of personal sovereignty and self-expression that we saw dramatized in Kulmann's oscillation between textual invention and figural self-effacement.[60] Such concerns would achieve some of their most poignant expressions in the translational work of Felicia Hemans and in particular her "German Studies," which were a planned series of translations and commentaries on the new literature coming out of the German states and which initially appeared in *The New Monthly Magazine* between 1831 and 1834. Where male writers seemed repeatedly drawn to Goethe's "awful and irregular" *Faust,*

as Hemans called it, Hemans chose to profile the plays of Goethe's earlier classical period, *Iphigenia at Tauris* and *Torquato Tasso*. "The spirit of the
imaginary personages," writes Hemans referring to Goethe's *Iphigenia*, "as
well as of the reader, here moves acquiescently within the prescribed circle
of events, and is seldom tempted beyond, to plunge into the abyss of general speculations upon the lot of humanity."[61] The enclosures of being that
Hemans foregrounds here are as much a call to classical values of harmony
and symmetry as they are to isolation and exile, "the bitter taste of another's
bread, the weary steps by which the stairs of another's house are ascended,"
as she would write in her later piece about *Tasso* (2:353). Like Elise von
Hohenhausen's choice of translating Childe Harold's farewell song, "Good
Night," from the first canto which began with the words, "'Adieu, adieu! My
native shore,'"[62] Iphigenia and Tasso were similarly also banished figures,
under the control of patrons like Thoas and Antonio and not agents of their
own wandering like Faust (whose patron was also his servant). Exile and
silence intersect in Hemans's thinking about women, writing, and translation, a fact suggested through her choice of translating the following lines of
Tasso's speech to Princess Leonora (act 2, scene 1, lines 797–800):

> But, alas!
> The more I listen'd still the more I sank
> In mine own eyes;—I seem'd to die away
> As into some faint echo of the rocks,—
> A shadowy sound—a nothing! (2:355)

> Doch ach je mehr ich horchte, mehr und mehr
> Versank ich vor mir selbst, ich fürchtete
> Wie Echo an den Felsen zu verschwinden,
> Ein Widerhall, ein Nichts mich zu verlieren.

Hemans takes the doubling at work in Goethe's image of sinking before
oneself—"before" in both a spatial and temporal sense—and transforms
it through the pun of eyes/I's into a reflection about the dissolution of self
through multiplicity ("the more I sank in mine own eyes," itself an echo
of a previous citation from *Tasso* in Hemans's essay, where she writes of
"the harvest of the quiet eye"). In transforming Goethe's "Widerhall" (re-
verberation) into the consonant catachresis of "shadowy sound," we can
see how Hemans transforms the acoustic doubling of the passage's visual
doublings into an act of rhetorical doubling as well. The doubling of metaphor through the use of mixed metaphor here underscores the greater rep-

resentational crisis that surrounds the threefold figure of poet, translator, and woman. Translation and transnationalism emerge in Hemans's translations as crucial tools to reflect on problems of self and self-expression, figured for example in her translation of Camões "Sonnet 239," itself a translation of Psalm 137, where she writes: "How shall our voices, on a foreign shore / (We answer'd those whose chains the exile wore,) / The songs of God, our sacred songs, renew?" (1:175). For Hemans, who had already written powerful reflections on the public place of the female poet in such poems as "Corinne at the Capitol," displacement as both a geographic and communicative imperative served as the grounds of poetic renewal.[63]

Overheard in Translation: Sophie Mereau, *La Princesse de Clèves* and the Loose Confession

If the translational work of Hemans and others illustrated various nodes within a larger problematic of women, translation, print, and publicity, the translational work of Sophie Mereau provides us with a single extended engagement with the entire range of these concerns, one that transpires across a variety of languages, genres, and historical periods. Mereau's "original" work has been some of the most researched of all romantic women writers of any national tradition, and yet her body of translations, which constitute almost half of her entire literary output, have been almost uniformly passed over.[64] Mereau is in this sense a classic example of the oversights that ensue when we take a historically contingent notion of authorship and apply it to new categories of authors in order to make room for those new authors. In our attempts to understand Mereau as an author and to include her as a major author of the romantic canon, we have reproduced a notion of authorship that the translations themselves repeatedly call into question.

According to Britta Hannemann, whose recent study of Mereau's translations now represents the most definitive available,[65] Mereau's translations included, among others, unpublished portions of Corneille's *Le Cid*, published editions of Mme de Lafayette's *La Princesse de Clèves*, selections of Ninon de Lenclos's letters, Boccaccio's *Fiammetta* and three tales from the *Decameron*, parts of María de Zayas's *Novelas amorosas y ejemplares* (also attributed to Clemens Brentano), and a translation of John Nott's *Sappho* (based on Ovid's *Heroïdes*), although scholars now suspect that her sister, Henriette Schubart, did most of that translation. Taken as a whole, Mereau translated works by both men and women; works that spanned broad cultural spaces, from the late Italian middle ages to the Spanish and French baroque; works that encompassed a range of genres, from letters, to dramas, to novellas; and works that were about sexual transgressions (Lenclos and Zayas) as well as feminine isolation and suffering (Lafayette, Boccaccio, and Nott).

In a key article that opened up Mereau's translations to scholarly inquiry, Daniel Purdy has argued that her translations aimed to create a continuity of female authorship, that by translating earlier women's writing Mereau was constructing a literary heritage for her own production.[66] Indeed, translation can function as a way for an author to establish precursors and a literary landscape in which to work; in this sense, translation is similar to the act of editing and literary collection, as a translator selects these texts and not those texts to construct a particular heritage. Yet when we look more closely at the entire range of work Mereau translated, it is precisely this notion of textual continuity that was repeatedly framed as problematic. The choice of Lenclos as one of Mereau's patron saints was itself a revealing one, as her life, which we learn in Mereau's biography of her published in Mereau's periodical, *Kalathiskos*, was marked by a genealogical crisis as the older and sexually adventurous Lenclos ultimately ends up sleeping with her own son. The very challenge to romantic poetics that Purdy sees in Mereau has much to do with such transmissional aberrations.

Die Prinzessin von Cleves. Frei nach dem Französischen bearbeitet. Von Sophie Mereau appeared in Dieterich's *Roman-Kalender* for 1799, an abridged translation of Mme de Lafayette's well-known novel, *La Princesse de Clèves* (1678). By the time of the translation Mereau was already a familiar poet to readers, with her work appearing regularly in Schiller's *Horen* and *Musenalmanach*. At the same time, *Die Prinzessin von Cleves* was also not her first translation. She had already translated Corneille's *Cid*, which remained unpublished, as well as two stories from Boccaccio's *Decameron*, which had appeared in *Die Horen* (to which I will return later). But in some sense the translation of Lafayette's work marked an important breakthrough for Mereau, not only through the emphatic placement of her name on the title page—an issue which would remain an issue throughout her career—and not only in the aggressively and openly cavalier way she treated her source text through her "Bearbeitung." Rather, the Lafayette translation, which followed closely on her translation of portions of Ninon de Lenclos's letters, marked a key moment in her emerging concern with problems of access, openness, and control that surrounded bibliographic culture. It established a capacious literary argument about the possibilities and pitfalls of women's translational and transitional occupations.

Lafayette's work was set at the sixteenth-century court of Henry II and concerned the story of a wife who confesses to her husband that she is in love with another man, but who never consecrates the affair. In placing the confession at the heart of the courtly romance, Lafayette's work has repeatedly been read as a kind of founding text of both the modern novel and, indeed, a strain of modern literature more generally. As Roland Galle has suggested, the exceptionality of the speech-act of "confession" at the center of the novel marked a revolutionary break between a courtly aesthetics of dissimulation and an Enlightenment aesthetics of authenticity and sincerity.[67] Confession, according to Peter Brooks, "is the kind of speech in which the individual authenticates his inner truth. . . . [It] creates the inwardness of the person."[68] Indeed, one can see how the very exceptionality at the heart of the speech-act of confession was then underscored in this scene by the way the confession was framed by its speaker: "I am going to make you a confession which no one has ever made to her husband" (Je vais vous faire un aveu, que l'on n'a jamais fait à son mari).[69] To make a unique confession, however, was a tautology. All confessions were by definition unique, not just because they belonged by nature to an individual but because they signaled an exceptional moment in that individual's own life. The confession was the exception within the exception.

In a further amplification of such exceptionality at the core of Lafayette's novel, the private confession takes place not at court but away in the woods at the Princess's remote country estate at Coulommiers, as we can see the confession's exceptionality radiating out to encompass a range of aspects of the novel, from utterance, to character, to setting,[70] making it little wonder that exceptionality would go on to function as one of the primary organizing principles shaping the novel's reception. It provided the very terms of both the novel's initial critique in the hands of seventeenth-century critics— who saw the implausibility of the novel's plot (what wife would ever do this?) as an affront to a reigning aesthetics of novelistic *vraisemblance*—and its subsequent valorization within both a new critical framework of the literary as a form of self-expression *and* a feminist tradition that saw in the Princess's committed adherence to an alternative "script" an ideal form of feminine resistance.[71] The exceptionality staged by the novel thus facilitated its own exceptional status and entry into the literary canon.

It is important to see, however, what such exemplary readings leave out: namely, the act of overhearing, the fact that during the confessional moment *someone else* is also there. A third person, indeed the very object of the confession, occupies this otherwise dyadic confessional space between husband and wife. The crucial element of this scene, then, is not its exceptionality or "unheardofness," in Goethe's terms, but precisely how it is *overheard* and then circulated throughout a larger social system. What matters to the economy of the novel is the way the confessional discourse is incorporated into a more complex circuit of social communication. M. de Nemours will tell the Vidame what he has overheard, who in turn tells his mistress, Mme de Martigues, who passes the story on to Mme la Dauphine. The crucial moment will occur when the Princess hears her own story told back to her in front of M. de Nemours: "If Mme de Clèves had at first been saddened by the thought that she had played no part in this adventure, Mme la Dauphine's last words brought her to despair as her role was now all too evident" (*PC*, 350). Confession thus gives way in the novel more properly speaking to the speech-act of digression—to the accumulation of narrative voices as we increasingly move from forms of direct to indirect speech. Such digressive speech will gradually narratively fan out as large portions of the novel concern characters' tales of losing something, whether a letter, a portrait, a lover, or of course a confession. As April Alliston has argued, in Lafayette the spatial breaks of digressive speech capture the temporal fault lines that surrounded the transmission of women's writing and that were figured in the untimely death of the Princess's mother.[72] But a key aspect of this substitution of digressive speech for confessional speech is the way it reformulates speech more generally not as an authentication of some inner, personal truth but as an invocation of the way speech itself always involves the pressure of an other. Seen in this light, confession's truth in Lafayette is not the truth of the confession, but how it is deployed, circulated, and reused—how private speech is publicized and the exploration of the social uncertainties that follow. The truth of the confession is in that figure of the third term standing for the social channel.

If we turn more specifically to Mereau's translation, I think we can find some crucial pointers that draw attention to Mereau's interest in amplifying the availability of speech at the heart Lafayette's work. On the one hand, Mereau's translation does much to accommodate the work to her romantic audience. She renames her heroine "Marie" and cuts many of the digressions concerning courtly life, offering her largely bourgeois female readers someone just like themselves. Her work seems in this regard to underscore the singularity of her heroine. But on the other hand, Mereau's translation also amplifies at key junctures precisely the novel's attention to the circulatory nature of such singular utterances. If we turn to the novel's close, we see that Lafayette's text ends on the words:

She passed part of the year in this religious home and the other part at her own home; but she did so in retirement, occupying herself with tasks even more severe than the most austere of convents; her life, which was brief, provided inimitable examples of virtue. (*PC*, 390)

Elle passait une partie de l'année dans cette maison religieuse et l'autre chez elle; mais dans une retraite et dans des occupations plus saintes que celles des couvents les plus austères; et sa vie, que fut assez courte, laissa des exemples de vertu inimitables.

Mereau ends hers this way:

Marie enjoyed for a time a spiritual life; her soul took pleasure in her love for heaven and for her fellow man, and the number of happy souls increased in the region where she lived.[73]

Marie genoß noch eine Zeit lang ein geistiges Daseyn; ihre Seele ergoß sich in Liebe gegen den Himmel und die Menschen, und die Zahl der Glücklichen mehrte sich in der Gegend, wo sie lebte.

In her study of Mereau's translations, Britta Hannemann has commented upon how similar these two endings appear to be.[74] And yet the differences between the two passages are significant, even if subtle. Where Lafayette's original emphasizes the plurality of virtuous *acts* as an index of her continued exceptionality—and thus inimitability—Mereau on the other hand chooses to emphasize the plurality of those affected by her—not the acts, but the recipients of those acts. The Princess does not leave things behind, as in the French verb *laisser*, but multiplies them and shares them, as in the German verb *sich mehren*. In place of a model of exceptionality as a form of feminine defiance, as in Nancy K. Miller's reading of Lafayette,[75] the final idea that Mereau's translation performs highlights instead the transmittability, and thus translatability, of her recirculated heroine. It reverses, in other words, the damaging effects of the loose confession to a woman's identity and replaces it instead with a morally infused model of feminine circulation. It is the heroine's translatability—and *not* her exceptionality—that becomes the grounds in Mereau for the engendering of a female community.

Such an emphasis on the translatability of her source text is registered even earlier in Mereau's translation when she has the narrator, and not the Princess, say that this is the most singular confession in the history of literature (a point that Hannemann leaves out of her discussion). Where Lafayette writes, "I will make you a confession which no woman has ever made to her husband," Mereau writes, "His doubts, his concerns rose until finally the most singular confession that a wife has ever made to her husband crossed her lips" (Seine Zweifel, seine Besorgnisse stiegen, bis endlich das seltenste Geständnis, welches ein Weib ihrem Gatten je gethan hat, über ihre Lippe schwebte) (263). Instead of having the confessor directly announce her confession ("*I* will make you a confession"), Mereau tells it from the perspective of the external narrator. Mereau's recourse to indirect speech, like her alteration of the conclusion, enacts a particular interpretation of Lafayette's work. She places the emphasis not on the confessional logic of the Princess's primary utterance but instead on the crucial role that the borrowing of that confession plays in the novel, that the act of confession is always implicated in the control of the confession by another. In a novel about overhearing, Mereau enacts her own gesture of overhearing at the narratological level by shifting the control of the Princess's confession from the "I" of the character to the "I" of the narrator. Her translation highlights at discrete points the appropriatability of narrative that was at the heart of this novel and that was the very precondition of translation itself.[76]

María de Zayas's *Novelas amorosas y ejemplares* and the Betrayal of Writing

María de Zayas's *Novelas amorosas y ejemplares* (1637), which Mereau collaboratively translated with Clemens Brentano, appeared as part of her edited collection, *Spanische und Italienische Novellen* (1804).[77] To move to it from Madame de Lafayette's *La Princesse de Clèves* is to remain within similar thematic concerns while extending those concerns to new terrain. If the crisis that *La Princesse de Clèves* enacted was that of hearing your own story told back to you—that your personal narrative was something you could lose control of—then the crisis of Zayas's *Novelas amorosas y ejemplares* was not *recognizing* your own story when it was told back to you.

Zayas was one of the most popular writers of the Spanish Golden Age, referred to by one contemporary as the "Sibyl of Madrid," and her book sales were surpassed only by Cervantes and Quevedo.[78] By the nineteenth century, however, her salacious tales of torture, rape, dismemberment, murder, and, most of all, infidelity, had drifted into obscurity and disrepute.[79] In resurrecting Zayas as a supplement to Cervantes as the central romantic precursor, Mereau was in some sense doing for the Spanish Golden Age what Dorothea Tieck would do for Shakespeare by translating his sonnets in full. (Tieck would continue in the same vein with Cervantes himself by translating his late novel, *Los trabajos de Persiles y Sigismunda* [The Trials of Persiles and Sigismunda, original 1617, translation 1837], as a counterweight to the romantic canonicity of *Don Quixote*, which her father had translated). The challenge Mereau's translation posed to the romantic literary establishment was not simply a matter of gender, however, but was also importantly one of genre and form. As one reviewer exclaimed, "What? the Mad. Mereau who was once so celebrated by us is now writing Spanish novellas, is writing sonnets, burlesques? She too inclines to that invidious school? Down with her immediately!"[80] Once again it was the sonnet, embedded as it was in numerous places within Zayas's novella collection, that did not "fit" the (male) romantic corpus, posing problems of both propriety and unity. But one can also begin to see here how a third scandalous aspect of Mereau's resurrection of this text was neither its genre nor its content, but the communicative poetics that it promoted.

Zayas's novella collection belongs to the popular early-modern genre of feminine rewritings of Boccaccio's *Decameron*, with a few key differences: it is set at court and not at a country estate, two tales are told per evening instead of ten, poetry plays a much larger role within the novellas, the plague has become a "fever" for the main character, Lisis, who is love sick, and the narrators all crucially lack parents—the men have no mothers, the women no fathers. As in Lafayette, where the Princess's mother dies early, leaving her without a moral compass to navigate the social intrigues in which she becomes embroiled, the genealogical crisis in Zayas is similarly intertwined with problems of overhearing and communicative uncertainty. But where the act of overhearing follows the confession in Lafayette and then functions as the organ that publicizes it, the overheard story in the first tale of the opening night of Zayas precedes and produces the confession. Establishing a paradigm for all of the later tales, the first story of the first night begins with a young man, Fabio, who is walking in the mountains when he overhears a voice singing a song. "Scarcely had he caught his weary breath when there came to his ears a soft delicate voice whose low tones seemed not too distant, suggesting that their source was not far away."[81] The disembodied voice leads the young man to search out the song's source: "The time, the place, desire, and the mountains made him want to continue. His only consolation for the fact that [the song] did not last longer was the thought that he might soon delight his eyes and his soul with this sight just as the voice had delighted his ears" (14–15, translation modified from original; 34, 21). It is in such moments where one can see just how attractive Zayas's work might have been to romantic writers and readers. The redirection of desire staged by this scene—from the realm of nature to the body of the poet—almost perfectly prefigured a romantic poetics that was moving from a representational to a constructive theory of language, where the speaker was the ultimate referent of speech.

Instead of an identifiable poetic body, however, Fabio discovers a body that resists identification. "I found you and I notice that in your face and in your bearing you are not what your dress indicates: your face does not match your clothes, nor do your words go with the disguise you wear" (16; 36; 24). The cross-dressed body that represents a problem of address—of the relationship between speaker and speech—is then undressed through the performance of his/her confessional discourse. As the narrator tells us, this character will make Fabio into the "archive of her secrets" (archivo de sus secretos, Archiv ihrer Geheimnisse, omitted in the English translation; 13; 19). The singer confesses that "he" is a woman, a widow named Jacinta, who has disguised herself as a shepherd boy. The widow continues to tell Fabio her story about being betrayed by her lover, and it appears that the confessional moment is consecrated and the biographical project—the attribution of song to person—complete. The legibility of lyric is made coeval with the legibility of the body.

When we turn to the second novella of the first night, however, we encounter an altogether inverted problem. Once again, we have the tale of a woman's betrayal, this time of Aminta by her lover, Jacinto. And as in the first story, we have another act of cross-dressing, as Aminta will change her name to Jacinto and become the page to her unfaithful lover by the same name. Aminta/Jacinto will then sing a song to Jacinto, her lover, about a certain "Jacinto" who has betrayed his lover. But in a reversal of the first night, Jacinto will assume, like Fabio, that the object of the lyric narrative (Jacinto) is the speaker not the addressee—Jacinto the cross-dressing page and not Jacinto the unfaithful man. Unlike in Lafayette, where the Princess hears her own story told back to her and the tellers are unaware whose story it is, in the second story of the first night of Zayas someone hears his own story told back to him, but he does not know that it is his story.

The significance of Zayas's work for Mereau, I want to suggest, lay in the way it conflates erotic betrayal with a communicative practice of betrayal, the way speech and sex continually overlap here. To betray *someone* is to be unfaithful to him or her, but to betray *something* is to reveal information that is not supposed to be revealed. As an act of communication, betrayal is an act of unwanted, or unauthorized, disclosure. Like overhearing, the story of betrayal concerns the depiction of a social space in which the control of communication has become highly problematic, a space that dramatizes the incomplete possession of one's own speech. As Goethe would write in his "translation" of the medieval Persian poet, Hafez, in the *West-East Divan,* "In vain is the poet silent / Writing poetry is indeed betrayal" (Dichter ist umsonst verschwiegen / Dichten selbst ist schon Verrath).[82]

In reviving these early-modern courtly tales about erotic and communicative infidelities for a romantic audience, Mereau was, on the one hand, addressing—or rather redressing—a longstanding intersection of femininity, infidelity, and translation captured in the well-known phrase, *les belles infidèles,* that referred to a seventeenth-century school of loose French translation. These cross-dressing tales of women's constancy and men's infidelity were in some sense an attempt to legitimize women's writerly identities, to reposition them away from a moral, linguistic, and aesthetic looseness.

But not completely. Woman's erotic constancy here is still married to an important element of communicative infidelity. Jacinta of the first story gives away more than she wishes, disclosing her location, her identity, and ultimately her story. Aminta of the second tale will give away more than *he* wishes, disclosing his and her story without him realizing this. Mereau's interest in the early modern, then, goes beyond a concern for a historical period when women were afforded a greater range of public identities, a period that predated a historical consensus surrounding the purely domestic identity of femininity. Instead, Mereau's pointing to courtly literature incorporates an interest in the modes of communication through which such public identities were articulated and retained. Mereau's engagement with the figure of betrayal in her translations of early modern texts becomes, in this sense, a means of thinking about the relationship of the act of translation to public speech at a moment when the conditions of publicity were shifting overwhelmingly away from the immediate environment of courtly life towards a highly mediated space of social interaction through books. Pairing translation with betrayal was not simply an identification of the ways a translator was unfaithful to her original; it was a way of identifying translation—and the realm of written public speech to which it belonged as part to whole—as an experience of losing control of one's speech. Translation was not only where an author lost control of his or her own words—where he or she was "betrayed" by the translator—it was also the space where the translator persistently betrayed some textual surplus: the language and culture of the original. As in the tales of Zayas's betrayed and betraying women, there was a referential crisis that surrounded the practice of translation, one that contained an important commentary on women's complicated position as professional writers. There were risks to such looseness—as in the first tale of the discovered Jacinta or the oppressed Princess from Lafayette—but there was also power in the pairing of dissimulation and disclosure, as in the figure of Aminta from Zayas's second tale of the first night who disclosed *without* revealing, indeed who disclosed someone else's story without him recognizing either her identity or his story. Understanding bookish culture as a space of perpetual betrayal—as a space marked by acts of dis-closure—was not only a challenge to traditional ways of thinking about books as bounded universes of words. It was also a means of developing strategies for women to go public and to make new publics in the process.

Boccaccio, Privacy, and Partiality: *Fiammetta* and *Decameron* 10.3

Mereau's final translation before her untimely death in childbirth was of Boccaccio's *Fiammetta*—the first-person story of a woman who has been betrayed in love but who steadfastly refuses to betray her own identity. This final translation constituted a kind of answer to the problem of communicative surplus that Mereau saw at the heart of bookish publics. It offered a book-length lesson in the poetics of privacy. That it was, or had to be, culled from a pre-print bibliographic heritage was all the more to the point of identifying an alternative way of thinking about books. If Zayas and Lafayette had gestured towards surplus as a precondition of publicness—a surplus that posed both an opportunity and a problem—Boccaccio served as a site for Mereau to interrogate a related yet different aspect of bibliographic publics: that of partiality.

For German romantic readers, *Fiammetta* had been popularized through Friedrich Schlegel's well-known review essay on the available works of Boccaccio,[83] who Schlegel sought to resurrect by assimilating him to the larger romantic fascination with the topos of unrequited love as a form of idealization and the absolute. One could see such thematic concerns at work in Mereau's circle through the translation by her sister, Henriette Schubart, of John Nott's novelistic adaptation of Ovid's tale of Sappho from the *Heroïdes*.[84] But where for Schlegel *Fiammetta* was reducible to a story of pure love—"everything is grand and universal, there is only love, nothing but love"[85]—a crucial element of the story was the way it coupled confession with illegibility, the way it dramatized revelation without transparency. "Even though I am writing things that are very true," Fiammetta declares, "I have arranged them in such a way that, except for the one who knows everything as well as I do (for he is the cause of them all), no one else, no matter how sharp his intellect, could discover who I am."[86]

In her translation of the line, "no one else . . . could discover who I am," Mereau renders the Italian *conoscere* (to recognize or know someone) as the

German *errathen* (to guess). Mereau's choice of words here not only nicely echoes the central role that *verrathen* (to betray) had played in Zayas—indeed, in the passage concerning the discovery of Jacinta in the first night Mereau had explicitly used the verb *verrathen* in place of the Spanish verb *mostraba* (to demonstrate or point). It also established the notion of *errathen* as a negative ideal—where the verb *raten* (to advise or give counsel) coupled with the prefix *er-* (suggesting the completion of an action) conveyed a sense of full communion with another. Privacy and nondisclosure emerged as the aims of writing in *Fiammetta*. When Mereau translated Fiammetta's *vaga penna* (vague, but also graceful or beautiful pen) as *zärtlich* (tender), she was drawing together the dual literary ideals of elegance and anonymity under the rubric of the feminine.[87] If translation was marked in Zayas and Lafayette by a something more—a linguistic and cultural surplus—in Mereau's Boccaccio translation it was marked by an equal and opposite "never enough"—the impossibility of accessing a textual and linguistic elsewhere.

In her study of the notion of privacy in eighteenth-century literature, Patricia Meyer Spacks has noted the urgency with which women writers thought about and depicted forms of privacy in their writing. "Because of women's comparative lack of freedom," writes Spacks, "their strategies for privacy display special ingenuity, and sometimes a certain desperation."[88] As Helga Meise has suggested, the notion of "innocence" that surrounded femininity in the eighteenth century participated in creating a social reality in which women were never left alone, that they were always subject to forms of social surveillance and control and thus always at risk of being overheard.[89] In this context, one can see just how attractive the idea of *not* being overheard could be to a woman writer, how powerful it would have been for a woman to truly be alone.

But it is important to see how such valorization of privacy was not a retreat to the private, but rather, as Spacks has argued, that it contained a decidedly public and political dimension. Freedom *from*, in Spacks's words, also implied a freedom *to*.[90] Such privacy understood as an alternative writerly space, a space of one's own, emerged in this sense as a powerful technique for creating a new public. In place of the androgyny that critics have noted as a characteristic of Mereau's "original" writing,[91] her translations were marked by a fundamental awareness of sexual and communicative difference. *Fiammetta* helps us see how the more general "subjectlessness" of her writing, in Christa Bürger's words,[92] assumes an important political dimension because of the paradoxical capacity of the self's illegibility to carve out a distinctly female literary public. The plaintive genre of the *heroïdes* to which *Fiammetta* belonged was framed not as the breakdown of community in Mereau—as a sign of women's atomism and isolation[93]—but as the means of establishing greater correspondences among women. Resistance to overhearing—aloneness and illegibility—became profoundly empowering and profoundly feminine in the work of Mereau, prefiguring in many ways the discourse of the room of one's own that Virginia Woolf would construct a century later.

In order to understand the extent to which Mereau was invested in these questions of the partiality of books, and the way Boccaccio would repeatedly serve as the literary site where she would explore such concerns, we need to turn to one final piece of evidence, her translation of the third story from the tenth day of Boccaccio's *Decameron*, which appeared in Schiller's journal *Die Horen* in 1797.[94] All of the stories from the tenth day in Boccaccio concern the larger theme of *magnificenzia*, which we might translate as "magnanimity," or the question of giving and reciprocity. This particular tale concerns Nathan and Mithridanes, where Nathan is the most generous man in the world and Mithridanes wishes to imitate him. Upon realizing the impossibility of his task, however, Mithridanes decides to murder Nathan, and in his generosity, Nathan, who learns of the plot, decides to give his life to Mithridanes. But Mithridanes decides he cannot go through with it. In return for his generosity of offering Mithridanes his life, Nathan asks Mithridanes in return if Mithridanes could instead become Nathan so that his generosity could be extended beyond his corporeal limits. This too Mithridanes in the end refuses. He cannot "take" Nathan's life in either sense of the word.

Mereau's translation of this short tale by Boccaccio offered readers a thought-provoking allegory of translation and, by extension, writing understood as a process of translation (a fact already encoded in Boccaccio's original through the name Mithridanes that diverged through a single letter from the famed Roman emperor, Mithridates, who it was said could speak all twenty-two languages of the nations he ruled and therefore did not require an interpreter). Where the texts by women that Mereau had translated seemed to authorize overhearing and intervention—that is, their translatability—the texts by her male source authorized the *limits* of overhearing: what others could not take and what one could not give. In her translation of Lafayette, Mereau had made the inimitable Princess imitable. In her translation of Zayas, Mereau had selected a work that revolved around the problem of betrayal, around the openness and too-muchness of communication. In both cases, Mereau had underlined the translatability of writing. In the work Mereau translated from the *Decameron*, however, one could never completely take someone else's story and make it one's own. Just as Mithridanes could never be Mithridates, *his* story (Boccaccio) could never completely be *her* story (Mereau). In *Fiammetta*, we encountered a text whose author remained explicitly opaque to us, as *her* story could never completely be made *our* story.

In placing the figure of overhearing (and its opposite, privacy) at the heart of her corpus of translations, Mereau was making a powerful argument about the relationship of translation to the work of women writers. Her work identified how an engagement with the foreign, whether of language, historical period, or gender, could serve as a productive source of writerly work and initiate new literary geographies and new literary publics. It placed dis-closure and dis-placement at the center of women's writing. But in her attention to the figure of overhearing, Mereau was also making an argument about the relationship of women writers to the bookish public sphere more generally in which translation functioned as an important initiatory literary practice. Translation was not only a means of getting into print. It was also a means of thinking about the nature of print and the printed book. Interlacing the categories of translation, the book, and overhearing offered a way of thinking about bookish publics as fundamentally open, authorizing women writers to participate in debates and discourses not addressed to them. Conceptualizing translation as a practice of overhearing afforded a position of power to women writers, allowing them to use the growing availability of printed books to "talk back" to institutions organized to exclude them.[95] It identified openness—in both the communicative and moral sense—as a constitutive feature of modern book culture, opening up the book to heretofore excluded members.

At the same time, Mereau's work consistently pointed to the costs, as well as the dangers, of this imagined openness of the book. In the partiality that surrounded the soundscape of overhearing—whether it was the Princess's story that no one knew referred to her, Jacinto's story that he did not know referred to himself, or, most significantly, Mithridanes who could not in the end become Nathan (or his precursor Mithridates)—Mereau was identifying the way public knowledge was always a form of incomplete knowledge.[96] To overhear was not only to participate in that which had not necessarily been addressed to you. It was also to overhear in the sense of to "overlook," to miss or skip something. The partiality of the overheard story drew attention to another key feature of modern publicness—that "the" public always gave way to numerous publics.[97] The advantage of this was that such partiality allowed new groups and new public identities to emerge; it offered the precondition of creating a new literature of one's own.

The disadvantage was that as every opening facilitated ever more openings, the openness of both publicness and the book meant that these spaces also gradually fell to pieces. In an age of too many books, one never knew, could never know, the whole story.

Mereau's *Fiammetta* was thus a sign of the growing partiality of book culture during and after romanticism. But it was also a sign of the desire to put an end to this constant culture of disclosure. As Peter Brooks would argue almost two centuries later about modern media more generally, "Contemporary society's apparent demand for transparency . . . has created a situation in which there is no evident end to the confessional process, no ritual of closure."[98] *Fiammetta* was precisely such a ritual of closure. Openness was ultimately about not just access *for* individuals but also access *to* individuals. The book's increasing availability, according to Mereau, was always a function of the increasing availability of the self. Whether it was the embattled Princess or the discovered and disclosed Jacinta, the continual possibility of being overheard posed a significant threat to a notion of individual sovereignty. Publicness was a dangerous space for private selves. The prescience and insight of Mereau's translational work was precisely its diagnosis of this dialectic of the book: the way the openness of the printed book constituted both a fundamental contribution as well as a basic challenge to any personal or political order.

CHAPTER SIX

Adapting

Word and image are correlates that eternally search for one another.

—J. W. Goethe

Romantic Lines

With the publication of *The Wild Ass's Skin* in August 1831, Honoré de Balzac not only emerged as one of the major literary figures of the nineteenth century, he also invented the visual epigraph (fig. 6.1).[1] It was a citation of the wavy line from volume 9 of Laurence Sterne's *The Life and Opinions of Tristram Shandy, Gentleman* (1759–67), which was made by a flourish of Corporal Trim's stick in the air in a conversation with Uncle Toby on the perils of marriage (fig. 6.2). In citing *Tristram Shandy*, Balzac was of course citing a work that had become famous for its visual elements, from the blank, black, and marbled pages, to its pagination jokes, to the various typographical events of asterisks and dashes (9,560 of them).[2] Sterne's own wavy line was itself a citation, or parody, of Hogarth's notion of the serpentine line as the line of beauty from the *Analysis of Beauty* and was thus integrally tied to eighteenth-century debates about the relationship between lines, the visual arts, and social distinction. But in fusing the scriptural and the visual through the device of the visual epigraph, a move that was accentuated by turning the vertical line on its side to have it look more like script, Balzac was also drawing attention to what had become one of the crucial features of the romantic bibliographic universe: the dynamic interaction between text and image through the proliferation of illustrated books. The wavy line not only captured an ancient notion of narration in the figure of Ariadne's

LA

PEAU DE CHAGRIN,

ROMAN PHILOSOPHIQUE,

PAR M. DE BALZAC.

(Sterne, *Tristram Shandy*, chap. cccxiii.)

TOME PREMIER.

PARIS,

CHARLES GOSSELIN, LIBRAIRE,
RUE SAINT-GERMAIN-DES-PRÉS, N° 9;

URBAIN CANEL, LIBRAIRE,
RUE DU BAC, N° 104.

M DCCC XXXI.

Figure 6.1   The visual epigraph from the title page of Honoré de Balzac, *La Peau de Chagrin*, vol. 1 (1831). Courtesy of the Pierpont Morgan Library, New York.

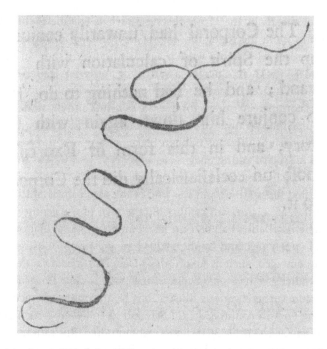

Figure 6.2   Corporal Trim's flourish from Laurence Sterne, *The Life and Opinions of Tristram Shandy, Gent.* (1767), 9:17. Courtesy of the Rare Books and Special Collections Division, McGill University Library.

thread,[3] which was itself addressed by Sterne in a series of visual jokes about his digressive style (volume 6, chapter 40). More importantly, the wavy line marked a fundamental threshold between visual and linguistic signs. The wavy line as epigraph was in some sense *the* image of the interaction between text and image, an expression of an increasingly sophisticated intermedial sensibility that was emerging in romantic readers and writers.

The explosion of the number of illustrated books and the number of illustrations in books is often dated to the republication of *Gil Blas* by Victor Paulin in 1835 that contained over 600 wood-engraved vignettes designed by Jean Gigoux.[4] But early-nineteenth-century readers were well aware that major illustrated French editions of Goethe and Walter Scott from the 1820s had helped pave the way for this later expansion.[5] Balzac's own homage to *Tristram Shandy* was preceded by another piece of Sterneana, Charles Nodier's *Histoire du Roi de Bohême et de ses sept chateaux* (1830), which was based on an untold story of Corporal Trim's (volume 8, chapter 19) and which contained fifty vignettes by Tony Johannot, illustrator of Balzac's *The Wild Ass's Skin*. But in book markets that were less shaken by the French

Revolution, already by the 1790s observers such as Friedrich Schlegel were complaining about the vogue for "Kupferstichromane," or illustrated novels, and treatises were being written against the new trend.[6] In England, by the late 1780s there emerged a variety of authorial "galleries" which served as both spaces of public exhibition for the visualization of literature and as commercial outlets for the sale of prints and illustrated books.[7] Such popular mobilization of readers as seers coincided with illustrative experiments such as those of William Blake, whose forty-three engravings adorned a reissue of Young's *Night Thoughts* (1797), as well as the translation into English of Lavater's *Essays on Physiognomy* (1792) that contained eight hundred illustrations and was one of the most important illustrated books of the late eighteenth century. By the turn of the century, German and French miscellanies had become key sources for the circulation of often allegorical engravings, and by the 1820s a new genre of illustrated travel books had emerged, such as Jakob Alt's *Malerische Donaureise* (1818–23), Charles Nodier's *Voyages pittoresques et romantiques dans l'ancienne France* (1820f.), and Turner's various illustrations to a number of "picturesque" tours of the English countryside. *Gil Blas* and its followers—such as the illustrated *Don Quichotte* (1836) with its eight hundred illustrations designed by Johannot—were thus much more the culmination of a process of equating reading with seeing than its beginning.

If one of the key aspects of illustrated books at the turn of the nineteenth century was the sheer number of illustrations that began to populate text, another important feature was the heterogeneity of such illustrations. Romantic book illustration seemed to mirror the larger romantic experimentations with form, producing a visual equivalent to Lukacs's "Gattungsverschlungenheit." Whether it was the revival of classical outline illustrations, medieval marginal illustrations, early-modern wood engraving and the use of decorated letters and head-pieces, or the introduction of new visual technologies such as steel-plate engraving and lithography and new types of illustrated books such as landscape books, authorial galleries, personal albums, and sketch-books, looking at books encompassed a vast array of visual experience during the romantic period. Indeed, the growing overlap between seeing and reading was accompanied by a larger expansion of visual culture more generally. As William St. Clair has written on the romantic period, "The explosion of the reading of literary texts was accompanied by an explosion in the viewing of engraved pictures,"[8] a point that would be adroitly exploited in Goethe's *Elective Affinities* (1809) and visually rendered in Georg Emanuel Opiz's watercolor series on the Leipzig Book Fair from the 1820s with its depiction of elegant crowds pressing in on the stalls for new prints. And as Gillen D'Arcy Wood has shown, such expanding visual commodities were not only limited to an emerging mass-market for prints but were part of an expanding public culture of spectacle that included theaters, museums, panoramas, and popular exhibits of oriental novelties.[9]

Despite this overwhelming diffusion of visual culture during the romantic period, or perhaps precisely because of it, histories of romanticism have tended to adhere to a fundamental narrative of romantic iconoclasm. Whether it is Gerhard Neumann's notion of a romantic "media crisis" between the "optical-imaginary" and the "conceptual-scriptural,"[10] Manfred Schneider's dialectic of a romantic *Bildersturm* and *Bilderflut* (iconoclasm *and* flood of images),[11] W. J. T. Mitchell and James Heffernan's notion of a "paragonal" relationship between text and image more broadly,[12] Alexandra Wettlaufer's study of the "pen vs. paintbrush" in postrevolutionary France,[13] or D'Arcy Wood's argument about the "shock of the real" and romanticism's development in reaction to popular visual culture,[14] all of this work maintains a basic structural antagonism between the romantic—and the notion of literature it has bequeathed us—and the image. Literature after 1800 emerges, and arguably continues to be thought of, as radically antipictorial.

In place of emphasizing its aversion to popular visual culture, I am interested in this chapter in drawing out romantic literature's deep interaction with the image—and one type of image in particular, book illustration.[15] If one of the key historical realities of the turn of the nineteenth century was the growing prevalence of illustrated books—and the number of illustrations in illustrated books—my aim here is to understand how the texts within and around those books were engaging with this increasingly visual bibliographic experience. At the same time, I want to explore how illustrations in books were themselves addressing through the use of new graphic practices the intermedial origins of visual art, the way the romantic image and the modes of envisioning that it promoted were crucially indebted to the medium of the printed book.

The illustrated book offers us one of the most emphatic examples of the intermedial nature of the early-nineteenth-century bibliographic imagination. How could these overlapping spaces of text and image function not solely as arenas of anxiety and disgust but importantly as spaces of creativity and innovation as well? How can the romantic engagement with the reproducible illustration be read as part of a larger engagement with the problem of reproducibility itself that was gradually shaping the romantic bibliocosmos? And how might romantic reflections on such intermedial problems as "translation," "caption," and "illustration" address contemporary concerns about the interpretability, and thus captionability, of our ever-expanding image world?[16] That is to say, if one of the key possibilities opened up by digital writing today is the saturation of text with images—and the urgent question of their dual legibility—how can the romantic book serve as an instructive guide in understanding the creative potential of this marriage of media?

In bringing together the oft-addressed question of ekphrasis—verbal representations of visual representations—and the under-addressed field of book illustration, this chapter tries to identify a number of ways that romantic writers and artists were exploring how the practices of reading and seeing increasingly inflected one another at the turn of the nineteenth century and how such inflections could serve as sources of creative and epistemological innovation. The book as an object of inquiry becomes a key tool in breaking down disciplinary divisions that have traditionally walled-off literary and art historical discourses from one another. At the same time, it reintroduces an important readerly experience that has too often been bracketed from literary study. What happens when we read Balzac with Tony Johannot, Goethe with Moritz Retzsch, Nepomuk Strixner, and Eugen Neureuther, and Stendhal with himself? For such writers questions of illustration, illustrative writing, and technologies of illustration were essential for their development as writers. An engagement with bibliographic pictorialism was the starting point for thinking about writing and the book. As Samuel Coleridge would say, "Without drawing I feel myself but half invested in language."[17]

In order to approach this romantic concern with the question of illustration, I will begin, following Balzac, with the figure of the line. If, as Garret Stewart has shown, the wavy line became the fundamental sign of the book within a painterly tradition of reading,[18] what did the wavy line mean in a literary-bibliographic tradition of seeing? The story of the romantic line will take us deep into the cultural terrain of the romantic age, bringing together a diverse range of illustrative practices from the late eighteenth and early nineteenth centuries, from the vogue for silhouette and outline drawings, to the rising fascination with the sketch (both visual and verbal), to popularized notions of the arabesque, to scientific breakthroughs such as Chladni's planar representations of sound, Goethe's work on plants, Fourier's trigonometric solutions to the problem of heat diffusion, and Humboldt's cartographical work on global isotherms. And it will draw together a range of textual experiments, from Balzac's Wild Ass's Skin (1831) and his "Unknown Masterpiece" (1831–47), both of which appeared in parts in the illustrated serial L'Artiste; to Goethe's novella "St. Joseph the Second," which initially appeared in Cotta's illustrated Ladies' Pocket-Book (1810) and then later in

Wilhelm Meister's Travels (1821/29); to Stendhal's illustrated handwritten autobiography, *The Life of Henry Brulard* (1835).

As we will see, such romantic interest in the line depended on the fundamental capacity of the line to straddle visual and scriptural representation, its ability to capture a notion of the "graphic" that was simultaneously legible as both writing and image. Where the wavy line functioned as the quintessential eighteenth-century figure of distinction (whether social or medial), the romantic line by contrast participated in fostering an *intermedial* and *intersocial* literacy at a historical juncture that witnessed the dramatic expansion and availability of both visual imagery and textual material, very often in the same bibliographic place. Whether wavy or straight, the line seemed to be a key figural place where romantic writers and artists explored the breakdown of a variety of categories, indeed, of the categorical itself. As William Blake would dramatically declare, "Leave out the line and you leave out life itself."[19] Following the line through the romantic bibliocosmos reveals a series of lines that consistently resist the line's twin identities as a marker of either distinction (the outline) or linearity (teleology). The historical significance of this particular investment in the line should not be overlooked if we remember that the serpentine line of the Laocoön statue served as one of *the* major visual sites in the eighteenth century to motivate a differentiation between the visual and the literary arts. William Blake's engraving that reconfigured Laocoön surrounded by a sea of aphorisms was perhaps the most pointed example of this romantic rejection of such distinguishing lines. The romantic interest in the line was a way of exploring the possibility of textual and visual simultaneity, a simultaneity that nevertheless always bordered on illegibility at the moment of such synthesis. Medial simultaneity was always poised on a temporal threshold, constantly threatening to move from one space to another and thus losing the availability (and visibility) of this other medial space. The romantic line persistently, and paradoxically, tended to represent a vanishing point, a point that I will take up at the close of the chapter by looking at how the contemporary German writer W. G. Sebald refashions the line of beauty— the line as a sign of distinction—into a mark of extinction.

Afterimages: Goethe and the Lily

At six-thirty in the morning on May 17, 1807, Goethe began dictating the opening chapter of *Wilhelm Meister's Travels* with the words, "In the shade of a mighty cliff sat Wilhelm . . ."[20] In place of God's command, "Let there be light!" (in Luther's translation: "Es werde Licht!"), Goethe began his sequel

with his hero sitting in the shade, a mixed visual space of both light and dark
that simultaneously conjured a range of intertextual references. The shade
not only offered an alternative creation myth to that of the Judeo-Christian,
where a biblical poetics of revelation was being displaced by a poetics of cumulative mediation. As a novel intimately concerned with ways of knowing,
the opening words also recalled philosophy's origins in Plato's cave, where
the wanderer sitting beneath an outdoor cliff was situated in a far different
space of projected knowledge than that of the enclosed philosopher's cave.
At the same time, the shade also pointed towards the shades of classical
mythology, those spectral representatives of the dead (written as *Erinnen*
in Goethe's first version of *Iphigenia* to conjure up the notion of *erinnern* or
remembering) who represented what Fritz Breithaupt has called "embodied
debt."[21] Writing a sequel in old age, such remembering of the dead seemed
an appropriate way to begin one's last novel. The novel as sequel—indeed
one could say the novel in general for Goethe—was in some sense a larger
exploration of what it meant to come afterwards. Beginning in the shade
was a sign of beginning in the second degree.

If the shade conjured a visual space with a complex set of archetypal
textual associations, it also drew upon what Robert Rosenblum has identified as one of the most important trends in the visual arts at the turn of the
nineteenth century: the rising fascination with outline drawings (*Umriß* in
German), which were closely linked to the vogue for silhouette drawings
(*Schattenriß*).[22] Beginning with John Flaxman's illustrations to Homer that
appeared in Italy in 1793 and later in Leipzig in 1804 and London in 1805,
outline drawings began a vigorous life as a form of textual illustration in a
double sense: as an illustrative practice that most often appeared in books
and as a practice that also derived from books.[23] Flaxman's designs were
indebted to a classical tradition of Greek vase illustration which he had
studied through the publication of Wilhelm Tischbein's illustrated edition
of Sir William Hamilton's vase collection, a collection which Goethe himself had seen during his Italian journey.[24] In its explicit rejection of what
Rosenblum called "that rich variety of spatial, luminary, and atmospheric
values" of a post-medieval painterly tradition,[25] Flaxman's illustrative practice was part and parcel of a greater romantic fascination with the primi-
tive and the fragment, prefiguring an aesthetic prioritization of the verbal
and visual "sketch." A. W. Schlegel would praise the outline illustration's
capacity for "light intimations,"[26] and Goethe too would later say that the
"ruins" of such outlines were enormously productive for his imagination.[27]
In translating an illustrative practice from one epoch to another (ancient to
modern) and from one medium to another (vase to book), Flaxman was

not only drawing upon a larger European fascination with cultural origins. He was also drawing upon a very specific myth of the origin of the visual arts themselves, where, according to the story of the Corinthian Maid, painting was said to begin when the maid traced the outline of her lover's shadow in order to remember him after his departure.

Such historical and mythological sources for Flaxman's undertaking, however, elided a more immediate source for this new illustrative style: that of the book, the very place that served as the new space of this recycled visual practice and that supplied the raw material for the content of such illustrations. In those heavy, straight black lines of Flaxman's drawings of literary texts (Dante or Aeschylus) that were set against a preponderance of white space, one could see the poignant way that the book was overtaking the visual imagination in the years around 1800. In reactivating a mythology of drawing's origins in the outline, the romantic book of outline drawings doubly fashioned itself as the new source of the visual arts, as both its vehicle and its object. Beginning in the shade in Goethe's sequel thus gestured towards yet another key originary myth, this time of visual representation in a bookish world.

Readers have often pointed out how Goethe's subtitle for the opening chapter of his novel "The Flight to Egypt" drew upon a key iconic tradition in the history of painting. In this sense, Goethe's novel stood at the outset of what Éric Bordas has identified as an emerging self-consciousness of the nineteenth-century novel as a painterly genre, the way the painterly and the writerly were intimately intertwined after 1800.[28] But what readers have not addressed is the way this scenic opening also drew attention to a particular type of representation and a particular type of representational technology. It was not just a painterly tradition and its influence on Western culture that Goethe was investigating here. It was also a technological tradition of printed images that Goethe was after, one in which outline drawings were playing an increasingly important role. A year after Goethe published his opening chapters of the *Travels* in 1810, he would receive twelve outline illustrations to his *Faust* by Moritz Retzsch.[29] Retzsch's outline illustrations eventually appeared in book form in 1816 and served as the basis of numerous subsequent *Faust* translations, marking the origin of a wave of *Faust* illustrations that flooded the nineteenth century (over 1,500 in all).[30] With Faust's medieval garb in outline form, the outline drawing as a classical origin had metamorphosed into a source of national origins, remarkably traversing the shift from classic to romantic schools as the thick, steady strokes of Flaxman turned to the fluid and overpopulated lines of Retzsch (fig. 6.3). In that mimetic rendering of the snake in the upper corner of the plate,

Figure 6.3   Plate 21 from Moritz Retzsch, *Umrisse zu Goethe's Faust*
(1816). Courtesy of the Klassik Stiftung Weimar, HAAB/F3487.

one could see Retzsch paying homage to the serpentine line from which
his work drew. In a sign of the line's capaciousness, Retzsch's style would
then be translated back into classical form in France with Girodet's sinuous,
twisting linear illustrations to his *Aeneid* (1825–27) one decade later.

As Michael Baxandall has deftly shown in his study *Shadows and Enlightenment*, the concept of the shadow played a crucial role in eighteenth-century
thought, standing as a necessary counterpart to the prioritization of visual
and epistemological illumination.[31] The importance of shadow in Goethe's
development of his theory of colors was but one example of this. But the rise
of outline drawings and Goethe's engagement with the outline suggested a
gradual shift away from thinking about shadow as an index of color and
contour—as a sign of three-dimensionality—and instead as a sign of what
Baxandall has called "linear coding," the "edge-seeking thrust of the visual
system" (35). The outline drawings that derived from an eighteenth-century
shadow discourse became in romantic hands a technique to learn how to
read edges, to read the line's interposition between lines of text and lines
of image. Reading in the shade contained, in other words, a fundamental
lesson about reading books in an age of illustrated books.

I want to turn in greater detail to the opening chapters of the *Travels* that appeared in Cotta's miscellany and in particular to the chapter entitled "St. Joseph the Second."[32] In his explicit secondarity, St. Joseph II offered readers a general reflection on questions of the sequel and a temporal afterwards that were of increasing value to the romantic literary marketplace. And yet in his numerous engagements with a visual tradition, St. Joseph II was also a figure who foregrounded questions of a visual elsewhere, of what it meant to come after images. The "afterimage" or "Nachbild" has repeatedly been identified as one of *the* crucial figures of thought in Goethe's theory of physiological perception that would influence nineteenth-century theories of visual perception more generally.[33] But what I want to suggest is that in the figure of St. Joseph II the "afterimage" ceases to be simply a matter of the physiology of perception and becomes instead a means of exploring the larger impact of the image's psychological and cultural residue. What happens to human subjectivity and literary creativity in a world of proliferating, reproducible images? St. Joseph II emerges as a key character in Goethe's corpus because he allows Goethe to explore a definition of the self in an age of the image's increasing reproducibility,[34] to explore what it meant to move from the chromatic tradition of painting and its fundamental singularity to the black and white tradition of print and its essential reproducibility and intermediality.

"St. Joseph the Second" was in this sense a key starting point for a series of reflections in Goethe's late work on the interactions between text, image, and reproducibility more generally, work which would largely appear in his periodical *On Art and Antiquity* and that in at least two key cases coincided with the initial publication of the *Travels* in 1821. In projects such as *The Paintings of Philostratus* (1818), which was a redescription by Goethe of a famous classical case of ekphrastic descriptions of lost ancient paintings, *Wilhelm Tischbein's Idylls* (1821), which was a series of prose commentaries to poetic commentaries to prints by Goethe's friend Tischbein, and *Engraved Leaves after Drawings by Goethe* (1821), for which Goethe produced poems to accompany reproductions of his earlier drawings, we can see Goethe playing with the status of a textual afterwards, both in terms of time (texts referring to engravings that were produced in previous cultural or personal epochs) as well as representation (prose texts that came after poetic texts that came after printed images that came after drawings). *Tischbein's Idylls* and *Engraved Leaves after Drawings by Goethe* were closely situated with one another in *Art and Antiquity* and also surrounded by a number of other texts about linguistic translation, from reviews of German translations of Calderon and Lucretius to a review by Goethe of an English translation of Goethe's review of Leonardo da Vinci. The problem of moving from image to text was subsumed in Goethe's late work under larger questions of translation more generally. In this we can see how the program of world literature at the heart of Goethe's late work was dependent not only on the international circulation of texts and the practice of linguistic translation but also on the circulation and mental availability of visual images through the practice of ekphrasis. Like translation, ekphrasis was conceived in Goethe's late work not as an act of substitution but rather as an arrow that pointed to, and thus made available, a visual and cultural elsewhere.

Of the numerous visual encounters dramatized in the St. Joseph story, I want to focus on one in particular that concerns a lily stem and thus intersects with a key linear icon in the history of painting. St. Joseph II, we are told, has organized his life around his ancestor, becoming a carpenter and living in a chapel with murals on the walls depicting the original Joseph story. His wife, called Mary, is not a virgin but a widow, who is found by Joseph after her carriage has been overrun by bandits and her husband severely wounded on a mountain pass. Joseph immediately falls in love with her and waits to hear the fate of her husband. Joseph's first emotional struggle is to contend with the conflicting desire for the husband to live (out of human kindness) and for him to die (to satisfy his erotic attraction to his wife). When the husband does eventually pass away, Joseph sits all night before the window of the house watching the silhouette figures of the wife and her midwife "moving on the curtains." Eight days later (one day after the biblical week), Joseph is allowed to visit, and now through "half-opened" curtains he sees the widow. The midwife, Frau Elisabeth, reaches into the bed and presents Joseph with the baby. It is at this moment that Joseph, who is telling his story to Wilhelm, remarks that he thought of the image of the lily stem or stalk (*Lilienstängel*) that stood between Joseph and Mary. "Frau Elisabeth held [the baby] exactly between me and the mother, and in that place the lily stem occurred to me, which in the image raises itself out of the earth between Joseph and Mary as a witness of a pure relationship. From that moment all of my troubles fell from my heart; I was certain of my happiness."[35] Joseph and Mary eventually marry and live in the chapel together as the story of immaculate conception turns to one of secular adoption.

Central to this story is the way St. Joseph II's visual encounters with the object of his desire are shaped by a shifting engagement with the line and its theatricality, from the outline figures that dance on the curtains during his moment of crisis to the straight line of the "lily stem" that captures the anticipation of his happiness to the curtain that is half-pulled back, which could be a visual reference to Dürer's *St. Jerome in his Study* (1511) and its heroicization of the saint as translator. As Garret Stewart has remarked, the framing of the image as stage—as a portal to a three-dimensional, lived universe—is one of the oldest devices used to endow the planar space of the painted book with an imagined "depth."[36] The visual plenitude of the book, however, that is promised here by the framework of the theatrical and the series of narrative "entries" performed in this passage is nevertheless persistently interrupted as the visual field in "St. Joseph the Second" is continually marked by signs of division. The lily stem—and it is important that it is called the lily *stem* and not just lily—becomes a visual stroke of distinction itself. And yet as we saw in the first chapter, where the cut was reformulated as connection, the mark of distinction here is used to facilitate a series of social and medial connections. Not only will Joseph's narration of the increasingly illegible imagery in the chapel provide the backdrop for Mary's agreement to marry him. But the lily stem that takes the place of the baby ("in that place the lily stem occurred to me") explicitly draws the reader's attention to a visual elsewhere, one that is over-coded, as we will see, with bibliographic meaning. In order to understand the stakes of this categorical move from the out-line to the lily-line in Goethe's text, we need to read out from Goethe's work to a larger visual field in which he was writing and to which his writing points us.

In codex collections of lithographs of European painting that were becoming increasingly popular after 1800, one could find ample evidence of the lily's iconic place as a figure of mediation in cycles of the Mary paintings that assumed a prominent position in such collections. Consider, for example, this print by Nepomuk Strixner of the *Annunciation* (fig. 6.4) from the collection of Sulpiz and Melchior Boisserée (wrongly attributed at the time to Jan van Eyck), which was singled out by Goethe in his essay on early-nineteenth-century lithography as one of the finest examples of the new art form.[37] The *Annunciation* offered a paradigmatic visual tradition in which one could see this intersection of the stem, the book, and the gesturing hand, an iconic overlap of the practices of deixis, writing, and naming that were already foregrounded in the opening pages of the *Travels* (when Felix asks his note-taking father, "What do you call this stone?").[38] The lily in this particular print represents a quintessential dividing line, not only through its almost impossible magnitude that challenges the perspectival order of the entire image but also in the way it is amplified through a variety of other vertical lines in the image, from Gabriel's staff, to the two characters' outstretched forefingers, to numerous folds in the angel's cloak, to that overly strong line marking the outer edge of Mary's cloak, which finds its

Figure 6.4 Lithograph of *The Annunciation* by Johann Nepomuk Strixner
from *Sammlung Alt- Nieder- und Ober-Deutscher Gemälde der Brüder Sulpiz
und Melchior Boisserée und Johann Bertram* (1821–34), 1:2. Courtesy
of the Bildarchiv Preussischer Kulturbesitz/Art Resource, NY.

mirror image in the half-pulled back curtain of the bed (suggesting yet another source for Goethe's choice of narrative imagery in "St. Joseph the Second"). If the lily served a crucial function in dividing the visual plane, especially between the chromatic spaces of light and dark, it also functioned as a pointer both within and without that visually bounded space. One can see how the two uppermost flowers of the lily, which remain not fully in bloom and thus capture an important element of futurity here, mirror the angle of the two gesturing hands of Mary and Gabriel (in the orans position or posture of prayer). The iconography of the hand that emerges in this bookish space is neither that of the grasping nor the greeting hand that we saw in earlier chapters, but now that of the praying or beseeching hand. The lily points in this sense to an entire social scene of verbal pointing, to the dual experience of calling and being called at the heart of the Christian church and at the basis of which stood the book. In making his *Wilhelm Meister* series explicitly about the theme of work or *Beruf* (one's calling), Goethe was translating this Christian bibliographic drama into secular terms.

Mary's arm encircles the Bible in a curvilinear gesture, as her outstretched thumb, in yet another echo of the lily, marks, and thus points to, a passage in the book of books. The bookishness of the entire domestic scene is then amplified through the visual echoes of the open book's turning leaf in the numerous open shudders of the room's windows (a common device among Annunciation imagery).[39] One could go still further in underscoring the bookishness of both this image and the lily at its center by highlighting, as Erwin Panofsky has done, that such Dutch Annunciation imagery was crucially indebted to a tradition of manuscript illustration by the Boucicaut Master.[40] As in the example of the *Annunciation* in a *Book of Hours* by a follower of the Boucicaut Master (ca. 1410) held in the Getty Museum,[41] one can see how the curling top of the winding speech scroll that was so common to manuscriptural illustration both mirrors the lily's drooping flower and points directly towards it. The straight line of the lily morphs in this bibliographic iconic tradition into the wavy line of the word, gesturing towards the line's capacity to become both an image and an image that bears the (legible) line of writing.

The turning (and illegible) page of numerous painted *Annunciations* serves as a visual echo of the turns of the speech scrolls that populated illuminated medieval books, one more move in a long chain of remediation that surrounded the lily's mobilization within Christian iconography, from the written scroll's appearance in the illuminated manuscript book, to the printed book's appearance in the easel painting, to painting's appearance in the lithographed book. Strixner's lithographed reproduction of a painted *Annunciation* that appeared in codex form thus pointed towards the image's own bibliographic origins—origins which themselves pointed in subtle ways to their pre-codicological medial sources. But it also pointed towards its bibliographic *future* as the book was lionized through this chain of interlocking bibliographic references. The book is framed as *the* medium for the continued circulation and cultural potency of the image. Goethe's narrated scene of seeing at the center of which stood the lily stem cites a quintessential icon that stands for a bibliographic heritage. The lily's chain of remediations discloses a temporalized notion of intermediality, exploring the larger problematic of the afterimage in a double sense: what it meant to come after images and what the cultural status of the afterimage, the visual residue, was.

The lily stem's capacity to function in the early nineteenth century as a visual shorthand for an intermedial scene of reading—as an incorporation of the line's potential to generate both writing and image, whether simultaneously or in succession—was given one of its most memorable incarnations by Philipp Otto Runge in his illustrations to Ludwig Tieck's collection of medieval love songs, *Minnelieder aus der schwäbischen Zeitalter* (1803), which I discussed in chapter 3 and which represented a key landmark of romantic interlingual and intermedial translation (fig. 6.5). Runge's illustrative work was extremely popular in romantic books, and one can see in his intense attraction to the lily further confirmation of this figure's intermedial associations. Where the pointedness of the lily from Tieck's *Minnelieder* seemed to embody the lily's identity as a kind of intermedial arrow, it was also the lily's *bowedness*, which one could see on display in Runge's print masterpiece, *The Seasons* (1806), and which Runge sent to Goethe in April 1806 roughly a year before Goethe began work on the *Travels*,[42] that pointed to another crucial scene of romantic intermediality: that of arabesque marginal illustration.[43] The straightness of the lily stem in Strixner or Tieck was at the same time linked in *The Seasons* to a visual revival that depended on an attention to an unceasing curvilinearity surrounding floral imagery. With the disproportionate heaviness of its head, the floral became an ideal representation not of uprightness but of a bowed, elliptical, or vorticular fluidity. The curvilinear visual line in the book's margins translated the discrete nature of the letter and the line of writing—and of the sense of self that they captured— into a figure of continuity and connectivity.[44] One of the key manifestations of this renewed interest in the bowed intermedial floral line was the appearance in 1808 of lithographed reproductions, again by Nepomuk Strixner, of the prayer book of Kaiser Maximilian I, for which Dürer had designed the elaborate arabesque marginal illustrations. Goethe

Figure 6.5   Lily stem by Philipp Otto Runge from plate 2 of Ludwig Tieck's *Minnelieder aus dem schwäbischen Zeitalter* (1803). Courtesy of the Klassik Stiftung Weimar, HAAB/Dl1-161.

would then enthusiastically review in the *Allgemeine Literatur Zeitung* this interesting case of a book that reproduced an earlier book through the new visual technology of lithography.[45] Goethe's promotion of this work and the general romantic enthusiasm for it would then lay the groundwork for the later publication of one of the most stunning illustrated editions of Goethe's ballads by Eugen Neureuther that appeared in 1829 (fig. 6.6).

The genre of the ballad would become a key source for illustrated books

Figure 6.6 Eugen Neureuther, "Der König von Thule," *Randzeichnungen zu Goethes Balladen und Romanzen* (1829). Courtesy of the Klassik Stiftung Weimar, HAAB/BH 1502.

Figure 6.7   Detail of Eugen Neureuther, "Der König von Thule," *Randzeichnungen zu Goethes Balladen und Romanzen* (1829). Courtesy of the Klassik Stiftung Weimar, HAAB/BH 1502.

in the nineteenth century, and as I discussed in chapter 3, this had much to do with the ballad's intermedial origins as both oral song and illustrated broadsheet from the early modern period. But where the illustrated broadside ballad had positioned itself as a form of popular entertainment, the illustrated ballad collection on the other hand was fast becoming a vehicle of social acculturation, a liminal form that introduced readers not just to reading itself but to a reading practice that depended on seeing images through text. The ballad's continued initiatory identity—as the privileged generic threshold to a world of reading—now served, in the form of the illustrated edition, the new cause of intermedial literacy, of associating reading with seeing and vice versa.

Once again, it was the floral stem, this time of the water lily, that provided the visual backdrop for such literary mobilizations. In this example taken from Goethe's ballad "The King of Thule," one can see how it is precisely the floral origins of the image's wavy lines that give birth to the script of poetry (fig. 6.7). As David Wellbery has shown, few works were more poetically insistent on the notion of containment than "The King of Thule," with its central image of the king's chalice that cannot be bequeathed and that will eventually be thrown into the water in a moment of heightened self-consumption: the figure of containing fluidity, the chalice, is itself consumed in a fluid grave.[46] Neureuther's visual handling of the poem, however, seemed to draw upon the poetic revisions that Goethe's later work was performing against his earlier, moving away from a poetics of the self-contained genius and towards those of the networked media artist. Not only does one have to search very hard to even find the chalice in this illustration, but Neureuther chooses to represent the container here neither in the moment of its thrownness nor in its fluid consumption, but instead straddling the horizon line floating half above and half below the watery surface. Like all of the objects that break through the horizon line between the elements of earth and water in Neureuther's illustration, the three-dimensional part above gradually decomposes into a planar sketch and then into the single dimension of the line below. The container no longer contains fluid but is itself *made* fluid as it dissolves into nothing but lines; it no longer stands for the self as something whole or unique—as a three-dimensional body in space—but instead captures a self that becomes script.

Stems, Spirals, and the New Scientific Graphics

The arabesque marginal illustration thus marked one of the most popular romantic translations of Sterne's initial intermedial wavy line, and it rested in important ways on the figure of the lily and its fundamentally bibliographic identity. I want to turn now to another key manifestation of the wavy line—the spiral line of Goethe's late poetry and scientific notebooks—which unites the vertical and curvilinear identities of the lily. It is here, in this axial fusion that also incorporates the problem of time, where we can see a new paradigm of scientific illustration coming into view in the opening decades of the nineteenth century. The wavy line served not only as an impetus to creative innovation in the romantic age but also as a key component of new forms of knowledge. As we will see in the cases of Goethe's contemporaries, Ernst Florens Friedrich Chladni, Joseph Fourier, and Alexander von Humboldt, the story of scientific illustration is integral to the larger story of the intermedial work of the romantic line.

Under the heading "Chinesisches" (Chinese Matters), Goethe published a series of translations of poetic portraits of mythical Chinese women in his journal *On Art and Antiquity* (1827) that had initially appeared in English translation by Peter Perring Thoms in 1824. In the opening poem, "Fräulein See-Yaou-Hing," we are told the story of the origins of the bound foot, which is compared at the close of the poem to the lily.[47] Once again the lily emerges as a key figure of Goethe's thought, and in aligning the linear figure of the lily with the spiral cloth of the bound foot, one could see how the lily, as that quintessential figure of intermediality, was being subsumed in Goethe's translation within a larger problematic of translation and transculturality more generally. Such intersections highlighted just how intimately related the fields of intermedial and interlingual translation were in Goethe's late work. Like the winding of the turban in "Come, love, come," from Goethe's *West-East Divan* (1819), the spirally bound object (the book as text/ile) embodied a transcultural textual imaginary.

In the identification of the lily with the spiral line of the bound object, this new metaphorical constellation brought together the vertical and the bowed line in a single image. It identified the lily as a key figure of translation. But if the lily's association with the spiral line served on the one hand to address a concern with problems of cultural and linguistic translation — with the problem of the "orient" or "Morgenland"—it pointed towards an even more fundamental problem of *representational* translation as well. The spiral gestured not just towards the problem of how the two-dimensional line could participate in the making of a perspectival three-dimensional reality.[48] It also explored how the static nature of the image could capture the dynamic variable of time (intimating why the temporalized notions of "occident" and "orient" in German, *Abendland* and *Morgenland*, figured so prominently in Goethe's thinking here). For Goethe, the spiral was one of the two fundamental forms of botanical growth that enabled the formal change that lay at the heart of all nature.[49] As he would write in his late essay, "On the Spiral Tendency" (1829), which accompanied the publication of his *On the Metamorphosis of Plants* published in a dual German and French edition in 1831, "We must assume: there presides in vegetation a universal spiral tendency through which, in connection with vertical striving, all structures of plants and their development are completed through the law of metamorphosis."[50] The spiral was a figure of movement in both time and space and encoded a basic potentiality for change and "development."

When we look at the illustrations that accompanied Goethe's notes to this essay, we can see how Goethe was visually trying to come to terms with this problem of the simultaneous representation of time and space within a single graphic practice. In this first example of a drawing meant to capture botanical growth, taken from his folder of notes from 1829 on the spiral tendency (fig. 6.8), we can see how the wavy line is placed within a spatially and temporally arranged grid, updating the abstract curvatures that Goethe used in 1787 to capture his inspiration that "all is leaf" (fig. 0.1). In this second example, however, entitled "Spiral Insertion on the Stem" (fig. 6.9), we can see Goethe moving away from the direct representation of the spiral through curvilinear form and towards something far more indirect. In the

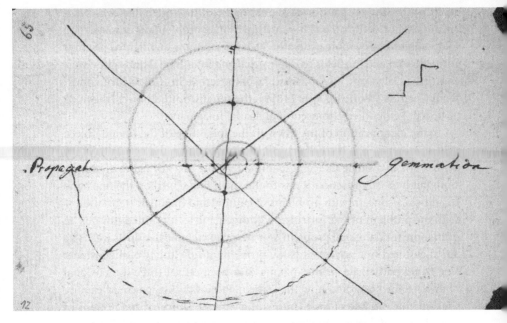

Figure 6.8   Goethe's sketch, "Spiraltendenz der Vegetation" (1829). |
Courtesy of the Klassik Stiftung Weimar, GSA 26/LXI, 7, Bl. 65.

second drawing, Goethe represents the knots where leaves grow on an un-
folded plant stem in order to identify their spiral-like structure of growth.
The spiral, which was itself imagined as the visual translation of a temporal
process into an image, is translated here back into a pattern of *straight* lines
as the three-dimensionality of the plant in the fourth dimension of time
is graphically captured in two-dimensional space through a series of one-
dimensional disconnected lines. Once again it is crucial that it is the "stem"
where these problems of visual translation and intermediality get worked
out. According to Goethe's graphical notations of spiral growth on the stem,
the spiral is a line that the mind must imaginatively reconstruct from observing a series of straight lines. The spiral comes to stand for a graphic
regime that is increasingly removed from the strictly mimetic rendering of
observed reality.

Although he does not cite Goethe's botanical work in his study, the media historian Bernhard Siegert has argued that such graphic abstractions
would become a defining feature of a new scientific visual paradigm that
emerged at the turn of the nineteenth century.[51] A growing interest in representing oscillating natural phenomena such as sound, heat, electricity, and
light led to the conceptualization of new mathematical and visual forms

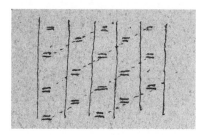

Figure 6.9   Goethe's sketch, "Spirale
Insertion am Stengel" (1829). Courtesy
of the Klassik Stiftung Weimar,
GSA 26/LV, 3, 3, Bl. 4.

of abstract representation. Of particular importance in this genealogy was Ernst Florens Friedrich Chladni, whose *Discoveries on the Theory of Sound* (1787), which was later the basis of the first handbook on acoustics (1802), would become a landmark romantic book because of the way it visually represented the medium of sound (fig. 6.10). Just as important as the intermedial translations in Chladni's work (from sound to image), however, were the *spatial* translations performed by his illustrations of wavy lines, the way he translated the eighteenth-century problem of representing the vibrating string (the moving line) into a problem of planar representation.[52] As Chladni would write in *Acoustics*, "With the descriptions of the vibrations of a plate, bell, etc. that appear in this and the following sections, we will not be observing curved lines of vibration [*krumme Schwingungslinien*], but curved planes [*krumme Flächen*], which are curved in more than one direction, and on which the parts to be found on the opposing side of the axis are not separated from one another by fixed points, but fixed lines, which one could also name lines of intersection [*Knotenlinien*]."[53] In referring to the wavy sound lines represented on his vibrating plates as *Knotenlinien* (which referred to the intersection of two planar phenomena more generally), Chladni was refashioning acoustical thinking, and the wavy line at its heart, away from one dimensional strings and towards two-dimensional planes that intersected in three-dimensional space.

If Chladni's ecliptic lines represented a double translation from sound to image and from a linear to planar theory of sound, Joseph Fourier's work on the diffusion of heat in three-dimensional bodies marked another essential mobilization of the wavy line, this time as sine and cosine curve as the source of translational knowledge about natural phenomena. Fourier would become one of the most influential figures in the history of math-

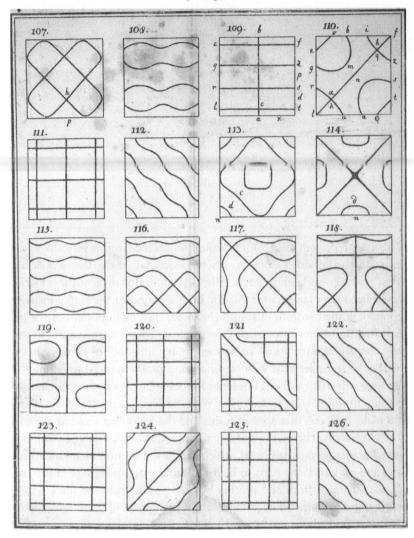

Figure 6.10   Table IX from E. F. F. Chladni, *Entdeckungen über die Theorie des Klanges* (1787). Courtesy of the Thomas Fisher Rare Book Library, University of Toronto.

ematics, with his work finding numerous subsequent applications that are still fundamental to the field of mathematical engineering today. But it was the more local identification of temperature as a central field of natural inquiry that marked Fourier's significance for a romantic audience. As Fourier would remark in his groundbreaking treatise, *Théorie analytique de la chaleur* (1822), whose genesis dated back to at least 1805, heat represented an other fundamental field of natural science akin to Newton's work on gravity and one that was as harmonic, regular, and measurable as the motion of physical bodies in space although it was not directly available to our visual senses.[54] Like Chladni's work on sound, Fourier's work on heat diffusion had emerged out of eighteenth-century debates about the problem of the periodic analysis of the vibrating string. But where Chladni's intervention was to challenge the linearity of eighteenth-century acoustic thought, Fourier's contribution was precisely to linearize with greater rigor all periodic functions. No matter how complex or discontinuous, Fourier saw that any periodic function could be broken down into the sum of simple functions representable through sine and cosine waves. "Through convergent series or definite integrals," Fourier argued, "we have represented separate parts of different functions or discontinuous functions between certain limits, for example as in the measure of the ordinate of a triangle. Our proofs leave no doubt of the exact truth of these equations" (587). Every straight or even broken line contained the possibility of being reformulated as a continuous wavy line. As the historian of mathematics, Ivor Gratton-Guinness, has remarked, Fourier's work marked "the birth of an era of linearization in the development of mathematical physics."[55]

Fourier's attention to heat and the problem of measuring its diffusion was not an isolated case, however. His work had an important parallel in that of Alexander von Humboldt, whose research on plotting isotherms[56]— lines connecting points of equal temperature across space—found its visual articulation in the landmark atlas project of Heinrich Berghaus (fig. 6.11). The popularization of the hand atlas would serve as one of the key new genres of illustrated books in the early nineteenth century, and one could see in those wavy lines of temperature that Humboldt's research supported a prime example of a new attention to the connectivity and the circulatory aspect of space. Such concerns dated back to Humboldt's own cartographic experiment in his *Tableau physique des Andes et Pays voisins*, which was published as part of his *Essay on the Geography of Plants* (1807).[57] As in the *Tableau physique*, in which the identities of plant species were defined through their position relative to a variety of external factors, the isotherm challenged the static linear coding of the traditional cartographic grid, overlaying such visual lattices with a series of dynamic, boundary-crossing wavy lines. According to such cartographic practices, the line became the means not only of establishing new geographic constellations but also of redefining the very identity of such constellations as relationally determined. The various remappings that Humboldt undertook during his career marked a significant contribution to a greater reorientation of spatial thought in the

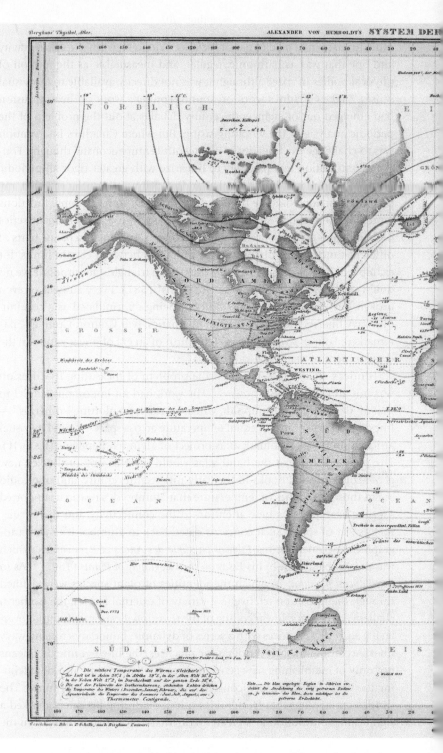

Figure 6.11   Alexander von Humboldt, "System der Isotherm-Kurven," from Heinrich Berghaus, *Physikalischer Atlas* (1837). Courtesy of the Klassik Stiftung Weimar, HAAB/Th.A 1:10(a).

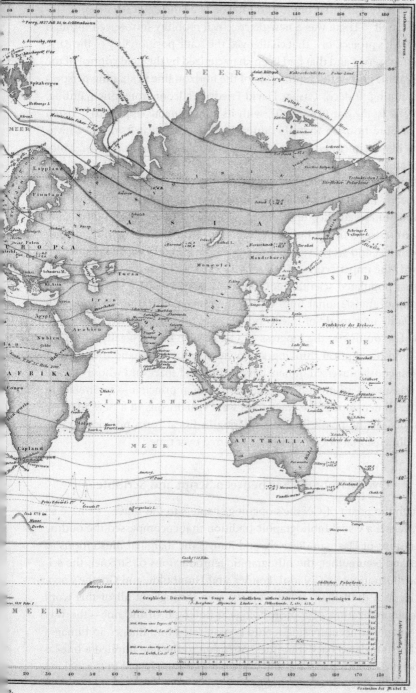

nineteenth century that one could categorize as the delocalization of "location" itself.[58] There was a new perspectival mobility introduced through Humboldt's project, one that challenged the static positionality of the early modern observer and that had been characterized by the rigid control of the cartographic grid or the central role of the horizon line in shaping perspectival painting. Indeed, Caspar David Friedrich's iconic romantic painting, *The Monk by the Sea* (1808–10), with its simultaneous appeal to a visual field of pure horizon that also threatened to disappear from the canvas (much like the pictured observer himself), could be read as a key instance of this shifting visual protocol.

Whether as stem, spiral, or wave, then, the wavy line emerged in a context of early-nineteenth-century scientific illustration as a key component of romantic intermediality, understood no longer as the problem of moving between text and image but as the more fundamental problem of moving between text and world *via* the image, of how to render visible that which escaped "the imperfection of our senses" in Fourier's words (xv). The wavy line that populated scientific editions became a key figure within a larger program of translational lines during the nineteenth century, capturing a profoundly new mode of linear thought that no longer rested on the closures of an outline or the progress of a telos. Such lines crucially depended on a kind of elliptical thinking, one whose indirections and dislocations simultaneously traversed dimensions of time and space and whose "meaning" was always a function of some translational principle—a correlate in another dimension. These wavy lines were visual icons of a new adaptive mentality, of the possibility of rendering in linear form nonvisualizable three-dimensional phenomena that occurred over time.

Overwriting: Balzac between Script and Scribble

Through the prism of Goethe's opening chapters to the *Travels*, we have so far traversed a visual bibliographic tradition that encompassed the outline illustrations of Flaxman, Retzsch, and Runge, the marginal illustrations of Dürer and Neureuther, the lithographic reproductions of Strixner, the scientific illustrations of Chladni, Fourier, and Humboldt, and Goethe's own practice as a draftsman. What we have seen throughout all of this work is the dramatization of a morphological potential of the line—the way early-nineteenth-century lines could be translated into images and images could be translated back into lines. Attention to the line implied a bifocal perspective of both the visual and scriptural that participated in the making of this larger category of text/image.

I want to turn now from the German scene of adaptation to the French, a cultural shift that will also entail a shift in design, from the German vogue for outlines and arabesque lines to the French wave of wood-engraved vignettes that began to infiltrate the printed page. But such a shift will also mark an important continuum, because at stake in the rise of the "vignette"—the illustration that winds itself (like a vine) around the stem of the text—was always the question of the serpentine line and its intermedial identity. The two central characters in this part of the story are Balzac and the illustrator Tony Johannot, who was referred to by Gautier as the king of illustrators and whose work would become one of the most recognizable visual signatures of the age.[59]

The bound foot in Goethe's "Chinese Matters" from the previous section nicely leads us to the wavy line in Balzac, not only to the visual line from The Wild Ass's Skin with which I began (fig. 6.1) but also to the mass of ekphrastic lines that would appear in the painterly portrait of Balzac's masterpiece on lines, "The Unknown Masterpiece," whose only "legible" visual element was ultimately a woman's foot. What happens when Goethe's lines that become images turn to Balzac's images that become lines? What are the stakes of these serial de- and re-compositions that are at the heart of romantic composition? How does this movement across national borders help tell us something more about the delimiting meaning of the enigmatic scribble and, by extension, the romantic book that contained such scribbling (and scribblers)?

Few texts have been more important for a modernist visual tradition than Balzac's "Unknown Masterpiece." As a work *about* the visual arts, it has experienced an enormously vibrant afterlife *in* the visual arts.[60] Read according to its aesthetic *fortuna*, "The Unknown Masterpiece" appears as a kind of modernist manifesto motivating an iconoclastic visual trajectory eventually culminating in abstract expressionism.[61] But as the work of Ségolène Le Men has done so much to show,[62] when we read this central tale of Balzac's oeuvre backwards into his formative writerly experiences of the late 1820s, we begin to see how it marked a very different culmination, one that captured Balzac's own exploration of the productive possibilities proposed by the interaction of text and image initiated by the expanding field of book illustration. As Le Men writes, "Balzac integrates his distinctive form of art within the collective matrix of the editorial team, continually combining word and image within the fraternity of the writer-journalist and the draftsman-journalist."[63] Both The Wild Ass's Skin and "The Unknown Masterpiece" would appear in parts in 1831 in the illustrated serial L'Artiste, and it was precisely this new illustrated space—along with related publications such as *La Caricature, La Mode,* and *La Silhouette*—that provided the bibliographic backdrop for Balzac's reflections on the relationship between text, image, revision, and excess—a constellation of ideas that always circled around the larger problem of illegibility and identity.[64] Seldom read in conjunction with one another, I want to argue that "The Unknown Masterpiece" and *The Wild Ass's Skin* constitute an important conceptual pair in Balzac's work, a fact underscored by the way these two works would remain bibliographically linked throughout their future permutations in Balzac's various acts of reprinting.

Sterne's wavy line that was chosen for the epigraph of Balzac's breakthrough novel assumes particular significance here when we consider that this would be the only novel by Balzac that was later republished as an illustrated edition under a larger plan to produce an entire edition of illustrated Balzac novels.[65] It assumes even more significance when we consider that at the level of content this is a novel intimately concerned with the figure of the *outline*. The novel's hero, Raphaël, will repeatedly draw a line around the magical skin, hung on the wall, that allows his desires to come true. Raphaël's outline drawing nicely recalls the myth of the Corinthian Maid and the origins of the pictorial arts, but with a crucial difference. While the Corinthian Maid froze her lover's outline on the wall, the wild ass's skin *shrinks*. Outline and object never perfectly coincide in Balzac because of the factor of time.

The skin's connection to the figure of the outline and the problem of time was deftly depicted in Johannot's frontispiece that adorned the first volume of Balzac's novel and that was initially printed in *L'Artiste* (fig. 6.12). On the one hand we see the outline of the skin separated from the remainder of the drawing by a swath of white space, as it functions as a visual mirror or window, itself mirrored in the framed image that stands opposite it. As an articulation of the self's desires, the skin assumes a double quality of narcissistic reflection and imaginative portal. When we scan the image more completely, however—when we work against the absorbed gaze of the image's own pictured viewers—we see in the various objects strewn about the antiquarian's store, from the skeletal torso and skull to the fragmented armor to the oriental tomb, how Johannot draws upon the popular visual genre of the "Still Life with Book."[66] In these very recognizable *memento mori,* Johannot's image portrays the passage of time so central to the skin's identity, visually dramatizing that aspect of time that Lessing had argued was the primary concern of text.

I say "Still Life with Book" here because the "skin" that they are looking at crucially contains a text, one said to be in "Sanskrit" (actually in Arabic),

Figure 6.12   Frontispiece, Honoré de Balzac, *La Peau de Chagrin*, vol. 1
(1831). Courtesy of The Pierpont Morgan Library, New York.

which is printed in Balzac's novel in its original form and translated into
French. In Johannot's image, however, the skin's text is no longer legible,
replaced instead by a few vertical wavy lines that give the skin a certain
perspectival contour. (In Balzac the skin is said to be composed of "rayures
capricieuses" (capricious stripes),[67] echoing the skin's visual relations to
the distorted caricatures of the baroque Italian *capriccio*). The illegible wavy
lines of writing on the skin that are then translated into legible words in
the text (as the image of writing becomes the language of text) are then
translated in the frontispiece back into visually illegible wavy lines, as the
frontispiece becomes a mirror image of the illegible wavy line of the visual

epigraph opposite it on the title page. In both the image (of a text) and the text (of an image), the wavy line of writing denotes a simultaneous opacity and transparency, a window onto the world and an obstruction to that very imaginative plenitude. We have here an ideal example of Garret Stewart's argument that the point of painted text—so often denoted as an illegible wavy line—is to mirror a larger cultural investment in the reader's unavailability, in the imagining of a subject, in Stewart's words, that is "not all there."[68] The reading self becomes an ideal self in the western painterly tradition precisely because it is an absorbed self. Such absorption is a function of a private, and thus personalized, legibility of the textual/visual line.

If Johannot's drawing gestured through its content towards this painterly tradition of pictured reading and the "removed self" (again Stewart), his stylistic innovations also pointed in a vastly different direction. Here the frontispiece to the second volume of *The Wild Ass's Skin* will be of help, also preprinted in *L'Artiste* (fig. 6.13). If the frontispiece to the first volume was marked by the figure of the outline and a simultaneous filling-up of the visual field surrounding the scene's two reader-observers, the frontispiece to the second volume took Johannot's style of intersecting wavy lines in the opposite direction towards a gradual emptying out of the visual plane. The first frontispiece visually motivated an attentive look that was also an act of reading, one that stood in stark contrast to the image's overall visual field that was marked by an unmistakable material excess. As in numerous other scenes of reading, the attentiveness of reading was figured as a resistance to a greater overabundance of material objects that invited one's gaze.

The second frontispiece by contrast signaled a kinetic act of looking that gradually moved into an unbounded void. Where the eyes in the first frontispiece are concentrated on a single visual plane (the line of sight figured as precisely that, a straight line), in the second we traverse a spiral-like form of observation that begins in the hero's feet and gradually follows the characters' points of view that culminate in looking at a mirror which is only half-represented and in which the observer could not possibly see herself—in other words, in which she is effaced. Looking in the second frontispiece is framed as an act of looking away. Such a visual aesthetics of effacement, which is integrally related to the curvilinear line that does not assume definite form (that does not close), is captured in that extraordinarily thick serpentine outline of the hero's outer leg, where the heaviness of the line is used by contrast to convey the gradual emaciation of the main character's entire body. The substantive self is gradually reduced in Johannot's "reading" of Balzac to a single wavy line.

As in the wavy lines that were at the heart of the romantic revival of the

Figure 6.13   Frontispiece, Honoré de Balzac, *La Peau de Chagrin*, vol. 2
(1831). Courtesy of the Pierpont Morgan Library, New York.

arabesque—and we cannot be far from such arabesque thinking in the ori-
entalism of Balzac's text—there is a temporality of viewing that is being dramatized in the second frontispiece, an acknowledgment of the embodied eye
that travels along the lines of the image. The more an image decomposed,
the more time it took to take it all in. Abstraction captured an all-important
temporality of looking, at the very moment that looking was being refigured as reading. The accumulation of those curving, disarticulated lines in
the second frontispiece now depicts a fundamental problem of attention.
Like the frontispiece's own viewers, the eye is no longer allowed to rest or
focus. The two frontispieces staged, in other words, that quintessential art-

historical opposition in Norman Bryson's terms between the "glance" and the "gaze," between two forms of seeing that depended on radically different principles of paying attention.[69] Johannot's designs not only captured a new velocity of illustration—images could easily populate textual space, thanks both to the relative quickness of wood engraving and the time saved by printing the engravings on the same press used to print a book's text. They also captured a new velocity of looking, and by extension, reading, which was integrally related to the rising tide of books, and the novel's role in par-ticular, in such proliferation. Johannot's style of wavy lines that adorned the romantic book highlighted a particular theory of romantic visuality (and a visually informed literacy) that depended not on a rapt attention of either book or image but instead on a glance that suggested at the same time a glancing *away*. The romantic anxiety about the capacity of book illustration to control and ultimately deplete readers' imaginations—a concern that continues to resonate into the present—missed the point of such illustrations that were in fact designed to draw the eye *off* the page. The legitimation of the mobile glance, which was tied to a larger nineteenth-century aesthetic investment in the "sketch,"[70] was thus integrally related to a culture of novel reading that depended not on spending too much time with a page of text but on a certain ocular velocity. The wavy line that adorned the romantic book not only signaled a certain opacity to the reading process—the enigmatic nature of the book—it also denoted a greater cultural hurriedness that came to surround bibliographic life more generally.

That such concerns between gazing and glancing figured in Johannot's visual illustrations were also concerns of the text can be seen in one of the central features attributed to the skin itself—the impossibility of its being stretched. On one level, we can read the "skin" at the center of Balzac's novel as a sign that harkens back to a bibliographic tradition before books were made of paper. Indeed, the central aspiration of David Sechard, one of the two heroes of *Lost Illusions* (1837), was to discover a new raw material for paper, a fact that nicely underscores Balzac's larger obsessions with the medium of paper and sets the skin in opposition to the new culture of paper.[71] To make the point wittily obvious, Balzac at one point even has the skin destroy a "press" that is applied to it in order to stretch it.

But we could read the bibliographically laden sign of the skin another way, where this enemy of the press was not a sign of nostalgia but instead a counter-ideal to an imagined print future, one that would be crucially worked out in Balzac's bibliographic experiment of *The Human Comedy*.[72] A key feature of Balzac's creative practice was precisely the stretching of his texts within ever larger bibliographic worlds, not to mention stretching the texts themselves as he continually rewrote and repositioned them. Indeed, as Kevin McLaughlin has shown, the skin assumed precisely this quality of openness in *Louis Lambert*, which Balzac began a year after *The Wild Ass's Skin*.[73] Here again the first edition of *The Wild Ass's Skin* proposes an important piece of paratextual evidence that strengthens its position as a threshold to Balzac's mature work.[74] Despite the placement of the title on the title page, in the initial version it functioned solely as the title to the first section and did not appear as a running header throughout the novel, replaced instead by the titles of each subsequent part (a fact not reproduced in the critical edition, for example). The title of this particular work is broken down into parts, much in the way that the title more generally in Balzac would always be figured as a part and not a whole. Such partialization of the whole is performed through the interruption of the *typographical* line of the running header, an early indication of the important intersections that the visual and the typographic would assume in Balzac's project. The paratextual devices of Balzac's *Human Comedy* were continually designed to invite the reader's eye to look towards a textual elsewhere.

Gerhard Neumann has argued that "anamorphosis"—the deformed but also stretched gaze—would emerge as one of the central features of a romantic visual poetics, embodied in the writer who would function as one of Balzac's most significant influences, E. T. A. Hoffmann.[75] Critics have returned again and again to Balzac's indebtedness to Hoffmann,[76] but they have largely overlooked a crucial practice that Balzac seems to have learned from his source, namely the bibliographic experimentation with textual replacement that I discussed in chapter 2. The anamorphic image, like the anamorphic text, was one that required the reader-viewer to move one's eyes and body to make something legible. There was a corporal kinesis to this new principle of looking/reading, one that rested on a fundamental notion of textual and visual *displacement*. Whether visual or lectoral, legibility was achieved in this new bibliographic space at an angle, off-center, and in motion. Such kinetic looking that was dramatized in Johannot's second frontispiece was then captured in Balzac's text, as we learn how Raphaël looks at the skin "from all angles" (sous toutes les faces) (82) in order to understand it. In *The Wild Ass's Skin*, Balzac's vision of the secular printed book of stretchtext (with due acknowledgment here to Ted Nelson) replaced a passing tradition of the unstretchable text of the sacred book made of parchment.

All of this should help frame a rereading of "The Unknown Masterpiece" as both a companion to *The Wild Ass's Skin* and as a "masterpiece" itself about the romantic problem of the intermedial line. If the visual line of illegible script functioned as a key intermedial portal to Balzac's novelistic enterprise in *The Wild Ass's Skin*, the narrated line of an illegible image would become the ekphrastic heart, so to speak, of his short fictions of intermediality. "Sarrasine," for example, which was written shortly before "The Unknown Masterpiece," was a veritable homage to the shadowed lines of the facial crease and the textile fold, a prime figural example of Michel Serres's notion of the fold not as a form of separation but as an adding-in of energy.[77]

"The Unknown Masterpiece" begins with a drama of crossing a thresh-old—the door to Porbus's studio—and we watch as the young painter, Nicolas Poussin, gradually ascends the diagonal line of the staircase and halts before the arabesque lines of the "grotesque knocker" of Porbus's door (413). It is at this point where Poussin will be introduced to the novella's extraordinarily linearized hero, Master Frenhofer: "Set this head on a slender, feeble body, enwind it in lace sparkling with whiteness and intricately worked over, throw a great chain of gold over the old man's black doublet, and you will have an imperfect image of this person . . . like a work of Rembrandt walking silently and without a frame in the black atmosphere for which this great painter is known" (415). The serpentine lines across which figures move and through which they are constituted (stairs, knockers, lace, chain, and of course the folds of the black doublet) dissolve into pure shadow, the "black atmosphere" of Rembrandtian style. We are back at the opening of Goethe's novel in the shade, the starting point of romantic fiction designed to overcome the boundedness of the line. Upon entering the studio, Porbus's painting, *Mary of Egypt*, is described by Frenhofer as a "silhouette with only a single dimension" (une silhouette qui n'a qu'une seule face) (416), the painting's failure described as a failure of the outline: "It is only true in the interior [*dans les milieux*], your contours are false" (417). Frenhofer's completion of Porbus's painting will be the result of a few added lines ("here two strokes of the brush, here only one" [421]), lines that are in fact designed to break down the line as outline. "Look, my boy," continues Frenhofer, "it's only the last stroke of the brush that counts. . . . No one will thank us for what is underneath" (422). The line—and the last line in particular—acts as both a quintessential aperture onto an imaginary visual world *as well as* a gesture of division, a mark of the lack of access to a material depth ("no one will thank us for what is underneath"). The objective of the line for Frenhofer is to negotiate this axial balance between its effacement across the horizontal plane of the seen image and its essential opacity across the vertical plane of the accumulated marks of paint that coalesce in the image. "The human body isn't bounded by lines!" says

Frenhofer in words that were echoed by the writings of Balzac's painterly contemporary, Delacroix.[78] "Line is the means," says Frenhofer, "by which man accounts for the effect of light on objects, but in nature where all is continuous [*où tout est plein*] there are no lines" (424–25).

The very disappearance of the line that is called for here nevertheless results in a masterpiece that is composed solely of lines. Poussin and Porbus are shocked at what they see—or don't see—and their looking is described in the following way: "they examined the painting by moving first to the right, then to the left, then head-on [*de face*], lowering and raising themselves by turns [*tour à tour*]" (436). Their bodies engage in a kind of anamorphic looking, to locate the head that cannot be seen "head on." The linear nature of their movements that come one after another "by turns" (*tour à tour*), are also figured as a form of turning and torquing that was at the heart of anamorphosis. But no matter how they move their bodies, the image's referent does not take shape. All they see is "a multitude of bizarre lines" (436).

Garret Stewart's work on the painted tradition of reading will again be decisive here in understanding the meaning of these lines that are framed as resisting meaning to their narrated viewers. As Stewart has written about the pictorial tradition, "Print's pictured illegibility . . . is recognized as a way of keeping faith with painting's own nature."[79] Illegible printed lines in paint interpret and give meaning to the medium of paint by highlighting its dual claims to simulation and imprecision, to an imagined perspectival unity alongside a mass of detail that departs from such an absolute rendering of reality—and that are, in painting's fundamental tautology, necessary for the very practice of simulation. If print's pictured illegibility tells us something fundamental about the essence of painting, what is the essence of print, and the printed book, that is captured by painting's narrated illegibility?

Starting at the most basic level, what we have here is a text about a portrait, a move that would recur with enormous frequency throughout *The Human Comedy*. As Adrien Goetz has written, "the painted portrait haunts *The Human Comedy*."[80] Goetz cites a variety of reasons why the portrait provides such a compelling visual genre for Balzac's fictional work, from its role as a key site of exchange in the nineteenth century to its own internal aesthetic contradictions between copying and idealizing. The intermedial consequences of this choice, however, should also be apparent from my discussion in chapter 2 of the expansion of authorial portraits that began to adorn books around the turn of the nineteenth century and that of course would assume a prominent position within Balzac's own collected project. The portrait was not only a sign of the rising commercialism of art in a bourgeois age, it also signaled a decisive *bibliographism* of art in an age of too many books. Seen the other way around, with this traffic between portraits and books, the book also gradually transformed itself into a portrait, an accumulation of lines (of text) that added up to, and coalesced in, an image of the author's face. When Raphaël in *The Wild Ass's Skin* is said to examine the magical skin "sous toutes les faces," we can see in this pun the way his reading of the text is framed as a reading of the face(s) of the text, as the text is lent both faciality and three-dimensionality as an object of visualization. Indeed, faciality becomes the very precondition of reading practices that depended upon imaginative visualization and textual "depth."

Balzac's reduction of the text into face and the face into lines thus disclosed something essential about the intermedial drama that was at the heart of the "portrait" itself. It not only highlighted the bibliographic underpinnings of the pictorial arts in the nineteenth century just as it drew attention to the cultural work of the romantic book that asked to be read as a portrait. As Jean-Luc Nancy has reminded us in his extended reflection on the portrait,[81] with its derivation from the Latin *trahere*, "to pull," the portrait's aim was to pull us in like a line of thread, shifting the plane of representation from one of mimesis to that of methexis. The portrait composed solely of lines disclosed something fundamental about a particular type of looking (and reading) that was framed by the genre of the portrait. It does not ask us to piece it together into a legible whole, but to enter into its frame, into the imaginative hole or aperture that it marks out on the page. But the portrait composed of *illegible* lines was designed by contrast to block precisely this eroticized, attentive gaze, motivating instead the ergodic glancing staged in Johannot's second frontispiece for *The Wild Ass's Skin* as well as Porbus and Poussin's torquing bodies before this unknown (and illegible) masterpiece.

In her astute reading of Balzac's relationship to the image, Alexandra Wettlaufer has made the argument that this tale more than any other embodied a kind of Balzacian antipathy to the visual arts. Frenhofer's (and the painter's) failure is a sign, in Wettlaufer's reading, of Balzac's (and the writer's) success.[82] But such a reading seems to subordinate Balzac's tale and its "take" on the visual arts too much within the confines of the genre of parody. "The Unknown Masterpiece" does not read well as a parody, and it is hard to imagine that its enormous subsequent allure to future generations of visual artists would be possible if there was not something about this tale that articulated a deep affinity between author and subject. In place of seeing Frenhofer as the embodiment of a failure that Balzac writes against, I want to suggest that Frenhofer's failure is an embodiment of a certain kind of writerly success that Balzac projects. The narration of painting's failure should be understood as the promotion of a kind of intermedial literacy, one required to understand the medium of the printed book for which Balzac was writing and on which his success as a writer depended. The story of the overwritten portrait—image as line and line as image—was about residing *between* text and image, a collapsing of two distinct representational spaces into one single visual-lectoral experience. These lines crucially push and pull, embodied (literally) in the only form of the portrait that is legible, the foot, which here stands for (again literally) such corporeal and sensorial mobility.

To support this point we need only look at two final pieces of para-textual evidence from the tale. The first are the two dates that frame the story: "1845," which is placed underneath the dedication "À un Lord," and "février 1832," which is placed at the story's close. As William Paulson has suggested, the differential dating that frames the story discloses the way this written work explicitly marks itself by the work of "overwriting" enacted in the pictorial project of the novella's hero.[83] There is an equivalence here between the dual images of authorship and "paintership" that the text makes available, proposing on some level an identification between the two. The second and more interesting piece of evidence is the illegible dedication above the opening date of 1845, which was added to the Furne edition of *The Human Comedy* and was composed, in Sternean fashion, of five lines of points. What was a dedication doing atop this single tale within the larger whole, especially from an author who had said that the age of dedications was past?[84] And more significantly, why was it illegible? How did the metamorphosis of type into an image (through the illegible line of type) fit within the novella's larger concern with the relationship between reading and seeing via the illegible line of drawing?

The positioning of the dedication assumes its significance, I want to suggest, through the way it visually stands in for two other paratextual devices that were common to the romantic book but that were *not* there in this case: the epigraph and the illustrated head-piece. The illegible dedication replaces, but also conjoins, the visual and the textual paratext. Such paratextual echoes (can one speak of the intertext of the paratext?) suggest the extent to which this particular paratextual device was invested with a crucial intermedial identity, much like the wavy line on the title page of *The Wild Ass's Skin*. Indeed, the illegible typographical line (of discrete points) translates the (handwritten and handcut) continuous line into the new media technology of print. In this sense, the dedication, which one could not read, was not a dedication at all, but functioned instead as another visual epigraph. The final version of "The Unknown Masterpiece" thus drew one more line of connection with its counterpart, *The Wild Ass's Skin*, that also initially appeared in the intermedial space of *L'Artiste*. Far from insulating the typographic from the image, as Le Men has argued in her study of Balzac's controlling relationship to his illustrators during the making of *The Human Comedy*,[85] it was precisely the typographic that was being transformed here into an image—and not just any image, but *the* image of romantic intermediality, the illegible line.

Parallels, or Stendhal and the Line of the Self

Balzac's text about illegible visual lines would receive its most prominent translation into the visual arts through Pablo Picasso's illustrated edition of Balzac's tale that appeared with Ambroise Vollard in 1931.[86] Such a textual-linear foundation of modern art would then go on to inspire some of the major subsequent artistic projects of the twentieth century from Cy Twombly to Brice Marden. (Goethe's own implication in this story was nicely captured by Twombly's six-part series, "Goethe in Italy.") That Picasso acutely understood the importance of the intermedial line (both typographic and wavy) could be seen in the fifty-five wood engravings of line drawings for his text that were entitled "En manière d'introduction par Pablo Picasso" and that consisted of numerous wavy lines connected by a series of points.

Where Picasso's work marked a watershed moment of the translation of Balzac's intermedial program into a visual tradition of the artist's book, I want to look at the way such Balzacian writing also gets *rewritten* in the twentieth century, principally through the intermedial poetics of the German writer W. G. Sebald. Sebald would become one of the most important postwar writers working with text and image, and his books have arguably done more than any other contemporary writer to reinvigorate our literary memory to attend to the history of visual and textual adaptation that has transpired across the page of the printed book. That Balzac's work would mark a key influence on Sebald's is thus hardly surprising. Sebald was not only one of the most literarily self-conscious of writers, Balzac's intense interest in the intersections of erasure and visualization through the overlapping lines of writing and image also foreground some of the basic concerns of Sebald's oeuvre. In the novella "Max Aurach," from *The Emigrants* (translated as "Max Ferber" in the English edition), we are told about the making of a portrait, one that could have come straight out of "The Unknown Masterpiece":

He drew with vigorous abandon, frequently going through half a dozen of his willow-wood charcoal sticks in the shortest of time; and that process of drawing and shading on the thick, leathery paper, as well as the concomitant business of constantly erasing what he had drawn with a woolen rag already heavy with charcoal, really amounted to nothing but a steady production of dust, which never ceased except at night. Time and again, at the end of the working day, I marveled to see that Ferber, with a few lines and shadows that had escaped annihilation, had created a portrait of great vividness.[87]

At the end of this romantic tradition of the wavy line we see how "a few lines and shadows that had escaped annihilation" work instead to create a portrait of "great vividness," a sympathy of observation that marks a direct reversal of Balzac's alienated, shifting, and stretching viewers who see "nothing." And it was precisely this possibility of the sympathy of the trace, the possibility of recovering a subjectivity from a few illegible lines, that was one of the main aims of Sebald's own work, emerging as it did within a German cultural matrix shaped by the postwar, postmodern, and postholocaust.

Before we move completely from Balzac to Sebald and the question of the vanishing line of subjectivity, however, we must first move back to one of Balzac's contemporaries and Sebald's most significant sources, Stendhal, whose illustrated autobiography would serve as a key handbook for Sebald's writerly beginnings. The opening chapter of Sebald's first prose work, *Vertigo* (1990), was entitled "Beyle, or Love is a Madness Most Discrete," and it contained several images of illustrations from Stendhal's autobiography, *Vie de Henry Brulard* (1835/36), a work which would serve as one of the major romantic reflections on the nature of the intermedial line. Stendhal, and his intermedial reflections on life writing, would become the principal portal to Sebald's prose.

Stendhal's autobiography was never published during his lifetime, and its manuscriptural form, which as we will see played a crucial role in shaping its meaning, nicely draws attention to the important way that "the romantic book" was not exclusively synonymous with "the printed book." Sketchbooks, notebooks, commonplace books, workbooks, albums, ledgers, police records—these were all bookish spaces in the romantic era that were not printed spaces. The manuscriptural in Stendhal is both figured as a pretext—he repeatedly refers to its future printing—as well as an endpoint. With its numerous incorporations of print conventions, Stendhal's manuscript book self-consciously remediates the printed book. But at the same time, it also walls off the technology of print through the overwhelming significance of the line drawings that populate the book and of the way the letter plays a role as both image and text. As numerous subsequent editors of Stendhal's work have remarked, one cannot produce a print edition of this work without effacing the important continuities staged in the book between the line of writing and that of drawing.[88]

The illustrations that populate *Henry Brulard* are marked by a high degree of heterogeneity, traversing letters, signatures, objects, topographical plans (of rooms, roads, and rivers), and landscape views most often of some horizon line (precipices, bridges, or mountains).[89] Through the proliferation of lines, whether literal or visual, life writing in Stendhal is invested with an essential graphic element, and such attention to the intersections of autobiography and vision are complemented by Stendhal's inclusion of a number of engraved images that were bound together with the manuscript pages and that were often indebted to Rosenblum's "international style" of outline illustration.[90] The various visual elements of Stendhal's autobiography thus situated readers within a shifting perceptual framework between looking over, looking at, and looking through, even as such looking was always intimately bound up with the act of reading. The line drawing was never very far from, indeed was often concomitant with, the line of writing.

Turning to the opening illustration in the autobiography, we read the following entry that accompanies it: "The other day while musing on life on the lonely road above Lake Albano I discovered that my life could be summarized in these names, and thus I wrote their initials in the dust like Zadig with my walking stick, sitting on the small seat behind the Stations of the Cross of the *Minori osservanti* built by Urban VIII's brother, Barberini, next to those two beautiful trees enclosed by a small circular wall."[91] Stendhal proceeds to list the first names of his lovers, and on the verso of the preceding leaf (page twenty-two), Stendhal gives us the work's first illustration, which would later be included in Sebald's *Vertigo*. Here we see a landscape drawing of where Stendhal was sitting when he experienced this epiphany. Five manuscript pages later, he will describe the same scene, but in place of drawing the scene he will draw the lovers' initials (plus a numerical coefficient that corresponded to the number of sexual encounters) as he said he did that day in September (fig. 6.14).

While Voltaire is said to be the immediate reference point for Stendhal ("like Zadig"), there is something decidedly Sternean going on here, not only with the stick that becomes a writing instrument, but more significantly in the wavy line captured in the scriptural "Z" of the proper name that is said to be the literal/literary referent point for this entire scene.[92] The shift from one graphic mode to another, from the horizontal to the

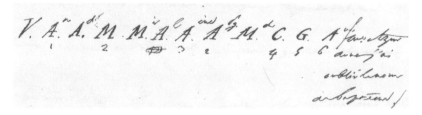

Figure 6.14   Initials in the sand from Stendhal, *Vie de Henry Brulard* (1835/36),
1:23. Courtesy of the Bibliothèque Municipale de Grenoble, France.

topographical (as we move from looking at the mountainside above the lake to looking down at letters written in the sand), also represents a shift in representational codes, from the mimetic to the paraphrastic, that transpires through the line(s) of text that also serve as an image of literal lines. Much like Sterne's wavy line with its capacity to summarize a series of arguments against marriage, these initials in the sand are said to play a paraphrastic role, standing for the entirety of Stendhal's "life." At the same time, in their function as code, not words, they also assume an elliptical nature, signs that stand for information that is not revealed, much like Trim's flourish that stands in, as image, for a text we cannot read. In each case, the line wavers between the two rhetorical devices of ellipsis and paraphrasis, standing in for something more and leaving something else out (standing for what is not there).

This precious balance between the legibility and illegibility of the line in the dust is itself doubled in the signs' capacity to function as both image and text. They are at once letters and images (of letters), and Stendhal's intermedial game is crucially tied to the particular medium of the book in which he is working. It is the manuscriptural nature of Stendhal's project that allows for this slippage between text and image within the text itself. Those manuscriptural letters can look like both images and writing in a way that they could not in a printed edition, where the typographic letters of the text would amplify, rather than parallel, those handwritten letter's visual aspect.[93] And it is precisely this hovering between the seen and the read that allows the line of script to function like code, to be both opaque and meaningful at the same time. Once again we can see how handwriting remains a key locus of the romantic bibliographic imaginary, only now it serves to address the question of the book's dual identity as a pictorial and literary medium.

The significance of the ambiguous legibility of the line emerges even more clearly when we attend to another detail from the manuscript—that

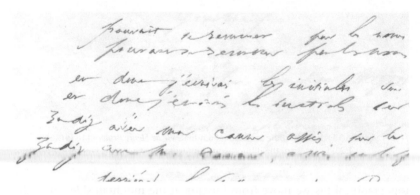

Figure 6.15   "Zadig" from Stendhal, *Vie de Henry Brulard* (1835/36),
1:28. Courtesy of the Bibliothèque Municipale de Grenoble, France.

Stendhal has written each of the lines of the above passage *twice*, the second
more neatly than the first (fig. 6.15). Stendhal would repeatedly return to
the question of the legibility of his handwriting in his autobiographical
work,[94] and such concerns would enter into his novelistic writing at the moment in *The Red and the Black* (1830) when Julien Sorel's upward mobility is
threatened by a case of misspelling "cela" with two l's while copying letters
for the Marquis (which Stendhal later recounts about himself in chapter 40
of *Henry Brulard*). Indeed, it is significant that Julien's mistake is revealed
during a moment of pouring over an eighty-volume edition of Voltaire's
works, a "masterpiece of the best bookbinder in London."[95] Attention to the
book is interrupted by an attention to the letter. Mediacy and literacy are, in
The Red and Black, mutually dependent upon one another.

Returning to the autobiography, we can see how the doubled lines of
text here disclose a key fact about the *dual* function of the coded letters
to which the lines refer and which are intended to be both legible and
illegible to subsequent readers—legible as image (we can read these letters as signs), but illegible as text (we cannot read the names and stories
attached to them). And here again the question of the letters' medial resonance is crucial: in the carefully serifed flourishes of the coded initials we
can see Stendhal endowing the coded manuscript letters with a *typographical*
identity (and thereby turning his lovers into "types"). The illegibility of the
manuscriptural scribble embodied in the "Z" of Zadig that had to be rewritten is replaced by the legibility of the curvilinear typographical line of the
serif that must be decoded. The manuscript letter requires a reperformance
and repetition, while the typographical letter requires interpretation and
undoing. In each case, it is the curvilinear flourish that lends meaning to

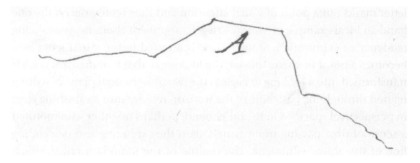

Figure 6.16   The horizon of the duel from Stendhal, *Vie de Henry Brulard* (1835/36), 2:484. Courtesy of the Bibliothèque Municipale de Grenoble, France.

the letter as sign, whether as tale or serif. In yet another recall of that Sternean line, it is precisely the tale *loop* of the rewritten "Z" in Stendhal that transforms it from squiggle to letter. The proper understanding of the letter passes through a particular graphic practice.

If these coded letters were in some sense the premier sign of the intermedial line in Stendhal—between text and image, between manuscript and typography—it is important to attend to the way the wavy horizon line would also assume a privileged visual identity in Stendhal's various attempts to capture the problematic convergence of writing and life through the figure of the line. It is precisely in such moments in Stendhal where we can see a new relevance being lent to Balzac's gesture of turning Sterne's wavy line on its side. In a description of a duel (is there any more prevalent romantic notion of life than the duel?), Stendhal describes his experience in the following manner:

> There the pistols were loaded; a number of horrifying paces were measured, perhaps twenty, and I said to myself, here is the moment to have courage. I don't know why, but Odru was to fire first, I looked fixedly at a small piece of rock in the shape of a trapezoid that was above point A, the same one one sees from the window of my aunt Elisabeth's next to the roof of the St. Louis church. (*HB*, 2:771)

As we can see in Stendhal's illustration (fig. 6.16), the letter "A" is enclosed by a line drawing of the trapezoid-shaped rock which trails off in a squiggle in the lower right-hand corner. Once again we are in the presence of the coded letter, only now the letter no longer is an image but accompanies the image of the line as a form of interpretation or "key." The letter marks out a point of visual attention and thus represents on the one hand an ideal example of Murray Krieger's argument about the spatializing tendency of ekphrastic writing.[96] Time is arrested in the visual letter as it becomes a point in space. Indeed, the looking *at* that it dramatizes is itself transformed into a looking *through* as the two dimensional plane of writing figured through the basic line of the horizon recedes into a vanishing *point* in perspectival space.[97] On the other hand, perhaps no other icon captured a sense of time passing more acutely than the ascending and descending line of the alpine silhouette. The outline of the mountain range, which also appears for example in numerous places in Coleridge's notebooks to denote visual vanishing points,[98] captured something that was also *missing* from view. The prevalence of such forms in Stendhal's autobiography articulated a notion of life defined by the figure of the "turn," by a narrative of a rise and fall. Indeed, Stendhal would use this same visual figure at a later point to capture a sense of decline, only in the second example it lacks the focalizing energy of the letter and is instead marked by the serial force of numbers and dates (*HB*, 2:809). This overlap of a notion of life with that of the "turn" was of course already disclosed through the central alphabetic sign of the "Z" that provided the literary and visual frame for his entire work and that derived in important ways from Trim's flourish and Balzac's epigraphic reappropriation.

The wavy line of the horizon marked by a coded letter thus captured the contradictions of the autobiographical pact itself: how to represent the mobile subject of "the life" in the single moment of its fixation on the page? Conversely, how could the writer identify precisely those singular "moments" that assumed paraphrastic significance—that could "summarize" the entirety of random events in a single visual/textual stroke? The moment of conflict (the duel) that was represented through the letter as a point of focalization and framed by the infinite oscillations of the wavy horizon line captured this latent conflict between the stretched-out moment (the anamorphic *bow*) and the condensed whole (the paraphrastic *point*). Such antinomies of life, line, image, and writing would arguably achieve their most profound moment of synthesis in the figure of yet another crucial line in Stendhal, that of the *parallel* line, to which I want to turn next.

Mathematics marked an essential ingredient of both Stendhal's own life and the way he tried to understand that life. But what emerges over the course of the autobiography is the way math is repeatedly used to capture the *divergence* between the line of writing and the line of life.[99] Musing on the importance of mathematics in his life, Stendhal writes:

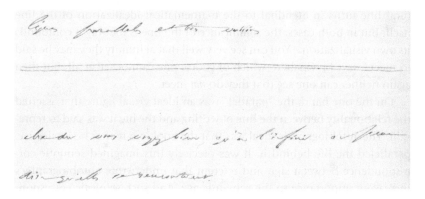

Figure 6.17   The parallel line from Stendhal, *Vie de Henry Brulard* (1835/36),
3:58. Courtesy of the Bibliothèque Municipale de Grenoble, France.

If − × − = + had caused me much sorrow [*chagrin*], one can imagine the blackness that took hold of my soul when I began Louis Monge's *Statics*. . . . At the beginning of geometry it says: We give the name of *parallels* to two lines which, when extended to infinity, would never meet. But right at the beginning of the *Statics* the famous animal Louis Monge has written something like this: Two parallel lines can be considered to meet if they are extended to infinity. (*HB*, 3:155)

Stendhal continues by recounting how he had asked his teacher, M. Chabert, for an explanation, who tells the young Beyle, after drawing an image of parallel lines on the blackboard, which Stendhal reproduces in his autobiography (fig. 6.17), "You can see very well that at infinity they may be said to meet" (*HB*, 3:155).

In this seemingly banal anecdote about the ignorance of his contemporaries, Stendhal is once again on Sternean terrain, for in volume 6, chapter 40 of *Tristram Shandy*, Shandy tells us that his narrative aspires, after so much indirection, to the straightness of the straight line. "If I mend at this rate," writes Shandy, "it is not impossible—by the good leave of his grace of *Benevento's* devils—but I may arrive hereafter at the excellency of going on even thus; [image of straight line] which is a line drawn as straight as I could draw it, by a writing-master's ruler, (borrowed for that purpose) turning neither to the right hand or to the left."[100] At stake in both Sterne and Stendhal—in the nonfictional replaying of the fictional autobiography—is ultimately the possibility of the straight line and its significance for the autobiographic project. Sterne's typographical idealization of the manuscriptural line turns in Stendhal to the mathematical idealization of the line itself. But in both cases, the significance of the line is the way it confounds its own visualization. "You can see very well that at infinity they may be said to meet," says M. Chabert, which of course one cannot see at all. But then again neither can one see that they do *not* meet.

On the one hand, the "parallel" was an ideal visual figure that asserted the relationality between the line of writing and the life it was said to represent. The autobiographic ideal was that the book, no matter how selective, paralleled the life behind it. It was precisely this imagined semiotic correspondence between sign and referent that underwrote autobiography's increasing importance to the romantic age. And such semiotic correspondence was then amplified in Stendhal by an asserted parallel between textual and visual signs. Their intermedial interchangeability paralleled that between book and self. But on the other hand, the parallel line ultimately represented a graphic impossibility, whether of text or image. Like Shandy's feigned naïveté, M. Chabert's seeming ignorance revealed a deeper truth. The parallel line—the line that was identical to itself—was as impossible to see as the text that was identical to the self. And the confounding variable in this graphic conundrum was always the function of time. Only the unrepresentable category of infinity would allow the truth of the parallel line (either its convergence or failure to converge) to emerge into view. The parallel line paralleled the autobiographical project precisely because it captured just such graphic vanishing *points*—the ultimate lack of coincidence between the line (whether of text or image) and the self.

Coda: Sebald's Bibliographic Vanishing Points

With the introduction of the paradox of the line as the figure of an intermedial and autobiographical vanishing point, we are now finally on Sebaldian terrain and in this sense at the outer edges of the romantic bibliographic imaginary. The combustion that was at the heart of Stendhal's autobiographical pseudonym (*brûler* = to burn) would of course become a key element of Sebald's project of writing after the Holocaust, and it suggested a decided limit to the imagined efficacy or continued vitality of the book. While so much of Sebald scholarship has turned on his relationship to the photograph to the point that we now have a monograph on photography *after* Sebald,[101] we should not overlook just how important the graphic line was for Sebald's visual and textual poetics, an investment whose lineage, we can now see, stretches back from Stendhal to Balzac, Goethe, and Sterne. I do not have room to unravel all of the ways that the line functions in Sebald,

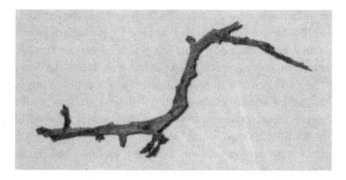

Figure 6.18   The crystalline line from W. G. Sebald, "Max Aurach," *Die Ausgewanderten: Vier lange Erzählungen*, 320. © Eichborn AG, Frankfurt am Main, 1992.

but to the question of where the intermedial wavy line goes after Stendhal, I want to supply the following image from the "Max Aurach/Ferber" chapter of Sebald's *Emigrants* (fig. 6.18), which bears a familial resemblance to those wavy lines in Sterne and his followers.

The narrator is visiting the Kissingen salt-frames, and the illustration is a drawing of the process of salt crystallizing in pools of water as a result of passing over blackthorn twigs attached to the walls of the mine. Crystallization was an idea that Sebald had taken from Stendhal's theory of love from *De l'Amour*, which opens with a description of the Salzburg salt mines.[102] But in Sebald's rewriting, the visual transparency of the saline crystal, which had stood in Stendhal as the prism of love, is transformed into a metaphor of ossification and death. It is no longer the branch or bough ("rameau d'arbre" in Stendhal) that becomes crystallized, but the water itself crystallizes—the fluid becomes fixed—in a form that *looks like* the bowed line of the tree branch. In the crystalline line's paralleling of the line of the tree branch, we can see how the line in Sebald hovers between the visual registers of mimesis and abstraction, indeed an act of mimesis that negates itself to become an abstraction. The crystalline line is capable of imitating nature (a mirror of the twigs on the wall) and, in the narrator's words, "sublating" it as well, as those very twigs are gradually denaturalized by so many years of being covered by mineral water. Mimesis eventually effaces the very object it aims to represent. The crystalline line becomes the sign of the dual capacity of nature to imitate itself and destroy itself in the process. It marks a poignant reversal of the aspirational potential of Goethe's spiral line.

The wavy line is, once again, marked by an extraordinary degree of legibility (the crystal) and illegibility (death), and similarly assumes an intermedial resonance in Sebald. In the narrator's reflections immediately following this image of nature imitating itself to death, we learn of the narrator's inability to write the story of his subject, Max Aurach (whose name combines an echo of both a lament, *Ach,* and the word for smoke, *Rauch*). Such concern will result, according to the narrator, in hundreds of pages of illegible "pen and pencil scribbles" (*Bleistift- und Kugelschreibergekritzel*).[103] The crystalline line of self-destruction is translated into the wavy line of the narrator's graphite/graphic scribble. When the narrator refers to his problems as the result of his own moral "Skrupulantismus" (scrupilism), we can see in this German neologism how even the narration of his incapacity to narrate is gradually infected by a certain degree of illegibility, an illegibility, it should be added, that is a function of an ingrained mimetic desire to accurately render the subjectivity of his object of study through writing. The more he wants to capture Aurach on the page, the more illegible the writing becomes.

The intermedial identity of the wavy line that I have been tracing over the course of this chapter and that seems to end in an act of vanishing rather than bringing into view emerges most visibly, so to speak, in Sebald's engagement with yet another culturally laden line, that of the train line. In an earlier novella from *The Emigrants,* "Paul Bereyter," we learn the story of a quarter-Jewish school teacher who is banned from teaching during the Nazi years and who eventually throws himself to his death onto train tracks many years later after the war. At a crucial moment in the narrative, we are presented with a drawing of train lines that contains the text, "So it is since October 4, 1949" (So ist es seit dem 4.10.1949). Only the presence of text in the image (which remains untranslated in the English version) draws our attention to what is missing in the image, namely the prior organization of the town's train line for the deportation of Jews. Neither the subjects who were carried by this medium nor the institutional organization of the medium itself are visible any longer. The line of text in the image serves as a caption to the line of drawing, but it does not caption what is depicted in the image but what it leaves out. Once again lingual and medial translation mutually highlight one another, as the untranslatable caption in the image illustrates not only the limits of translating images but also the limits of visual illustration itself. With the image of the disappearing tracks that would eventually mark the space of Bereyter's own death with which the novella begins (fig. 6.19), we can see the most emphatic instance of how Sebald takes the serpentine line—the quintessential eighteenth-century figure of beauty and grace—and transforms it into the most recognizable twentieth-century sign of extinction. It comes to represent the loss of person and with it, the loss of story and knowledge.

Figure 6.19 The train line from W. G. Sebald, "Paul Bereyter," *Die Ausgewanderten: Vier lange Erzählungen*, 41. © Eichborn AG, Frankfurt am Main, 1992.

This then marks the endpoint of the romantic bibliographic imagination. The wavy line that captured the precarious emergence of intermedial knowledge in the romantic book turns into a sign marking the vanishing point of knowledge in the postmodern book. At the moment of its threatened obsolescence in the late twentieth century, the book is refigured as a marker of just such a medial threshold. The book as universe that was transformed in the romantic period to a universe of books is refigured in this subsequent turn of the century as a dividing line that marks off a receding bibliographic horizon, as that which we can no longer see, read, or directly experience. Unlike the hero and heroine of Goethe's "Man of Fifty" whose joints touch each other in secret as they jointly hold and read a book, the book in Sebald is reimagined as the marker of things permanently out of reach, whether a self, a culture, or even the book itself. And yet if one can draw a sense of hope from Sebald's intermedial project of vanishing points (which is hardly self-evident) it might be this: that the intermedial interactions between text and image in the book propel us to search out the otherwise invisible intermedial interactions that take place beyond the boundaries of the book with *other* media. It is there, in this entanglement, where the book's identity—and the remnants of its vanishing—are to be found.

Next to the Book

He talked. After a while she began to understand what she was hearing. It took many levels of perception. It took whole social histories of how people listen to what other people say.

—Don DeLillo, *The Body Artist*

Lection/Selection

In July 1999 at a castle in Elmau, Bavaria, the German philosopher Peter Sloterdijk delivered a talk to an audience of Christian and Jewish theologians entitled "Rules for the Human Zoo: An Answer to Heidegger's *Letter on Humanism.*"[1] The theme for the conference was "Exodus from Being," and at the heart of Sloterdijk's polemical talk was the assertion that the project of humanism and humanistic learning had come to an end in a world dominated by mass media. For Sloterdijk, humanism had emerged out of and intimately depended upon a culture of the printed book. The book's growing marginality signaled the waning power of the humanities to socialize individuals. "Social synthesis is no longer—no longer even apparently—primarily a matter of books and letters."[2] The future of the humanities, and by extension the human itself, were crucially tied in Sloterdijk's vision to the future of the book.

Sloterdijk's talk went on to become a sensation in the German press, with numerous articles, interviews, and public letters being issued on the topic in the months leading up to the turn of the millennium.[3] On the one hand, Sloterdijk's talk was little more than a garden variety tale of the end of the book that was becoming increasingly popular by the mid to late 1990s, a genre that owed much to the initial popularity of works like Sven Birkerts's

Gutenberg Elegies (1994). But on the other hand, what drove the talk's peculiarly vibrant afterlife was Sloterdijk's original association of media technology and biotechnology, his assertion that the book had played a crucial role as an "anthropotechnology" of human domestication. In identifying the "humanizing power of reading classics," Sloterdijk placed the book within a much longer trajectory of technologies of human engineering. "Reading and selection" (*Lektionen und Selektionen*), argued Sloterdijk using words designed to get the attention of his German and German-Jewish listeners, "have more to do with one another than any cultural historian has been capable or willing to consider."[4] The book was to be understood as a precursor of a (necessary) biotechnological future. As Sloterdijk later said in an interview, "Man has always been made."[5] Genetic engineering silently emerged as the implied successor to the vanishing book.

Dreaming in Books is conceived as an answer to answers like Sloterdijk's to the increasingly unsettled relationship between the future of the book and the future of the humanities, between the shifting terrain of media, intellectual, and literary history today. How we understand the history of the book will determine how we understand the book's future role in society as a medium of both knowledge and creativity. As Sloterdijk vividly pointed out in his talk, the identity of the humanities and their pedagogical efficacy *are* intimately linked to the identity of the printed book. We simply cannot understand how modern societies have made knowledge—and made intellectual making itself, *poiesis*—without understanding the changing relationship between individuals and their books. But by reconceptualizing the history of the book not as a narrative of rise and fall but precisely as a series of social, historical, and technological negotiations, we can begin to see in a more critical light the negotiations that are underway today in revaluing our relationship to the book. Rather than prophesy (yet again) the end of the book, the point would be to rethink (yet again) the place of the book within the humanities, both as an object of study and a mode of communication. My aim is to reposition the "nextness," in Michael Joyce's words,[6] that suffuses media studies with a move towards the "next to," what I want to call a "translational humanism."

"Book was there, it was there."—Gertrude Stein

At a key moment in Goethe's novella "The Man of Fifty," a guest of the beautiful widow reaches for a book of poetry upon the arrival of the Major, the so-called man of fifty, who will soon become the widow's lover. The grasping of the book (*greifen* in German) that this scene stages, the act of bringing the book closer to oneself, poignantly mirrored the social grasping that was about to transpire between the widow and the unsuspecting major. In doing so, it also captured a fundamental identity of the book itself, one that depended upon a physical as well as conceptual proximity to the self. Being next to the book was what allowed one to understand (*begreifen*) the book's contents, a metaphorical constellation that one could trace back to Augustine's own bibliographic epiphany that was induced by the voice of a child, "tolle lege, tolle lege" (take up and read, take up and read).[7] As I have tried to show in numerous places throughout this book, the book was repeatedly endowed during the romantic era with a notion of being "at-hand." Whether it was the greeting, grasping, giving, beseeching, or even striking hand, such handedness that surrounded the romantic book partook in a much larger alignment of grasping and reading that has crucially shaped the book's meaning in the Western tradition.

Such dramas of being next to the book in Goethe were nevertheless subtly being transformed in his work by a very different notion of bibliographic next-to-ness, one that has important implications about how we might think about the book in the future. When the guest in "The Man of Fifty" takes up the book, she also sets in motion an increasingly complex exchange of texts and textual containers. After requesting that the Major recite his poem of "the hunt," which he refuses, the widow then hands him an embroidered case (*Brieftasche*) as a "deposit" so that he will return it with a handwritten copy of his poem inside. As we later learn, the widow's "case" is not quite complete (it is referred to as her Penelopean work), and she tells us that she worked on it while "overhearing" the conversations of others. Upon returning home and looking through his papers, the Major will place a "fair copy" of his poem (a term denoting a manuscript prepared for printing) in the case and will then decide to place a verse translation of a passage from Ovid (about Arachne, the weaver of webs) as an epigraph to the poem. The case that was composed while listening to or listening in on the stories of others contains and transmits the story of another (about a man on a hunt), which is itself framed by the translation of yet another text (about women and webs). Upon delivering the bound object the Major wonders to himself whether his meaning has not in fact gotten away from him. In exchange for his efforts, the widow will one day return a case of letters that the Major has written but that were not addressed to the widow but to his sister regarding the planned marriage of their children to one another. None of these cases will ever be "finished," as the novella itself does not come to a conclusion but is only completed later within the novel in which it is embedded.

As "The Man of Fifty" nicely illustrates, the book was being refigured by Goethe as an increasingly shared and syncretic textual space—a distinct rejection of the popularized notion of the book as a closed and socially isolating mediaspace that still endures today. Texts in books were imagined to be participants in larger social dramas, their discrete specificity ("book was there, it was there" in Gertrude Stein's words) seen as increasingly dispersed and problematic. Goethe's short work was part of a much larger romantic investment in addressing what I would call a "crisis of address," of making sense of the sense of the book's newfound ubiquity at the turn of the nineteenth century. Far from marking out a world that was then superseded by the "mass media" of the twentieth century, as Sloterdijk suggested in his Gutenbergian elegy, the world of the romantic book was intimately concerned with the shifting alignment of the broadcast and the interpersonal. Being open to the ways in which the book addressed questions of communicative and social disclosure in the past can allow us to see how it might continue to do so in the future under new circumstances.

If Goethe's fiction gestured towards a growing textual heterogeneity, both within and among books, it also drew attention to a technological heterogeneity as well as the characters in the novella continually shifted between various forms of textuality, from the printed book, to the fair copy manuscript, to handwritten letters, to the woven case. Writing, and the social interactions it made possible, were taking place in Goethe between various medial registers. Such romantic dramas of intermediality should stand as important reminders today as we think about conditions of new media not in terms of replacement but as renegotiation.[8] In Lisa Gitelman's words, "The introduction of new media is never entirely revolutionary: new media are less points of epistemic rupture than they are socially embedded sites for the ongoing negotiation of meaning as such. Comparing and contrasting new media thus stand to offer a view of negotiability in itself."[9] *Dreaming in Books* has tried to recover precisely such sites of negotiability, not only in moving from one medium into another (from manuscript into print in the critical edition, for example), but also in moving from one medium *to* another (from manuscript to print in the miscellany or from text to image in the illustrated book). While translation may have emerged as a "basic structure of romantic thought," in Andreas Huyssen's words,[10] it significantly referred not only to the interlingual transfers of an increasingly open literary system that the book's expansion made possible but also to the intermedial transfers that were daily taking place between different forms of writing and different forms of representation. During this crucial period of media change, nextness was as much about the "next to" as it was about what came next. Understanding the future of the book depends upon a better understanding of the history of interactions between residual and new communications technologies.

Besides: Toward a Translational Humanism

At the conclusion of his talk, Sloterdijk proposed that the future humanist would soon be nothing more than an archivist. Books that were no longer read could no longer be considered to be in circulation. "It is their fate to stand in quiet stacks, like dead letters that are no longer retrieved from the post-office, representations—or misrepresentations—of a wisdom which contemporaries no longer succeed in believing in."[11] Books had sunk irretrievably into the "timelessness of the archive." Those who guarded over them were irrelevant, foolish, or just plain mad.

In place of the lonely figure of the bookish humanist as an archivist, wiseman, or madman—yet another variation on the myth of the ivory tower—I want to reimagine the humanist as a translatologist, as a scholar of those fields of negotiability that individuals like Gitelman and Bolter have identified in their work on the history of new media. The future humanist in this thought experiment is not an isolated and anachronistic figure—a deeply resonant leitmotif that has been associated with the printed book from its inception (as in the canonized images of Messina's *St. Jerome in His Study* [1475] or Dürer's *Erasmus of Rotterdam* [1526]). Rather, this humanist would be multiply situated across linguistic, disciplinary, and communicative spaces. This humanist breaks down what Espen Aarseth has called the "media chauvinism" of the humanities into media-specific disciplines (art history, literature, film, theater),[12] at the same time that s/he would also avoid the pitfalls of the discourse of "convergence" that surrounds so much recent new media theory.[13] Instead of either separating or effacing the communicative differences between media, the humanist as translatologist studies the losses, breaks, ruptures, discoveries, additions, negotiations, and doublings that occur in moving from one medium to another. In this vision of the humanist, the study of literature is reconceived as a linguistic performance across multiple media channels, requiring something akin to Alan Liu's notion of a new "transliteracy."[14]

How does this impact the study of the history and future of the book? It would mean first and foremost reaffirming the importance of *history*. Next to the book refers, as it did for Goethe, to the ability of the scholar to get close to the physical book, to grasp it in both senses of the word. As much as the study and engagement with digital media has brought into sharper relief the unique qualities of the printed book, exemplified in studies such as Jerome McGann's *Radiant Textuality: Literature after the World Wide Web* or N. Katherine Hayles, *My Mother Was a Computer: Digital Subjects and Literary Texts*, such differential analysis cannot replace an encounter with historical material and the attempt to reconstruct the book as a lived experience.

At the same time, being next to the book implies moving beyond the teleologically oriented frameworks of studies such as McGann's with its exclusive emphasis on the "after," on how to move from book to web. Such work only reaffirms the hegemony of the computer and collapses otherwise diverse media spaces. When new media theories such as Lev Manovich talk about the "transcoding" of culture through the computer today,[15] they are identifying the powerful and pervasive ways that all media are increasingly influenced by the logic of computerization, whether it is in the form of digital cinema projectors, sound and image editing software, or basic word processing programs that facilitate, in the words of Michael Joyce, a "nomadic style" of cut-and-paste.[16] Such a view of the computerization of culture, however, overlooks the variety of *other* media that crowd our lives and between which we move every day. In our claims about it being a universal medium, the computer threatens to become the new book.

Instead, we need to make room for the spatially relational study of the book, of how the printed book and computer (but also handwriting, speech, video, sculpture, theater, and a host of other media) have existed and continue to exist side by side, with, as Goethe put it, "their joints touching quite naturally in secret." We need to account for what Mette Ramsgard Thomsen has called "mixed reality,"[17] not the way a single medium might absorb and consume us, but the way we incorporate various media into our interactions with and understanding of the world. Media are not simply forms of displacement, but also come with us. The point is to explore not just the different nature of marking systems (XML or type) or projection surfaces (screens or pages) but the way media themselves generate very different experiential spaces and encounters, whether intermedially or intramedially. In place of Friedrich Kittler's tripartite 1800/1900/2000 media paradigm of universality, differentiation, and convergence, this kind of research would draw attention to the persistent recurrence of media differentiation *and* interaction over time.

In highlighting these interactive, performative spaces, such work would explore the different ways that we express ourselves when using different media—when we write with our hands or our computers, when we speak to someone in person, over the phone, in a lecture hall, or into a microphone or a recording device. It would explore the different meanings that are conveyed when reading a book, listening to a radio play, or watching a podcast. In short, it would draw attention to what Hanjo Berressem has called the "dynamism of the signifier."[18] In doing so, it should offer a corrective to the book's perceived universality well into the nineteenth century as well as its perceived marginality at the turn of the twenty-first. It shows us how the romantic self can be understood as a precursor of the modern self who comes into being through numerous different channels of communication, as both sender and receiver. It will provide a useful framework to understand our own (and our students') future uses (or non-use) of the book, to begin to conceive of our work as multi-medially situated, increasingly reliant on both the separate and overlapping uses of text, speech, and image depending on the intellectual goals at hand.[19] It is time to conceive of visual translations of literary works and oral performances of reading experiences and not just more books about books.

Translational humanism orients scholarship towards the study and practice of how different individuals translate themselves into different media in different situations at different points in their lives. Indeed, it reframes the human itself not as something made, as an inert object, but as a translation, as a process. That such an understanding of the human is not exclusively an invention of the digital but already resident in bibliographic culture (and no doubt even earlier) can be seen on the second and third pages of Mallarmé's experimental book *Un coup de dés*, which begins with the command "Soit" ("be") in the upper left corner of the page and ends with the word "par" ("through") in the lower right.[20] Being is refigured as "being through" that takes shape not only across the page, but also across the fold between the verso and recto sides of separate leaves.

Ultimately, translational humanism will undertake to provide what John Durham Peters has called a "morphology of communication," to "seek to describe the communicative crafts that abound in our species."[21] It requires that we pay attention to the historical interactions between language and media and the various ways that such interactions have been thought about and conceived over time. The six categories of communicating that I have proposed in this book (networking, copying, processing, sharing, overhearing, and adapting) are intended as just such a preliminary morphology, with many more no doubt to be found in between.

Beckett's "Eff"

I want to conclude by way of reading, as well as listening to, a work that condenses precisely these concerns with media, language, and translation. In moving between these different forms of critical attention, I want to foreground a work that illustrates just how intimately connected all three of these categories are to one another as our lives increasingly become both more "connected" and "mediated." Samuel Beckett's *Embers* was produced as a radio play by the BBC in 1959, and its title provides us with another echo of Stendhal's *Brulard* (discussed in the last chapter) and the intermedial tradition to which it belonged. In Beckett's radio play, we are presented with a monologue of the main character, Henry, who is sitting by the sea and who has a conversation with his dead wife, Ada, at the same time that he hears incidents from the life of his absent daughter, whose name is Addie. In one incident Addie is attending a piano lesson with her Italian music instructor. After warming-up with a scale of A-flat major, she begins to play Chopin's Fifth Waltz in A-Flat Major, with the music instructor keeping time with a stick. When she plays an E instead of an F, we hear a "resounding blow," in the words of the stage directions, of the stick against the piano.[22] Addie stops playing and the following exchange ensues:

> MUSIC MASTER: (violently). Fa!
> ADDIE: (tearfully). What?
> MUSIC MASTER: (violently). Eff! Eff!
> ADDIE: (tearfully). Where?
> MUSIC MASTER: (violently). Qua! (He thumps note.) Fa!

Addie plays again and makes the same mistake. Another blow is followed by the instructor's repeated cries of "Eff! Eff! Eff! Eff!" Addie's subsequent crying is abruptly cut off as we return to the muffled sound of the sea.

In its staging of the character who hears voices in his head—in the ambiguous ontological status of the voice in general—Beckett's *Embers* would become famous for its capacity to draw attention to the impact of radio on human subjectivity. The radio listener finds his double in the character of Henry, who undergoes that rather revolutionary experience of no longer being able to place or physically visualize the voices that one hears. This particular scene with Addie is similarly out of place, with no verbal or acoustic cues as to its temporal location within Addie's life or its purpose within the plot of the radio play itself. It just appears, and then disappears with a sudden end to the sound, no fade-in or fade-out like the ebb and flow, the rising and falling of sound of the sea's waves that punctuate other characters' speech in *Embers*. As in E. T. A. Hoffmann's "Uncanny Guest," the ambiguous diegetic location of the voice occurs immediately following a "blow" (here the instructor's rhythm stick against the piano, in Hoffmann the knock at the door). The singular, shocking sound indicates a series of subsequent sounds that cannot be easily placed within a narrative order. In beginning with the enigmatic word "On," *Embers* indicates a foundational crisis of acoustic reference after radio, where the listener experiences an automatic tension of who speaks between the "turn on" of the narrator/technician and the "go on" of the weary old character. At the core of Beckett's radio play is a question about the place of sound and the meaning of words.

If the scene with Addie indicates a larger crisis of address, of where these sounds are coming from and where they were going to, I want to focus in particular on the work that the letter/word/sound "eff" performs in the course of this scene. The instructor begins by shouting "Fa!," a word used to denote the fourth note of the musical octave in a fixed system of solmization (solfège), which is commonly used in Romance language countries. But in a moveable system of solfège, which is typically used in English-speaking countries and would likely have been more familiar to Addie, "Fa" would refer to D-flat in the key of A-flat major. There is already a problem of translation being staged here even at the level of the syllable. In reply to Addie's cry of "what?"—of both not hearing something (what did you say?) and not understanding something (what did you mean?)—the instructor translates "Fa!" into "Eff!," a word for the alphabetic letter that denotes the musical note F. He moves from a word for a sound to a word for a letter for a sound, at which point Addie's problem of grasping what is going on is no longer expressed through the word "What?" but "Where?" The location of the note is the problem now (is he pointing to the piano keys or the sheet music?), to which the instructor replies, in Italian, "Qua!" The deictic "here!," in Italian, points to something that we cannot see and that Addie cannot hear, a multisensory misapprehension that is then amplified in the foreignness of the untranslated "Qua!" Our understanding of her misunderstanding is stretched across four possible levels—is it a function of language (Italian/English), sound (the sound of F versus E), the language of sound (the difference between Anglo and Romance solmization), or writing (misreading the sheet music)? The problem of translating between the media of sound and writing (the various moves from "Fa!" to "Eff!")—and the referential gap that ensues in moving between them—is tied to the problem of translating between sound and space (and the referential gap of pointing to a visual "here" on the radio), as both are ultimately tied to the problem of linguistic translation (in the misunderstood "Qua" and the instructor's accent that turns "Eff" into "Eff-e"). Addie's tears are the sign of the listener's exhaustion of having—and failing—to traverse the gaps between these various linguistic, acoustic, cultural, and medial registers.

There is of course one final resounding resonance in that word "Eff."

The one word we never hear in *Embers* is "Off," the counterpart to the play's opening word, "On." Precisely the problem that the sea poses is that one cannot drown it out; the sea drowns you, you do not drown it (there is a death by drowning that always hovers in the background of the characters' biographies). Henry's fascination with a drip at one point in the play is a sign of fantasizing about a sound—about sound in general—that is discrete and not continuous. It marks a direct reversal of the romantic fascination with the bow and an imagination of the discrete medium of the book as somehow continuous. The core identity of sounded existence in Beckett is precisely one of continuity and flow, that which cannot be turned off, as the sea wave becomes an ideal figure of the sound wave. Sound in Beckett captures something crucial about media traffic in general, that it is always there, whether we are or not. Media for Beckett pose a problem of arrest and resting. Just as the title word "Embers" refers, as we are told in the play, to a level of burning that one can neither hear nor see—a word that resists translation into a human sensory state, that resists sense itself—"eff" is a word that signifies both a wish for, and an impossible touching of, "off." The vowel shift—a shift of sound—not only signifies a shift of meaning, from a word that means a sound (eff) to a word that means not sound (off). It also signifies a displacement or an echo, a something that can never quite be reached. It is always next to, but never coincident with, a kind of acoustic tangent. Through sound, "eff" tries to approximate that which it cannot, "off." It hopes and fails. "Eff" is the sound of translation.

Embers ends with the figure of a book. In doing so, it marks a key turning point in my own book's portrayal of the bibliographic imagination and a key challenge to the contemporary imagination of how to think about the study of books today. Where there was still a pervasive sense of closeness to the book in the romantic age—despite, or perhaps because of, the flourishing circulation of the book—we can no longer be sure that the book is there anymore in Beckett's sounded universe. Unlike Goethe's dramas of grasping books that transpired in books—of being next to the book—the book in Beckett is always somewhere else. In one sense (hearing), the radio has superseded the book. But in another sense (touch), the book is still there, only now it is less substantial. It is this new, ambiguous relationality to the book that Beckett's radio drama challenges us to understand. The concluding words of the play are those of Henry reading aloud, as speech is used via the medium of the radio to both affirm and disown the continued presence of the book. The mediated relationship to the medium of the book is not imaginatively overcome but is rather painfully underscored as Henry reads from a calendar (a pocket-book) which is filled with "nothing":

Little book. This evening . . . Nothing this evening. Tomorrow . . . tomorrow
. . . plumber at nine, then nothing. Plumber at nine? Ah yes, the waste. Words.
Saturday . . . nothing. Sunday . . . Sunday . . . nothing all day. Nothing, all day
nothing. All day all night nothing. Not a sound. (Sea.)

We are left in Beckett with the task of interpreting an endless series of medial and lingual translations: an empty book that we hear, an invocation
of silence on the radio, and finally, a stage direction for a sound that is a
homonym of the verb for sight. Perhaps no other work shows us with such
clarity how to move forward from here.

NOTES

A note on translations: All translations are mine unless otherwise noted.

A note on editions: Where possible, I have cited texts from authorial critical editions for the sake of availability where the material aspects of the text do not play a role in the analysis. Otherwise, original editions have been cited. Citations from critical editions have in all cases been cross-checked with their originals.

INTRODUCTION

Epigraph: Sketch accompanying Goethe's notation, "Hypothese: Alles ist Blat" (1787). Courtesy of the Klassik Stiftung Weimar, GSA 26/LV, 13, Bl. 166v.

1. Wolfgang Menzel, "Die Masse der Literatur," in *Die deutsche Literatur*, vol. 1 (Stuttgart: Franckh, 1828), 1.

2. In his poem, "Deutschland—Ein Wintermärchen," Heine suggested that while the Russians and the French belonged to their land, the British to their sea, the Germans ruled nothing but the ethereal space of their dreams.

3. For its most canonized reading, see Michel Foucault, "The Fantasia of the Library," in *Language, Counter-Memory, Practice*, ed. D. Bouchard (Ithaca: Cornell University Press, 1977), 87–109.

4. Thomas Carlyle, *Sartor Resartus: The Life and Opinions of Herr Teufelsdröckh*, in *Collected Works*, vol. 1 (London: n.p., 1872), 167.

5. Victor Hugo, *Notre-Dame de Paris*, ed. Jacques Seebacher and Yves Gohin (Paris: Gallimard, 1975), 173.

6. Stephan Schütze, "Des Buches Ursprung," in *Der Wintergarten* (Frankfurt/Main: Wilmans, 1816), 9–11, and Leigh Hunt, "Old Books and Bookshops," in *Literary Criticism*, ed. Lawrence Huston Houtchens and Carolyn Washburn Houtchens (New York: Columbia University Press, 1956), 47.

7. Friedrich Schlegel, "Brief über den Roman," in *Kritische Friedrich-Schlegel-Ausgabe*, vol. 2, ed. Ernst Behler (München: Schöningh, 1958), 332.

8. Honoré de Balzac, "De l'état actuel de la Librairie," in *Oeuvres diverses*, vol. 2, ed. Pierre-Georges Castex (Paris: Gallimard, 1996), 663.

9. Edgar Allan Poe, "Berenice," in *The Collected Works of Edgar Allen Poe*, ed. Thomas Olive Mabbott, vol. 2 (Cambridge, Mass.: Belknap Press of Harvard University Press, 1978), 210.

10. Karl Immermann, "Memorabilien," in *Werke*, vol. 5, ed. Harry Maync (Leipzig: Bibliographisches Institut, 1906), 316.

11. See also the narrator's discussion in Poe's "Berenice," where he speaks of his "monomania" and "that nervous intensity of interest." Edgar Allan Poe, "Berenice," in *The Collected Works of Edgar Allen Poe*, 211.

12. For a discussion of Hunt's essay along with a number of other romantic examples of "book-love," see Deidre Shauna Lynch, "'Wedded to Books': Bibliomania and the Romantic Essayists," *Romantic Libraries: Praxis Series—Romantic Circles;* http://www.rc .umd.edu/praxis/libraries/lynch/lynch.html.

13. Isaac D'Israeli, "The Bibliomania," in *Curiosities of Literature: Consisting of Anecdotes, Characters, Sketches, and Observations, Literary, Critical, and Historical* (London: Murray 1791), 19–20, and Charles Nodier, "Le Bibliomane," in *Paris; ou Le livre des cent-et-un*, ed. Pierre-François Ladvocat, vol. 1 (Paris: L'advocat, 1831), 87–108. For a discussion of Romantic bibliomania, see Ina Ferris, "Bibliographic Romance: Bibliophilia and the Book-Object," *Romantic Libraries: Praxis Series—Romantic Circles.* http://www.rc.umd .edu/praxis/librairies/ferris/ferris.html.

14. For a discussion of romantic literature's invention or at least deep investment in addiction narratives, see Clifford Siskin, "Romantic Addictions," in *The Historicity of Romantic Discourse* (Oxford: Oxford University Press, 1988), 179–94.

15. Johann Wolfgang Goethe, *Aus meinem Leben: Dichtung und Wahrheit*, in *Sämtliche Werke*, vol. 14, ed. Klaus-Detlef Müller (Frankfurt/Main: Deutscher Klassiker Verlag, 1986), 36–37.

16. Clifford Siskin, *The Work of Writing: Literature and Social Change in Britain, 1700–1830* (Baltimore: Johns Hopkins University Press, 1998), and Paul Keen, *The Crisis of Literature in the 1790s: Print Culture and the Public Sphere* (Cambridge: Cambridge University Press, 1999).

17. For bibliographic information concerning the production of writing and literature during this period, for France, see Carla Hesse, *Publishing and Cultural Politics in Revolutionary Paris, 1789–1810* (Berkeley and Los Angeles: University of California Press, 1991), Martyn Lyons, *Le Triomphe du livre: Une histoire sociologique de la lecture dans la France du XIXe siècle* (Paris: Promodis, 1987), and James Smith Allen, *Popular French Romanticism: Authors, Readers, and Books in the Nineteenth Century* (Syracuse: Syracuse University Press, 1981); for England, James Raven, *The Business of Books: Booksellers and the English Book Trade, 1450–1850* (New Haven: Yale University Press, 2007), and William St. Clair, *The Reading Nation in the Romantic Period* (Cambridge: Cambridge University Press, 2004); for the German states, Ilsedore Rarisch, *Industrialisierung und Literatur* (Berlin: Colloquium, 1976), and Albert Ward, *Book Production, Fiction, and the German Reading Public* (Oxford: Clarendon, 1974); and for the United States, see John Tebbel, *A History of Book Publishing in the United States*, 4 vols. (New York: Bowker, 1972–81), and *A Checklist for American Imprints* (Metuchen: Scarecrow, 1972).

18. On reading clubs, see Otto Dann, "Die Lesegesellschaften des 18. Jahrhunderts und der gesellschaftliche Aufbruch des deutschen Bürgertums," in *Buch und Leser*, ed. Herbert G. Göpfert (Hamburg: Hauswedell, 1977), 160–93; on lending libraries, see Georg Jäger, "Die deutsche Leihbibliothek im 19. Jahrhundert: Verbreitung— Organisation—Fall," in *Buch und Leser*, 194–202; on private libraries, see James Raven, "Modes of Reading and Writing in the Eighteenth-Century Private Library," in *Lesen und Schreiben im 17. und 18. Jahrhundert*, ed. Paul Goetsch (Tübingen: Gunter Narr, 1994), 49–59, and Marcel Lajeunesse, "Personal Libraries and Bibliophilia," *History of the Book in Canada*, vol. 1: *Beginnings to 1840*, ed. Patricia Lockhart Fleming,

Gilles Gallichan, and Yvan Lamonde (Toronto: University of Toronto Press, 2004), 202–206. For images of British private libraries, see John Cornforth, *English Interiors, 1790–1848* (London: Barrie and Jenkins, 1978), and for German reading interiors, see the paintings of Georg Friedrich Kersting in Werner Schnell, *Georg Friedrich Kersting* (Berlin: Verlag für Kunstwissenschaft, 1994).

19. See Thomas Jentzsch, "Verlagsbuchhandel und Bürgertum um 1800: Dargestellt am Beispiel der Buchhändler Familie Vieweg," *Archiv für Geschichte des Buchwesens* 37 (1992): 167–251, at 169.

20. We spent over $25 billion on books in 2007, the most recent year available for statistics, versus $10.3 billion on music, the next most purchased medium (box office grosses were just over $9 billion and video games were $7.4 billion). For information on contemporary book-buying, see Dave Bogart, ed., "Table 1: Estimated Book Publishing Industry Sales, 2002, 2003–2005," *The Bowker Annual Library and Book Trade Almanac*, 51st ed. (New York: Information Today, 2006), 522 and for 2007 numbers, http://www.publishers.org/main/IndustryStats/indStats_02.htm. For motion picture information, "Research and Statistics," *Motion Picture Association of America* (24 April 2008): http://www.mpaa.org/researchStatistics.asp. For sound recording, "Research & Data: Marketing Information, 2007 Consumer Profile," *Recording Industry Association of America* (24 April 2008): http://www.riaa.com/keystatistics.php. For video games, no new figures were available for 2007: "2006 Sales, Demographic and Sales Data: Essential Facts about the Computer and Video Game Industry," *Entertainment Software Association* (24 April 2008): http://www.theesa.com/archives/files/ESA-EF%202007.pdf.

21. While U.S. book publishing has reported steady gains in recent years, it should be noted European publishing has, despite the higher sales, declined. Eurostat Pocketbooks, *Cultural Statistics, 2007 Edition* (Luxembourg: Office for the Official Publications of the European Communities, 2007), 78–87; http://epp.eurostat.ec.europa.eu/cache/ITY_OFFPUB/KS-77-07-296/EN/KS-77-07-296-EN.PDF.

22. For academic libraries, see "Academic Libraries: 2000," *National Center for Education Statistics: Library Statistics Program* (Washington: U.S. Dept. of Education, 2003), 7, and for public libraries, see "Public Libraries in the United States: 2004," *National Center for Education Statistics: Library Statistics Program* (Washington: U.S. Dept. of Education, 2006), 82.

23. Jonathan Sterne, *The Audible Past: Cultural Origins of Sound Reproduction* (Durham: Duke University Press, 2003), 8.

24. The crucial date for the "birth" of the codex is AD 300, when we think it achieved parity with the scroll. See Colin H. Roberts and T. C. Skeat, *The Birth of the Codex* (London: British Academy, 1983), 75.

25. As Jon Klancher has written, "In an unusually intense time of expounding and castigating texts, the audiences emerging in the nineteenth century were not only exercising vastly different 'tastes.' They were also, more critically, taking shape as diverging collective interpreters whose 'readings' of the social and intellectual world opened unbridgeable cultural conflicts." Jon P. Klancher, *The Making of English Reading Audiences, 1790–1832* (Madison: University of Wisconsin Press, 1987), 5.

26. James Raven, *The Business of Books*, 30.

27. Although it still remains within a single linguistic field, an important new work in this direction is Richard B. Sher, *The Enlightenment and the Book: Scottish Authors and the Publishers in Eighteenth-Century Britain, Ireland, and America* (Chicago: University of Chicago Press, 2006).

28. Karl S. Guthke, *Die Erfindung der Welt: Globalität und Grenzen in der Kulturgeschichte der Literatur* (Tübingen: Francke, 2005), 53. For a discussion of cosmopolitan discourse around 1800, see Andrea Albrecht, *Kosmopolitismus: Weltbürgerdiskurse in Literatur, Philosophie und Publizistik um 1800* (Berlin: de Gruyter, 2005). For a theoretical discussion of the study of "world literature," see David Damrosch, *What is World Literature?* (Princeton: Princeton University Press, 2003).

29. David Thorburn and Henry Jenkins, eds., *Rethinking Media Change: The Aesthetics of Transition* (Cambridge, Mass.: MIT Press, 2003), and Jay David Bolter and Richard Grusin, *Remediation: Understanding New Media* (Cambridge, Mass.: MIT Press, 1999).

30. Carla Hesse, "Books in Time," in *The Future of the Book*, ed. Geoffrey Nunberg (Berkeley and Los Angeles: University of California Press, 1996), 28.

31. See Espen Aarseth, *Cybertext: Perspectives on Ergodic Literature* (Baltimore: Johns Hopkins University Press, 1997), 18.

32. In this I am offering an alternative to the ever growing body of work that aims to codify the differences between digital and print media. For recent examples, see Sabine Eckmann and Lutz Koepnick, eds., *[Grid< >Matrix]* (St. Louis: Kemper Art Museum, 2008); Pat Harrigan and Noah Wardrip-Fruin, eds., *Second Person: Role-Playing and Story in Games and Playable Media* (Cambridge, Mass.: MIT Press, 2007); Marie-Laure Ryan, *Avatars of Story* (Minneapolis: Minnesota University Press, 2006); N. Katherine Hayles, *My Mother Was a Computer: Digital Subjects and Literary Texts* (Chicago: University of Chicago Press, 2005); Lev Manovich, *The Language of New Media* (Cambridge, Mass.: MIT Press, 2001); Jerome McGann, *Radiant Textuality: Literature after the World Wide Web* (New York: Palgrave, 2001); as well as the ongoing work of Rita Raley (http://raley.english.ucsb.edu/), the "electronic book review" (http://www.electronicbookreview.com/), and "dichtung-digital" (http://www.dichtung-digital.de/).

33. For the now canonical position on this shift, see Adrian Johns, where he writes: "This book contends that what we often regard as essential elements and necessary concomitants of print are in fact rather more contingent than generally acknowledged." Adrian Johns, *The Nature of the Book: Print and Knowledge in the Making* (Chicago: University of Chicago Press, 1998), 2.

34. As John Durham Peters has helped us to see, "mass communication" and the issues it raises should in no way be exclusively linked to electronic media, indeed, to any one medium in particular, but instead to a set of practices and mentalities. As Peters writes, "Mass communication—a concept too long seen as the historically recent production of electronic media—is in fact an old form, maybe the most basic form of communication." John Durham Peters, "The Gaps of Which Communication is Made," *Critical Studies in Mass Communication* 11, no. 2 (June 1994): 117–40, at 132.

35. Jerome McGann, *Radiant Textuality*, 151.

36. Priscilla Coit Murphy, "Books are Dead, Long Live Books," in *Rethinking Media Change*, ed. Thorburn and Jenkins, 81–94.

37. Mario Vargas Llosa, "Why Literature? The Premature Obituary of the Book," *The New Republic*, May 4, 2001.

38. Seth Lerer, "Epilogue: Falling Asleep over the History of the Book," *PMLA* 121, no. 1 (Jan. 2006): 230.

39. Friedrich Schlegel, "Brief über den Roman," 335.

40. N. Katherine Hayles, *Writing Machines* (Cambridge, Mass.: MIT Press, 2002), 23.

41. Jerome McGann, *Radiant Textuality*, 138.

42. Joseph Tabbi writes: "With all its devotion to the generation of complexity, con-

sciousness, and reflexive understanding at the level of the signified, [literary activity] has depended on a stable, simplified, largely forgotten page as a material carrier capable of fixing language at the level of the signifier." Joseph Tabbi, "The Processual Page," in *The Future of the Book*, ed. Nunberg, 207.

43. For various theoretical approaches in this direction, see Sean Gurd, *Iphigenias at Aulis: Textual Multiplicity, Radical Philology* (Ithaca: Cornell University Press, 2005); Dieter Mersch, "Ereignis und Aura: Radikale Transformationen der Kunst vom Werkhaften zum Prozesshaften," *Kunstforum* 152 (2000): 94–103; D. C. Greetham, *Theories of the Text* (Oxford: Oxford University Press, 1999); Stephen G. Nichols, "Why Material Philology?" *Zeitschrift für deutsche Philologie* 116 (1997): 10–30; Peter L. Schillingsburg, "Text as Matter, Concept, and Action," *Studies in Bibliography* 44 (1991): 31–82; Joseph Grigely, "The Textual Event," in *Devils and Angels: Textual Editing and Literary Theory*, ed. Philip Cohen (Charlottesville: Virginia University Press, 1991), 167–94; and James McLaverty, "The Mode of Existence of Literary Works of Art," *Studies in Bibliography* 37 (1984): 82–105. On the thingness of literature, see Bill Brown, ed., *Things* (Chicago: University of Chicago Press, 2004).

44. F. W. Bateson, "Modern Bibliography and the Literary Artifact," in *English Studies Today*, ed. Georges A. Bonnard (Bern: Lang, 1961), 67–77.

45. For a discussion of the literary and scientific interlockings of such autopoetic discourse at the turn of the nineteenth century, see Helmut Müller-Sievers, *Self-Generation: Biology, Philosophy and Literature around 1800* (Stanford: Stanford University Press, 1997).

46. Martha Woodmansee, "On the Author Effect: Recovering Collectivity," and Peter Jaszi, "On the Author Effect: Contemporary Copyright and Collective Creativity," in *The Construction of Authorship: Textual Appropriation in Law and Literature*, ed. Woodmansee and Jaszi (Durham: Duke University Press, 1994), 1–15, 16–28.

47. Meredith McGill, *American Literature and the Culture of Reprinting, 1834–1853* (Philadelphia: University of Pennsylvania Press, 2003), 16.

48. Robert Darnton, *The Kiss of Lamourette: Reflections in Cultural History* (New York: Norton, 1990), 152–53.

49. Margaret Ezell, *Social Authorship and the Advent of Print* (Baltimore: Johns Hopkins University Press, 1999).

50. Michel Foucault, "What is an Author?" in *Language, Counter-Memory, Practice*, ed. D. Bouchard (Ithaca: Cornell University Press, 1977).

51. For an introduction into the problems surrounding the interdisciplinary overlaps in this field of inquiry, see Leslie Howsam, *Old Books and New Histories: An Orientation to Studies in Book and Print Culture* (Toronto: University of Toronto Press, 2006).

52. In this it should be clear just how different my approach is than that of someone like William St. Clair, whose "political economy" of the romantic book in *The Reading Nation* largely ignores what is in books.

53. Albrecht Koschorke, *Körperströme und Schriftverkehr: Mediologie des 18. Jahrhunderts* (München: Fink, 1999), 11.

54. Adrian Johns, *The Nature of the Book: Print and Knowledge in the Making* (Chicago: University of Chicago Press, 1998).

55. Garret Stewart, *Dear Reader: The Conscripted Audience in Nineteenth-Century British Fiction* (Baltimore: Johns Hopkins University Press, 1996), 6–7.

56. As Leah Price has suggested, a history of the book does not just give shape to an idea of literature, but a history of literature gives shape to an idea of the book. Leah Price, "Introduction: Reading Matter," *PMLA* 121, no. 1 (2006): 9–15.

57. M. M. Bakhtin, "The Problem of Speech Genres," in *Speech Genres and Other Late Essays*, trans. Vern W. McGee (Austin: University of Texas Press, 1986), 71, and Michel Serres, *The Parasite*, trans. Lawrence R. Schehr (Minneapolis: University of Minnesota Press, 2007). See also Rüdiger Campe, "Die Schreibszene Schreiben," in *Paradoxien, Dissonanzen, Zusammenbrüche: Situationen offener Epistemologie*, ed. H. U. Gumbrecht and K. Ludwig Pfeiffer (Frankfurt/Main: Suhrkamp, 1991), 759–72, where Campe speaks of the literary imperative of dramatizing "writing" to frame the protocols of communication that guide the literary work (764).

58. On the study of the intelligibility of media, see Lisa Gitelman, "Introduction," in *Always Already New: Media, History, and the Data of Culture* (Cambridge, Mass.: MIT Press, 2006), 1–18.

59. Bernhard Siegert, "Cacography or Communication? Kulturtechnik in German Media Studies," *Grey Room* 29 (Winter 2008): 33.

60. Percy Bysshe Shelley, *A Defense of Poetry*, in *The Complete Works of Percy Bysshe Shelley*, vol. 7, ed. Roger Ingwen and Walter Peck (London: Gordian, 1965), 135.

61. Charles Baudelaire, "Qu'est-ce que le romantisme?" in *Oeuvres complètes*, ed. Y. G. le Dantec (Paris: Gallimard, 1964), 879, and William Wordsworth, "Preface," *Lyrical Ballads*, ed. R. L. Brett and A. R. Jones (London: Routledge, 1996), 246.

62. Friedrich Kittler, *Discourse Networks, 1800/1900*, trans. Michael Metteer with Chris Cullens (Stanford: Stanford University Press, 1990), 140.

63. Ina Ferris, "Bibliographic Romance: Bibliophilia and the Book-Object."

64. Marc Redfield, *The Politics of Aesthetics: Nationalism, Gender, Romanticism* (Stanford: Stanford University Press, 2003), in particular p. 17f, where he discusses the simultaneous reliance on and disowning of media within aesthetic discourse.

65. See John Durham Peters, *Speaking into the Air: A History of the Idea of Communication* (Chicago: University of Chicago Press, 1999). My work is an attempt to expand into the field of literature the kind of analysis that Peters's book has initiated.

66. Roger Chartier, *The Order of Books*, trans. Lydia Cochrane (Stanford: Stanford University Press, 1992).

67. Walter Benjamin, "Der Erzähler," in *Gesammelte Schriften*, vol. 2.2, ed. Rolf Tiedemann and Hermann Schweppenhäuser (Frankfurt/Main: Suhrkamp, 1977), 443.

68. Raymond Williams, *Television: Technology and Cultural Form* (New York: Routledge, 2003), 77–120.

69. See J. W. Goethe, "Bezüge nach Aussen," in *Ueber Kunst und Alterthum*, 6.2, in *Sämtliche Werke*, vol. 22, ed. Anne Bohnenkamp (Frankfurt/Main: Deutscher Klassiker Verlag, 1999), 427f.

70. E. A. Poe, "Exordium to Critical Notices," in *Essays and Reviews* (New York: Library of America, 1984), 1027. For a discussion of Poe, see Meredith McGill, *American Literature and the Culture of Reprinting*, 141–86.

71. Kurt Mueller-Vollmer writes: "Romanticism embraced a distinct notion of internationalism of its own: to be sure, not one that could serve as the basis for a program of universalist cultural politics, as was characteristic for the Enlightenment. It manifested itself instead in the creation and dissemination of a new cultural discourse that was both international and transcultural in nature, while at the same time extolling the individuality of the participating national cultures." Kurt Mueller-Vollmer, "On Germany: Germaine de Staël and the Internationalization of Romanticism," in *The Spirit of Poesy*, ed. Richard Block (Evanston: Northwestern University Press, 2000), 150–66, at 151.

72. Madame de Staël, *Corinne, ou L'Italie,* in *Oeuvres complètes,* vol. 2, pt. 3, ed. Simone Balayé (Paris: Champion, 2000), 237.

73. "When it has once been written down, every discourse rolls about everywhere, reaching indiscriminately those with understanding no less than those who have no business with it, and it doesn't know to whom it should speak and to whom it should not." Plato, *Phaedrus,* trans. Alexander Nehamas and Paul Woodruff (Indianapolis: Hackett, 1995), 81. For the way this concern with the address of speech is at the heart of the foundation of the romantic science of hermeneutics, see Paul Ricoeur, who writes that in writing "the narrowness of the dialogical relation explodes. Instead of being addressed just to you, the second person, discourse is revealed as discourse in the universality of its address. . . . It no longer has a visible auditor. An unknown, invisible reader has become the unprivileged addressee of the discourse." Paul Ricoeur, *Hermeneutics and the Human Sciences,* trans. John B. Thompson (Cambridge: Cambridge University Press, 1981), 202.

74. As Goethe famously remarked to his friend Friedrich Soret in 1832, "My oeuvre is that of a collective being and that bears the name Goethe." J. W. Goethe, *Briefe, Tagebücher und Gespräche, 1823–1828,* in *Sämtliche Werke,* vol. 37, ed. Horst Fleig (Frankfurt/Main: Deutscher Klassiker Verlag, 1993), 522. On Scott as a "joint-stock business," see Fiona Robertson, *Legitimate Histories: Scott, Gothic, and the Authorities of Fiction* (Oxford: Clarendon, 1994), 12.

75. See Mathew Fuller, *Media Ecologies: Materialist Energies in Art and Technoculture* (Cambridge, Mass.: MIT Press, 2005); Jay David Bolter and Richard Grusin, *Remediation;* Jörg Helbig, ed., *Intermedialität: Theorie und Praxis eines interdisziplinären Forschungsgebietes* (Berlin: Erich Schmidt, 1998); Dick Higgins, *Horizons: The Poetics and Theory of Intermedia* (Carbondale: Southern Illinois University Press, 1984); and the work of my research group, *Interacting with Print: Cultural Practices of Intermediality, 1700–1830,* http://interactingwithprint.mcgill.ca. Such work aims to add a mediological dimension to Emily Apter's call for translation to be at the heart of a new comparative literature. See Emily Apter, *The Translation Zone: A New Comparative Literature* (Princeton: Princeton University Press, 2006).

76. E. R. Curtius, "The Book as Symbol," in *European Literature and the Latin Middle Ages,* trans. Willard R. Trask (Princeton: Princeton University Press, 1973), 302–47.

CHAPTER ONE

1. Jochen Golz, "Das Goethe- und Schiller-Archiv in Geschichte und Gegenwart," in *Das Goethe- und Schiller-Archiv 1896–1996,* ed. Jochen Golz (Weimar: Böhlau, 1996), 13–70, at 37.

2. Ibid., 35.

3. Dieter Borchmeyer, "Sophiens Reise von Weimar nach München," *Goethe Jahrbuch* 106 (1989): 230–39, at 232.

4. Hermann Grimm, "Vorwort," *Goethes Werke,* vol. 1 (Weimar: Böhlau, 1887), xi.

5. Bernhard Suphan, "Vorbericht," *Goethes Werke,* vol. 1 (Weimar: Böhlau, 1887), xvii–xix.

6. The most prominent late-nineteenth-century articulation of such a theoretical position was Wilhelm Scherer, "Goethe-Philologie (1877)," in *Aufsätze über Goethe* (Berlin: Weimar, 1900), 1–28.

7. Hermann Grimm, *Goethe: Vorlesungen gehalten an der kgl. Universität zu Berlin* (1874/75), 2 vols. (Stuttgart, 1903), 1:8.

8. J. W. Goethe, *Aus meinem Leben: Dichtung und Wahrheit*, in *Sämtliche Werke*, vol. 14, ed. Klaus-Detlef Müller (Frankfurt/Main: Deutscher Klassiker Verlag, 1986), 310.

9. J. W. Goethe, *Wilhelm Meisters Wanderjahre*, in *Sämtliche Werke*, vol. 10, ed. Gerhard Neumann (Frankfurt/Main: Deutscher Klassiker Verlag, 1989), 329. Parenthetical citations use the abbreviation *WMT.*

10. The collective consisted of the scribes Johann John, Friedrich Kräuter, Johann Schuchardt, the philologists Friedrich Riemer and Karl Göttling, the art historian Johann Meyer, Goethe's faithful secretary Eckermann and even Wilhelm Reichel, Cotta's corrector in his Augsburg print shop. For a discussion of the relationship of the personal archive to the work of the writer, see Goethe's essay, "Archiv des Dichters und Schriftstellers" (1823).

11. For a discussion of Goethe's collecting practices, see Erich Trunz, "Goethe als Sammler," *Goethe-Jahrbuch* 89 (1972): 13–61.

12. J. W. Goethe, *Briefe, Tagebücher und Gespräche, 1823–1828*, in *Sämtliche Werke*, vol. 37, ed. Horst Fleig (Frankfurt/Main: Deutscher Klassiker Verlag, 1993), 522.

13. Heinz Fröbe, "Die Privilegierung der Ausgabe 'letzte Hand' Goethes sämtlicher Werke," *Archiv für Geschichte des Buchwesens* 2 (1960): 187–229.

14. In his letter to the *Bundesversammlung*, Goethe writes: "Nevertheless, the means for an individual author to maintain his acknowledged intellectual property emerged soon after the discovery of the printing press whereby in light of a general deficiency of laws, one turned to individual privileges." J. W. Goethe, *Briefe, Tagebücher und Gespräche, 1823–1828*, 239.

15. Goethe writes in the same letter: "Should not the noble Bundestag, the union of all German sovereignties, be equally inclined to exercise itself as a totality today, in a similar fashion to the individuals who were and continue to be afforded such rights? And would not such an act powerfully exercise the most decisive influence on German literature and spiritual development?" J. W. Goethe, *Briefe, Tagebücher und Gespräche, 1823–1828*, 239.

16. This problem has been much commented on by later critics. See Ernst Grumach, "Prolegomena zu einer Goethe-Ausgabe," in *Beiträge zur Goetheforschung*, ed. Ernst Grumach (Berlin: Akademie, 1959), 1–34. For discussions of how the lastness that the editors thought they were reproducing in their focus on the octavo edition was not in fact completely accurate, see Waltraud Hagen, "Der Erstdruck von Goethes Faustfragment," in *Beiträge zur Goetheforschung*, 59–78, and Waltraud Hagen, "Goethes Ausgabe letzter Hand. Entstehung und Bedeutung," *Marginalien* 99 (1985): 1–22. The octavo was published along with portions of the *Taschenausgabe* so that a strict last-wishes edition would have to include elements from both of these editions. Hagen's painstaking work has been focused on reconstructing the temporality of production of these two final editions to identify what would have been the last authorized changes.

17. Siegfried Unseld, *Goethe and his Publishers*, trans. Kenneth J. Northcott (Chicago: University of Chicago Press, 1996); Dorothea Kuhn, ed., *Goethe und Cotta: Briefwechsel, 1797–1832* (Stuttgart: Cotta, 1979–1983); Wolfgang Bunzel, *Poetik und Publikation: Goethes Veröffentlichungen in Musenalmanachen und literarischen Taschenbüchern; Mit einer Bibliographie der Erst- und autorisierten Folgedrucke literarischer Texte Goethes im Almanach (1773–1832)* (Köln: Böhlau, 1997); and finally, the numerous works by Waltraud Hagen, principally, Waltraud Hagen, ed., *Die Gesamt- und Einzeldrucke von Goethes Werken*, supplementary vol. 1 (Berlin: Akademie, 1956); Waltraud Hagen, ed., *Quellen und Zeugnisse zur Druckgeschichte von Goethes Werken*, parts 1 and 2 (Ber-

lin: Akademie, 1966, 1982); and Waltraud Hagen, *Die Druck von Goethes Werken* (Berlin: Akademie, 1971).

18. Regarding the dating of texts that appeared in miscellanies here and in subsequent chapters, because they were sold the year before their printed publication date, when I speak of the actual date of publication for texts within the miscellanies I will use the prior year from the stated date on the title page whereas when I refer to the publication itself I will use the given publication date in parentheses. For studies on the publication history of the novel, see Erhard Bahr, *The Novel as Archive: The Genesis, Reception and Criticism of Goethe's "Wilhelm Meisters Wanderjahre"* (Camden: Camden House, 1998), and Hans Reiss, *"Wilhelm Meisters Wanderjahre:* Der Weg von der ersten zur zweiten Fassung," *Deutsche Vierteljahrsschrift* 39 (1965): 34–57, although the latter is far more interested in identifying the stylistic and not bibliographic changes between the two versions.

19. The seeds of such a project of identifying the novel's communicative poetics were planted in Manfred Karnick's *"Wilhelm Meisters Wanderjahre," oder die Kunst des Mittelbaren* (München: Fink, 1968). See also Gerhard Neumann's commentary to the *Frankfurter Ausgabe*, where he focuses on the novel's media-theoretical interest in the idea of the "proper distance."

20. Hermann Broch, "James Joyce und die Gegenwart," in *Schriften zur Literatur*, 2 vols. (Frankfurt/Main: Suhrkamp, 1975), 1:63–94.

21. For explicit comparisons to Joyce, see Ehrhard Bahr, *"Wilhelm Meisters Wanderjahre," Goethes Erzählwerk*, ed. Paul Michael Lützeler and James E. McLeod (Stuttgart: Reclam, 1985), 363–93, and Walter Muschg, *Goethe als Emigrant* (Frankfurt/Main: Insel, 1996), 161. For an emphasis on a modern poetics of openness promoted by the novel's heterogeneity as well as irony, see Erhard Bahr, *Die Ironie im Spätwerk Goethes* (Berlin: Schmidt, 1972), 88–130; Jane K. Brown, *Goethe's Cyclical Narratives* (Durham: University of North Carolina Press, 1975); Hans Vaget, "Johann Wolfgang von Goethe: *Wilhelm Meisters Wanderjahre,"* in *Romane und Erzählungen zwischen Romantik und Realismus*, ed. Paul Michael Lützeler (Stuttgart: Reclam, 1983), 136–64; and most recently, Christina Salmen, *"Die ganze merkwürdige Verlassenschaft": Goethes Entsagungspoetik in "Wilhelm Meisters Wanderjahre"* (Würzburg: Königshausen und Neumann, 2003), who refers to the novel's "fractal form" (19). For the counterargument that Goethe's novel is antimodern, see Hannelore Schlaffer, *Wilhelm Meister: Das Ende der Kunst und die Wiederkehr des Mythos* (Stuttgart: Metzler, 1980). For a reading of the novel that does not look forward to a future tradition but rather looks backward to its origins in eighteenth-century ironic novels by Fielding, Sterne, Voltaire and Wieland, see Benjamin Bennett, *Beyond Theory: Eighteenth-Century German Literature and the Poetics of Irony* (Ithaca: Cornell University Press, 1993), 14–63.

22. For studies that argue for this novel's importance in its capacity to address "discursive" and intellectual shifts at the turn of the nineteenth century, see Franziska Schößler, *Goethes Lehr- und Wanderjahre: Eine Kulturgeschichte der Moderne* (Tübingen: Francke, 2002), 357; Irmgard Egger, *Diätetik und Askese: Zur Dialektik der Aufklärung in Goethes Romanen* (München: Fink, 2000), 13; Henriette Herwig, "Schule der Entsagung? Zur Kritik der moral-pädogogischen Instrumentalisierung von Goethes *Wanderjahren,"* in *Spuren-Signaturen-Spiegelungen: Zur Goethe-Rezeption in Europa*, ed. Anke Bosse (Köln, 2000), 541, based on her earlier study, Henriette Herwig, *Das ewig Männliche zieht uns hinab: "Wilhelm Meisters Wanderjahre"; Geschlechterdifferenz, sozialer Wandel, historische Anthropologie* (Tübingen: Francke, 1997); Erhard Bahr, *The Novel as Archive*, 99; and Klaus Detlef Müller, "Lenardos Tagebuch: Zum Romanbegriff in Goethes

Wilhelm Meisters Wanderjahre," Deutsche Vierteljahresschrift 53, no. 2 (1979): 275–99, who writes that the novel represents the "totality of forms of written communication" (298). According to these readings, Goethe's novel is understood as a cultural archive, a complete record of the changes that modern intellectual institutions and their genres were undergoing at the turn of the nineteenth century, a point that is amplified by the fact that the archive is itself a key theme of the *Travels*. The current interest in the novel as archive dates back to Volker Neuhaus, "Die Archivfiktion in *Wilhelm Meisters Wanderjahre*," *Euphorion* 62 (1968): 13–27.

23. Ernst Behler, "Goethes Wilhelm Meister und die Romantheorie der Frühromantik," *Études Germaniques* (Oct./Dec. 1989): 409–28.

24. Novalis, *Werke, Tagebücher und Briefe*, ed. Hans-Joachim Mähl and Richard Samuel (München: Hanser, 2005), 2:504.

25. Friedrich Schlegel, "Philosophische Fragmente: Zweite Epoche; II," in *Kritische Friedrich-Schlegel-Ausgabe*, vol. 18, ed. Ernst Behler (München: Schöningh, 1963), 364.

26. As Schlegel wrote in his review of *Wilhelm Meister's Apprenticeship*, "Through such continuing education [*Fortbildung*] is the coherence and through such enclosure is the diversity of the individual masses guaranteed and confirmed; in this way each necessary part of this single and indivisible novel a system unto itself." Friedrich Schlegel, "Über Goethes Meister," in *Kritische Friedrich-Schlegel-Ausgabe*, vol. 2, ed. Ernst Behler (München: Schöningh, 1963), 135. It should become apparent in the course of this chapter, however, just how extensively Goethe's novelistic work will experiment with Schlegel's notion of the indivisibility of the novel.

27. J. W. Goethe, *Briefe, Tagebücher und Gespräche, 1828–1832*, in *Sämtliche Werke*, vol. 38, ed. Horst Fleig (Frankfurt/Main: Deutscher Klassiker Verlag, 1993), 199.

28. Novalis, *Werke, Tagebücher und Briefe*, 2:838. See Friedrich Schlegel's media theoretical understanding of the novel in his *Brief über den Roman*, where he writes: "A novel is a romantic book [*Ein Roman ist ein romantisches Buch*].—You will pass this off as a meaningless tautology. But I want first and foremost to draw your attention to the fact that with a book one already thinks of a work, a totality existing for itself [*ein für sich bestehendes Ganze*]." Friedrich Schlegel, "Brief über den Roman," in *Kritische Friedrich-Schlegel-Ausgabe*, vol. 2, ed Ernst Behler (München: Schöningh, 1958), 335.

29. See Manuel Castells, *The Rise of the Network Society*, 2d ed. (London: Blackwell, 2000); Darin Barney, *The Network Society* (Cambridge: Polity, 2004); and Alexander Galloway and Eugene Thacker, *The Exploit: A Theory of Networks* (Minnesota: University of Minnesota Press, 2007).

30. Following on the work of network theorists Alexander Galloway and Eugene Thacker, I understand a network as both an apparatus that facilitates interrelationality and a logic that governs how things are done with that apparatus. See Alexander Galloway and Eugene Thacker, "Protocol, Control, and Networks," *Grey Room* 17 (Fall 2004): 6–29, at 9.

31. For a history of networked thought, see Sebastian Gießmann, *Netze und Netzwerke: Archäologie einer Kulturtechnik, 1740–1840* (Bielefeld: Transcript, 2006).

32. On the evolutionary aspect of networks, see Hartmut Böhme, who writes: "[Networks] are capable of learning, they develop new connections and differences, nodes and relays. They process mistakes, interruptions, crises and catastrophes." Hartmut Böhme, "Netzwerke: Zur Theorie und Geschichte einer Konstruktion," in *Netzwerke: Eine Kulturtechnik der Moderne*, ed. Jürgen Barkhoff, Hartmut Böhme, and Jeanne Riou (Köln: Böhlau, 2004), 23. On the collectivity of Goethe's late poetics, see Safia

Azzouni, *Kunst als praktische Wissenschaft: Goethes "Wilhelm Meisters Wanderjahre"
und die Hefte "Zur Morphologie"* (Köln: Böhlau, 2005). On the "playability" and "per-
formability" of networked fiction, see Noah Wardrip-Fruin, "Writing Networks: New
Media, Potential Literature," *Leonardo* 29, no. 5 (1996): 355–73, and N.
Katherine Hayles, "Translating Media," *My Mother Was a Computer: Digital Subjects and Literary
Texts* (Chicago: University of Chicago Press, 2005), 89–116. Such concepts are related in diverse ways to the centrality of "contingency" that also emerged during the
romantic period. See David Wellbery, "Contingency," in *Neverending Stories: Toward
a Critical Narratology*, ed. Ann Fehn, Ingeborg Hoesterey, and Maria Tatar (Princeton:
Princeton University Press, 1992), 237–57. On the ludic tradition to which Goethe's
"playable" novel is indebted, see Benjamin Bennett, *Beyond Theory*, 14–63. On the
novel's emphasis on the importance of a kind of readerly openness, see Hans Vaget,
"Johann Wolfgang von Goethe: *Wilhelm Meisters Wanderjahre*," 136–64, and Birgit
Baldwin, "*Wilhelm Meisters Wanderjahre* as an Allegory of Reading," *Goethe Yearbook*
5 (1990): 213–32. Finally, on the centrality of the navigational to digital networked
narratives, see Rita Raley, "Reveal Codes: Hypertext and Performance," *Postmodern
Culture* 12, no. 1 (2001): Par. 19. http://muse.jhu.edu/journals/pmc/v012/12.1raley
.html. For the relationship between cartography and the novel, see Andrew Piper,
"Mapping Vision: Goethe, Cartography and the Novel," in *Spatial Turns: Space, Place,
and Mobility in German Literary and Visual Culture*, ed. Jaimey Fisher and Barbara Mennel (Amsterdam: Rodopi, forthcoming 2009).

33. For recent examples of this approach, see Leah Price, *The Anthology and the Rise of the
Novel* (Cambridge: Cambridge University Press, 2000), David Brewer, *The Afterlife of
Character, 1726–1825* (Philadelphia: University of Pennsylvania Press, 2005), and
Thomas Keymer and Peter Sabor, *Pamela in the Marketplace: Literary Controversy and
Print Culture in Eighteenth-Century Britain and Ireland* (Cambridge: Cambridge Uni-
versity Press, 2005).

34. Steven Connor, "Topologies: Michel Serres and the Shapes of Thought," *Anglistik* 15
(2004): 105–17.

35. As Galloway and Thacker write, "What matters [in a network] is less the character of
individual nodes than the topological space within which and through which they
operate as nodes. . . . To be a node is to exist inseparably from a set of possibilities
and parameters." Alexander Galloway and Eugene Thacker, *The Exploit: A Theory of
Networks*, 40.

36. Wolfgang Bunzel, "'Das ist eine heillose Manier, dieses Fragmente-Auftischen': Die
Vorabdrucke einzelner Abschnitte aus Goethes *Wanderjahre* in Cottas *Taschenbuch für
Damen*," *Jahrbuch des freien deutschen Hochstifts* (1992): 36–68, at 36.

37. Leah Price, *The Anthology and the Rise of the Novel: From Richardson to George Eliot*
(Cambridge: Cambridge University Press, 2000).

38. Wolfgang Bunzel "'Das ist eine heillose Manier, dieses Fragmente-Auftischen,'" 45.

39. *Taschenbuch für Damen* (1810), viii.

40. Goethe writes in *Dichtung und Wahrheit*, "We removed ourselves to a spacious alcove
and I read a fairy-tale aloud, to which I subsequently appended the title of 'The New
Melusina.' It relates to 'The New Paris' roughly like the adolescent does to the boy,
and I would insert it here if I was not afraid of harming the bucolic reality and simplicity that pleasantly surrounds us here through such bizarre plays of fantasy." J. W.
Goethe, *Aus meinem Leben: Dichtung und Wahrheit*, 485.

41. Cited in Wolfgang Bunzel, "'Das ist eine heillose Manier, dieses Fragmente-
Auftischen,'" 68.

42. Cited in ibid.

43. Meredith McGill, *American Literature and the Culture of Reprinting, 1834–1853* (Philadelphia: University of Pennsylvania Press, 2003).

44. In one of the few monograph studies on the literary sequel, Paul Budra and Betty Schellenberg write of "the sequel's inherent potential for stabilization through repetition across textual boundaries." "Introduction," *Part Two: Reflections on the Sequel* (Toronto: University of Toronto Press, 1998), 12.

45. Thomas Wolf, *Pustkuchen und Goethe: Die Streitschrift als produktives Verwirrspiel* (Tübingen: Niemeyer, 1999).

46. For a discussion of the novel's reception, see Klaus F. Gille, *Wilhelm Meister im Urteil der Zeitgenossen (Assen: Van Gorcum, 1971)*

47. J. W. Goethe, "Geneigte Theilnahme an den *Wanderjahren*," *Ästhetische Schriften, 1821–1824*, in *Sämtliche Werke*, vol. 21, ed. Stefan Greif and Andrea Ruhlig (Frankfurt/Main: Deutscher Klassiker Verlag, 1998), 290–92.

48. J. W. Goethe, *Wilhelm Meisters Lehrjahre*, in *Sämtliche Werke*, vol. 9, ed. Wilhelm Voßkamp (Frankfurt/Main: Deutscher Klassiker Verlag, 1992), 823.

49. J. W. Goethe, "Anzeige von Goethe's Sämmtlichen Werken vollständige Ausgabe letzter Hand," *Ästhetische Schriften, 1824–1832*, in *Sämtliche Werke*, vol. 22, ed. Anne Bohnenkamp (Frankfurt/Main: Deutscher Klassiker Verlag, 1999), 759.

50. Ibid., 762.

51. Friedrich Schütz, *Kritik der neuesten Cotta'schen Ausgabe von Goethe's Werken, nebst einem Plane zu einer vollständigen und kritisch geordneten Ausgabe derselben* (Hamburg: Nestler, 1828), 44.

52. See Waltraud Maierhofer, *"Wilhelm Meisters Wanderjahre" und der Roman des Nebeneinander* (Bielefeld, 1990), who writes about "das Fehlen eines Kontinuitätsprinzips" within the novel (15).

53. See Barbara Piatti, who refers to the Lago Maggiore as a "bildgewordener Landschaft." Barbara Piatti, "Wasserreisen: Vierwaldstättersee und Lago Maggiore als literarische Landschaften," in *Romantik und Exil*, ed. Claudia Christophersen and Ursula Hudson-Wiedenmann (Würzburg: Königshausen und Neumann, 2004), 279–93, at 287.

54. For a discussion of such recursive poetics, see Joseph Vogl, *Kalkül und Leidenschaft: Poetik des ökonomischen Menschen* (München: Sequenzia, 2002), 37.

55. Hannelore Schlaffer, *Wilhelm Meister: Das Ende der Kunst und die Wiederkehr des Mythos* (Stuttgart: Metzler, 1980), 22.

56. Genette writes: "By hypertextuality I mean any relationship uniting a text B to an earlier text A upon which it is grafted in a manner that is not that of commentary" (5). Or further: "It may yet be of another kind such as text B not speaking of text A at all but being unable to exist, as such, without A, from which it originates through a process I shall provisionally call transformation, and which it consequently evokes more or less perceptibly without necessarily speaking of it or citing it" (5). Against this definition, Genette defines intertextuality as "a relationship of copresence between two texts or among several texts. . . . In its most explicit and literal form, it is the traditional practice of quoting" (1–2). Gérard Genette, *Palimpsests: Literature in the Second Degree*, trans. Channa Newman and Claude Doubinsky (Lincoln: University of Nebraska Press, 1997). This contrasts with Kristeva's notion of intertextuality, see where she writes that intertextuality refers to "a mosaic of quotations; any text is the absorption and transformation of another. The notion of intertextuality replaces that of intersubjectivity, and poetic language is read as at least double." Julia Kristeva,

"Word, Dialogue, Novel," in *The Kristeva Reader,* ed. Toril Moi (New York: Columbia University Press, 1986), 37.

57. J. W. Goethe, *Die Leiden des jungen Werthers: 2. Fassung,* in *Sämtliche Werke,* vol. 8, ed. Waltraud Wiethölter (Frankfurt/Main: Deutscher Klassiker Verlag, 1994), 199.

58. For a reading of this passage that emphasizes the opacity of these signs' meaning and thus occludes the very reading process that they are designed to motivate, see Wolfram Malte Fues, *"Wanderjahre* im Hypertext," in *Klassik und Anti-Klassik,* ed. Ortrud Gutjahr and Harro Segeberg (Würzburg: Königshausen und Neumann, 2001), 137–56, where he writes: "What kind of small piece of paper? What kind of illustrated arrow, when and where was it drawn, on what occasion and to what end? Readers of the *Travels* in its final version are once again confronted with a riddle, one that they have already often encountered" (143).

59. See Emil Staiger, *Goethe* (Zürich: Artemis, 1959), 3:136.

60. In a reading of Goethe's interest in cartography, Gerhard Neumann has emphasized the importance of the category of the "gap" *(die Lücke)* in Goethe's thinking about maps, that mapping is fundamentally defined by what it leaves out *(Nichtwissen).* Gerhard Neumann, "Naturwissenschaft und Geschichte als Literatur: Zu Goethes Kulturpoetischen Projekt," *MLN* 114, no. 3 (1999): 471–509. What the passage that I have discussed here indicates is the way such concerns with omission are always linked with the simultaneous practice of pointing towards something else *(Mehrwissen).*

61. J. W. Goethe, "Über Naturwissenschaft im Allgemeinen, einzelne Betrachtungen und Aphorismen," in *Werke,* sect. 2, vol. 11, ed. Bernhard Suphan and Rudolf Steiner (Weimar: Böhlau, 1893), 148. For a discussion of Goethe's relationship to magnetism, see Klaus H. Kiefer, "Goethe und der Magnetismus," *Philosophie naturalis* 20, no. 3 (1983): 264–311. The obvious attraction (excuse the pun) of magnetism for Goethe was the way it captured Goethe's belief in the polarity of being. See J. W. Goethe, *Aus meinem Leben,* 520.

62. Wilhelm Emrich, "Das Problem der Symbolinterpretation im Hinblick auf Goethes *Wanderjahre," Deutsche Vierteljahrsschrift* 26 (1952): 331–52, at 339. Debates about Goethe's theory of the symbol are legion. For a résumé, see Michael Titzmann, "Allegorie und Symbol im Denksystem der Goethezeit," in *Formen und Funktionen der Allegorie,* ed. Walter Haug (Stuttgart: Metzler, 1979), 642–65, and Birgit Baldwin, "*Wilhelm Meisters Wanderjahre* as an Allegory of Reading," 213–32.

63. On the alignment of literature and the riddle, see Daniel Tiffany, "Lyric Substance: On Riddles, Materialism, and Poetic Obscurity," in *Things,* ed. Bill Brown (Chicago: University of Chicago Press, 2004), 72–98, and Manfred Fuhrmann, "Obscuritas: Das Problem der Dunkelheit in der rhetorischen und literarästhetischen Theorie der Antike," in *Immanente Ästhetik—Ästhetische Reflexion: Lyrik als Paradigma der Moderne,* ed. Wolfgang Iser (München: Fink, 1966), 47–72.

64. Walter Benjamin, *Das Passagen Werk,* in *Gesammelte Schriften,* vol. 5, ed. Rolf Tiedemann (Frankfurt/Main: Suhrkamp, 1982), 461. For a discussion of the genre of the riddle, see André Jolles, "Rätsel," in *Einfache Formen* (Tübingen: Max Niemeyer, 1968), 126–49.

65. Walter Benjamin, *Ursprung des deutschen Trauerspiels* (Berlin: Ernst Rowohlt Verlag, 1928), 173.

66. Michael McKeon, *The Secret History of Domesticity: Public, Private, and the Division of Knowledge* (Baltimore: Johns Hopkins University Press, 2007), 506–46, 598–614, 631–59.

67. On the dating of Balzac's transition to thinking about his works as one complete whole, see Claude Duchet and Isabelle Tournier, eds., *Balzac, œuvres complètes: Le moment de "La comédie humaine"* (Vincennes: Presses universitaires de Vincennes, 1993).

68. Friedrich Schütz, *Kritik der neuesten Cotta'schen Ausgabe*, 38.

69. Irmgard Egger, *Diätetik und Askese*; Safia Azzouni, *Kunst als praktische Wissenschaft*; and Henriette Herwig, *Das ewig Männliche zieht uns hinab*.

70. Simon Richter, *Laocoön's Body and the Aesthetics of Pain: Winckelmann, Lessing, Herder, Moritz, Goethe* (Detroit: Wayne State University Press, 1992).

71. Clifford Siskin, *The Historicity of Romantic Discourse* (Oxford: Oxford University Press, 1988), 140–41.

72. Irmela Marei Krüger-Fürhoff, *Der versehrte Körper: Revisionen des klassistischen Schönheitsideals* (Göttingen: Wallstein, 2001).

73. Barbara Maria Stafford, *Body Criticism: Imaging the Unseen in Enlightenment Art and Medicine* (Cambridge, Mass.: MIT Press, 1991), 47.

74. Albrecht Koschorke, *Körperströme und Schriftverkehr: Mediologie des 18. Jahrhunderts* (München: Fink, 1999). See also Marie-Luise Angerer, *Body Options: Körper. Spuren. Medien. Bilder* (Wien: Turia & Kant, 2000); Annette Keck and Nicolas Pethes, *Mediale Anatomien* (Bielefeld: Transcript, 2001); Andrew Piper, "'Korpus: Brentano, das Buch, und die Mobilisierung eines literarischen und politischen Körpers,'" *Textbewegungen 1800/1900*, ed. Till Dembeck and Matthias Buschmeier (Würzburg: Königshausen & Neumann, 2007), 266–86; and of course the classic example, Marshall McLuhan, *Understanding Media: The Extensions of Man* (Cambridge, Mass.: MIT Press, 1994).

75. For a discussion of the significance of Vesalius's book, see Katharine Park, *Secrets of Women: Gender, Generation, and the Origins of Human Dissection* (New York: Zone, 2006).

76. In a telling example of the often reductive kind of literary analysis that discursive readings can generate, Irmgard Egger reads Wilhelm's interaction with the arm as nothing more than a sentimental "Einfühlung" in the object of study and thus a resistance to the "objektive Präzision" at the heart of experimental science. However true this may be, it overlooks the elaborate figural structure of the entire scene that is the subject of my reading here and that produces much different conclusions about the chapter's significance. Irmgard Egger, "'Verbinden mehr als Trennen': Goethe und die plastische Anatomie," *Germanisch-romanische Monatsschrift* 51, no. 1 (2001): 45–53. For an explication of the historical references embedded in this scene that similarly overlook its narrative structure, see Moritz Baßler, "Goethe und die Bodysnatcher," *Von der Natur zur Kunst zurück*, ed. Moritz Baßler et al. (Tübingen: Niemeyer, 1997), 181–97.

77. Erich Blackall, *Goethe and the Novel* (Ithaca: Cornell University Press, 1976), 248.

78. See J. A. Schmoll, "Zur Genesis des Torso-Motivs," *Das Unvollendete als künstlerische Form*, ed. J. A. Schmoll (München: Francke, 1959), 117–39, and Maria Neusser, "Die Antikenergänzungen der Florentiner Manieristen," *Wiener Jahrbuch für Kunstgeschichte*, vol. 6 (1929), 27f.

79. J. W. Goethe, *Leben des Benvenuto Cellini*, in *Sämtliche Werke*, vol. 11, ed. Hans-Georg Dewitz and Wolfgang Proß (Frankfurt/Main: Deutscher Klassiker Verlag, 1998), 384f.

80. Jacob and Wilhelm Grimm, *Deutsches Wörterbuch*, vol. 20 (München: dtv, 1994), 691.

81. For a discussion of the centrality of the "prototype" today, see Scott Lash, *Critique of Information* (London: Sage, 2002), 22.

82. The technological identity of the work of art in the novel is usually underplayed by critics in favor of an emphasis on an organic notion of continuity. For examples of readings of this chapter that emphasize the overcoming of death and the triumph of nature—that align it with a larger Christian metaphorics of resurrection—see Safia Azzouni, *Kunst als praktische Wissenschaft*, 95–105, and Irmgard Egger, *Diätetik und Askese*, 35f. For a thought-provoking reading that draws attention to the role of the technological here not as something to be valorized but as an implicit critique of the "violence of technicity" behind any aesthetic underpinnings of modern nation states, see Marc Redfield, "The Dissection of the State: *Wilhelm Meisters Wanderjahre* and the Politics of Aesthetics," in *Aesthetic Ideology and the Bildungsroman* (Ithaca: Cornell University Press, 1996), 124.

83. J. W. Goethe, *Briefe, Tagebücher und Gespräche, 1823–1828*, 551.

CHAPTER TWO

1. The story was recounted by Johann Gottfried Gruber, friend of Wieland and future editor of the *Allgemeine Enzyklopädie der Wissenschaften*. Cited in Siegfried Unseld, *Goethe und seine Verleger* (Frankfurt/Main: Insel, 1991), 148. For the English translation, see Siegfried Unseld, *Goethe and his Publishers*, trans. Kenneth J. Northcott (Chicago: University of Chicago Press, 1996).

2. See Manfred Sommer, *Sammeln: Ein philosophischer Versuch* (Frankfurt/Main: Suhrkamp, 1999) and Justin Stagl, "Homo collector: Zur Anthropologie und Soziologie des Sammelns," in *Sammler—Bibliophile—Exzentriker*, ed. Aleida Assmann, Monika Gomille, and Gabriele Rippl (Tübingen: Günter Narr, 1998), 37–54.

3. Elizabeth L. Eisenstein, *The Printing Press as an Agent of Change: Communications and Cultural Transformations in Early-Modern Europe*, 2 vols. (Cambridge: Cambridge University Press, 1979), and Alvin Kernan, *Samuel Johnson and the Impact of Print* (Princeton: Princeton University Press, 1989).

4. Philip Connell, "Bibliomania: Book Collecting, Cultural Politics, and the Rise of Literary Heritage in Romantic Britain," *Representations* 71 (2000 Summer): 24–47. See also Susan A. Crane, *Collecting and Historical Consciousness in Early Nineteenth-Century Germany* (Ithaca: Cornell University Press, 2000).

5. Print for Anderson not only operated on such spatial planes to promote national mentalities; its creation of such collective heritages was also a crucial component of the national imaginary. "If nation-states are widely conceded to be 'new' and 'historical,'" writes Anderson, "the nations to which they give political expression always loom out of an immemorial past, and, still more important, glide into a limitless future." Benedict Anderson, *Imagined Communities: Reflections on the Origin and Spread of Nationalism* (New York: Verso, 1991), 11.

6. Marjorie Swann, *Curiosities and Texts: The Culture of Collecting in Early Modern England* (Philadelphia: University of Pennsylvania Press, 2001).

7. For a discussion of Göschen's undertaking, see Wolfgang von Ungern-Sternberg, "C. M. Wieland und das Verlagswesen seiner Zeit," *Archiv für Geschichte des Buchwesens* 14 (1974): 1213–1534, Dietmar Debes, *Georg Joachim Göschen: Die typographische Leistung des Verlegers* (Leipzig: Institut für Buchgestaltung, 1965), and Stephan Füssel, *Studien zur Verlagsgeschichte und zur Verlegertypologie der Goethe-Zeit* (Berlin: de Gruyter, 1999).

8. For a discussion of Scott, see Jane Millgate, *Scott's Last Edition: A Study in Publishing History* (Edinburgh, 1987). For Goethe, see my previous chapter. For Balzac, see Claude Duchet et Isabelle Tournier, eds., *Balzac, œuvres complètes: Le moment de La*

comédie humaine (Vincennes: Presses universitaires de Vincennes, 1993). And for Henry James, see Philip Horne, "Henry James and the Cultural Frame of the New York Edition," in *The Culture of Collected Editions*, ed. Andrew Nash (New York: Palgrave Macmillan, 2003), 95–110, and David McWhirter, *Henry James's New York Edition: The Construction of Authorship* (Cambridge: Cambridge University Press, 1999).

9. According to the annual catalogue to the Leipzig book fairs, for example, the yearly production of collected works in German went from an annual average of roughly five to seven in the years around 1800 to fifty-one by 1830. See the *Allgemeines Verzeichniß der Bücher* (Leipzig: Weidman, 1760–1850).

10. For a recent study on the format, see Andrew Nash, ed., *The Culture of Collected Editions* (New York: Palgrave Macmillan, 2003). While there have been numerous studies on individual authors' editions, there has been relatively little work drawing attention to this format itself and its impact on writing and the shape of literary texts. In her work on the culture of reprinting in the nineteenth century, Meredith McGill has nicely illustrated how posthumous collected editions often elided the diverse publishing practices of nineteenth-century authors. See Meredith McGill, "Unauthorized Poe," in *American Literature and the Culture of Reprinting, 1834–1853* (Philadelphia: University of Pennsylvania Press, 2003), 141–86. And yet by the early nineteenth century, the collected edition itself was an important example of such dramas of republication. It was not just an aftereffect that effaced a variety of other practices, but was one of those practices as well, one that influenced nineteenth-century writers in important and complex ways.

11. Tanselle writes: "But printed books . . . even when similarly mass-produced, are often seen to be in a class apart, exempt from the human urge to tinker and, more significantly, from the human inability to do the same thing twice." G. Thomas Tanselle, *A Rationale of Textual Criticism* (Philadelphia: University of Pennsylvania Press, 1989), 49. For William St. Clair it was less of a universal problem and more of a bibliographic fact that moveable type—as opposed to stereotype—tended to promote variety and not continuity between editions of a work during the romantic period. St. Clair writes: "The growth in books and reading brought about by the coming of print, by contrast, took the form of the production of more texts rather than of more copies of existing texts." William St. Clair, *The Reading Nation in the Romantic Period* (Cambridge: Cambridge University Press, 2004), 22.

12. E. A. Poe, "Magazine-Writing," *Collected Writings*, vol. 3, ed. Burton R. Pollin (New York: Gordian, 1986), 137. Friedrich Schlegel, "Vom kombinatorischen Geist," *Lessings Gedanken und Meinungen* (1804), in *Kritische Friedrich-Schlegel-Ausgabe*, vol. 3, ed. Hans Eichner (München: Ferdinand Schöningh, 1967), 79–85.

13. See Christine Haynes, "An 'Evil Genius': The Construction of the Publisher in the Postrevolutionary Social Imaginary," *French Historical Studies* 30, no. 4 (Fall 2007): 559–95.

14. Hillel Schwartz, *The Culture of the Copy* (Cambridge: Zone, 1996).

15. It is important to note here how, contra Benjamin, the romantic book precedes photography as a key medium for contemporaries to reflect upon the problem of technological reproducibility.

16. Dietmar Debes, *Georg Joachim Göschen*.

17. Siegfried Unseld, *Goethe und seine Verleger*, 147.

18. Ibid.

19. Waltraud Hagen, "Goethes Ausgabe letzter Hand: Entstehung und Bedeutung," *Marginalien* 99 (1985): 1–22.

20. Siegfried Unseld, *Goethe und seine Verleger*, 147.

21. Georg Reimer to A. W. Schlegel, March 20, 1826. Cited in Doris Reimer, *Passion und Kalkül: Der Verleger Georg Andreas Reimer* (Berlin: de Gruyter, 1999), 148.

22. Tom Mole, "Ways of Seeing Byron," in *Byron: The Image of the Poet*, ed. Christine Kenyon Jones (Newark: University of Delaware Press, forthcoming).

23. Gilles Deleuze and Félix Guattari, "Year Zero: Faciality," in *A Thousand Plateaus: Capitalism and Schizophrenia*, trans. Brian Massumi (Minneapolis: University of Minnesota Press, 1987), 167–191.

24. Ibid., 170.

25. Ibid., 180.

26. Nathaniel Hawthorne, "The Minister's Black Veil: A Parable," *Tales and Sketches* (New York: Library of America, 1982), 372.

27. *Oeuvres de J. J. Rousseau, avec des notes historiques*, 22 vols. (Paris: Lefèvre, 1819).

28. *Collection complète des œuvres de J. J. Rousseau, Citoyen de Genève*, 33 volumes (Genève, 1782).

29. *Oeuvres de J. J. Rousseau, avec des notes historiques* (1819), 1:xviii (emphasis in original).

30. *The Works of Lord Byron, with his Letters and Journals, and His Life, by Thomas Moore, esq.*, 14 vols. (London: Murray, 1832), 7:vi.

31. J. W. Goethe, *Aus meinem Leben: Dichtung und Wahrheit*, in *Sämtliche Werke*, vol. 14, ed. Klaus-Detlef Müller (Frankfurt/Main: Deutscher Klassiker Verlag, 1986), 310.

32. Christof Windgätter, *Medienwechsel: Vom Nutzen und Nachteil der Sprache für die Schrift* (Berlin: Kadmos, 2006), 61.

33. *Oeuvres de J. J. Rousseau, avec des notes historiques*, 1:i (emphasis in original).

34. Wolfgang von Ungern-Sternberg, "C. M. Wieland und das Verlagswesen seiner Zeit."

35. On copyright and reprinting in Germany, see Heinrich Bosse, *Autorschaft ist Werkherrschaft: Über die Entstehung des Urheberrechts aus dem Geist der Goethezeit* (München: Schöningh, 1981).

36. Wolfgang von Ungern-Sternberg, "C. M. Wieland," 1472. Göschen's other tactic, again driven by the need to comply with legal norms, was to encourage Wieland to rewrite *Agathon* as much as possible. "Thus I implore you," wrote Göschen, "change, improve, and increase the third part as much as possible." Cited in Wolfgang von Ungern-Sternberg, "C. M. Wieland," 1500.

37. Johann Gottlieb Fichte, "Beweis der Unrechtmäßigkeit des Büchernachdrucks," *Sämtliche Werke*, vol. 8 (Berlin: Veit und Comp., 1846), 223–44.

38. Wolfgang von Ungern-Sternberg, "C. M. Wieland," 1502.

39. Doris Reimer, *Passion und Kalkül*.

40. E. T. A. Hoffmann, *Die Serapionsbrüder*, in *Sämtliche Werke*, vol. 4, ed. Wulf Segebrecht (Frankfurt/Main: Deutscher Klassiker, 2001), 11. Parenthetical citations of *SB* are to this edition.

41. Meredith McGill, *American Literature and the Culture of Reprinting, 1834–1853* (Philadelphia: University of Pennsylvania Press, 2003).

42. Andreas Gailus, "Poetics of Containment: Goethe's *Conversations of German Refugees* and the Crisis of Representation," *Modern Philology* 100, no. 3 (February 2003): 436–74.

43. Johann Peter Eckermann, *Gespräche mit Goethe*, in J. W. Goethe, *Sämtliche Werke*, vol. 39, ed. Christoph Michel (Frankfurt/Main: Deutscher Klassiker Verlag, 1999), 221.

44. Friedrich Schlegel, "Nachricht von den poetischen Werken des Johannes Boccaccio,"

Kritische Friedrich-Schlegel-Ausgabe, vol. 2, ed. Hans Eichner (München: Schöningh, 1967), 394.

45. Ludwig Tieck, *Schriften*, vol. 11 (Berlin, 1829), lxxxiv–xc. Cited in Josef Kunz, ed., *Novelle* (Darmstadt: Wissenschaftliche Buchgesellschaft, 1968), 53.

46. Alfred de Vigny, "Lettre à Lord * * * sur la soirée du 24 Octobre 1829 et sur un système dramatique," in *Oeuvres complètes*, v. 1 (Paris: Gallimard, 1986), 409.

47. Friedrich Schlegel, "Athenäums-Fragmente," in *Kritische Friedrich-Schlegel-Ausgabe*, 2:219.

48. Ernst Behler, "Von der romantischen Kunstkritik zur modernen Hermeneutik," in *Ästhetische Moderne in Europa*, ed. Vieltz und Kemper (München: Fink, 1998), 127–50.

49. For a review of this reception, see Uwe Japp, "Das serapiontische Prinzip," *Text + Kritik* (1992): 63–75, and, more recently, H. M. Brown, *E. T. A. Hoffmann and the Serapiontic Principle: Critique and Creativity* (Rochester: Camden House, 2006).

50. Sigmund Freud, "The Uncanny," in *The Standard Edition of the Complete Psychological Works*, trans. and ed. James Strachey, vol. 17 (London: Hogarth Press, 1955), 220.

51. This turn to look at the exteriorities and utterances *in* Hoffmann should be understood as an explicit reversal of canonical readings of Hoffmann inspired by Friedrich Kittler that have been aimed at understanding the technical conditions of such interiorities but that nonetheless still aim exclusively at unearthing a "psychological discourse." Kittler writes: "It will be shown that Literature's descent into interiority is only the interior aspect of an exteriority that prescribed an entire literary epoch to speak psychologically." Friedrich Kittler "'Das Phantom unseres Ichs' und die Literaturpsychologie: E. T. A. Hoffmann—Freud—Lacan," in *Urszenen*, ed. Friedrich Kittler (Frankfurt/Main: Suhrkamp, 1977), 139.

52. Hoffmann to Reimer, January 2, 1821. Cited in Hoffmann, *E. T. A. Hoffmanns Briefwechsel*, 3 vols., ed. Friedrich Schnapp (München: Winkler, 1968), 2:282.

53. As Hoffmann has his characters tell us, this Serapion is not to be confused with the fourth-century Egyptian bishop, Serapion of Thmius, whose death would not have overlapped with the life of Emperor Decius (ca. AD 201–51). But there is a remarkable similarity between the fate of "Serapion" here and the historical fate of Cyprian, the bishop of Carthage, who shares the same name as the tale's narrator.

54. Peter von Matt, *Die Augen der Automaten* (Tübingen: Niemeyer, 1971), 16. For the argument that Serapion is chosen because he represents an alternative to the materialist position represented in the frame figure of Rat Krespel, who dissects violins to find out the secret of their sound, see Dorothea von Mücke, *The Seduction of the Occult and the Rise of the Fantastic Tale* (Stanford: Stanford University Press, 2003), 148–96.

55. On the shaping of reading as repetition in the romantic period, see Deidre Shauna Lynch, "Canons Clockwork," in *Bookish Histories*, ed. Ina Ferris and Paul Keen (New York: Palgrave, forthcoming).

56. See Natalie Zemon Davis, *The Return of Martin Guerre* (Cambridge, Mass.: Harvard University Press, 1983).

57. Eva Horn, "Prothesen: Der Mensch im Lichte des Maschinenbaus," *Mediale Anatomien*, ed. Annette Keck und Nicolas Pethes (Bielefeld: Transcript, 2001), 193–210.

58. For an overview, see Andrew J. Webber, *The Doppelgänger: Double Visions in German Literature* (Oxford: Clarendon, 1996), and Christof Forderer, *Ich-Eklipsen: Doppelgänger in der Literatur seit 1800* (Stuttgart: Metzler, 1999).

59. See "Quellen und Anregungen" in E. T. A. Hoffmann, *Fantasiestücke in Callot's Manier*,

in *Sämtliche Werke*, vol. 2.1, ed. Hartmut Steinecke (Frankfurt/Main: Deutscher Klassiker Verlag, 1993), 727–30.

60. H. R. Jauss, *Studien zum Epochenwandel der ästhetischen Moderne* (Frankfurt/Main: Suhrkamp, 1989). A similar argument is made about the ways in which the genre of the fantastic promotes a divided subjectivity that does not completely know itself in Dorothea von Mücke, "Unheimliche Verdoppelungen," in *Germanistik und Komparatistik: DFG-Symposium*, ed. Hendrik Birus (Stuttgart: Metzler, 1993), 160–87.

61. Jürgen Barkhoff, "Inszenierung—Narration—his story: Zur Wissenspoetik im Mesmerismus und in E. T. A. Hoffmanns 'Das Sanctus,'" in *Romantische Wissenspoetik*, ed. Gabrielle Brandstetter and Gerhard Neumann (Würzburg: Königshausen und Neumann, 2004), 91–122, at 93.

62. Christof Forderer, *Ich-Eklipsen*, 25.

63. In referring to the doubling function of "the uncanny," Freud describes this act of psychological projection as "the subject's narcissistic overvaluation of his own mental processes." Sigmund Freud, "The Uncanny," *Standard Edition*, 17:263.

64. Friedrich Kittler, "Romanticism—Psychoanalysis—Film: A History of the Double," in *Literature, Media, Information Systems*, ed. John Johnston (Amsterdam: G & B Arts, 1997), 90.

65. On the position of mesmerism within a history of communication and not just psychohistory, see Jürgen Barkhoff, "Die Anwesenheit des Abwesenden im Netz: Kommunikative Vernetzung im Mesmerismus," in *Netzwerke: Eine Kulturtechnik der Moderne*, ed. Jürgen Barkhoff, Hartmut Böhme, und Jeanne Riou (Köln: Böhlau, 2004), 69–86.

66. Koschorke writes: "The treatment can proceed wordless, without the need for mediating semiotic elements, through the immediate relaying of magnetic current." Albrecht Koschorke, *Körperströme und Schriftverkehr*, 112.

67. Ibid.

68. For Hoffmann's connection to the rise of nineteenth-century hermeneutics, see David Wellbery, "E. T. A. Hoffmann and Romantic Hermeneutics: An Interpretation of Hoffmann's 'Don Juan,'" *Studies in Romanticism* 19 (Winter 1980): 455–73.

69. For a discussion of the figure of the third as a figure of the channel, see Michel Serres, *The Parasite*, trans. Lawrence R. Schehr (Minneapolis: University of Minnesota Press, 2007), 34–39. For an extrapolation of Serres's argument, see Bernhard Siegert, "Cacography or Communication? Cultural Techniques in German Media Studies," *Grey Room* 29 (Winter 2008): 26–47.

70. Meredith McGill, *The Culture of Reprinting* 156, 160.

71. For Neumann, it was the trope of "Anamorphose" that stood for the deformation and multiplication of perspective central to both Hoffmann's writing and the fundamental reorganization of perception in the nineteenth century, which the work of Jonathan Crary has done so much to identify. Gerhard Neumann, "Romantische Aufklärung: Zu E. T. A. Hoffmanns Wissenschaftspoetik," in *Aufklärung als Form: Beiträge zu einem historischen und aktuellen Problem*, ed. Helmut Schmiedt und Helmut J. Schneider (Würzburg: K & N, 1997), 106–48; Gerhard Neumann, "Anamorphose: E. T. A. Hoffmanns Poetik der Defiguration," in *Mimesis und Simulation*, ed. Andreas Kablitz and Gerhard Neumann (Freiburg, 1998), 377–417; and Gerhard Neumann, "Narration und Bildlichkeit: Zur Inszenierung eines romantischen Schicksalsmusters in E. T. A. Hoffmanns Novelle Doge und Dogaresse," in *Bild und Schrift in der Romantik*, ed. Gerhard Neumann (Würzburg: Königshausen und Neumann, 1999), 107–42.

72. Nathaniel Hawthorne, "My Kinsman, Major Molineaux," in *Tales and Sketches* (New York: Library of America, 1982), 83.

73. Bakhtin writes: "But any utterance, when it is studied in greater depth under the concrete conditions of speech communication, reveals to us many half-concealed or completely concealed words of others with varying degrees of foreignness." M. M. Bakhtin, "The Problem of Speech Genres," in *Speech Genres and Other Late Essays*, trans. Vern W. McGee (Austin: University of Texas Press, 2002), 93.

74. Steven Connor, "Dickens, The Haunting Man (On L-iterature)," Paper delivered at the Institute for English Studies, July 25–27, 2002: http://www.bbk.ac.uk/english/skc/haunting/.

75. That this condition of availability is a key feature of environments of mass communication is argued by John B. Thompson: "The products of the media industries are available in principle to a plurality of recipients. They are produced in multiple copies or transmitted to a multiplicity of receivers in such a way that they are available in principle to anyone who has the technical means, abilities and resources to acquire them." John B. Thompson, *Media and Modernity* (Cambridge: Polity Press, 1995), 30.

CHAPTER THREE

1. Cited in Rainer Kolk, "Liebhaber, Gelehrte, Experten: Das Sozialsystem der Germanistik bis zum Beginn des 20. Jahrhunderts," in *Wissenschaftsgeschichte der Germanistik im 19. Jahrhundert*, ed. Jürgen Fohrmann und Wilhelm Voßkamp (Stuttgart: Metzler, 1994), 48–114, at 60.

2. Benedict Anderson, *Imagined Communities: Reflections on the Origin and Spread of Nationalism* (London: Verso, 1991), 71.

3. Friedrich von der Hagen, ed., *Der Nibelungen Lied* (Berlin: Unger, 1807), n.p.

4. Hans Ulrich Gumbrecht, "'Un souffle d'Allemagne ayant passé': Friedrich Diez, Gaston Paris, and the Genesis of National Philologies," *Romance Philology* 40, no. 1 (August 1986): 1–37.

5. For the relationship of translation to editing, see Bodo Plachta and Winfried Woesler, eds., *Edition und Übersetzung: Zur wissenschaftlichen Dokumentation des interkulturellen Texttransfers* (Tübingen: Max Niemeyer, 2002).

6. Georg Lukacs, *Goethe und seine Zeit* (Bern: Francke, 1947), 32.

7. J. W. Goethe, *Wilhelm Meisters Wanderjahre*, in *Sämtliche Werke*, vol. 10, ed. Gerhard Neumann (Frankfurt/Main: Deutscher Klassiker Verlag, 1989), 610, 601.

8. Friedrich Nietzsche, "Wir Philologen," in *Werke: Kritische Gesamtausgabe*, sect. 4, vol. 1, ed. Giorgio Colli and Mazzino Montinari (Berlin: de Gruyter, 1967), 133.

9. For a history of editing, see D. C. Greetham, *Textual Scholarship: An Introduction* (New York: Garland, 1994), Bernard Cerquiglini, *In Praise of the Variant: A Critical History of Philology*, trans. Betsy Wing (Baltimore: Johns Hopkins University Press, 1999), and Hans Ulrich Gumbrecht, *The Powers of Philology: Dynamics of Textual Scholarship* (Champaign: University of Illinois Press, 2003).

10. Nietzsche said of Leopardi, "Leopardi is the modern ideal of a philologist; German philologists cannot do anything." Friedrich Nietzsche, "Wir Philologen," 98. For a discussion of Leopardi's work, see Hans Ludwig Scheel, *Leopardi und die Antike* (München: Max Hueber, 1959), and Sebastiano Timpanaro, *La filologia di Giacomo Leopardi* (Rome: Laterza, 1997).

11. Discussed in G. Lothholz, *Das Verhältnis Wolfs und Wilhelm von Humboldts zu Göthe und Schiller* (Wernigerode: Angerstein, 1863). This is an area of Goethe scholarship

that has received surprisingly little attention. Nietzsche seems to be one of the few to have discussed Goethe's relationship to philology: "The greatest events that have impacted philology are the appearances of Goethe, Schopenhauer and Wagner." And: "The demise of the philologist-poets lies in good measure in their personal debasement; their kind continues later, as, for example, Goethe and Leopardi are just such phenomena." Friedrich Nietzsche, "Wir Philologen" 110, 120.

12. See Goethe's diary entries from December 4, 8, 9, 1820. J. W. Goethe, *Werke*, sect. 3, vol. 8 (Weimar: Böhlaus, 1896), 255–56.

13. Debates about whether the rise of German philology around 1800 constituted a methodological origin or merely a continuation are practically infinite. For overviews, see Sebastiano Timpanaro, *The Genesis of Lachmann's Method* (Chicago: University of Chicago Press, 2004), Lothar Bluhm, *Die Brüder Grimm und der Beginn der deutschen Philologie* (Hildesheim: Weidmann, 1997), and Harald Weigel, *"Nur was du nie gesehn wird ewig dauern": Carl Lachmann und die Entstehung der wissenschaftlichen Edition* (Freiburg: Rombach, 1989). For the argument that the only thing new about these editors was their "Publikationswut" and "Bibliomanie," see Ulrich Hunger, "Die altdeutsche Literatur und das Verlangen nach Wissenschaft," in *Wissenschaftsgeschichte der Germanistik im 19. Jahrhundert*, ed. Jürgen Fohrmann und Wilhelm Voßkamp (Stuttgart: Metzler, 1994), 236–63. Ulrich Wyss has emphasized the pre-professional, dilettantish practice of early-nineteenth-century editors. Ulrich Wyss, *Die wilde Philologie: Jacob Grimm und der Historismus* (München: Beck, 1979). The centrality of the amateur to the early-nineteenth-century editorial landscape was captured in Walter Scott's portrayal in *The Antiquary* of the collector who produces a folio, "on which he gazed from time to time with the knowing look of an *amateur*" (my emphasis). Walter Scott, *The Antiquary*, ed. David Hewitt (Edinburgh: Edinburgh University Press, 1995), 9. Still other historians have argued for the intermixing of tendencies that is characteristic of any emergent system, that the practices of the amateur and the scholarly expert existed side by side in the early nineteenth century and quite often in the same person. See Rainer Kolk, "Liebhaber, Gelehrte, Experten: Das Sozialsystem der Germanistik bis zum Beginn des 20. Jahrhunderts."

14. Jerome McGann, *Radiant Textuality: Literature after the World Wide Web* (New York: Palgrave, 2001), 169.

15. Joseph Körner, *Nibelungenforschungen der deutschen Romantik* (Leipzig: Haessel, 1911), 78.

16. Rüdiger Krohn, "'das Alles Allen verständlich sey . . .': Die Altgermanistik des 19. Jahrhunderts und ihre Wege in die Öffentlichkeit," in *Wissenschaftsgeschichte der Germanistik im 19. Jahrhundert*, 277. For the French, see Michael Glencross, "Relic and Romance: Antiquarianism and Medievalism in French Literary Culture, 1780–1830," *Modern Language Review* 95 (2000): 337–49.

17. "Words that are entirely incomprehensible in our language," writes Tieck, "are thus left out, but not those that we continue to use in a slightly altered sense or those whose meaning is easily surmised through analogy." Ludwig Tieck, "Die altdeutschen Minnelieder," *Kritische Schriften*, vol. 1 (Leipzig: Brockhaus, 1848; rpt. Berlin: de Gruyter, 1974) 187–214, at 212. For example, Tieck tells us that "schwachen" is left because it simply means "schwach machen" (make weaker) while "Schwere" (difficulty, in new high German) and "Sehnen" (desire, in n.h.G.) are left as they are, even though they mean "Trauer" (mourning) and "Leid" (suffering) respectively, which Tieck assumes can be gleaned from the context.

18. Ludwig Tieck, "Die altdeutschen Minnelieder," 211.

19. Ann Radcliffe, *Gaston de Blondeville* (Chicago: Valancourt, 2006), 27.

20. From Scott's review in the *Edinburgh Review* (1804), reprinted in *Prose Works of Walter Scott*, vol. 21 (Edinburgh: Cadell, 1836), 32.

21. Joseph Görres, *Altteutsche Volks- und Meisterlieder* (Frankfurt/Main: Wilmans, 1817), xvii, and Jacob Grimm, "Vorwort," *Deutsche Sagen* (1817), in *Kleinere Schriften*, vol. 8 (Hildesheim: Olms, 1965), 12.

22. It should be noted just how much Tieck's translational editorial poetics contradicts Kristina Hasenpflug's thesis of his work's "Primat der Allgemeinverständlichkeit." Kristina Hasenpflug, "'Denn es gibt doch nur eine Poesie': Tiecks Minnelieder—ein romantisches Literaturprogramm," in *Edition und Übersetzung: Zur wissenschaftlichen Dokumentation des interkulturellen Texttransfers*, ed. Bodo Plachta und Winfried Woesler (Tübingen: Max Niemeyer, 2002), 326.

23. F. A. Wolf, *Prolegomena to Homer*, trans. Anthony Grafton et al. (Princeton: Princeton University Press, 1985), 192.

24. Cited in Sebastiano Timpanaro, *The Genesis of Lachmann's Method*, 55.

25. Clemens Brentano to Achim von Arnim, January 16, 1813. Cited in Clemens Brentano, *Sämtliche Werke und Briefe*, vol. 33, ed. Konrad Feilchenfeldt (Stuttgart: Kohlhammer, 2000), 11.

26. See note 3.

27. Wilhelm Grimm, *Kleinere Schriften*, vol. 1, ed. Gustav Hinrichs (Berlin: Dümmler, 1881), 73.

28. Ibid., 76.

29. *Journal des Savants* (1830): 196. Cited in Michael Glencross, "Relic and Romance," 345.

30. For a discussion of the production of this text, see Lothar Bluhm, "Der Wissenschaftskrieg zwischen Friedrich von der Hagen und den Brüdern Grimm," in *Romantik und Volksliteratur*, ed. Lothar Bluhm and Achim Hölter (Heidelberg: Universitätsverlag Winter, 1999): 49–70.

31. Friedrich von der Hagen, *Lieder der älteren oder Sämundischen Edda* (Berlin: Haude & Spencer, 1812).

32. Wilhelm and Jacob Grimm, *Lieder der alten Edda* (Berlin: Realschulbuchhandlung, 1815).

33. *Morgenblatt* 221 (September 14, 1821), cited in Bluhm, "Der Wissenschaftskrieg zwischen Friedrich von der Hagen und den Brüdern Grimm," 62.

34. Friedrich von der Hagen, ed., *Der Nibelungen Lied, zum erstenmal in der ältesten Gestalt aus der St. Galler Handschrift mit Vergleichung der übrigen Handschriften* (Breslau: Max, 1816). While Hagen's 1810 version was already supposed to be a "critical edition," Hagen writes in the preface to the 1816 edition: "This edition of the *Nibelungen-Lied* is less a second printing of the first edition that appeared in 1810 as it is a completely new book" (iii).

35. Karl Lachmann, *Kleinere Schriften*, vol. 1, ed. Karl Müllenhoff (Berlin: Reimer, 1876), 83.

36. See Sebastiano Timpanaro, *The Genesis of Lachmann's Method*, 70–74. As Timpanaro shows, Lachmann and his contemporaries' valuation of recension emerged out of an eighteenth-century field of classical philology (Friedrich August Wolf) and biblical exegesis (Johann Albrecht Bengel).

37. Hermann Reichert, ed., *Das Nibelungenlied: Nach der St. Galler Handschrift* (Berlin: de Gruyter, 2005).

38. François-Juste-Marie Raynouard, *Choix des poésies originales des troubadours* (Paris: Didot, 1816–21), 5:iv.

39. Friedrich Diez, *Die Poesie der Troubadours: Nach gedruckten und handschriftlichen Werken derselben dargestellt* (Zwickau: Schumann, 1826), xi.

40. Christof Windgätter, *Medienwechsel: Vom Nutzen und Nachteil der Sprache für die Schrift* (Berlin: Kadmos, 2006), 60.

41. Karl Lachmann, *Kleinere Schriften*, 1:84

42. Karl Lachmann, "Vorrede," *Iwein*, 2d ed. (1843), v.

43. For a discussion of the emphasis on moving away from originals and towards recovering manuscripts as historically specific documents as events, see Steven Nichols, "Introduction: Philology in a Manuscript Culture," *Speculum* 65 (1990): 1–10, and Seth Lerer, "Medieval English Literature and the Idea of the Anthology," *PMLA* 118, no. 5 (2003): 1251–62.

44. See for example, Heinsius' edition, Ovid, *Pub. Ovidii Nasonis Opera. Daniel Heinsius textum recensuit. Accedunt Breves Notae ex collatione codd. Scaligeri et Palatinis Iani Gruteri* (Leiden, 1629). See also his "Amice Lector," where he recounts the previous authoritative editions his edition and emendations are based upon. As Evelyn Tribble has illustrated in discussions of sixteenth-century Horace editions, such a practice was by no means an anomaly in the early modern period. Tribble cites a 1546 Horace edition with fifteen different names on its title page. Evelyn B. Tribble, *Margins and Marginality: The Printed Page in Early Modern England* (Charlottesville: University of Virginia Press, 1993).

45. See Johannes Saltzwedel, "Der Herausgeber als Titan," *Der Spiegel*, December 16, 2000.

46. Helmut-Müller Sievers, "Tales of the Crypt," Talk delivered at Deutsches Haus, Columbia University, November 21, 2003.

47. Goethe to Carlyle, June 15, 1828. Cited in *Correspondence between Goethe and Carlyle*, ed. Charles Eliot Norton (New York: Cooper, 1970), 92.

48. For a record of Goethe's work, see J. W. Goethe, *Volkslieder in Elsaß aufgezeichnet: Faksimile-Ausgabe*, ed. Louis Pinck (Heidelberg: Elsaß-Lothringische Wissenschaftliche Gesellschaft, 1932).

49. On the translatability of bardic and balladic imaginaries from one local culture to another, see Katie Trumpener, *Bardic Nationalism: The Romantic Novel and the British Empire* (Princeton: Princeton University Press, 1997).

50. Hannelore Schlaffer, "Gitarre und Druckerei: Clemens Brentanos Schwierigkeiten beim Publizieren," in *Bildungsexklusivität und volkssprachliche Literatur*, ed. Klaus Grubmüller und Günter Hess (Tübingen: Niemeyer, 1986), 51–58.

51. See Reinhold Steig, ed., *Achim von Arnim und die ihm nahe standen*, vol. 1 (Stuttgart: Cotta, 1894), 95, where Arnim writes to Brentano during his trip to London in July 1803 about buying a copy of Scott's *Minstrelsy*.

52. For a recent treatment of the ballad's role in the development of romantic poetry, see Steve Newman, *Ballad Collection, Lyric, and the Canon: The Call of the Popular from the Restoration to the New Criticism* (Philadelphia: University of Pennsylvania Press, 2007).

53. See David Wellbery, "Primordial Orality," *The Specular Moment: Goethe's Early Lyric and the Beginnings of Romanticism* (Stanford: Stanford University Press, 1996), 187–221, and Maureen McLane, "Ballads and Bards: British Romantic Orality," *Modern Philology* 98, no. 3 (2001): 423–43.

54. J. W. Goethe, "Ballade: Betrachtung und Auslegung," in *Ästhetische Schriften, 1816–1822*, in *Sämtliche Werke*, vol. 21, ed. Stefan Greif und Andrea Ruhlig (Frankfurt/Main: Deutscher Klassiker Verlag, 1998), 39.

55. Paula McDowell, "'The Manufacture and Lingua-facture of Ballad-Making': Broadside Ballads in Long-Eighteenth-Century Ballad Discourse," *The Eighteenth Century* 47, nos. 2/3 (2006): 151–78.

56. See Maureen McLane, "Tuning the Multi-Media Nation, or, Minstrelsy of the Afro-Scottish Border ca. 1800," *European Romantic Review* 15, no. 2 (June 2004): 289–305.

57. Celeste Langan, "Understanding Media in 1805: Audio-Visual Hallucination in *The Lay of the Last Minstrel*," *Studies in Romanticism* 40, no. 1 (2001): 49–70.

58. Steve Newman, *Ballad Collection, Lyric, and the Canon* 185.

59. Susan Stewart, "Notes on Distressed Genres," *The Journal of American Folklore* 104 (1991): 5–31.

60. See the recent study by Ann Rowland in which this teleological relationship between the ballads and the novels in Scott is reformulated as individual development, as the ballads capture the oral, childhood origins of the newly psychologized subject. Ann Wierda Rowland, "'The fause nourice sang': Childhood, Child Murder, and the Formalism of the Scottish Ballad Revival," in *Scotland and the Borders of Romanticism*, ed. Leith Davis, Ian Duncan, and Janet Sorensen (Cambridge: Cambridge University Press, 2004), 225–44. For an example of this process outside of Scott, see Susan Stewart, "The Ballad in *Wuthering Heights*," *Representations* 86 (Spring 2004): 175–97.

61. "However he was placed, however he was dated, the minstrel raised methodological problems of dating and placing." Maureen McLane, "The Figure Minstrelsy Makes: Poetry and Historicity," *Critical Inquiry* 29, no. 3 (2003): 429–52, at 434.

62. Franco Moretti writes that Scott's historical novels produce a "phenomenology of the border." Franco Moretti, *Atlas of the European Novel, 1800–1900* (London: Verso, 1998), 35. On nationalism in Scott, see Ian Duncan, special issue on Scott, Scotland, and Romantic Nationalism, *Studies in Romanticism* 40, no. 1 (2001). On transnationalism and Scott, see Katie Trumpener, *Bardic Nationalism*, and Leith Davis, Ian Duncan, and Janet Sorensen, eds., *Scotland and the Borders of Romanticism*. Judith Wilt has invoked the "quarrel of languages" as a defining characteristic of Scott's work. Judith Wilt, *Secret Leaves: The Novels of Walter Scott* (Chicago: University of Chicago Press, 1985). Wilt's suggestion is a productive extension of Bakhtin's notion that it is precisely a surplus of languages (heteroglossia) that constitutes the novel form. There are numerous other studies on the role of multiple languages in Scott. See David Murison, "The Two Languages in Scott," in *Scott's Mind and Art*, ed. A. Norman Jeffaries (Edinburgh: Oliver and Boyd, 1969), 206–29; Graham Tulloch, *The Language of Walter Scott* (London: Deutsch, 1980); David Hewitt, "The Phonocentric Scot/t," in *Scott in Carnival*, ed. J. H. Alexander et al. (Aberdeen: Association for Scottish Literary Studies, 1993), 581–92; as well as the debate between James Buzard and Ina Ferris on the role of translation in Scott: James Buzard, "Translation and Tourism: Scott's *Waverley* and the Rendering of Culture," *Yale Journal of Criticism* 8, no. 2 (1995): 31–59, and Ina Ferris, "Translation from the Borders," *Eighteenth-Century Fiction* 9, no. 2 (1997): 203–22.

63. See Katie Trumpener, *Bardic Nationalism*; Fiona Robertson, *Legitimate Histories: Scott, Gothic, and the Authorities of Fiction* (Oxford: Clarendon, 1994); Ian Duncan, *Modern Romance and Transformations of the Novel: The Gothic, Scott, and Dickens* (Cambridge: Cambridge University Press, 1992); and Ina Ferris, "From 'National Tale' to 'Historical

Novel': Edgeworth, Morgan and Scott," in *The Achievement of Literary Authority: Gender, History and the Waverley Novels* (Ithaca: Cornell University Press, 1991), 105–36.

64. Cited in J. G. Lockhart, *Memoirs of the Life of Sir Walter Scott, Bart.*, 9 vols. (Boston: Ticknor and Fields, 1861), 2:39. For discussion of the making of the ballad edition, see Jane Millgate, "The Early Publication History of Scott's Minstrelsy of the Scottish Border," *The Papers of the Bibliographical Society of America* 94, no. 4 (2000): 551–64.

65. *Prose Works of Walter Scott*, 21:101.

66. Percy writes: "The word Minstrel is derived from the French Menestrier; and was not in use before the Norman conquest. . . . The Minstrels continued a distinct order of men, and got their livelihood by singing verses to the harp, at the houses of the great." Thomas Percy, ed., *Reliques of Ancient English Poetry: Consisting of Old Heroic Ballads, Songs, and Other Pieces of our Earlier Poets (Chiefly of the Lyric Kind); Together with some few of later Date*, 3 vols. (London: Dodsley,1765), xv–xvi.

67. Achim von Arnim, "Von Volkslieder." Cited in Clemens Brentano, *Sämtliche Werke und Briefe*, vol. 6, ed. H. Rölleke (Stuttgart: Kohlhammer, 1975), 423.

68. In the fourth edition, which was reissued in 1794, Percy writes: "The scene of the finest Scottish Ballads is laid in the South of Scotland; which should seem to have been peculiarly the nursery of Scottish Minstrels" (lii).

69. For a discussion of the difference between Herder's project and later editions of ballads and folksongs, see Max Kommerell, "Das Volkslied und das deutsche Lied," *Jahrbuch des freien deutschen Hochstifts* (1922/23): 3–51.

70. The choice of the border assumes even more richness given that a majority of the ballads Scott included in his collection were from the northern regions of Scotland, although we do not know whether Scott was aware of this fact. See David Buchan, *The Ballad and the Folk* (London: Routledge, 1972).

71. Max Kommerell, "Das Volkslied und das deutsche Lied," 17.

72. J. G. Lockhart, *Memoirs of the Life of Sir Walter Scott*, 2:214.

73. Walter Scott, *Minstrelsy of the Scottish Border*, 2 vols. (Kelso: Ballantyne, 1802), 1:4.

74. For other instances of Scott family appearances in the ballads, see the introduction to "The Battle of Otterbourne," where Sir Walter Scott is said to be present at the battle; "Kinmont Willie," where Robert Scott plays a role in rescuing Willie; "Jamie Telfer" and the death of Willie Scott; "The Broom of Cowdenknows" and the assertion that Cowdenknows is located in Ettrick Forest; and finally, in "Sir Patrick Spens," which was not included in the first edition, Sir Michael Scott is said to receive Margaret. Also, the entire collection is dedicated to Henry, Duke of Buccleuch, from whose family Scott's family was supposed to descend. Scott's obsession with establishing the legitimacy of property ownership surrounded him his entire life (from his aggressive land acquisition around Abbotsford to his intense pursuit of acquiring aristocratic titles) and would become a central issue in his fiction as well. For a discussion of Scott's biographical interest in property, see John Sutherland, *The Life of Walter Scott: A Critical Biography* (Oxford: Blackwell, 1995), 155f., 209–11, and 224–25.

75. Karl Lachmann, *Kleinere Schriften*, 1:1–48.

76. J. G. Lockhart, *Memoirs of the Life of Sir Walter Scott*, 2:214.

77. Gérard Genette, *Paratexts: Thresholds of Interpretation*, trans. Jane E. Lewin (Cambridge: Cambridge University Press, 1997), 178–94.

78. "The term 'legitimate,' therefore, most immediately conjures up the political context of Scott's work, asking what counts as a legitimate history for Britain within the

rapidly changing European framework of Scott's time." Fiona Robertson, *Legitimate Histories*, 12.

79. Ina Ferris, *The Achievement of Literary Authority*.

80. Gilles Deleuze and Félix Guattari, *A Thousand Plateaus: Capitalism and Schizophrenia*, trans. Brian Massumi (Minneapolis: University of Minnesota Press, 1987), 84.

81. Albrecht Koschorke, *Körperströme und Schriftverkehr: Mediologie des 18. Jahrhunderts* (München: Fink, 1999).

82. Andrea Henderson, "Centrality and Circulation in *The Heart of Mid-Lothian*," in *Romantic Identities: Varieties of Subjectivity 1774–1830* (Cambridge: Cambridge University Press, 1996), 130–62. See also Ina Ferris's article on linguistic and corporeal ҏⲏⲁⲛⳓⲩ ⲓⲛ Ꮪⲥⲟⲧⲧ Ina Ferris, "The Indefatigable Word," in *Scott in Carnival*, ed. J. H. Alexander et al. (Aberdeen: Association for Scottish Literary Studies, 1993), 19–26.

83. Deidre Shauna Lynch, *The Economy of Character: Novels, Market Culture, and the Business of Inner Meaning* (Chicago: University of Chicago Press, 1998).

84. *Marmion*'s characters break down between the faithful Constance, Clare, and Wilton and the unfaithful Friar John, Lady Heron, and Marmion himself. Indeed, such competing groups of actors of mobility were reflected in competing scenes of mobility in the poem's convents of Whitby versus Holy Isle (home of the "one of the most mutable and unreasonable saints in the Calendar").

85. Jane Millgate, *Walter Scott: The Making of the Novelist* (Toronto: University of Toronto Press, 1980), 159.

86. Charlotte Sussmann, "The Emptiness at the Heart of Midlothian: Nation, Narration and Population," *Eighteenth-Century Fiction* 15, no. 1 (2002): 103–26; Caroline McCracken-Flesher, "Narrating the (Gendered) Nation in Scott's *The Heart of Mid-Lothian*," *Nineteenth-Century Contexts* 24, no. 3 (2002): 291–316; David Hewitt, "*The Heart of Mid-Lothian* and the People," *European Romantic Review* 13, no. 3 (2002): 299–309.

87. Walter Scott, *The Heart of Mid-Lothian*, Edinburgh Edition of the Waverley Novels, ed. David Hewitt and Alison Lumsden (Edinburgh: Edinburgh University Press, 2004), 14. Parenthetical citations in this section are to this edition.

88. It should be noted that it is always "direction" which poses a problem in *Mid-Lothian*. For example: "But the last observation of the procurator-fiscal was too much of the nature of a direct interrogatory, and it broke the charm accordingly" (154), or: "As this was spoken with a menacing tone and gesture, Jeanie hastened to protest her total innocence of purpose in the accidental question which she had asked, and Madge Wildfire went on somewhat pacified. 'Never ask folk's names, Jeanie—it's no civil'" (276).

89. James Chandler, *England in 1819: The Politics of Literary Culture and the Case of Romantic Historicism* (Chicago: University of Chicago Press, 1998), 304–5.

90. Walter Scott, *The Bride of Lammermoor*, Edinburgh Edition of the Waverley Novels, ed. J. H. Alexander (Edinburgh: Edinburgh University Press, 1995), 248. Parenthetical citations in the paragraph are to this edition.

91. J. G. Lockhart, *The Poetical Works of Sir Walter Scott*, 12 vols. (Edinburgh, 1833–34), 1:iv–v.

CHAPTER FOUR

1. Johann Wolfgang von Goethe, *The Man of Fifty*, trans. Andrew Piper (London: Hesperus Press, 2004), 12.

2. For questions of dating in the miscellanies, see chap. 1, note 18.

3. Barbara Benedict, *Making the Modern Reader: Cultural Mediation in Early Modern Literary Anthologies* (Princeton: Princeton University Press, 1996), 40.

4. Leah Price, *The Anthology and the Rise of the Novel: From Richardson to George Eliot* (Cambridge: Cambridge University Press, 2000), 3.

5. Ina Ferris, "Antiquarian Authorship: D'Israeli's Miscellany of Literary Curiosity and the Question of Secondary Genres," *Studies in Romanticism* 45, no. 4 (Winter 2006): 523–42.

6. See Kathryn Ledbetter, "A Woman's Book: The Keepsake Literary Annual" (Ph.D. diss., University of South Carolina, 1995) and a number of subsequent articles by her; Meredith McGill, "Common Places: Poetry, Illocality, and Temporal Dislocation in Thoreau's 'A Week on the Concord and Merrimack Rivers,'" *American Literary History* 19, no. 2 (Summer 2007): 357–74; Paul Gerhard Klussmann and York-Gotthart Mix, eds., *Literarische Leitmedien: Almanach und Taschenbuch in kulturwissenschaftlichen Kontext* (Wiesbaden: Harrassowitz, 1998); Hans-Jürgen Lüsebrinck, "La littérature des almanachs: Réflexions sur l'anthropologie du fait littéraire," *Études françaises* 36, no. 3 (2000): 47–63; Stephen G. Nichols and Siegfried Wenzel, eds., *The Whole Book: Cultural Perspectives on the Medieval Miscellany* (Ann Arbor: University of Michigan Press, 1996); Seth Lerer, "Medieval English Literature and the Idea of the Anthology," *PMLA* 118, no. 5 (2003): 1251–62; Armando Petrucci, "From the Unitary Book to Miscellany," in *Writers and Readers in Medieval Italy: Studies in the History of Written Culture* (New Haven: Yale University Press, 1995), 1–18; and Ségolène Le Men, "Quelques définitions romantiques de l'album," *Art et métiers du livre* (Jan. 1987): 40–47.

7. Leigh Hunt, "Pocket-Books and Keepsakes," in *The Keepsake* (London: Hurst, Chance & Co., 1828), 4–5.

8. On the importance of the series for mass media environments, see Umberto Eco, "Serialität im Universum der Kunst und Massenmedien," in *Streit der Interpretationen* (Konstanz: Universitäts-Verlag, 1987), 49–65. On the relationship between seriality and nationality, see Benedict Anderson, who writes: "The idea of the sociological organism moving calendrically through homogenous, empty time is a precise analogue of the idea of the nation, which is also conceived as a solid community moving steadily down (or up) history." Benedict Anderson, *Imagined Communities: Reflections on the Origin and Spread of Nationalism* (London: Verso, 1991), 26.

9. Philip G. Altbach and Edith S. Hashino, eds., "The Paperback," in *International Book Publishing: An Encyclopedia* (New York: Garland, 1995), 262.

10. Sigfred Taubert, *Bibliopola: Pictures and Texts about the Book Trade* (Hamburg: E. Hauswedell, 1966), 2:297.

11. Writing of the emergence of the modern, commercial function of the Christmas holiday, Nissenbaum writes: "Books were on the cutting edge of a commercial Christmas, making up more than half of the earliest items advertised as Christmas gifts." Stephen Nissenbaum, *The Battle for Christmas* (New York: Vintage, 1997), 140.

12. For discussions of the feminization of literature in pocket books, see Kathryn Ledbetter, "Lucrative Requests: British Authors and Gift Book Editors," *Papers of the Bibliographical Society of America* 88, no. 2 (1994): 207–16; Laura Mandell, "Hemans and the Gift-Book Aesthetic," *Cardiff Corvey* 6 (2001): unpaginated; and Lydia Schieth, "'Huldigung der Frauen'—Frauentaschenbücher in der ersten hälfte des 19. Jahrhunderts," in *Literarische Leitmedien: Almanach und Taschenbuch in kulturwissenschaftlichen Kontext*, ed. Paul Gerhard Klussmann and York-Gotthart Mix (Wiesbaden: Harrassowitz, 1998), 83–100.

13. Martha Woodmansee, "The Genius and the Copyright: Economic and Legal Conditions of the Emergence of the 'Author,'" *Eighteenth-Century Studies* 17, no. 4 (1984): 425-48, and idem, *The Author, Art, and the Market: Rereading the History of Aesthetics* (New York: Columbia University Press, 1994). See also Mark Rose, *Authors and Owners: The Invention of Copyright* (Cambridge, Mass.: Harvard University Press, 1993); Heinrich Bosse, *Autorschaft ist Werkherrschaft: Über die Entstehung des Urheberrechts aus dem Geist der Goethezeit* (München: Schöningh, 1981); Joseph Loewenstein, *The Author's Due: Printing and the Prehistory of Copyright* (Chicago: University of Chicago Press, 2002); and Jody Greene, *The Trouble with Ownership: Literary Property and Authorial Liability in England, 1660-1730* (Philadelphia: University of Pennsylvania Press, 2005). For a discussion of contemporary issues in copyright, see Peter Jaszi, "Toward a Theory of Copyright: The Metamorphoses of 'Authorship,'" *Duke Law Journal* (1991): 455-500. For a discussion on the common rights of copyright, see Trevor Ross, "Copyright and the Invention of Tradition," *Eighteenth-Century Studies* 26, no. 1 (1992): 1-28.

14. Natalie Zemon Davis, "Beyond the Market: Books as Gifts in Sixteenth-Century France," *Transactions of the Royal Historical Society* 5, no. 33 (1983): 69.

15. At the time of writing, at any given moment over ten million people are engaged in the act of sharing content over the Internet, and there are currently well over 1 *billion* songs available online for sharing. Yet parallel to such practices one finds their increasing criminalization through laws such as the Digital Millennium Copyright Act, the Piracy Deterrence and Education Act, or the recent Supreme Court ruling in *MGM v. Grokster*. The Recording Industry Association of America has accordingly filed over 6,000 lawsuits against individuals, and yet even as increasingly concerted legal efforts are used to restrict file sharing, its practice continues to rise.

16. "Let us speak of a work of art as *autographic* if and only if the distinction between original and forgery of it is significant; or better, if and only if even the most exact duplication of it does not thereby count as genuine. . . . Thus painting is autographic, music non-autographic, or *allographic*." Nelson Goodman, *Languages of Art: An Approach to a Theory of Symbols* (Indianapolis: Hackett, 1976), 113.

17. Two of the most important recent critiques are Siva Vaidhyanathan, *Copyrights and Copywrongs: The Rise of Intellectual Property and How It Threatens Creativity* (New York: New York University Press, 2003), and Lawrence Lessig, *Free Culture: How Big Media Uses Technology and the Law to Lock Down Culture and Control Creativity* (New York: Penguin Press, 2004).

18. Kenneth Monkman, "The Bibliography of the Early Editions of *Tristram Shandy*," *Library: A Quarterly Journal of Bibliography* 25 (1970): 11-39.

19. See for example, *A Miscellany of Poems by Several Hands* (1731), *Hibernicus's letters: or, a philosophical miscellany . . . written by several Eminent Hands* (1734), *A Collection of Poems, Mostly Original, by Several Hands* (1789), or less literally, Coleridge's collection, *Sonnets from Various Authors* (1794-95).

20. See William H. Sherman, *Used Books: Marking Readers in Renaissance England* (Philadelphia: University of Pennsylvania Press, 2008); Robin Meyers, Michael Harris, and Giles Mandelbrote, eds., *Owners, Annotators and the Signs of Reading* (New Castle, Del.: Oak Knoll Press, 2005); David McKitterick, *Print, Manuscript, and the Search for Order 1450-1830* (Cambridge: Cambridge University Press, 2002); H. J. Jackson, *Marginalia: Readers Writing in Books* (New Haven: Yale University Press, 2001); Roger Chartier, "Le manuscrit à l'âge de l'imprimé (XVe-XVIIIe siècles)," *La lettre clandestine*

7 (1998): 175–93; and Anthony Grafton, "Is the History of Reading a Marginal Enterprise?" *Papers of the Bibliographical Society of America* 91 (1997): 139–57.

21. Margaret J. M. Ezell, *Social Authorship and the Advent of Print* (Baltimore: Johns Hopkins University Press, 1999), 25. For other studies of early modern manuscript literary practices, see Harold Love, *Scribal Publication in Seventeenth-Century England* (Oxford: Oxford University Press, 1993), and Jonathan Goldberg, *Writing Matter: From the Hands of the English Renaissance* (Stanford: Stanford University Press, 1990).

22. Tamara Plakins Thornton, *Handwriting in America* (New Haven: Yale University Press, 1996); Meredith McGill, "The Duplicity of the Pen," in *Language Machines: Technologies of Literary and Cultural Production*, ed. Jeffrey Masten, Peter Stallybrass, and Nancy Vickers (New York: Routledge, 1997), 39–71; Stephen Colclough, "Recovering the Reader: Commonplace Books and Diaries as Sources of Reading Experience," *Publishing History* 44 (1998): 5–37; and Bernhard Siegert, *Relays: Literature as an Epoch of the Postal System*, trans. Kevin Repp (Stanford: Stanford University Press, 1999). See also Ray Nash, *American Penmanship, 1800–1850* (Worcester: American Antiquarian Society, 1969), and William St. Clair, *The Reading Nation in the Romantic Period* (Cambridge: Cambridge University Press, 2004), 224. I also wish to extend my thanks for helpful emails to Patricia Crain and Philip Martin, who is at work on a history of handwriting in the eighteenth and nineteenth centuries.

23. J. W. Goethe, *Wilhelm Meisters Wanderjahre*, in *Sämtliche Werke*, vol. 10, ed. Gerhard Neumann (Frankfurt/Main: Deutscher Klassiker Verlag, 1989), 339.

24. For an explicit and exemplary argument of the differentiation of script and print in their evolution, see Thornton, who writes that Americans around the turn of the nineteenth century "came to understand handwriting in contradistinction to print and to make handwriting function in contradistinction to the press, as the medium of the self." Tamara Thornton, *Handwriting in America*, 30. See also Michael Warner, *The Letters of the Republic: Publication and the Public Sphere in Eighteenth-Century America* (Cambridge: Harvard University Press, 1990), 7–9.

25. Leigh Hunt, "Pocket-Books and Keepsakes," 16.

26. Desiderius Erasmus, *The Adages of Erasmus*, selected by William Barker (Toronto: University of Toronto Press, 2001).

27. For a discussion of authors' and readers' dedications, see Gerard Genette, *Paratexts: Thresholds of Interpretation*, trans. Jane Lewin (Cambridge: Cambridge University Press, 1997), 123f. For a discussion of actual readers' inscriptions, see Cindy Dickinson, "Creating a World of Books, Friends, and Flowers: Gift Books and Inscriptions, 1825–1860," *Winterthur Portfolio* 31, no. 1 (1996): 53–66.

28. Leigh Hunt, "Pocket-Books and Keepsakes," 17.

29. Citing Balzac's words, "Madame, the time of dedications is past," Genette writes: "Tending to disappear at the beginning of the nineteenth century, therefore, are two features, obviously connected: the most direct (economic) social function of the dedication, and its expanded form of laudatory epistle." Gerard Genette, *Paratexts*, 123.

30. For an excellent discussion of the socialization of writing in the eighteenth and nineteenth centuries that nevertheless does not touch on the role of the miscellanies, see Patricia Crain, *The Story of A: The Alphabetization of America from The New England Primer to The Scarlet Letter* (Stanford: Stanford University Press, 2000).

31. For example, see *Dean's Universal Penman* (1808), where the author advises: "Sit at a convenient distance, avoid leaning hard on the pen, and incline the left side of the

body toward the desk, without leaning upon, or even touching it. . . . The forefinger should lie on the top of the pen, and be just as low as the top of the nail of the second finger. . . . Lay the third or ring finger, over the little finger inward, and when writing, rest lightly on the end of the little finger" (unpaginated). It was also not uncommon for manuals to call for a system of tying-up pupils' limbs. See Ray Nash, *American Penmanship*, 33.

32. Carlyle writes to his mother in 1827: "News came directly after breakfast that the packet from Goethe had arrived in Leith! . . . In the box containing the necklace [for Mrs. Carlyle], and in each pocket of the pocket-book were cards, each with a verse of poetry on it in the old master's own hand." Charles Eliot Norton, ed., *Correspondence between Goethe and Carlyle* (London: Macmillan, 1887), 20.

33. For an excellent material example of this intersection of accounting and fiction, see Borges's manuscript of "The Library of Babel" that was written on ledger paper. On the relationship of bookkeeping to modernist fiction, see Stanley Corngold, "Book-keeping in the Modernist Novel," in *Approaching Modernism*, ed. Astradur Eysteinsson and Vivian Liska (Amsterdam: Benjamins, 2007), 367–81.

34. For a discussion of commonplace books, see Ann Moss, *Printed Commonplace-Books and the Structuring of Renaissance Thought* (Oxford: Clarendon, 1996), and Barbara Benedict, *The Making of the Modern Reader*, chap. 1. It should be pointed out that, as William St. Clair has shown, miscellanies did not actually replace commonplace books but rather had the opposite effect of increasing their sales. William St. Clair, *The Reading Nation in the Romantic Period*, 224. And as Stephen Colclough has shown, the excerpts that readers wrote in their commonplace books were very often taken from the miscellanies themselves. Stephen Colclough, "Recovering the Reader," 5–37.

35. For a discussion of the relationship between the hand and the gift, see Jacques Derrida, "Geschlecht II: Heidegger's Hand," in *Deconstruction and Philosophy*, ed. John Sallis (Chicago: University of Chicago Press, 1987).

36. J. W. Goethe, *The Man of Fifty*, 48.

37. Edgar Allan Poe, "The Pit and the Pendulum," in *The Gift: A Christmas and New Year's Present* (Phil.: Carey and Hart, 1843), 145. Parenthetical citations in the paragraph are to this edition.

38. Washington Irving, "Rip van Winkle," in *The Sketch Book of Geoffrey Crayon, Gent.*, ed. Haskell Springer (Boston: Twayne, 1978), 37.

39. "This new shock was too great for her already overstrained intellects. A giddiness seized upon her; every thing seemed to whirl before her eyes; she gasped some incoherent words, and sunk senseless upon the ground. Days—weeks—elapsed before Inez returned to consciousness." Washington Irving, "The Student of Salamanca," in *Bracebridge Hall or the Humourists: A Medley*, ed. Herbert F. Smith (Boston: Twayne, 1977), 150. The only variant with the first American edition was the use of commas instead of dashes for "days, weeks, elapsed." [Washington Irving], "The Student of Salamanca," in *Bracebridge Hall or the Humourists: A Medley*, by Geoffrey Crayon, Esq., 2 vols. (New York: C. S. van Winkle, 1822), 1:341.

40. "Textual Commentary," *Bracebridge Hall*, ed. Smith, 433, 351.

41. On Irving as father of the American short story, see Eugene Current-Garcia, "Soundings and Alarums: The Beginning of the Short Story in America," *Midwest Quarterly* 17 (1976): 311–28.

42. On Irving as ambiguous patriarch, see Edward Wagenknecht for a summary of this

position: "Irving's position in American literature is a rather odd one. So far as his name goes, he is still one of the most famous American authors. There is also a conventional honor paid to him as the Father of American Literature. Yet the living body of his work is small, and in the critical estimate generally placed upon his effort as a whole, he now ranks below any of the others who enjoy a comparable fame." Edward Wagenknecht, *Washington Irving: Moderation Displayed* (Oxford: Oxford University Press, 1962), ix.

43. Paul Giles, "Burlesques of Civility: Washington Irving," in *Transatlantic Insurrections: British Culture and the Formation of American Literature, 1730–1860* (Philadelphia: University of Pennsylvania Press, 2001), 142–63, at 143. For a discussion of Irving in a similar vein through a reading of his biographies of English writers, see James Chandler, *England in 1819: The Politics of Literary Culture and the Case of Romantic Historicism* (Chicago: University of Chicago Press, 1998).

44. Michael Warner, "Irving's Posterity," *ELH* 67, no. 3 (2000): 773–99.

45. Washington Irving, "An Unwritten Drama of Lord Byron," in *The Gift* (Philadelphia: Carey & Hart, 1836), 166–71. Reprinted in Washington Irving, "An Unwritten Drama of Lord Byron," in *Miscellaneous Writings, 1803–1859*, vol. 2, ed. Wayne R. Kime (Boston: Twayne, 1981), 88–90.

46. "Textual Commentary," in Irving, *Miscellaneous Writings 1803–1859*, 2:394.

47. For a discussion of the sources of both Byron's and Irving's work, see Charles E. Robinson, "The Devil as Doppelgänger in the *Deformed Transformed*: The Sources and Meanings of Byron's Unfinished Drama," in *The Plays of Lord Byron: Critical Essays*, ed. Robert Gleckner (Liverpool: Liverpool University Press, 1997), 321–46. Robinson's move from calling it an "unwritten" drama to an "unfinished" one in his essay indicates the generic ambiguity that the term "unwritten" could provoke.

48. See Garrett Stewart, *Dear Reader: The Conscripted Audience in Nineteenth-Century British Fiction* (Baltimore: Johns Hopkins University Press, 1996).

49. Christof Forderer, *Ich-Eklipsen: Doppelgänger in der Literatur seit 1800* (Stuttgart: Metzler, 1999), 25.

50. Washington Irving, "An Unwritten Drama of Lord Byron," in *Miscellaneous Writings, 1803–1859*, 2:90.

51. Laura Mandell, "Hemans and the Gift-Book Aesthetic," unpaginated.

52. Edgar Allan Poe, *Essays and Reviews*, ed. G. R. Thompson (New York: Library of America, 1984), 575 (emphasis in original).

53. "Textual Commentary," in Irving, *Miscellaneous Writings, 1803–1859*, 2:394.

54. Edgar Allan Poe, *Essays and Reviews*, 571.

55. Edgar Allan Poe, "The Philosophy of Composition," in *Essays and Reviews*, 17.

56. Andrew Piper, "Korpus: Brentano, das Buch, und die Mobilisierung eines literarischen und politischen Körpers," *Textbewegungen 1800/1900*, ed. Till Dembeck and Matthias Buschmeier (Würzburg: Königshausen & Neumann, 2007), 266–86.

57. Sarah Wadsworth, *In the Company of Books: Literature and its 'Classes' in Nineteenth-Century America* (Amherst: University of Massachusetts Press, 2006).

58. Mrs. S. A. H. Chamberlain, "Jottings from an Old Journal," in *The Rose of Sharon: A Religious Souvenir*, ed. Mrs. C. M. Sawyer (Boston: Tompkins and Mussey, 1852), 59–65, at 59. For a discussion of the immense popularity of Mitchell's *Reveries* for women readers, see Lisa Spiro, "Reading with a Tender Rapture: *Reveries of a Bachelor* and the Rhetoric of Detached Intimacy," *Book History* 6 (2003): 57–94.

59. "Textual Commentary," in Irving, *Miscellaneous Writings 1803–1859*, 2:394.

CHAPTER FIVE

1. Alexander Nikitenko, "Lebensbeschreibung von Elisabeth Kulmann," in *Elizabeth Kulmanns Sämmtliche Gedichte in vier Theilen*, ed. Alexander Nikitenko (St. Petersburg: Kaiserliche Russische Akademie, 1839), 2.

2. See Joan DeJean, "Sex and Philology: Sappho and the Rise of German Nationalism," *Representations* 27 (Summer 1989): 148–71. Early nineteenth-century reception of Sappho emphasized her heterosexuality and her unrequited love, which depended in large measure on the limited corpus of fragments available at the time.

3. For the foundational works, see Andreas Huyssen, *Die frühromantische Konzeption von Übersetzung und Aneignung* (Zürich: Atlantis, 1969); Friedmar Apel, *Sprachbewegung: Eine historisch-poetologische Untersuchung zum Problem des Übersetzens* (Heidelberg: Winter, 1982); Antoine Berman, *L'épreuve de l'étranger: Culture et traduction dans l'Allemagne romantique* (Paris: Gallimard, 1984); and José Lambert and André Lefevere, eds., *La traduction dans le développement des littératures* (New York: Peter Lang, 1993).

4. Clemens Brentano, *Godwi* (Stuttgart: Reclam, 1995), 294.

5. J. W. Goethe, "German Romance," *Ästhetische Schriften, 1824–1832*, in *Sämtliche Werke*, vol. 22, ed. Anne Bohnenkamp (Frankfurt/Main: Deutscher Klassiker Verlag, 1999), 434.

6. Ezra Pound, *Literary Essays* (Norfolk: New Directions, 1954), 35.

7. See Franco Moretti, *Atlas of the European Novel, 1800–1900* (London: Verso, 1998), chap. 3. Moretti also highlights the way nations erase linguistic difference at the local level: "State-building requires streamlining . . . of physical barriers, and of the many jargons and dialects that are irreversibly reduced to a single national language" (45). Much recent translation theory concentrates today on the translation's role as a form of domestication and accommodation. See, for example, Lawrence Venuti *The Scandals of Translation* (New York: Routledge, 1998), who writes: "The very function of translating is assimilation, the inscription of a foreign text with domestic intelligibilities and interests" (11).

8. See Peter Burke, *Language and Community* (Cambridge: Cambridge University Press, 2004), 66–81.

9. *The Edinburgh Review* 55 (April 1832): 63.

10. J. W. Goethe to Thomas Carlyle, July 20, 1827, in *Correspondence between Goethe and Carlyle*, ed. Charles Eliot Norton (New York: Cooper, 1970), 18.

11. David Damrosch, *What is World Literature?* (Princeton: Princeton University Press, 2003).

12. Margaret Cohen and Carolyn Dever, eds., *The Literary Channel: The Inter-National Invention of the Novel* (Princeton: Princeton University Press, 2002), 19.

13. On the work of early-modern women as translators, see Margaret P. Hannay, ed., *Silent But for the Word: Tudor Women as Patrons, Translators, and Writers of Religious Works* (Kent: Kent State University Press, 1985), and Tina Krontiris, *Oppositional Voices: Women as Writers and Translators of Literature in the English Renaissance* (New York: Routledge, 1992).

14. Sherry Simon, *Gender in Translation: Cultural Identity and the Politics of Transmission* (New York: Routledge, 1996), 39.

15. Lori Chamberlain, "Gender and the Metaphorics of Translation," in *The Translation Studies Reader*, ed. Lawrence Venuti (New York: Routledge, 2000), 314–30.

16. See Barbara Godard, "Theorizing Feminist Discourse/Translation," in *Translation, History and Culture*, ed. Susan Bassnett and André Lefevere (London: Pinter, 1990),

87–96; Suzanne de Lotbinière-Harwood, *Re-Belle et Infidèle: La traduction comme pratique de réécriture au féminin/The Body Bilingual: Translation as Rewriting in the Feminine* (Toronto: University of Toronto Press, 1991); Luise von Flotow, *Translation and Gender: Translating in the Era of Feminism* (Ottawa: University of Ottawa Press, 1997); Sabine Messner and Michaela Wolf, *Mittlerin zwischen den Kulturen—Mittlerin zwischen den Geschlechtern? Studie zu Theorie und Praxis feministischer Übersetzung* (Graz: Institut für Translationswissenschaft, 2000); Annie Brisset, "Alterity in Translation: An Overview of Theories and Practices," in *Translation/Translation*, ed. Susan Petrilli (Amsterdam: Rodopi, 2003), 101–32.

17. Catherine Gallagher, *Nobody's Story: The Vanishing Acts of Women Writers in the Marketplace, 1670–1820* (Berkeley and Los Angeles: University of California Press, 1994); Susanne Kord, *Sich einen Namen machen: Anonymität und weibliche Autorschaft, 1700–1900* (Stuttgart: Metzler, 1996); Joan DeJean and Nancy K. Miller, *Displacements: Women, Tradition, Literatures in French* (Baltimore: Johns Hopkins University Press, 1991); and Margaret J. M. Ezell, *Social Authorship and the Advent of Print* (Baltimore: Johns Hopkins University Press, 1999). Ezell writes: "We still need histories of authors and readers—often women—who resided away from the centers of publishing and technology of 'modern' authors. In short, we still need studies that are not focused on the 'advanced' or modern concept of authorship during this period of transition but instead on all the varied aspects of the material culture of literature" (11–12).

18. Carla Hesse, *The Other Enlightenment: How French Women Became Modern* (Princeton: Princeton University Press, 2003); Elizabeth Eger, Charlotte Grant, Clíona ó Gallchior, and Penny Warburton, eds., *Women, Writing and the Public Sphere, 1700–1830* (Cambridge: Cambridge University Press, 2001); and Margaret Cohen, *The Sentimental Education of the Novel* (Princeton: Princeton University Press, 1999), where the latter's project depends on recovering the vast archive of popular women's novels from the nineteenth century.

19. Elizabeth Goldsmith and Dena C. Goodman, *Going Public: Women and Publishing in Early Modern France* (Ithaca: Cornell University Press, 1995).

20. See the work of the Montreal-based research group, Making Publics: Media, Markets, and Association in Early Modern Europe: http://makingpublics.mcgill.ca.

21. Novalis, "Fragmente," *Schriften*, vol. 2, ed. Richard Samuel (Stuttgart: Kohlhammer, 1983), 646. See also Hölderlin's programmatic statement in the notes to his Sophocles translation, "Everything is speech against speech, which mutually sublimates itself." Friedrich Hölderlin, "Anmerkungen," *Die Trauerspiele des Sophokles* (1804), in *Sämtliche Werke und Briefe*, vol. 2, ed. Jochen Schmidt (Frankfurt/Main: Deutscher Klassiker Verlag, 1994), 856.

22. Deidre Shauna Lynch, "The (Dis)locations of Romantic Nationalism: Shelley, Staël, and the Home-Schooling of Monsters," in *The Literary Channel: The Inter-National Invention of the Novel*, ed. Margaret Cohen and Carolyn Dever (Princeton: Princeton University Press, 2002), 194–224, and April Alliston, *Virtue's Faults: Correspondences in Eighteenth-Century British and French Women's Fiction* (Stanford: Stanford University Press, 1996), where she writes: "Novels of women's correspondence already plot themselves over, against, and about their own complex relationship to the boundaries of nation and tradition" (9).

23. For a thoughtful discussion about contemporary practices of technological overhearing, see Patrick Radden Keefe, *Chatter: Dispatches from the Secret World of Global Eavesdropping* (New York: Random House, 2005).

24. Honoré de Balzac, *Le Père Goriot: histoire parisienne*, vol. 1 (Paris: Werdet, 1835).

25. Tom Mole, *Byron's Romantic Celebrity: Industrial Culture and the Hermeneutic of Intimacy* (New York: Palgrave, 2007).

26. For a comparison with eighteenth-century writers' investment in establishing, and not worrying over, a poetics of privacy, see Patricia Meyer Spacks, *Privacy: Concealing the Eighteenth-Century Self* (Chicago: University of Chicago Press, 2003).

27. For discussions of translation as an act of cultural overhearing formulated as a form of appropriation and empowerment, see James T. Siegel, *Fetish, Recognition, Revolution* (Princeton: Princeton University Press, 1997). "Independence [in Indonesia]," writes Siegel, "will appear as the result of the history of hearing and overhearing that went on between groups of the Indies and between the Indies and the world" (6). For a study of overhearing in the nineteenth-century novel, see Ann Gaylin, *Eavesdropping in the Novel from Austen to Proust* (Cambridge: Cambridge University Press, 2002).

28. Cited in Heinz Hamm, *Goethe und die französische Zeitschrift 'Le Globe'* (Weimar: Böhlaus, 1998), 161.

29. On translating Schiller, see Peter Mortensen, "Robbing *The Robbers*: Schiller, Xenophobia, and the Politics of British Romanticism," *Literature and History* 11, no. 1 (2002): 41–61; on translating Kotzebue, see Matthew Scott, "The Circulation of Romantic Creativity: Coleridge, Drama, and the Question of Translation," *Romanticism on the Net* 2 (May 1996): n.p.; on the Minerva Press, see Deborah Ann McLeod, "The Minerva Press" (Ph.D. diss., University of Alberta, 1997). Wordsworth's statement is in "Preface," *Lyrical Ballads*, ed. R. L. Brett and A. R. Jones (London: Routledge, 1996), 249.

30. *Critical Review* (June 1807), cited in James Raven, "An Antidote to the French? English Novels in German Translation and German Novels in English Translation, 1770–1799," *Eighteenth Century Fiction* 14, nos. 3/4 (2002): 715–33, at 717.

31. Based on my counts from Wolfgang Rössig, *Literaturen der Welt in deutscher Übersetzung: Eine chronologische Bibliographie* (Stuttgart: Metzler, 1997).

32. Norbert Bachleitner, "Übersetzungsfabriken: Das deutsche Übersetzungswesen in der ersten hälfte des 19. Jahrhunderts," *IASL* 14 (1989): 1–49.

33. José Lambert, "Théorie de la littérature et théorie de la traduction en France, 1800–1850," *Poetics Today* 2, no. 4 (1981), 161–70; Lieven D'Hulst, "La traduction en France à l'époque romantique et l'évolution de la culture française," in *La traduction dans le développement des littératures*, ed. José Lambert and André Lefevere (New York: Lang, 1993), 159–64; José Lambert, Lieven D'Hulst, and Katrin van Bragt, "Translated Literature in France, 1800–1850," in *The Manipulation of Literature: Studies in Literary Translation*, ed. Theo Hermans (London: Croom Helm, 1985), 149–63; and Katrin van Bragt, *Bibliographie des traductions françaises, 1810–1840* (Louvain: Presses universitaires de Louvain, 1995).

34. Based on my counts from Liselotte and Karl Epting Bihl, *Bibliographie französischer Übersetzungen aus dem Deutschen, 1487–1944*, vol. 1 (1487–1870) (Tübingen: Niemeyer, 1987).

35. Scott Holland Goodnight, *German Literature in American Magazines Prior to 1846* (Madison: Bulletin of the University of Wisconsin, 1907).

36. Frank Luther Mott, *A History of American Magazines, 1741–1850* (Cambridge, Mass.: Belknap Press of Harvard University Press, 1966), 402.

37. William Cullen Bryant, "The Brother Jonathan and its 'Extra Novels'" (master's thesis, Columbia University, 1940), 8.

38. Based on my counts from Rinderknecht for American imprints and Wright for American novels. Carol Rinderknecht and Scott Bruntjen, eds., *A Checklist of American Imprints for 1840* (Metuchen: Scarecrow, 1990), and Lyle H. Wright, *American Fiction, 1774–1850: A Contribution Toward a Bibliography*, rev. ed. (San Mareno: Huntington, 1948).

39. William Cullen Bryant, "The Brother Jonathan and its 'Extra Novels,'" 28–29.

40. William St. Clair, *The Reading Nation in the Romantic Period* (Cambridge: Cambridge University Press, 2004).

41. The now-classic study of such international flows is Robert Darnton, *The Forbidden Bestsellers of Pre-Revolutionary France* (New York: Norton, 1996). But it is important to see how this problematic extends well beyond the Enlightenment into the nineteenth century and how translation is part and parcel of that story of international deregulation.

42. Norbert Bachleitner, "Übersetzungsfabriken."

43. Wilhelm Hauff, "Die teutschen Übersetzungsfabriken," in *Sämtliche Werke*, vol. 3, ed. Sibylle von Steinsdorff (München: Winkler, 1970), 260.

44. See Roland Mortier, *Diderot in Deutschland, 1750–1850* (Stuttgart: Metzler, 1967).

45. Goethe to Schiller, April 25, 1805, in *Der Briefwechsel zwischen Schiller und Goethe*, ed. Emil Staiger (Frankfurt/Main: Insel, 1966), 1051.

46. Hedwig Hülle, *Irrfahrten des Odysseus in vier und zwanzig Gesängen: Freie Nachbildung in gereimten Strophen nach Homer von Hedwig Hülle, geborne Hoffmeier* (Bremen, 1826).

47. F. G. Klopstock, "Vom deutschen Hexameter," in *Gedanken über die Natur der Poesie: Dichtungstheoretische Schriften*, ed. Winnfried Menninghaus (Frankfurt/Main: Insel, 1989), 60–156.

48. For an overview in English, see Jonathan Arac, "The Impact of Shakespeare," in *The Cambridge History of Literary Criticism*, vol. 5, ed. Marshall Brown (Cambridge: Cambridge University Press, 2000), 272–96.

49. See Christa Jansohn, ed., *Shakespeares Sonette in der Übersetzung Dorothea Tiecks* (Tübingen: Francke, 1992).

50. Friedhelm Kemp, *Das europäische Sonett*, 2 vols. (München: Wallstein, 2002), and Stuart Curran, "The Sonnet," in *Poetic Form and British Romanticism* (Oxford: Oxford University Press, 1986), 29–55.

51. As Margreta de Grazia has demonstrated in her work on the history of editing Shakespeare, the sonnets persistently occupied a troubled position within Shakespearean editions and criticism well into the twentieth century. Margreta de Grazia, *Shakespeare Verbatim: The Reproduction of Authenticity and the 1790 Apparatus* (Oxford: Clarendon, 1991).

52. Joel Fineman writes: "The first few sonnets seem deliberately to deploy grammatical markers of personality—personal pronouns, demonstrative adjectives, i.e., deictics—in such a way as . . . to point up the famished absence of the poet's self." Joel Fineman, *Shakespeare's Perjured Eye: The Invention of Poetic Subjectivity in the Sonnets* (Berkeley and Los Angeles: University of California Press, 1986), 202.

53. J. W. Goethe, "Zum Shakespeares Tag," in *Sämtliche Werke*, vol. 18, ed. Friedmar Apel (Frankfurt/Main: Deutscher Klassiker Verlag, 1998), 11.

54. J. W. Lever, *The Elizabethan Love Sonnet* (New York: Barnes and Noble, 1974), 188.

55. See for example A. W. Schlegel's reply to his publisher in response to Ludwig Tieck's editing of his Shakespeare translation: "I have no monopoly. Everyone has the right to translate Shakespeare . . . indeed even to correct my Shakespeare: either in hand-

writing in the margin of his copy or in print through reviews, etc. But to correct in the translation itself, no one can do this without my express permission." Cited in Reinhard Tghart, *Weltliteratur: Die Lust am Übersetzen im Jahrhundert Goethes* (Marbach: Deutsche Schillergesellschaft, 1982), 153.

56. [Wilhelmine von Gersdorf], *Redwood: Ein amerikanischer Roman von Cooper* (Wien: Kaulfuß und Krammer, 1825).

57. [Therese Huber], *Emilie von Varmont: Eine Geschichte in Briefen von Herrn Louvet; Nebst einem Anhang aus dem Französischen übersetzt und mit einer Vorrede begleitet vom Verfasser des heimlichen Gerichts* (n.p. [Altenburg: Richter], [1793?] 1794).

58. Valérie Cossy, *Jane Austen in Switzerland* (Genève: Slatkine, 2006).

59. ~~Margaret Cohen, The Sentimental Education of the Novel, 6~~

60. Barbara Becker-Cantarino, *Der lange Weg zur Mündigkeit: Frau und Literatur, 1500–1800* (Stuttgart: Metzler, 1987).

61. Felicia Hemans, *The Complete Works of Mrs. Hemans*, 2 vols. (New York: D. Appleton & Co., 1853), 2:360. Parenthetical citations are to this edition.

62. Elise von Hohenhausen, "Lord Byron's Abschied vom Vaterlande," *Morgenblatt für gebildete Stände*, no. 98 (April 24, 1820).

63. One could see this principle at work in Hemans's choice of translating Schiller's "Thekla: Ein Geisterstimme," which was supposedly written by Schiller in response to readers' (and theatergoers') disappointment about the disappearance of Thekla from *Wallensteins Tod* and which begins with the words (in Hemans's version): "Ask'st thou my home?" (1:546). The poem as literary supplement serves as an occasion to explore the translator's supplementary place within literature.

64. See Daniel Purdy, "Sophie Mereau's Authorial Masquerades and the Subversion of Romantic Poesie," *Women in German Yearbook* 13 (1997): 29–48, and Britta Hannemann, *Weltliteratur für Bürgertöchter: Die Übersetzerin Sophie Mereau-Brentano* (Göttingen: Wallstein, 2005).

65. Britta Hannemann, *Weltliteratur für Bürgertöchter*. See also Katharina von Hammerstein, ed., *Liebe und allenthalben Liebe: Sophie Mereau-Brentano; Werke und autobiographischen Schriften in drei Bänden* (München: DTV, 1997), and Gisela Schwarz, *Literarisches Leben und Sozialstrukturen um 1800: Zur Situation von Schriftstellerinnen am Beispiel von Sophie Mereau-Brentano geb. Schubart* (Frankfurt: Lang, 1991).

66. Daniel Purdy, "Sophie Mereau's Authorial Masquerades and the Subversion of Romantic Poesie" 30.

67. Roland Galle, *Geständnis und Subjektivität: Untersuchungen zum französischen Roman zwischen Klassik und Romantik* (München: Fink, 1986), 33–54.

68. Peter Brooks, *Troubling Confessions: Speaking Guilt in Law and Literature* (Chicago: University of Chicago Press, 2000), 4, 2.

69. Madame de Lafayette, *La Princesse de Clèves*, in *Oeuvres complètes*, ed. Roger Duchêne (Paris: Bourin, 1990), 342. Parenthetical citations are to this edition.

70. On the function of the woods and getting lost, see Kurt Weinberg, "The Lady and the Unicorn, or M. de Nemours à Coulommiers: Enigma, Blazon and Emblem in *La Princesse de Clèves*," *Euphorion* 71, no. 4 (1977): 306–35; on spatial poetics see Keren M. Smith, "Towers and Mirrors: Aspects of Space in *La Princesse de Clèves*," *Mosaic* 33, no. 1 (2000): 113–31.

71. For a summary of Lafayette's reception, see Nancy K. Miller, "Emphasis Added: Plots and Plausibilities in Women's Fiction," in *Subject to Change: Reading Feminist Writing* (New York: Columbia University Press, 1988), 25–46.

72. April Alliston, "What the Princess Left; or, Exemplary Faults in *La Princesse de Clèves*,"

in *Virtue's Faults: Correspondences in Eighteenth-Century British and French Women's Fiction* (Stanford: Stanford University Press, 1996).

73. Sophie Mereau, *Die Prinzessin von Clèves: Frei nach dem Französischen bearbeitet; Romanen = Kalender für das Jahr 1799* (Göttingen: Dieterich, 1799), 312.

74. Britta Hannemann, *Weltliteratur für Bürgertöchter*, 125.

75. Nancy K. Miller, "Emphasis Added."

76. For a reading of the importance of the turn and transformation in Mereau's writing more generally, see Gabriele Brandstetter, "'Die Welt mit lachendem Mut umwälzen': Frauen im Umkreis der Heidelberger Romantik," in *Heidelberg in säkularen Umbruch: Traditionsbewußtsein und Kuturpolitik um 1800*, ed. Friedrich Strack (Stuttgart: Klett-Cotta, 1987): 282-300.

77. Hannemann has uncovered evidence that suggests Mereau initially worked from a French translation of Zayas, but she doubts Mereau's participation in the final print version because of suppositions about her lack of knowledge of Spanish (*Weltliteratur für Bürgertöchter*, 49-51). Nonetheless, knowing as we do how much Brentano infringed upon Mereau's career as a writer, and how such involvement constantly threatened her ability to claim authorship (see Hannemann's discussion of the elaborate exchange of letters with Achim von Arnim about whether or not she should appear on the title page as translator of her translation of Boccaccio's *Fiammetta* [258-66]), without absolutely firm evidence we should be careful about continuing the critical tradition of disinheriting Mereau of texts she worked on. We know for certain she *was* involved in this project, and thus it serves as an important record of her translational work however collective such practices were.

78. Marina S. Brownlee, *The Cultural Labyrinth of María de Zayas* (Philadelphia: University of Pennsylvania Press, 2000), 7.

79. For a research review, see Judith A. Whitenack, "Introduction," in *María de Zayas: The Dynamics of Discourse*, ed. Amy R. Wilkinson and Judith A. Whitenack (Madison, N.J.: Fairleigh Dickinson University Press, 1995), 1-11.

80. *Der Freimüthige* 118 (June 14, 1804).

81. María de Zayas, *The Enchantments of Love*, trans. H. P atsy Boyer (Berkeley and Los Angeles: University of California Press, 1990), 13; María de Zayas y Sotomayor, *Novelas amorosas y ejemplares*, in *Obra narrativa completa*, ed. Estrella Ruiz-Gálvez Priego (Madrid: Castro, 2001), 32; Sophie Mereau, ed., *Spanische und Italienische Novellen*, vol. 1 (Penig: Dienemann, 1804), 19. All subsequent references will be made with the English translation cited first, the Spanish original second, and Mereau's German third.

82. J. W. Goethe, *West-östlicher Divan*, in *Sämtliche Werke*, vol. 3.1, ed. Hendrik Birus (Frankfurt/Main: Deutscher Klassiker Verlag, 1994), 417.

83. Friedrich Schlegel, "Nachricht von den poetischen Werken des Johannes Boccaccio," *Kritische Friedrich-Schlegel-Ausgabe*, vol. 2, ed. Hans Eichner (München: Schöningh, 1967), 373-96.

84. [Henriette Schubart], *Sapho und Phaon: Ein Roman* (Aschaffenburg: Etlinger, 1806).

85. Friedrich Schlegel, "Nachricht von den poetischen Werken des Johannes Boccaccio," 389.

86. Giovanni Boccaccio, *The Elegy of Lady Fiammetta*, trans. Mariangela Causa-Steindler and Thomas Mauch (Chicago: University of Chicago Press, 1990), 22; Giovanni Boccaccio, *Opere*, ed. Cesare Segre (Milano: Mursia, 1966), 965; *Fiametta: Aus dem Italienischen des Boccaccio übersetzt von Sophie Brentano* (Berlin: Realschulbuchhandlung, 1806), 51-52.

87. Boccaccio, *Opere*, 967, and Mereau, *Fiametta*, 57. On the history of the relationship of vagueness and beauty in Italian literature, Italo Calvino writes: "As far as I know Italian is the only language in which the word *vago* [vague] also means 'lovely, attractive.'" Italo Calvino, "Exactitude," in *Six Memos for the Next Millennium* (New York: Vintage, 1988), 57.

88. Patricia Meyer Spacks, *Privacy*, 25.

89. Helga Meise, *Die Unschuld und die Schrift: Deutsche Frauenromane im 18. Jahrhundert* (Berlin: Guttandin und Hoppe, 1983).

90. Patricia Meyer Spacks, *Privacy*, 14.

91. Katharina von Hammerstein, "Schreiben als Berufung: Sophie Mereau-Brentano, 1770 1806," in *Beruf: Schriftstellerin: Schreibende Frauen im 18. und 19. Jahrhundert*, ed. Karin Tebben (Göttingen: Vandenhoeck, 1998), 148.

92. Christa Bürger, "'Die mittlere Sphäre': Sophie Mereau—Schriftstellerin im klassischen Weimar," in *Deutsche Literatur von Frauen*, 2 vols., ed. Gisela Brinker-Gabler (München: Beck, 1988), 1:386.

93. See Joan DeJean, *Fictions of Sappho, 1546–1937* (Chicago: University of Chicago Press, 1989), 96–102.

94. [Sophie Mereau], "Nathan," *Die Horen*, vol. 7, no. 9 (1796), ed. Rolf Michaelis (Weimar: Böhlau, 2000), 85–94.

95. In Faye D. Ginsburg, Lila Abu-Lughod, and Brian Larkin, eds., *Media Worlds: Anthropology on New Terrain* (Berkeley and Los Angeles: University of California Press, 2002), the editors describe this idea of "talking back" as a kind of "cultural activism," the appropriation of mass media for local political and cultural goals within a contemporary global media context.

96. Ann Gaylin, *Eavesdropping in the Novel from Austen to Proust*, 9.

97. I am indebted for these insights to my conversations with the members of the *Making Publics* research group in Montreal: http://makingpublics.mcgill.ca.

98. Peter Brooks, *Troubling Confessions*, 168.

CHAPTER SIX

1. The visual epigraph is not to be confused with the literal vignette such as the printer's mark or xylographic title page. See Margaret M. Smith, *The Title Page: Its Early Development, 1460–1510* (New Castle, Del.: Oak Knoll Press, 2000), 113.

2. Peter J. de Voogd, "Tristram Shandy as Aesthetic Object," *Word and Image* 4, no. 1 (1988): 383–92, and J. Paul Hunter, "From Typology to Type: Agents of Change in Eighteenth-Century English Texts," *Cultural Artifacts and the Production of Meaning: The Page, the Image, and the Body*, ed. Margaret J. M. Ezell and Katherine O'Brien O'Keeffe (Ann Arbor: University of Michigan Press, 1994), 41–70.

3. J. Hillis Miller, *Ariadne's Thread: Story Lines* (New Haven: Yale University Press, 1992).

4. For histories of romantic book illustration, see John Harthan, *The History of the Illustrated Book: The Western Tradition* (London: Thames and Hudson, 1981); Gordon N. Ray, *The Illustrator and the Book in England from 1790 to 1914* (New York: Oxford University Press, 1976); Gordon N. Ray, *The Art of the French Illustrated Book 1700–1914* (New York/Ithaca: Pierpont Morgan/Cornell University Press, 1982); Arthur Rümann, *Das illustrierte Buch des XIX. Jahrhunderts in England, Frankreich und Deutschland, 1790–1860* (Leipzig, 1930); Theodor Kutschmann, *Geschichte der deutschen Illustration, vom ersten Auftreten des Formschnittes bis auf die Gegenwart, 2*

vols. (Berlin: F. Jäger, 1900); and Regine Timm, *Buchillustration im 19. Jahrhundert* (Wiesbaden: Harrassowitz, 1988).

5. Ségolène Le Men, "Balzac et les illustrateurs," in *Balzac et la peinture*, ed. Jean Germain (Tours: Musée des Beaux-Arts, 1999), 109.

6. Johann Georg Meusel, "Etwas über die Mode litterarische Producte mit Kupferstichen zu begleiten," in *Neue Miscellaneen artistischen Inhalts für Künstler und Kunstliebhaber*, no. 1 (Leipzig, 1795), 56.

7. Luisa Calè, *Fuseli's Milton Gallery: "Turning Readers into Spectators"* (Oxford: Oxford University Press, 2006).

8. William St. Clair, *The Reading Nation in the Romantic Period* (Cambridge: Cambridge University Press, 2004), 135.

9. Gillen D'Arcy Wood, *The Shock of the Real: Romanticism and Visual Culture, 1760–1860* (New York: Palgrave, 2001). Wood writes: "The conflict addressed in *The Shock of the Real* is not between M. H. Abram's mirror and lamp, but between the lamp and the magic lantern: between Romantic, expressive theories of artistic production . . . and a new visual-cultural industry of mass reproduction, spectacle and simulation" (7). For a study of the popularization of visual culture in France, see Petra ten-Doesschate Chu and Gabriel P. Weisberg, eds., *The Popularization of Images: Visual Culture under the July Monarchy* (Princeton: Princeton University Press, 1994).

10. Gerhard Neumann und Günter Oesterle, eds., *Bild und Schrift in der Romantik* (Würzburg: Königshausen und Neumann, 1999), 10. In this vein, see also Fritz Breithaupt's work that emphasizes an attention to "beyond the image": *Jenseits der Bilder: Goethes Politik der Wahrnehmung* (Freiburg: Rombach, 2000).

11. Manfred Schneider writes how the "unrepresentability of modernity articulates itself as an explosive overvisuality." Manfred Schneider, *Bildersturm und Bilderflut um 1800: Zur schwierigen Anschaulichkeit der Moderne* (Bielefeld: Aisthesis, 2001), 15.

12. W. J. T. Mitchell, *Picture Theory: Essays on Verbal and Visual Representation* (Chicago: University of Chicago Press, 1994), and James Heffernan, *The Museum of Words: Poetics of Ekphrasis from Homer to Ashbery* (Chicago: University of Chicago Press, 1993), and his more recent *Cultivating Picturacy: Visual Art and Verbal Interventions* (Waco: Baylor University Press, 2006).

13. Alexandra K. Wettlaufer, *Pen vs. Paintbrush: Girodet, Balzac and the Myth of Pygmalion in Postrevolutionary France* (New York: Palgrave, 2001). See also Keri A. Berg, "Contesting the Page: The Author and the Illustrator in France, 1830–1848," *Book History*, vol. 10, ed. Ezra Greenspan and Jonathan Rose (University Park: Pennsylvania State University Press, 2007), 69–102.

14. Wood writes: "The opinions of Lamb, Wordsworth and the conservative *Quarterly Review* show that, as late as the 1840s, the literary elite continued to actively resist the cultural influence of new visual media." Gillen D'Arcy Wood, *The Shock of the Real* 173.

15. For a recent example of this direction in scholarship, see Evelyn K. Moore and Patricia Anne Simpson, eds., *The Enlightened Eye: Goethe and Visual Culture* (Amsterdam: Rodopi, 2007).

16. For two recent thought-provoking investigations into the legibility and captionability of the image, see Susan Sontag, *Regarding the Pain of Others* (New York: Farrar, Straus and Giroux, 2003), and Robert Hariman and John Louis Lucaites, *No Caption Needed: Iconic Photographs, Public Culture and Liberal Democracy* (Chicago: University of Chicago Press, 2007).

286 / Notes to Pages 188–193

17. Samuel Taylor Coleridge, *The Notebooks of Samuel Taylor Coleridge*, ed. Kathleen Coburn (London: Routledge, 1957), vol. 1, §1554.

18. Garrett Stewart, *The Look of Reading: Book, Painting, Text* (Chicago: University of Chicago Press, 2006).

19. William Blake, *A Descriptive Catalogue of Pictures: Poetical and Historical Inventions Painted by William Blake* (London: Shury, 1809), 65.

20. J. W. Goethe, *Wilhelm Meisters Wanderjahre: Erstes Buch*. In *Taschenbuch für Damen* (Stuttgart: Cotta, 1810), iii.

21. Fritz Breithaupt, *Jenseits der Bilder*, 33.

22. Robert Rosenblum, *The International Style of 1800: A Study in Linear Abstraction* (London: Garland, 1976).

23. Sarah Symmons, *Flaxman and Europe: The Outline Illustrations and their Influence* (New York: Garland, 1984).

24. Sir William Hamilton and Johann Heinrich Wilhelm Tischbein, *Collection of engravings from ancient vases mostly of pure Greek workmanship discovered in sepulchres in the kingdom of the Two Sicilies but chiefly in the neighbourhood of Naples during the course of the years MDCCLXXXIX and MDCCLXXXX now in the possession of Sir Wm. Hamilton* (Naples, 1791–95), then published in German as *Umrisse griechischer Gemälde auf antiken, in den Jahren 1789 und 1790* (Weimar: Landesindustrie Comptoir, 1797).

25. Robert Rosenblum, *The International Style of 1800*, 1.

26. A. W. Schlegel, "Über Zeichnungen zu Gedichten und John Flaxman's Umrisse," in *Romantische Kunstlehre*, ed. Friedmar Apel (Frankfurt/Main: Deutscher Klassiker Verlag, 1992), 312. For a discussion of the critical reception of illustration around 1800, see Doris Schumacher, *Kupfer und Poesie: Die Illustrationskunst um 1800 im Spiegel der zeitgenossischen deutschen Kritik* (Köln: Böhlau, 2000).

27. J. W. Goethe to J. H. Meyer, September 15, 1809, in J. W. Goethe, *Werke*, sect. 4, vol. 21 (Weimar: Böhlau, 1896), 65.

28. Éric Bordas, "Balzac: Écriture et peinture," in *Balzac et la peinture*, ed. Jean Germain (Tours: Musée des Beaux-Arts, 1999), 119–31. See also Ann Jefferson, who writes that the object-centeredness of nineteenth-century novelism "hold[s] out the promise of a shared reading of social and moral concerns, and access to this general social truth is achieved through the novelist's insistent hermeneutic pressure on the visible surface of the world." Ann Jefferson, "Stendhal's Art History and the Making of a Novelist," in *Artistic Relations: Literature and the Visual Arts in Nineteenth-Century France*, ed. Peter Collier and Robert Lethbridge (New Haven: Yale, University Press 1994), 193. The central text that discusses Goethe's relationship to the visual arts is Ernst Osterkamp, *Im Buchstabenbilde: Studien zum Verfahren Goethescher Bildbeschreibungen* (Stuttgart: Metzler, 1991).

29. Moritz Retzsch, *Umrisse zu Goethe's Faust, gezeichnet von Retzsch* (Cotta: Stuttgart, 1816).

30. Viola Hildebrand-Schat, *Zeichnung im Dienste der Literaturvermittlung: Moritz Retzschs Illustrationen als Ausdruck bürgerlichen Kunstverstehens* (Würzburg: Königshausen und Neumann, 2004), 19.

31. Michael Baxandall, *Shadows and Enlightenment* (New Haven: Yale University Press, 1995).

32. The St. Joseph chapters of the *Travels* are generally read as a parody of the Nazarene school of romantics who wished to resacralize the visual arts. For the most thorough examples of this argument, see Gabrielle Bersier, "Goethe's Parody of 'Nazarene'

Iconography: The Joseph Story in *Wilhelm Meisters Wanderjahre*," *Goethe Yearbook* 9 (1999): 264–77, and Ernst Osterkamp, *Im Buchstabenbilde*, 224f.

33. For an introduction to the problem, see Frederick Burwick, *The Damnation of Newton: Goethe's Color Theory and Romantic Perception* (Berlin: de Gruyter, 1986). Most recently, see Clark S. Muenzer, "Fugitive Images and Visual Memory in Goethe's Discourse on Color," in *The Enlightened Eye*, 219–38, and of course Jonathan Crary, *Techniques of the Observer: On Vision and Modernity in the Nineteenth Century* (Cambridge, Mass.: MIT Press, 1990).

34. Hendrik Birus, "Der Entzug des Hier und Jetzt: Goethes *Ueber Kunst und Alterthum* an der Schwelle zum Zeitalter der technischen Reproduzierbarkeit des Kunstwerks" (January 22, 2004): http://www.goethezeitportal.de/db/wiss/goethe/birus_kunst .pdf.

35. J. W. Goethe, *Wilhelm Meisters Wanderjahre: Erstes Buch*, in *Taschenbuch für Damen*, xxx.

36. Garrett Stewart, *The Look of Reading*, 128.

37. The print by Nepomuk Strixner appeared in *Sammlung Alt- Nieder- und Ober-Deutscher Gemälde der Brüder Sulpiz und Melchior Boisserée und Johann Bertram, lithographiert von Johann Nepomuk Strixner* (München, 1821–34), 2:2. Goethe reviewed this image in his essay, "Über Lithographie," *Ueber Kunst und Alterthum*, 3, no. 2 (1821), in *Sämtliche Werke*, vol. 21, ed. Stefan Greif und Andrea Ruhlig (Frankfurt/Main: Deutscher Klassiker Verlag, 1998), 171.

38. For a discussion of this tradition, see Carol J. Purtle, *The Marian Paintings of Jan van Eyck* (Princeton: Princeton University Press, 1982).

39. Garret Stewart, *The Look of Reading*, 157.

40. Erwin Panofsky, *Early Netherlandish Painting*, 2 vols. (Cambridge: Cambridge University Press, 1966), 1:193.

41. An image of the "Annunciation" by a follower of the Boucicaut Master is available online at: http://www.getty.edu/art/gettyguide/artObjectDetails?artobj=3748.

42. Jörg Träger, *Philipp Otto Runge und sein Werk* (München: Prestel-Verlag, 1975), 360.

43. On the resurgence of the arabesque and its role in romanticism, see Günther Oesterle, "Arabeske, Schrift und Poesie in E. T. A. Hoffmanns Kunstmärchen, *Der goldne Topf*," *Athenäum* 1 (1991): 95.

44. Stefan Rieger, "Die Gestalt der Kurve: Sichtbarkeiten in Blech und Draht," in *Die Sichtbarkeit der Schrift*, ed. Susanne Strätling and Georg Witte (München: Fink, 2006), 119–38.

45. Johann Nepomuk Strixner, *Albrecht Dürers christlich-mythologische Handzeichnungen: Nebst Titel, Vorrede und Albrecht Dürers Bildnis, zusammen 23 Blätter, in lithographischer Manier gearbeitet von N. Strixner* (München, 1808). For Goethe's review, see J. W. Goethe, *Sämtliche Werke*, vol. 19, ed. Friedmar Apel (Frankfurt/Main: Deutscher Klassiker Verlag, 1998), 378–85.

46. David Wellbery, *The Specular Moment: Goethe's Early Lyric and the Beginnings of Romanticism* (Stanford: Stanford University Press, 1996), 233–46.

47. J. W. Goethe, "Chinesisches," *Ueber Kunst und Alterthum* 6:1 (1827), in *Sämtliche Werke*, vol. 22, ed. Anne Bohnenkamp (Frankfurt/Main: Deutscher Klassiker Verlag, 1999), 370.

48. Gerhart von Graevenitz, *Das Ornament des Blicks: Über die Grundlagen des neuzeitlichen Sehens, die Poetik der Arabeske und Goethes "West-östlichen Divan"* (Stuttgart: Metzler, 1994).

49. See Astrida Orle Tantillo, *The Will to Create: Goethe's Philosophy of Nature* (Pittsburgh: University of Pittsburgh Press, 2002), 168f.

50. J. W. Goethe, "Über die Spiraltendenz," *Schriften zur Morphologie*, in *Sämtliche Werke*, vol. 24, ed. Dorothea Kuhn (Frankfurt/Main: Deutscher Klassiker Verlag, 1987), 777.

51. Bernhard Siegert, *Passagen des Digitalen* (Berlin: Brinkmann und Bose, 2003). It should be noted that Siegert's story of scientific illustration falls between Stafford's accounts of eighteenth-century illustration and its emphasis on the substantive and Daston and Galison's recent work on nineteenth-century mechanically informed objectivity. See Barbara Maria Stafford, *Voyage into Substance: Art, Science, Nature and the Illustrated Travel Account, 1760–1840* (Cambridge, Mass.: MIT Press, 1984), and Lorraine Daston and Peter Galison, *Objectivity* (New York: Zone, 2007).

52. Dieter Ullmann, *Chladni und die Entwicklung der Akustik von 1750–1850* (Basel: Birkhäuser, 1996).

53. Ernst Florens Friedrich Chladni, *Die Akustik* (Leipzig: Breitkopf und Härtel, 1802), 117.

54. Joseph Fourier, *Théorie analytique de la chaleur* (Paris: Didot, 1822), i–ii.

55. I. Grattan-Guinness, *Joseph Fourier, 1768–1830: A Survey of His Life and Work* (Cambridge, Mass.: MIT Press, 1972), 145.

56. Alexander von Humboldt, "Des lignes isothermes et de la distribution de la chaleur sur le globe," *Mémoires de physique et de chimie de la Société d'Arcueil*, vol. 3 (Paris, 1817), 462–602.

57. Alexander von Humboldt, *Essai sur la Géographie des plantes, accompagné d'un Tableau physique des régions équinoxiales, et servant d'introduction à l'Ouvrage: Avec une Planche* (Paris: Schoell; Tübingen: Cotta, 1807). See also von Humboldt, *Essay on the Geography of Plants*, ed. Steven T. Jackson, trans. Sylvie Romanowski (Chicago: University of Chicago Press, 2009).

58. See Andrew Piper, "Mapping Vision: Goethe, Cartography and the Novel," *Spatial Turns: Space, Place, and Mobility in German Literary and Visual Culture*, ed. Jaimey Fisher and Barbara Mennel (Amsterdam: Rodopi, forthcoming, 2009).

59. Rachel Schmidt, "The Romancing of Don Quixote: Spatial Innovation and Visual Interpretation in the Imagery of Johannot, Doré and Daumier," *Word and Image* 14, no. 4 (1998): 354–70.

60. Catherine Coeuré and Chantal Massol, "Postérité du Chef-d'œuvre inconnu," in *Balzac et la peinture*, ed. Jean Germain (Tours: Musée des Beaux-Arts, 1999), 153–69.

61. Much of this reading depends on drawing a connection between Balzac's tale and a traditional reading of the iconoclasm of the German romantic tradition, evoked through the tale's initial subtitle as a "conte fantastique." For an example of the way such linkages continue to influence Balzac scholarship, see the following contribution to the special issue on Balzac and the image: Patrizio Collini, "'Le Chef-d'œuvre inconnu' et le romantisme allemand," *L'Année Balzacienne* 5, Balzac et l'image (2004): 75–86. Such readings are based on the standard work by Pierre Laubriet, who sees "The Unknown Masterpiece" as an embodiment of a romantic "abus de la réflexion," a looking that is always a looking-inside. Pierre Laubriet, *Un Catéchisme Esthétique: "Le Chef-d'oeuvre Inconnu" de Balzac* (Paris: Didier, 1961), 19.

62. Ségolène Le Men, "Balzac et les illustrateurs," in *Balzac et la peinture*, and idem, "Book Illustration," in *Artistic Relations*, ed. Peter Collier and Robert Lethbridge, 94–110.

63. Ségolène Le Men, "Balzac et les illustrateurs," 111.

64. On the importance of *L'Artiste* to French romanticism, see Suzanne Damiron, "La

Revue *L'Artiste:* Sa fondation, son époque, ses amateurs," *Gazette des Beaux-Arts* (Oct. 1954): 191–202.

65. Honoré de Balzac, *La Peau de Chagrin* (Paris: H. Delloye, 1838).

66. Garret Stewart, *The Look of Reading,* 31–80.

67. Honoré de Balzac, *La Peau de Chagrin,* in *La Comédie humaine,* vol. 10, ed. Pierre Citron (Paris: Gallimard, 1979), 82. Parenthetical citations are to this edition.

68. Garret Stewart, *The Look of Reading,* 49.

69. See Norman Bryson, *Vision and Painting: The Logic of the Gaze* (New Haven: Yale University Press, 1983), discussed in Garret Stewart, *The Look of Reading,* 117f.

70. See Richard C. Sha, *The Visual and Verbal Sketch in British Romanticism* (Philadelphia: University of Pennsylvania Press, 1998).

71. Kevin McLaughlin, *Paperwork: Fiction and Mass Mediacy in the Paper Age* (Philadelphia: University of Pennsylvania Press, 2005).

72. Claude Duchet and Isabelle Tournier, eds., *Balzac, œuvres complètes: Le moment de "La Comédie humaine"* (Vincennes: Presses universitaires de Vincennes, 1993).

73. Kevin McLaughlin, *Writing in Parts: Imitation and Exchange in Nineteenth-Century Literature* (Stanford: Stanford University Press, 1995), 70.

74. See Jeri DeBois King, *Paratextuality in Balzac's "Le Peau de Chagrin"* (Lewiston: Mellen, 1992).

75. Gerhard Neumann, "Narration und Bildlichkeit: Zur Inszenierung eines romantischen Schicksalsmusters in E. T. A. Hoffmanns Novelle *Doge und Dogaresse,*" in *Bild und Schrift in der Romantik,* ed. Gerhard Neumann und Günter Oesterle, 107–42.

76. In his introduction to the Pléiade edition, René Guise calls this tale "un pastiche d'Hoffmann." Honoré de Balzac, "Le Chef d'œuvre inconnu," in *La Comédie humaine,* ed. René Guise, vol. 10 (Paris: Gallimard, 1979), 401. Parenthetical citations are to this edition. For a recent example, see Sigbrit Swahn, "*Le Chef-d'oeuvre inconnu,* récit hoffmannesque de Balzac," *Studia Neophilologica* 76, no. 2 (2004): 206–14.

77. See Steven Connor, "Topologies: Michel Serres and the Shapes of Thought," *Anglistik* 15 (2004): 105–17.

78. Delacroix writes: "I am at my window and I see the most beautiful landscape: the idea of a line does not enter into my mind." Cited in Balzac, "Le Chef d'œuvre inconnu," 1422.

79. Garret Stewart, *The Look of Reading,* 66.

80. Adrien Goetz, "Une Toile de Rembrandt, marchant silencieusement et sans cadre: L'esthétique du portrait peint dans *La Comédie humaine,*" *L'Année Balzacienne* 2 (2001): 101. See also Isabelle Mimouni, *Balzac illusionniste: Les arts dans l'œuvre de l'écrivain* (Paris: Adam Biro, 1999), 26–53.

81. Jean-Luc Nancy, *Le Regard du portrait* (Paris: Galilée, 2000).

82. Wettlaufer writes: "Defining himself in contradistinction to the failures of painting, Balzac posits a counter-discourse to the reigning hierarchy of representation as formulated in the equivalence between seeing and knowing promoted by the physiologies." Alexandra K. Wettlaufer, *Pen vs. Paintbrush,* 172.

83. William Paulson, "Pour une analyse dynamique de la variation textuelle: Le Chef d'œuvre trop *connu,*" *Nineteenth-Century French Studies* 19, no. 3 (1991): 404–16.

84. Cited in Gerard Genette, *Paratexts: Thresholds of Interpretation,* trans. Jane Lewin (Cambridge: Cambridge University Press, 1997), 123.

85. Ségolène Le Men, *Une comédie inachevée: Balzac et l'illustration* (Tours: Bibliothèque municipale, 1999), 13.

86. Honoré de Balzac, *Le Chef-d'œuvre inconnu, Eaux-fortes originales et dessins gravés sur bois de Pablo Picasso* (Paris: Ambroise Vollard, 1931).

87. W. G. Sebald, *The Emigrants*, trans. Michael Hulse (New York: New Directions, 1996), 161–62.

88. Jacques Neefs, "Stendhal, sans fins," in *Le Manuscrit inachevé: Écriture, création, communication*, ed. Louis Hay (Paris: Édition du Centre National de la Recherche Scientifique, 1986), 15–43.

89. Martine Reid, *Stendhal en images: Stendhal, l'autobiographie et "La Vie de Henry Brulard"* (Genève: Librairie Droz, 1991), 124.

90. Sheila M. Bell, "Les Gravures de *La Vie de Henry Brulard*: Affaire Publique ou affaire privée?" *L'Année Stendhalienne* 4 (2005): 255–75.

91. Stendhal, *Vie de Henry Brulard, écrite par lui-même*. Edition diplomatique du Manuscrit de la Bibliothèque de Grenoble, ed. Gérald Rannaud, 3 vols. (Grenoble: Klincksieck, 1996), 1:109. Parenthetical citations are to this edition.

92. Gisèle Child-Olmsted, "Z/S: L'image de Zadig dans l'autobiographie de Stendhal," *Stendhal Club* 140 (1993), 281–94.

93. Thomas Stöber writes: "As a manuscript Stendhal's *écriture* can shift from writing to signification and from signification to writing. Writing and signification are in this sense not so much two separate sign systems as they are two sides of a single *tracement.*" Thomas Stöber, "Stendhals Auto-Graphie," in *Von Pilgerwegen, Schriftspuren und Blickpunkten: Raumpraktiken in medienhistorischer Perspektive*, ed. Jörg Dünne, Hermann Doetsch, and Roger Lüdeke (Würzburg: Königshausen und Neumann, 2004), 167.

94. On the role of "illisibilité" in Stendhal, see Martine Reid, *Stendhal en images*, 40–41.

95. Stendhal, *Le Rouge et le Noir*, in *Oeuvres romanesques complètes*, vol. 1, ed. Yves Ansel and Philippe Berthier (Paris: Gallimard, 2005), 568.

96. Murray Krieger, "The Ekphrastic Principle and the Still Moment of Poetry; or *Laokoön* Revisited," in *The Play and Place of Criticism* (Baltimore: Johns Hopkins University Press, 1967).

97. For the distinction between looking through and looking at in Stendhal's visual poetics see Michael Sheringham, "Visual Autobiography: Stendhal's *Vie de Henry Brulard*," *Paragraph* 11, no. 3 (1988): 249–73.

98. For Coleridge's fascination with the bow, see *The Notebooks of Samuel Taylor Coleridge*, vol. 1, §798.

99. See for example Stendhal's notation $25\sqrt{4} + \sqrt[3]{9}$ that is used to represent his age (53), but that of course contains a mistake (intentional or unintentional) (*HB*, 2:717). Mathematically it should be the square, not cube root of nine, but the point may be an emphasis on the unreliability of the numerical that would parallel Stendhal's love of the unreliability of the name through his incessant pseudonymity. In support of this latter reading, the passage is also tellingly reproduced in Sebald.

100. Laurence Sterne, *The Life and Opinions of Tristram Shandy, Gentleman*, in *The Florida Edition of the Works of Laurence Sterne*, vol. 2, ed. Melvyn New and Joan New (Gainesville: University Presses of Florida, 1978), 571–72. In the original: Laurence Sterne, *The Life and Opinions of Tristram Shandy, Gentleman*, vol. 6 (London, 1762), 154.

101. Christel Dillbohner, *Searching for Sebald: Photography after Sebald* (Los Angeles: Institute for Cultural Inquiry, 2006).

102. "At the salt mines of Saltzbourg [sic], they throw a tree branch made leafless by the winter into one of the abandoned pools of the mine. Two or three months later they retrieve it covered with shining crystals. . . . One can no longer recognize the original

branch. What I have called crystallization is a process of the spirit which draws from everything that presents itself the discovery of new perfections in the one we love." Stendhal, *De L'Amour*, in *Oeuvres complètes*, vol. 20, ed. Daniel Muller and Pierre Jourda (Paris: Champion, 1926), 20.

103. W. G. Sebald, *Die Ausgewanderten: Vier lange Erzählungen* (Frankfurt/Main: Fischer, 2000), 345; W. G. Sebald, *The Emigrants*, 230.

CONCLUSION

1. Later published as a special edition by Suhrkamp as Peter Sloterdijk, *Regeln für den Menschenpark: Ein Antwortschreiben zu Heideggers Brief über den Humanismus* (Frankfurt/Main: Suhrkamp, 1999).

2. Ibid., 14. Sloterdijk says further: "If this epoch appears today to have expired irretrievably, then it is not because man is no longer capable of fulfilling his literary task due to a kind of decadent mood; the epoch of national bourgeois humanism has reached its end because the art of writing love-inspiring letters to a nation of friends, even if it is still professionally practiced, can no longer suffice to link together the telecommunicative bonds between inhabitants of a modern mass society" (13).

3. Andrew Piper, "Project Übermensch: German Intellectuals Confront Genetic Engineering," *Lingua Franca* (December/January 2000): 74–77.

4. Peter Sloterdijk, *Regeln für den Menschenpark*, 43. Sloterdijk is drawing on Heidegger's association in his essay on "Logos" of the German *lesen* with its etymological root as an act of agricultural harvesting and gathering together, but also as an act of selecting out (*auslesen*) of the choicest fruits.

5. Andrew Piper, "Project Übermensch," 74.

6. Michael Joyce, *Othermindedness: The Emergence of Network Culture* (Ann Arbor: University of Michigan Press, 2000), 179f.

7. Saint Augustine, *Confessions*, trans. R. S. Pine-Coffin (London: Penguin, 1961), 177.

8. As Paul Duguid has cautioned us, end-of-the-book narratives depend on an impoverished notion of media change. Paul Duguid, "Material Matters: The Past and Futurology of the Book," in *The Book History Reader*, 2d ed., ed. David Finkelstein and Alistair McCleery (London: Routledge, 2006).

9. Lisa Gitelman, *Always Already New: Media, History, and the Data of Culture* (Cambridge, Mass.: MIT Press, 2006), 6.

10. Andreas Huyssen, *Die frühromantische Konzeption von Übersetzung und Aneignung* (Zürich: Atlantis, 1969) 121.

11. Peter Sloterdijk, *Regeln für den Menschenpark*, 55.

12. Espen Aarseth, *Cybertext: Perspectives on Ergodic Literature* (Baltimore: Johns Hopkins University Press, 1997), 16.

13. See, for example, Alexis Weedon's interesting new journal project, *Convergence: International Journal of Research into New Media Technologies*. For a useful critique of convergence discourse that nevertheless still uses the term, see Henry Jenkins, *Convergence Culture: Where Old and New Media Collide* (New York: New York University Press, 2006).

14. See the research group at the University of California, Santa Barbara: http://translit eracies.english.ucsb.edu.

15. "The computerization of culture gradually accomplishes similar transcoding in relation to all cultural categories and concepts. That is, cultural categories and concepts are substituted, on the level of meaning and/or language, by new ones that derive from the computer's ontology, epistemology, and pragmatics. New media thus acts

as a forerunner of this more general process of cultural reconceptualization." Lev Manovich, *The Language of New Media* (Cambridge, Mass.: MIT Press, 2001), 47.

16. Michael Joyce, *Othermindedness*, 3.

17. Mette Ramsgard Thomsen, "Positioning Intermedia: Intermedia and Mixed Reality," *Convergence* 8, no. 4 (2002): 38–45.

18. Hanjo Berressem, "Chaos/Control: Complexity," *Amerikastudien/American Studies* 45, no. 1 (2000): 5–21.

19. As Scott Lash has argued, "Informationcritique must be inside of information." Scott Lash, *Critique of Information* (London: Sage, 2002), 10.

20. Stéphane Mallarmé, *Oeuvres complètes*, vol. 2, ed. Henri Mondor and G. Jean-Aubry (Paris, Gallimard, 1998), 460.

21. John Durham Peters, "The Gaps of Which Communication is Made," *Critical Studies in Mass Communication* 11, no. 2 (June 1994): 135.

22. Samuel Beckett, "Embers," *Krapp's Last Tape and Other Dramatic Pieces* (New York: Grove, 1960), 107. References to the audio version of the play are to Samuel Beckett, *Works for Radio*, 4 CDs (London: British Library, 2006).

INDEX

Printed and bound by CPI Group (UK) Ltd, Croydon, CR0 4YY

13/04/2025

14656512-0004